Hawaii -
The Fake State

A Nation in Captivity

Aran Alton Ardaiz

Truth of God Ministry
Hawaiian Islands

Published by
Truth of God Ministry
Hawaiian Islands

Order this book online at www.trafford.com/08-0435
or email orders@trafford.com

Most Trafford titles are also available at major online book retailers.

General Delivery, (Box 62107)
Manoa Station, Island of Oahu
The Hawaiian Islands
(U. S. P. Z. Exempt)

Note for Librarians: A cataloguing record for this book is available from Library
and Archives Canada at www.collectionscanada.ca/amicus/index-e.html

Printed in Victoria, BC, Canada.

ISBN: 978-1-4251-7524-5

*We at Trafford believe that it is the responsibility of us all, as both individuals
and corporations, to make choices that are environmentally and socially sound.
You, in turn, are supporting this responsible conduct each time you purchase a
Trafford book, or make use of our publishing services. To find out how you are
helping, please visit www.trafford.com/responsiblepublishing.html*

*Our mission is to efficiently provide the world's finest, most comprehensive
book publishing service, enabling every author to experience success.
To find out how to publish your book, your way, and have it available
worldwide, visit us online at www.trafford.com/10510*

www.trafford.com

North America & international
toll-free: 1 888 232 4444 (USA & Canada)
phone: 250 383 6864 ♦ fax: 250 383 6804
email: info@trafford.com
The United Kingdom & Europe
phone: +44 (0)1865 722 113 ♦ local rate: 0845 230 9601
facsimile: +44 (0)1865 722 868 ♦ email: info.uk@trafford.com

10 9 8 7 6 5 4

Hawaii - The Fake State

A Manifesto and Exposé of a Nation in Captivity

This declaration and exposé reveals 115 years of United States Government deception; its unlawful activities of abuse as a colonial Pacific Ocean police power; its violations of the National rights of the Hawaiian People of the *neutral*, sovereign nation, **Ko Hawaii Pae Aina** *(The Hawaiian Islands);* and the concealment of that living nation.

This revelation documents the abuse of justice through court abuses of corrupt judiciaries, hidden facts of corrupt activities, violations of law and the oppressive double standard of the United States Government in regard to Hawaii.

This revelation exposes, the fraudulent conversion and capturing of people's birth names and birthrights silently condoned under the *"color of (U.S.) law"* by the United States Government functioning unlawfully on Hawaiian National soil.

Author: Aran Alton Ardaiz
Truth of God Ministry – Hawaii Nei
General Delivery, (Box 62107)
Manoa Station, Island of Oahu
Ko Hawaii Pae Aina
(U. S. P. Z. Exempt)
© Copyright 2008

Dedicated to my Lord and Saviour, Jesus the Christ and to all those who have given their all in obedience to Him. May His Truth now reveal to you knowledge (Hosea 4:6), and may He give you the Power of His Holy Spirit (Acts 1:8) to withstand that evil one and those who are deceived and who do evil and devious works. May His Grace abide with you always.

Aloha Ke Akua.

The Author extends his appreciation and Aloha to those loving Hawaiian National Citizens and friends, of the koko (blood) and not of the koko, who have been so helpful and considerate in providing critique and sharing understanding of loving Hawaiian values, customs, traditions, feelings, thoughts, and desires.

The Author also extends sincere appreciation to his Brother in Christ, Leon Siu of Hilo and Honolulu for his complete dedication and contribution to the many hours and days of assistance in order to assure that the Hawaiian People's history and culture is accurately and properly presented herein.

Aran Alton Ardaiz
The Truth of God Ministry - Hawaii
Common law Copyright Aran Ardaiz, 2008

BACKGROUND OF THE AUTHOR

The Author is Aran Alton Ardaiz, born in 1939 in the beautiful old City of Monterey, Monterey County, California Republic. He is the grandson of Gil Refugio Cano a law enforcement officer who served 37 years as Constable, Deputy Sheriff and Sheriff for Monterey County. Aran's mother, Martha Presentacion Cano Ardaiz was a court interpreter her whole life, and his uncle Gil Cano Jr. died in a car accident while serving as Monterey County Deputy Sheriff. Aran has two sons, Matthew and Nathan who both serve in the U. S. Military at this time.

In the late 1960's, Ardaiz became politically active in the tri-county area of Monterey, Santa Cruz and San Benito Counties California, resulting in new and improved, major housing, and county-housing authorities for the less fortunate. Aran also served as an Adviser on rural housing and Indian Affairs to then Governor Ronald Reagan and was a Member of the Republican State Central Committee. He was a Presidential Appointee and served briefly under the first Nixon Administration in the area of housing and small business development for the Office of Economic Opportunity, Western Region.

Ardaiz has owned and operated a successful consulting and contracting company in Hawaii for over 35 years.

Since 1971, Mr. Ardaiz has been living in the Hawaiian Islands *(Ko Hawaii Pae Aina)* enjoying his life with his lovely wife Nalani, and a faithful Beagle companion who is distantly related to Snoopy, of Charlie Brown fame.

TABLE OF CONTENTS

EXHIBITS

Introduction

This declaration is a revelation of Truth by a Christian Believer attempting to reflect the perspective of The Awesome, Living and Loving, Almighty God looking down upon His Creation that is functioning in disrespect and disobedience.

The shocking contents of this document are factual, revealing, informative and enlightening. Many situations related here you would think could not happen to you. If you are a typical product of the "dumbed-down" American educational system you probably won't come into conflict with these types of situations. That is, until you happen to wind up in a supposed U.S. court of law, trying to stand upon what you thought were your rights under the American Constitution.

The following events depicted herein have happened to me and to many others. These things could happen to you also!

It is with my knowledge of God's Word, the facts, knowledge of law and Aloha for the Hawaiian People that this Christian Man and Living Soul puts forth these findings of law and truth for your awareness and understanding.

This *declaration*[1] and *manifesto*[2] is an *exposé*[3] through first-hand knowledge of the deliberate actions of a major world power, the *Federal United States of America*, in open violation of International Law; violations being committed against the Citizens of

---

[1] *Declaration.* "In common-law pleading, the first of the pleadings on the part of the plaintiff in an action at law, being a formal and methodical specification of the facts and circumstances constituting his cause or action…" (Black's Law Dictionary, 6th Ed.)

[2] *Manifesto.* "A public declaration, usually of a prince, sovereign, or other person claiming large powers, showing his intentions, or proclaiming his opinions and motives in reference to some act done or contemplated by him as, a manifesto declaring the purpose of a prince to begin war, and explaining his motives." (Bouvier.)

[3] *Exposé.* "A statement; account; recital; explanation. The term is used in diplomatic language as descriptive of a written explanation of the reasons for a certain act or course of conduct. Exposure of discreditable matter concerning a person, government, etc." (Black's Law Dictionary, 6th Ed.)

the nation, the *Hawaiian Kingdom*.[4] This declaration takes into consideration the invasion and usurpation of the power and rights of the neutral Hawaiian Nation, through a conspiracy of **deception**.[5] That major world power, the United States, has brazenly imposed its foreign corporate, pseudo-corporate, and statutory laws upon the Hawaiian National populace.

After a hundred years of occupation, the *Federal United States* has, due to *Hawaiian* pressure, rendered a hollow, shallow and essentially meaningless **"Apology"** in the form of the **United States Public Law 103-150 of November 23, 1993 (See EXHIBIT A)**. The Apology was signed into law by President William Jefferson Clinton and formally accepted for value, by the God-fearing People of Hawaii (**See EXHIBIT B**). Of note is that this Apology was offered to the *Native Hawaiians* (the aboriginal people), not to the *Hawaiian Nationals* (the Citizens of the *Hawaiian Kingdom*).

The Apology openly acknowledges the international violation of law by the Federal United States but falls short of permitting proper restoration, restitution, reparations or consideration required of an honorable and sincere apology.

The fact is, the "Apology" lacks "virtue," because after its acceptance, there has not been any effort to return the authority, assets, rights and power taken, nor has there been a diminishment of the oppressive practices of the foreign-sustained de facto[6]

---

[4] The Hawaiian nation has two lawful Hawaiian names: *Ke Aupuni o Hawaii* refers to *The Hawaiian Kingdom*, the governing entity; *Kö Hawaii Pae 'Äina* refers to *"The Hawaiian Islands," the name of the country.*

[5] **Deception.** *1. The practice of making somebody believe things that are not true 2.* an act, trick, or device intended to deceive somebody. *Fraud.*

[6] **De facto government.** *"One that maintains itself by a display of force against the will of the rightful legal government and is successful, at least temporarily, in overturning the institutions of the rightful legal government by setting up its own in lieu thereof." Source:* Blacks Law Dictionary, 6th Edition. Therefore: The State of Hawaii is an unlawful, de facto, foreign instituted corporate entity on Hawaiian soil and is not a lawful State of the American Union of states. This fact is affirmed by **Title 4 U. S. C. Section 1,** which by law admits there are today, **only 48 States in the American Union** and by **Title 28 Section 91 of the U. S. Code,** which defines jurisdictional limitations of the U. S. Court for the Hawaii District, <u>**which excludes all of the major Islands of the Hawaiian Archipelago.**</u>

"STATE OF HAWAII" *"puppet government"*[7] instituted on Hawaiian National *Aina*[8] (or land) designed to oppress Hawaiian National interests.

Additionally the United States Government, since their virtue-less *"Apology,"* has continued to deny the lawful rights of properly documented Hawaiian Nationals to live as Hawaiian Nationals under their own national *common-law*, thus causing extreme duress. The *common-law* is the **de jure**[9] *National law* of **Ke Aupuni O Hawaii Nei** *(The Hawaiian Kingdom).* The *Federal United States Government* aids in the suppression of Hawaiian Nationals through its *"puppet government,"* a de facto, **non-state of the Union entity**[10] titled the *"STATE OF HAWAII"* which functions under *"color of U.S. law"*[11] *in violation of and in open defiance of United States Criminal Laws.*

---

[7] **Puppet (Government):** *"1 a: a small-scale figure (as of a person or animal) usu. With a cloth body and hollow head that fits over and is moved by the hand b: MARRIONETTE 2: doll 3: one whose acts are controlled by an outside force or influence –"* (Bold emphasis by Author. Source: Merriam-Webster's Collegiate Dictionary, Tenth Edition)

[8] *'Äina. This Hawaiian word "'Äina" is loosely translated in English as "land." But the word is used to denote not only the physical or geographical feature, but the nurturing, relational aspects in the broadest and deepest sense, as in "land of my birth" or "land that I love."*

[9] **De jure.** *"Descriptive of a condition in which there has been total compliance with all requirements of law. Of right; legitimate; lawful; by right and just title. In this sense it is the contrary of de facto (q.v.). It may also be contrasted with de gratia, in which case it means "as a matter of right," as de gratia means "by grace or favor," Again it may be contrasted with de æquitate; here meaning "by law," as the latter means "by equity."* (Source: Black's Law Dictionary 6th Edition, Page 425)

[10] **"non-state of the Union entity":** The U.S. President (Eisenhower) issued an Executive Order to create a "State of the Union." Under the united *"States Constitution,"* the President cannot create a State. Statehood can only be created by the **National Congress of the Republic,** in proper session, and not by the issuance of an *"Executive Order"* by a President as in the creation of the *"color of law [below],"* de facto, "State of Hawaii," which in reality is simply a federal corporation.

[11] **(Author's Note) Color of Law.** *"color of U. S. law"* is a violation of United States Criminal law and is affirmed by *Title 18 United States Criminal Code Sections 241 and 242.* Applies to corporate government and corporate citizens. The de facto **United States Court for the Hawaii District** and subordinate State of Hawaii Courts *(of incompetent jurisdiction)* do not honor United States laws except when appropriate for their purposes. *"Color of law"* is defined as follows:

Color of law. *"The appearance or semblance, without the substance, of legal right. Misuse of power, possessed by virtue of state law, and made possible only because the wrongdoer is clothed with authority of state, is action taken under "color of state law." Atkins v. Lanning, D. C. Okl., 415 F. Supp. 186, 188. Acts "under of color of any law" of a State include not only acts done by State officials within the bounds or limits of their lawful authority, but also acts done without and beyond the bounds of their lawful authority; provided that, in order for unlawful acts of an official to be done "under color of any law", the unlawful acts must be done while such official is purporting or pretending to act in the performance of his official duties; that is to say, the unlawful acts must consist in an abuse or misuse of power which is possessed by the official only because he is an official; and the unlawful acts must be of such a nature or character, and be committed under such circumstances, that they would not have occurred but for the fact*

The result is this de facto *(false)* government entity functions by systematic abuse of police power in violation of International Law. The STATE OF HAWAII harasses, oppresses, fines, arrests (without properly executed warrants), denies and ignores proper documentation presented or filed by *de jure* Hawaiian Nationals. The de facto "State" incarcerates *(without proper trial),* and physically abuses those incarcerated, evicts people by force of arms from their homes under false pretenses *(claiming abandonment when the home is in fact occupied).* The de facto "State" functions collusively with the Internal Revenue Service *(IRS)* and other government agencies *(U. S. Justice Department, FBI…)* to seize bank accounts, and raid homes and businesses on trumped-up charges, and confiscate *(take, steal)* items not listed on search warrants, and not return those items taken even if no charges are brought!

Unfortunately, under *"color of law"* the *de facto State* and *Federal U. S. Governments* do as they please to maintain their illegal military control, oppression and *genocide[12]* against the Hawaiian People. This abuse of "law and justice," to harass, suppress, diminish and discourage Hawaiian Nationals from functioning within their lawful national rights is designed to keep Hawaiians captive to the U.S. and disabling Hawaiian Nationals from honoring their own superior, de jure, positive *Common-law[13]* of the *Hawaiian Kingdom.* This ongoing abuse *(exercised by de facto local and "State" police, attorneys and judges)* under de facto-government oaths of office is knowingly condoned and protected by the *Federal United States Government.* The local federal judiciary, and *U. S. Justice Department*, et al, as agencies of the U.S., occupying the *National Lands* of the *Hawaiian Kingdom*, functioning contrary to and in violation of Hawaiian Kingdom and international law.

---

that the person committing them was an official when and there exercising his official powers outside the bounds of lawful authority. 42 U. S. C. A. Section 1983." (Source: Black's Law Dictionary, 6th Edition)

[12] **Genocide.** (Not in Black's Law Dictionary, 6th Edition) *"The deliberate and systematic destruction of a racial, political or cultural group."* (Source: Merriam-Webster's Collegiate Dictionary, 10th Ed.)

[13] Common-Law. Chapter LVII. An Act To Reorganize the Judiciary Department (of the Hawaiian Kingdom), (1892) **Section 5.** *"The common law of England, as ascertained by English and American decisions, is hereby declared to be the common law of the Hawaiian Islands in all cases, except as otherwise expressly provided by the Hawaiian Constitution or laws, or fixed by Hawaiian judicial precedent, or establish by Hawaiian national usage, provided however, that no person shall be subject to criminal proceedings except as provided by the Hawaiian laws."*

In 1893, an act of treason and sedition was committed by a small band of *haole*[14] businessmen — some were *Hawaiian Nationals,* the others were United States *Citizens,*[15] or other aliens residing in Hawaii. Their unlawful actions against the *National Government of the Hawaiian Kingdom,* was in direct violation of the sovereignty of the Hawaiian Kingdom, the *United State's* own *Constitution"* and *International Law (i.e. The Law of Nations, and conventional treaties).* The unauthorized hostile actions by the U.S. military, was later admitted by U.S. President Grover Cleveland to have been an unprovoked *"...act of war..."* against a friendly nation, and violated the existing, *non-abrogated*[16] *Treaty of 1850* (See EXHIBIT C) between the Hawaiian Kingdom and the United States of America.

ABOUT THE AUTHOR:

I, Aran Ardaiz, a student of biblical history and of U. S. and world history, am from a law abiding family and have experienced first-hand, the abuses and acts of genocide being inflicted upon the Citizens of Hawaii, a sovereign, neutral nation. These abuses against the Hawaiian Citizens are being committed by the United States in direct and willful violation of *International Law,* the *United State's Constitution* and, of course, *the Hawaiian Kingdom Constitution.* This Author and others have been arrested and jailed numerous times for honoring and asserting the distinction of being foreign, Hawaiian Nationals outside the jurisdiction of the *de facto State of Hawaii.*

This Author was born to one of America's de jure sovereign States, titled the *"California Republic"* and possesses dual Citizenship: as a natural-born, private *American National Citizen* and as a documented *Hawaiian National Citizen* (which the Author acquired by lawful filing with the *de jure Hawaiian National Government*).

---

[14] *Haole.* This Hawaiian term refers to Caucasians, primarily American or European.

[15] Actually, those *Hawaiian Kingdom National Citizens* who committed acts of treason and insurrection against the very government to whom they had pledged lawful allegiance *(these facts affirmed by the very existence of the U. S. Apology Bill, Public Law 103-150)* with the help of the then *United States Minister John L. Stevens,* while at the same time seeking protection via political and military support from the *Government of the United States* for their treasonous actions.

[16] **Non-Abrogated   Treaty.** *"Not annulled, cancelled, revoked, repealed or destroyed."*

This Author is also an *"Apostille,"* (neutral) under *The Hague Convention of 1961* (See **EXHIBIT D**) affirmed by the *Secretary of State* of the *de facto STATE OF HAWAII*, representing the *Federal United States Government*; the latter being a signatory party to the Convention *(Of concern is the fact that since the State of Hawaii is de facto, all elected officials, appointed officials, judges, attorneys, notaries, etc., are also de facto, and therein is created a question as to the creditability of any documentation filed within that closed system; especially since the State can only affirm its own Notary signature and not a lawful document).*

The *Federal United States Government* was properly served notice of this Author's lawful dual citizenship status with filing No. MC 05 00109 *(Apostille filing)* in the de facto *U. S. Court for the Hawaii District (Federal)* on April 21, 2005.

As a Minister, teacher and student of the Holy Scriptures, I desire to reflect *(to the best of my ability)* the will of my Lord Jesus Christ and His Truth. I make this public declaration and exposé with knowledge of His Truth and as affirmed by laws and documentation contained herein and elsewhere. Appropriate to state for this era in world history, is the following Holy Scripture:

> *"In transgressing and lying against the Lord, and departing away from our God, speaking oppression and revolt, conceiving and uttering from the heart words of falsehood. And judgment is turned away backward; for truth is fallen into the street and equity cannot enter. Yea, truth faileth; and he that departeth from evil maketh himself a prey. And the Lord saw it, and it displeased Him that there was no judgment (justice)."*
>
> (Isaiah 59: 13, 14, 15 KJV)

It is in the interest of righteousness that this book, *"Hawaii – The Fake State"* has been written. It is not written with the design to cause revolt, the taking up of arms or the oppression of others, but to educate and reveal those truths long-hidden from the People *(of all ethnic backgrounds)* of the Hawaiian Kingdom and the People of America since the overthrow of the de jure *"neutral,"* *Hawaiian National Government* on January 17, 1893; and, to reveal current abuses being perpetrated against Hawaiian Nationals by the *Federal United States Government* and the puppet *State of Hawaii.*

Disclaimer: This Author composed this document to the best of his knowledge and ability with available facts provided and documented; knowing he himself is not perfect and not the best of writers or users of the English language; having struggled with English classes and language classes as a youth. Of importance are the facts and common-sense issues of deception and corruption reflected, whether or not presented with any degree of eloquence.

For this book, this Author decided not to use diacritical marks for the Hawaiian words as they were not used in documents of the Hawaiian Kingdom. Diacritical marks are a modern device to assist non-Hawaiian speakers with pronunciation and distinguishing between identical or similar looking words.

Many terms, particularly those regarding types of governments and types of citizenships, have been deliberately written by this Author with specific capital/lower case, underlining and italics, etc., in order to maintain the distinctions between legal terms that may look and sound alike but have subtle or marked differences in meanings and jurisdiction.

Chapter 1

General Background

With Critique of The Newlands Resolution, The Organic Act and The Statehood Act

This manifesto and exposé is written to direct attention to a great deception committed by the United States Government, acting without honor or integrity in sustaining an abusive relationship with the inhabitants of a foreign nation, The Hawaiian Islands (properly titled, "Ko Hawaii Pae Aina") whose national government is known and commonly addressed as The Hawaiian Kingdom (Ke Aupuni O Hawaii Nei).

Foreign nations, specifically those with still-existing, valid *(non-abrogated[1])* international treaties with the Hawaiian Nation (i.e. Hawaiian Kingdom) (See EXHIBIT E), as well as the United Nations (noticed under separate cover) have been made aware of the false and misleading posture of jurisdictional claim by the United States Government, on the sovereign nation of the Hawaiian Islands, which geographically includes the entire Hawaiian Archipelago.

The U.S. Government, however, in order to keep control over the Hawaiian People and to control the Islands of the Hawaiian Archipelago and to justify the United States' unlawful existence and presence on the foreign national soil of the *Hawaiian Kingdom,* has deliberately dispersed disinformation through falsification of records and documents, manipulation of mass media and educational systems, exertion of abusive police power and economic policies. This was done to falsely claim that the Hawaiian People acquiesced to the present so-called *"Statehood"[2]* status (which they have not).

Those nations having treaties with *The Hawaiian Kingdom* were aware at the time of the overthrow, January 17, 1893, that the United States exercised "gunboat diplomacy" in violation of International Treaties and International Law and was a *conspiratorial*

---

[1] *Non-Abrogated Treaty.* "Not annulled, cancelled, revoked, repealed or destroyed."

[2] *Statehood. n. the status or condition of being a state, esp. a state of the U.S. (Source: Webster's Encyclopedic Unabridged Dictionary, 2001 Edition.)*

participant³ in the violation of the sovereignty of the *Hawaiian Islands,* an internationally declared *"neutral"* foreign nation. On that date, the United States Military *(activated, by U.S. Minister John L. Steven's unauthorized orders⁴)* directly supported treason and insurrection on Hawaiian National soil with military troops and weapons brought ashore from a U.S. warship in Honolulu Harbor. The U.S. participated as an invasive force on foreign soil in support of acts of treason by armed, racially white, insurrectionists⁵ violating their sworn oaths to uphold Hawaiian National laws, and who were not, as they falsely claimed, under threat or duress from the Hawaiian Kingdom or its people. At the time, only about three thousand American civilians lived (unthreatened) in all of the islands.

Under protest and to avoid needless bloodshed, Queen Liliuokalani, yielded her authority to the President of the United States (Benjamin Harrison) until the facts of the illegal insurrection could be determined and the Kingdom Government properly restored. Meanwhile the insurrectionists installed an illegal "provisional government" to conduct the affairs of the Hawaiian Kingdom and to consolidate their control.

U.S. President Harrison, in disregard for truth and righteousness, had presided over a deliberate, unsupportable, hostile action against the friendly, neutral nation, the Hawaiian Kingdom. President Grover Cleveland succeeded Harrison just after the U.S.' illegal actions against Hawaii. Following a formal protest by Queen Liliuokalani, the newly installed President Cleveland suspended deliberations in the U.S. Senate of the Treaty of Annexation of Hawaii and sent former U.S. Congressman James H. Blount as a Special Commissioner to investigate the situation. Months later, in his 1,397 page "Blount Report"⁶ he concluded that the United States' military *(Navy and Marine)* actions on foreign, Hawaiian Kingdom National soil was patently unlawful. Based upon the Blount Report, Cleveland withdrew the treaty of annexation stating in his Message to the U.S. Congress on December 18, 1894. I quote in part President Cleveland:

---

³ *U.S. actions are affirmed by its own United States' State Department Publication "Correspondence with Diplomatic and Naval Officers concerning The Relations of the United States to the Hawaiian Islands," Washington: Government Printing Office. 1893*

⁴ *Read the 1893 State Department Publication. (Supra)*

⁵ *Insurrectionist – One who favors or takes part in insurrection; an insurgent. (Webster's New Collegiate Dictionary, Second Edition)* Some of the insurrectionists were Hawaiian Citizens; some were dual citizens, some were foreigners domiciled in the Hawaiian Kingdom.

⁶ Report of the U.S. Special Commissioner James H. Blount to Secretary of State Walter Q. Gresham concerning The Hawaiian Kingdom Investigation [1893]

"The military demonstration upon the soil of Honolulu [participation in the overthrow of January 16th & 17th, 1893] was of itself an <u>act of war</u> [against a "friendly" and "neutral," treaty nation], unless made either with the consent of the Government of Hawaii or for the bona fide purpose of protecting the imperiled lives and property of citizens of the United States." (Emphasis/bracketed clarifications by Author)

Full text (due to the extensiveness of the report) can be read by online computer.

Because the U.S. had committed an unlawful military intervention to assist in a coup against the lawful government of a sovereign nation, the Hawaiian Islands, the U.S. had no lawful basis to annex that nation. Therefore, in the order to make it look like an "annexation," the U.S. arrogantly ignored numerous U.S., Hawaiian Kingdom and international laws, and unscrupulously and illegally took (stole) Hawaii. As a result, to this day, the U.S. claim to the Hawaiian Islands is not only defective it is outright fraudulent!

UNITED STATES CONGRESS AFFIRMS NO LAWFUL LAND CLAIM TO THE HAWAIIAN ARCHIPELAGO AND ITS ISLANDS:

The present United States Congressional jurisdictional statement in Title 28 U.S.C. § 91 defining the lawful authority of the U.S. District Court for Hawaii reflects the United States' Congressional limitations upon that court. <u>It is the only judicial district</u> of all the United States District Courts <u>where the area of jurisdiction</u> is described as being <u>outside of, and away from, the location of its court</u>!

More specifically, each of the United States court's jurisdictions reflects names of cities, counties, etc. <u>within</u> its boundaries of authority and jurisdiction yet; the Hawaii District Court does not. I quote 28 U.S.C. § 91:

"Title 28 U.S.C. § 91. Hawaii - Hawaii <u>constitutes</u> one judicial district which <u>includes</u> the Midway Islands, Wake Island, Johnston Island, Sand Island, Kingman Reef, Palmyra Island, Baker Island, Howland Island, Jarvis Island, Canton Island, and Enderbury Island: Provided, That the <u>inclusion</u> of Canton and Enderbury Islands in such judicial district shall in no way be construed to be prejudicial to the claims of the United Kingdom to said Islands in accordance with the agreement of April 6, 1939, between the Governments of the United States and of the United Kingdom to set up a regime for their use in common. Court shall be held <u>at</u> Honolulu." (Key word underlining by Author)

Notice that the list of islands in this "judicial district" does not include the main Islands of the Hawaiian Archipelago: Hawaii, Maui, Oahu, Kauai, Molokai, Lanai, Niihau and Kahoolawe!

Then *what* or *which "Hawaii"* is this U.S. Congressional Law alluding to? Is it:

1. *"Hawaii"* - *the largest Island on the southern part of the Hawaiian Archipelago?*

2. *"Hawaii"* - Ko Hawaii Pae Aina (the Hawaiian Islands), the lawful independent, sovereign nation? *The de jure Nation among Nations, under suppression by the colonial and military power of the* United States Federal Government?

3. *"Hawaii"* – *the illegal "State of Hawaii" corporation/puppet-government?* The "State of Hawaii" *is a corporation created in 1959 by "Executive (Order) Proclamation"* No. 3309, Aug. 21, 1959, 25 F.R. 6868, 73 Stat. c74),

OR, is it…

4. "Hawaii" – used just as a word, without its substance being defined, to describe the named (includes/inclusion) minor islands and reefs in the Pacific. Please note that it specifically excludes (omits) the main Islands of the Hawaiian Archipelago, but specifically includes the Midway Islands, Wake Island, Johnston Island, Sand Island, Kingman Reef, Palmyra Island, Baker Island, Howland Island, Jarvis Island, Canton Island, and Enderbury Island?

It appears that the latter application, #4, is appropriate and intentional, there being no other consideration possible without a clarifying definition provided for the word *"Hawaii."* The term *"Hawaii"* thus used is ambiguous. Because of its ambiguity, it is not to be considered a legal term, as it has not been defined or clarified within the code section or law. This appears to be the United States' description for their imaginary *Hawaii Judicial District* that does not lawfully exist!

Again, notice that the main islands of the Hawaiian Archipelago, are not specified anywhere in the text of this enabling law! Was this just a clerical error in drafting the "Statehood Act"? This is highly unlikely. But even if it was an error, it would mean that the Hawaiian Islands are not part of the *"Hawaii Judicial District."* The only plausible explanation for this irregularity is that the main Hawaiian Islands were specifically and deliberately (but very deviously) omitted from being designated as being under the United States jurisdiction!

Furthermore, the above law (Title 28 U.S.C. § 91) states that the *U.S. Court for the Hawaii District* is to be held *"at"* Honolulu instead of *"in"* Honolulu. The participle, *"at"* indicates a point or place but can mean: "in, about or near." If the Hawaiian Archipelago were the lawful possession of the United States, they would have used the possessive, *"in"* (*also a participle, but one that indicates "inclusion within a space, or a boundary, i.e. possession"*), as it does for Seattle, San Francisco, Los Angeles, Washington D.C. or other acceptable locations.

Other words of importance and their meanings:

"Constitutes." Not in Black's Law Dictionary, Sixth Edition.

In **Merriam Webster's Collegiate Dictionary,** *Tenth Edition, "constitutes" is defined as follows: "constitute: 1: to appoint to an office, function or dignity 2: SET UP, ESTABLISH: as a: ENACT b: found c (1): to give due or lawful form to (2): to legally process 3: MAKE UP, FORM, COMPOSE..."*

"Includes."– Source: Black's Law Dictionary, Sixth Edition.

(Lat. Inclaudere, to shut in, keep within.) *To confine within, hold as in an enclosure, take in, attain, shut up. Contain, enclose, comprise, comprehend, embrace, involve. Term may, according to context, express an enlargement and have the meaning of and or in addition to, or merely specify a particular thing already included within general words theretofore used. "Including" within statute is interpreted as a word of enlargement or of illustrative application as well as a word of limitation. Premier Products Co. v. Cameron, 240 Or. 123, 400 P.2d 227, 228.*

Therefore, **Title 28 U.S.C. § 91,** defining *"The United States Court for the Hawaii District"* is obviously and clearly an example of *"Admission by Omission,"*[7]

---

[7] **"Admission by Omission."** - The description does not include any Islands of the Hawaiian Archipelago; to wit: **"Inclusio unius est exclusio alterius"** which means, **"the inclusion of one is the exclusion of another"**... The certain designation of one person is an absolute exclusion of all others. This doctrine decrees that where law expressly describes (a). a particular situation to which it shall

revealing that the U.S. District Court for Hawaii possesses <u>no</u> lawful authority over the *Hawaiian Archipelago, i.e. Hawaiian Kingdom.* <u>THEREFORE</u>, it follows that the United States does not possess lawful jurisdiction over the *Hawaiian Islands* or *Hawaiian Nationals (Citizens or Subjects of Hawaii).*

What the United States Federal Government did and has done through deception, under *"color of law"[8]* in open violation of their own United States Laws and the "United States Constitution," was to create a colonial de facto state, with a foreign puppet government, using three distinct phases of deception and suppression. This was accomplished with complicity (often ignorant) from government leaders, the legal profession, business and economic leaders, the educational system, the average U.S. taxpayer, the major news media, and all strata of the American-colonized Hawaiian society.

The first phase started with the original treasonists (some being trusted government office-holders under oath) calling themselves, *"The Committee of Safety."[9]* Their primary motivation was to solidify and increase their financial interests in Hawaii through highly favorable business and trade policies.

The Committee of Safety in plotting and participating in the overthrow of the lawful Hawaiian Kingdom National Government were <u>afraid for their lives because, if their coup should fail, the penalty for their act of treason would be death</u>! They were only able to go through with their plans because the U.S. Foreign Minister John L. Stevens unlawfully, without U.S. government authority, ordered the landing of a fully armed detachment of U.S. Marines and Navy personnel to back the unlawful takeover. <u>Without this military intervention the coup would have failed.</u>

In the second phase, the rebels formed a "provisional government," took over control of Hawaii and immediately sought annexation to the U.S. The desire of these

---

apply, an irrefutable inference must be drawn that what is omitted or excluded was intended to be omitted or excluded." (Black's Law Dictionary, 6th Ed.)

[8] **Color of Law.** *(see introduction p. ix, footnote 11)*

[9] *The Committee of Safety. (Author's Note)* <u>These were of foreign, Caucasian, descent.</u> *Americans like Dole, Thurston, Cooper, Damon, Tenney, Brown, Smith, Castle(s), Dawson, Wilder, McCandless, Ashley, Bolte, Jones, King, Emmeluth, Morgan, Marsden, Waterhouse, Emerson, Jones, Spalding, Alexander, Young, Moore, Hobbs, Swinburne, Laird, Judd, Soper, Wilcox(s), Carter, Oleson, Coffman, Stelker, Bowen, Reeder, Macarthur, Belknap, Delameter, Day, Hoes, Simpson, Ludlow etc.) Some of these were outright Hawaiian National Citizens, and some National Citizens of dual U.S. and Hawaiian citizenship. Some were under Hawaiian Government oaths of Offi*ce. **Several were European citizens.** *All became treasonists and/or insurgents under Hawaiian Kingdom National Law.*

conspirators and traitors was for the United States to reward and protect them by making Hawaii, at the very least, a protectorate or territory under United States military control. This was sought in order that these wealthy merchants-turned-traitors could retain their assets, their power, and their lives! But at the end of 1893, when the facts of the unlawful military intervention were exposed, President Cleveland caused the Treaty of Annexation to be withdrawn from the U.S. Congress.

This triggered phase three, whereby the treasonists had to do something to save themselves. Hurriedly, in 1894 the traitors declared Hawaii to be a new country with a new (de facto) government called, *"The Republic of Hawaii."* This self-proclaimed manifestation of a government had no support and virtually no approval from the general populace of the Hawaiian Islands. In an ironic and amazing display of audacity the *Republic of Hawaii* warned the United States not to attempt to restore the Monarch or the Government of the Hawaiian Kingdom for to do so would amount to *interference in the internal affairs of this foreign nation! What hypocrisy!*

The Hawaiian National Citizens (the vast majority of the population) during this time had placed their trust in their beloved monarch, Queen Liliuokalani, and the rule of law, both domestic and international. In order to avert bloodshed, and expecting a swift diplomatic resolution, the Queen had ordered her small, inadequate military force and the people to not take up arms to resolve the usurpation. Instead, she temporarily yielded her authority to the President of the United States, trusting in the good will and character of the President as an emissary of righteousness and head of a supposedly Godly nation to honorably rectify the breach. The Queen's conditional yield to the President of the United States placed in his hands the right, the duty, the opportunity and the moral authority to restore to *power*[10] the Hawaiian Nation's proper and lawful government.

---

[10] *I, Liliuokalani, by the Grace of God and under the Constitution of the Hawaiian Kingdom, Queen, do hereby solemnly protest against any and all acts done against myself and the Constitutional Government of the Hawaiian Kingdom by certain persons claiming to establish a Provisional Government of and for this Kingdom.*

That I yield to the superior force of the United States of America whose Minister Plenipotentiary, His Excellency John L. Stevens, has caused United States troops to be landed at Honolulu and declared that he would support the Provisional Government. Now to avoid collision of armed forces, and perhaps the loss of life, I do this under Protest and impelled by said force yield my authority until such time as the Government of the United States shall, upon facts being presented to it, undo the action of its representatives and reinstate me in the authority which I claim as the Constitutional Sovereign of the Hawaiian Islands.

Done at Honolulu this 17th Day of January A.D. 1893."

Unfortunately, the Queen's and the Hawaiian people's trust was in vain. A significant fact is that small band of conspirators was of Caucasian descent; there was not one citizen of Hawaiian blood that participated in the removal of the Queen and the takeover of the Hawaiian Kingdom. In fact, many of the Hawaiian citizens of Caucasian descent, and virtually all those of Asian descent remained loyal to the Queen and their country, Hawaii.

The outgoing, "lame-duck" U.S. President Benjamin Harrison was receptive to annexing Hawaii, and supported the annexation treaty hastily proposed by the treasonous individuals who had usurped the Hawaiian Kingdom. The treaty was submitted to the U.S. Senate for acceptance. In the meantime, President Harrison rejected correspondence, proper petitions, appeals and personal emissaries of Queen Liliuokalani to the United States. By inaction, delay and other political machinations, President Harrison provided protection and time for the conspirators (consisting of United States citizens and several European foreigners) to consolidate with U.S. provided arms their treasonous actions. This is affirmed by many historical documents, including the U.S. State Department publication titled, *"Foreign Relations of the United States: Affairs in Hawaii - 1895, et al.*

Despite the efforts of the conspiracy, the formal protests filed by the Queen (see Footnote 10, of this Chapter), the lawful Hawaiian Kingdom Government, the Hawaiian people, and strong objections raised by certain U.S. Senators of integrity and conscience, helped to stall immediate passage of the Treaty.

By submitting the Treaty of Annexation to Congress, President Harrison and members of his administration, lacking any integrity, had deliberately ignored existing treaties; the overtly illegal and absurd actions of various conspirators; the treasonous *Committee of Safety in overthrowing the Hawaiian Kingdom; the U.S. Foreign Minister in providing unlawful recognition of the illegal Provisional Government for the Hawaiian Kingdom;* and *the hostile maneuvers by the U.S. Marines and Navy personnel on sovereign Hawaiian National soil.*

The incoming President, Grover Cleveland ordered an investigation. The resulting *"Blount Report"* found the actions of the parties of the *"Committee of Safety"*

"Therefore I, Liliuokalani of Hawaii, do hereby call upon the President (Benjamin Harrison) of that nation, to whom alone I yielded my property and my authority..." Source: "Hawaii's Story" by Queen Liliuokalani, 1898)

as unlawful and treasonous; and the unauthorized participation by *U.S. Minister Stevens* and the unauthorized invasion by the *U.S. Military (Navy and Marines)* on sovereign *Hawaiian National* soil, as unlawful under international law and contrary to the U.S. Constitution and foreign policy. President Cleveland ordered the Treaty of Annexation to be withdrawn from Congress and the rightful Hawaiian Government restored.

But for various unexplained reasons, the President of the United States failed to take affirmative action to restore to the Hawaiian Kingdom the lawful authority that had been temporarily yielded solely to the U.S. President in 1893.

The U.S. military had their own agenda. While the U.S. Government was directly supporting treason on foreign soil, and then "neglecting" to restore the proper and lawful *Hawaiian National Government,* the U.S. military was implementing its own designs to establish a U.S. naval base at Pearl Harbor. All that was needed was a plausible justification.

In 1897 another attempt was made to pass a treaty to annex Hawaii to the United States. Tremendous lobbying efforts by Queen Liliuokalani, numerous Hawaiian patriots, patriotic organizations, and a huge public groundswell in Hawaii, caused the treaty to be defeated again in the U.S. Congress. Despite this failure, a military need (plausible justification) immediately presented itself with the outbreak of the Spanish American War. Suddenly, Pearl Harbor became a crucial military coaling station and the islands an outpost to support America's expansion into the territories sought from Spain in the Western Pacific — the Philippines, Guam, and the Caroline Islands.

In 1898, the United States Government, using blatant deception via public disinformation, passed through Congress the *"Newlands Resolution"*[11] (See EXHIBIT F) as a supposed *"treaty of annexation"* to create and form a foreign United States puppet government by endorsing and negotiating with the de facto, treasonous *Republic of Hawaii.* A U.S. Resolution is a <u>congressional **suggestion** for internal (domestic) application</u>. It is only a formal statement or expression of preferred or

---

[11] ***Newlands Resolution.*** "Joint Resolution To Provide for annexing the Hawaiian Islands to the United States. Statutes At Large of the United States of America. Resolution No. 55, 2nd Session, 55th Congress, July 7, 1898; 30 Sta. At L. 750; 2 Supp. R. S. 895." (**Author's Note: A resolution only has effect in the country or jurisdiction passing it. The Hawaiian People never approved it by vote, nor did the de jure Hawaiian Kingdom Government accept annexation or submission of any kind to U.S. authority.**)

recommended policy. A resolution is not law on U.S., much less, foreign soil. It has no force of law!

The U.S. Government then utilized this internal document: *"Joint Resolution to Provide for Annexing the Hawaiian Islands to the United States,"* as the basis for a supposed treaty of annexation (*Newlands Resolution, supra*) to create the de facto *"Territory of Hawaii."* This, in its first paragraph stipulates, that the U.S. Government *(having already recognized as "de facto," the "Republic of Hawaii,")* now supposedly accepts from it as *"ceded"* … *"sovereignty of whatsoever kind…"* etc., (the stolen possessions of another). In truth, the *"Republic of Hawaii"* possessed nothing that it could lawfully *"cede"* to anyone.

Jurisdictionally speaking, the U.S. recognized "de facto" *"Republic of Hawaii"* possessed no *"sovereignty,"* and hence the usage of the ambiguous phrase, *"…of whatsoever kind…"* The treasonists most definitely did not possess, *"exclusive jurisdiction,"* over the lands and Hawaiian People. The treasonists only had stolen "rights." To this very day, these stolen "rights" are enforced through abuse of police power with full United States complicity and military support.

Section 1, of the *"Newlands Resolution,"* provided for the United States to financially bail out the indebted, de facto *"Republic of Hawaii"* by *"assuming"* its public debt to the tune of $4,000,000! The United States did not pay off that debt, but only loaned the de facto entity money. The *Newlands Resolution, § 1 Paragraph 7,* which affirms this fact, states:

> *"The public debt of the Republic of Hawaii, lawfully existing at the date of the passage of this joint resolution, including the amounts due to Depositors in the Hawaiian Postal Savings Bank, is hereby assumed by the Government of the United States; but the liability of the United States in this regard shall in no case exceed four million dollars. So long, however, as the existing Government (Republic of Hawaii) and the present commercial relations of the Hawaiian Islands are continued as hereinbefore provided said Government (Republic of Hawaii) shall continue to pay the interest on said debt."*

> *(Parenthesis and underlining clarifications by Author)*

This does not constitute, nor does it substitute for an acquisition! There was no purchase here! It was a loan (assumption of a debt) misrepresented to be payment for acquisition in order to create a basis for the upcoming *Organic Act*, which was then deviously and fraudulently misrepresented to the American and Hawaiian People.

Meanwhile, in Hawaii (i.e. the de facto *"Republic of Hawaii"*) the People were being misled and told publicly the following, through the de facto Legislative Body, and the media; I quote: (*Section 2, of the "Organic Act,"*)

> *"That the islands <u>acquired</u> by the United States of America under an Act of Congress entitled "Joint resolution to provide for annexing the Hawaiian Islands to the United States," approved July seventh, eighteen hundred and ninety-eight, shall be known as the territory of Hawaii." (Source: Organic Act Sessions Law of the Republic of Hawaii) (Underlined emphasis by Author)*

Contrary to the claim of the above excerpt, <u>the Hawaiian Islands were never "acquired"</u>! Such shrewd deception and misrepresentation was utilized to bolster the false official U.S. Government's position. The de facto courts in Hawaii, with judges appointed from within the de facto entity as prescribed in the *Organic Act,* continue to support the U.S.' fraudulent position.

The defective *Newlands Resolution* (1898) was the foundational basis for the creation of the *"Organic Act" (April 30, 1900, C 339, 31 Stat 14)*. The *Organic Act* contains deliberate misrepresentations to sway, obscure and otherwise cause a grand deception to con the general American public and private sectors; to demean and subjugate and suppress Hawaiian Nationals; and to establish future U.S. military control of the Hawaiian Islands.

CRITIQUE of the "THE ORGANIC ACT - An Act to Provide a Government for the Territory of Hawaii (Act of April 30, 1900, C 339, 31 Stat 141)"

The third phase of the chain of de facto governments was called the *"Territory of Hawaii,"* fraudulently created by the U.S. Federal Congress through passage of the *Organic Act of 1900*. This measure was used by the U.S. to carry out the so-called *"annexation"* of Hawaii initiated by the deficient 1898 Newlands Resolution. This annexation was unlawful from its inception because the U.S. entered into a contract with known treasonists *posing as the Republic of Hawaii,* who did not possess *"exclusive"* jurisdictional interest over the Hawaiian Nation. The vast majority (over 90%) of the population was openly opposed to annexation, and believed in the *rule of law* (instead of warfare) to receive justice. Their voice of protest and their cries for justice were ignored and trampled by racist discriminatory prejudices prevalent among the American leadership and general society. Hawaiian Nationals were allowed no platform for their voice then, or since; being unable to vote or participate in government unless they surrendered their Hawaiian Nationality and swore allegiance to the de facto *Republic of Hawaii* or *Territory of Hawaii* or *State of Hawaii* and the intimidating, intrusive *United States.*[12]

Let me be more specific about the United States-created, *"Organic Act."* In that Act, under *"Definitions,"* the United States openly maligns and insults Hawaiian Nationals of Hawaiian blood and mixed-blood heritage within the *Territory of Hawaii* (the subjugated and occupied de jure *Hawaiian Kingdom).* In the *Organic Act, § 1, "Definitions,"* we find the following:

> *"Hawaiian" and "native Hawaiian" mean any descendent of the races inhabiting the Hawaiian Islands prior to 1778."*

This new definition effectively introduced ethnicity (race) as a means of separating Hawaiians from their nationality. Defining Hawaiians by their ethnicity changed their status from Nationals (Private Citizens) of the Hawaiian Kingdom (a heretofore legitimate and recognized independent country), into members of an isolated ethnic, indigenous group. And what about those Hawaiian Nationals who were not "native Hawaiian" as defined above? For example, many Hawaiian Nationals were of Chinese, Japanese, English, German, French, Spanish, Portuguese *ethnicities.* They too, as Hawaiian Nationals, lost their country. All, had been citizens of the Hawaiian Kingdom, protected by International Treaties with other nations worldwide. By this very repugnant *Organic Act,* aboriginal Hawaiians *of the blood (koko)* and those of all other ethnicities have been relegated to non-Hawaiian-National-Citizenship status; in their own, recognized sovereign Nation.

Fact: Technically, all the lands of Hawaii are still the property of the national entity, the Hawaiian National Government, and its people. That has not lawfully changed.

---

[12] See Chapter 4, BIRTHNAMES, BIRTHRIGHTS AND CITIZENSHIP, *which describes how Hawaiians were moved into a legal but not lawful, foreign U.S. Federal judicial jurisdiction as* "citizens of Washington D.C." *thus becoming foreign,* "second-class immigration status," "U.S. federal citizens" *on their own birth soil.*

By redefining and recasting *Hawaiian Nationals (citizens of a sovereign nation)* as aboriginals *(native inhabitants of Hawaii)*, the land, according to accepted Euro-American colonial standards would be up for grabs by *conquest.*[13] That would put the treasonous entity, *the so-called Committee of Safety (later transformed into the Republic of Hawaii)*, in position to exercise (with U.S. support) a pretentious claim of conquest.

The act of the treasonists was internal, within the national "exclusive jurisdiction" of the Hawaiian Kingdom. It was the United States that committed an "act of war" as was admitted to by President Cleveland, as an unintended, regrettable violation that required immediate remedy and restoration. There was no declaration of war between Hawaii and the U.S., so conquest by warfare cannot to be used as a pretext for today's U.S. occupation of Hawaii. It is plain and simple *theft!*

The United States current occupation of Hawaii is based on a series of false and unlawful claims by illegal de facto governments from 1893 to the present day. The Hawaiian Kingdom was concealed, not "overthrown" or conquered. Since there has never been a lawful transition of governance following the initial takeover, according to international standards *(i.e. the Law of Nations, World Court, United Nations, etc.)*, the sovereignty of the nation of Hawaii has never been extinguished. **Therefore, the *Nation* of the *Hawaiian Islands*, and its governing entity, *the Hawaiian Kingdom*, still exist *in continuity*, as do the rights, privileges and duties of *Hawaiian National Citizens!***

The *Organic Act of 1900* is insulting, demeaning and oppressive to all Hawaiians, especially those who understand its purpose. Through this instrument, the U.S. supported a lawless group of treasonists functioning under abuse of police power. With blatant prejudice and disregard for law, they demote *Hawaiian Nationals* (Private Citizens of a recognized, progressive nation), to the status of *"native Hawaiians,"* insinuating an aboriginal tribal entity instead of an organized progressive nation.

I can only assume this was done as the result of the Americans' bias that Hawaiians (now downgraded by the Organic Act to only "blood quantum" *"native*

---

[13] **European Colonialism** is founded on the *"Doctrine of Discovery"* as expressed through the 1493 Papal Bull *Inter Caetera* and other pronouncements such as *Terra Nullis*. In essence, the Doctrine of Discovery maintains that non-Christians (heathens, pagans, Saracens) are merely occupiers of lands without lawful (Catholic Church-sanctioned) claim to the lands that they inhabit. Therefore, (particularly Catholic) European nations have the "God-given" right to conquer those lands and subject or eliminate the people that live there. Though not as overt, this *Doctrine of Discovery* is still a key factor in the attitude and operating policies for Western nations such as America.

Hawaiians") could not have the capacity to own their land, nor have the intelligence sufficient to operate their own nation. Of course this was absolutely not true. Except for a five-month period in 1843, Hawaii had always been self-governing for over a thousand years, and in 1840 had established a progressive, constitutional form of government. Hawaiian Nationals of this sovereign Hawaiian nation who were extremely well informed, articulate and fully proficient in self-governance.

The depiction by Americans of Hawaiians as "aborigines" was done to play on the ethno-centric prejudices of an ignorant American public (*i.e. non-white = savage, heathen, uncivilized*). Under this *Organic Act*, the newly created, U.S. implemented court system looked down upon the native Hawaiians, treating them as non-persons (similar to Blacks or American Indians), lacking European knowledge or education; and occupying, but having no "legal" rights to their land. Shame on America's politicians and Government!

The Twentieth Century (1900) dawned with the United States fully embarked on a new path of imperialism with its newly created, fraudulent governing entity replacing the fraudulent *Republic of Hawaii.* This time, the governing entity was titled the *"Territory of Hawaii,"* but it was still the result of a series of lies and deception to defraud both the American and Hawaiian people.

TERRITORIAL LAWS AND U.S. COURTS CREATED BY THE ORGANIC ACT

The U.S. courts on Hawaiian Kingdom soil and functioning under this Act are *de facto.* They cannot be anything else. The U.S. even created a *"Territorial Oath"* (See EXHIBIT M) for its federal judges under the Organic Act, who under this Act are to this date, appointed by the *President of the United States.*[14]

The *"Organic Act" (i.e. Territorial Act)* begins with deception and fraud. In *"Section 1", "Definitions."* the United States herein recognizes its own de facto creation (*The overthrow of the lawful Hawaiian Government was affected by the "Committee of Safety," which a year-and-a-half later changed itself into the "Republic of Hawaii"*). These are the same conspirators; only the name of their group had changed.

Section 1: (Organic Act)

---

[14] That particular oath consists of a combination of two oaths, which this Author cannot find legislation or promulgation for in order to substantiate its lawful existence- See Chapter 6, Hawaii's Courts...).

Section 1. Definitions. *"That the phrase "the laws of Hawaii" as used in this Act without qualifying words, shall mean the constitution and laws of the Republic of Hawaii, in force on the twelfth day of August, eighteen hundred and ninety-eight, at the time of the transfer of the sovereignty of the Hawaiian Islands to the United States of America."*

The use of the wording, *"transfer of the sovereignty…"* is a false and misleading statement that refers to a sovereignty that did not exist under the "Republic of Hawaii," and a transfer of power, authority, land and possessions that the Republic of Hawaii did not lawfully possess, and, therefore, did not (because they could not) lawfully transfer.

Section 2:

"Section 2" states that the Archipelago was *"acquired"* by the United States by an Act of Congress *("Newlands Resolution," supra)*, which is also false!

Section 2. Territory of Hawaii. *That the islands acquired by the United States of America under an Act of Congress entitled "Joint resolution to provide for annexing the Hawaiian Islands to the United States," approved July seventh, eighteen hundred and ninety-eight, shall be known as the Territory of Hawaii."*

Let's look back at the "Newlands Resolution" (Resolution No. 55, 2nd session, 55th Congress, July 7, 1898; 30 Sta. At L. 750; 2 Supp. R.S. 895) **(See EXHIBIT F)** and see what it says regarding the **"acquisition."** I quote Paragraph 7, of that Resolution:

> *Newlands Resolution: Paragraph 7. "The public debt of the Republic of Hawaii, lawfully existing at the date of the passage of this joint resolution, including the amounts due to depositors in the Hawaiian Postal savings Bank, is hereby assumed by the government of the United States; but the liability of the United States in this regard shall in no case exceed four million dollars. So long, however, as the existing Government and the present commercial relations of the Hawaiian Islands are continued as hereinbefore <u>provided said Government shall continue to pay the interest on said debt.</u>" (Underlined emphasis by Author)*

The above is the only reference to any monetary acquisition or supposed acquisition within the *"Newlands Resolution."* If you read the last sentence, you find that <u>this is a conditional loan</u>, subject to the necessity *that "…said Government shall continue to pay the interest on said debt."* Interest is only paid on a loan! Where was the acquisition? I cannot find one!

Let's be truthful here. You cannot lawfully purchase stolen goods *(i.e. The Hawaiian Kingdom)* from a thief, if in fact you know that that which you are acquiring is stolen! Secondly, there was no purchase involved, only a loan! In fact, the whole of the claim of United States' interest in *The Hawaiian Islands,* as its possession, is a fraud, deceptively false, and misleading <u>not just morally and diplomatically</u>, but <u>without any lawful foundation under any law!</u> U.S. actions regarding *The Hawaiian Islands* are an affront to righteousness and the very Constitution of the <u>u</u>nited *State's of America* that they, the politicians, attorneys and judges of that era, as well as the present era, say they honor! The Nation called *"America"* whose Federal Congress presently represents itself as being *"Under God"* operates with deviousness, deception and lies!

> **Section 4 of the Organic Act, states:** *"That all persons who were citizens of the <u>Republic of Hawaii</u> on August twelfth, eighteen hundred and ninety-eight, are hereby <u>declared to be citizens</u> of the United States and citizens of the Territory of Hawaii" (Underlined emphasis by Author).*

In essence, by this act the Federal United States grants immunity to those who participated in treason and revolt and were in illegal control of *The Hawaiian Islands* at the time. <u>This was an *"ex post facto"*[15]</u> law. This assumed law is not law. It is illegal in the United States, but even more so on foreign soil! This is very, very morally wrong, not just unlawful, but outright deception by the United States. It amounted to endorsement of an unlawful act of revolt and treason that the United States fostered in a foreign country and supported militarily, and now, through this Organic Act, grants immunity and rewards for those who did it! Again, the truth is distorted… America's politicians and Congress lies again!

U.S. presence is still maintained in Hawaii today by *abuse of police power.* The U.S. military presence has remained since the overthrow of the de jure Government of *The Hawaiian Kingdom* on January 16th and 17th of 1893. The United States just as easily could have, and should have acted as a friend and restored the *Hawaiian Kingdom Government* to its rightful status among the nations of the world. Unfortunately, its

---

[15] ***Ex post facto.*** "After the fact; by an act or fact occurring after some previous act or fact, and relating thereto; by subsequent matter; the opposite of ab initio. Thus, a deed may be good ab initio, or, if invalid at its inception, may be confirmed by matter ex post facto." (Black's Law Dictionary, 6th Edition)

Congress and President, both lacking integrity, chose not to do so because of the importance of Hawaii as a strategic military location in the Pacific as affirmed in their *U.S. State Department Publication of 1893.*[16] (Read the book footnoted below)

It is interesting that Pearl Harbor, needed as a *"coaling station,"* had already been leased to the U.S. prior to the overthrow of the lawful Hawaiian Kingdom National Government. Hawaii was considered a key component and opportunity by America's expansionists to exert its *"Manifest Destiny"* in the Pacific Ocean, from which to extend its new role as a world military power.

THE FRAUDULENT CONVERSION OF HAWAIIAN CITIZENS TO UNITED STATES CITIZENS OF WASHINGTON, D.C. - WHILE ON THEIR OWN HAWAIIAN NATIONAL LAND

United States Law *Title 8, United States Code, § 1405* (Quoted below) as referenced in **Section 4 of the Organic Act of 1900**, above, is a very interesting and non-applicable law. It was created and passed on June 27, 1952 in preparation for publicly creating the image, to the international community, of Hawaiian Nationals as having accepted their status as American citizens (albeit a foreign *"second-class, 14th Amendment, United States federal immigration status"* citizenship *under Article 1, § 8 of the United States' Constitution).* This U.S. law was never applicable to and never accepted by Hawaiian Nationals. This law has the explicit affect of granting American federal citizenship and immunity to all *citizens* of the unlawful *"Republic of Hawaii"* that overthrew the lawful *National Government of the Hawaiian Kingdom.* I quote that ex post facto law:

Source: 8 U.S.C. § 1405 (Also, *Immigration and Nationality Act. § 305*)

> "A person born in Hawaii on or after August 12, 1898, and before April 30, 1900 is declared to be a citizen of the United States as of April 30, 1900. A person born in Hawaii on or after 1900, is a citizen of the United States at birth. A person who was a citizen of the Republic of Hawaii on the date of August 12, 1898 is declared to be a citizen of the United States as of April 30, 1900."
> (Underlined Emphasis by Author)

---

[16] *"CORRESPONDENCE WITH DIPLOMATIC AND NAVAL OFFICERS* concerning the Relations of the United States to the Hawaiian Islands - Including a reprint of Senate Executive Documents No. 76 and No. 77, Fifty-Second Congress, Second Edition" (and which was printed by the) "WASHINGTON: Government Printing Office 1893."

First of all, a *"person"* is in this sense, a *public servant* or *corporate fiction* and not a living soul or private human being. <u>This pertains to the created, *"14th Amendment,"* *"Washington D.C.,"* *"Emancipated Slave,"* *"immigration status,"* "federal type" of citizenship</u>. This violates the American Constitution and International Law as well. You cannot just *'declare,'* *"All citizens of New Zealand are now United States <u>c</u>itizens."* You cannot just *'declare,'* *"All citizens of Canada are now United States <u>c</u>itizens (as of such and such a date)."* I don't believe that the Private Citizens or Governments of either New Zealand or Canada would take a very compassionate or appreciative view of such inappropriate U.S. Congressional legislation. Such absurd legislation would not have affected the *Citizenship of the People of the Hawaiian Kingdom* any more than it would the Citizens of New Zealand and Canada. <u>In effect, it says nothing</u>.

THE ADMISSION ACT CRITIQUE: (Hawaii Statehood Act of March 18, 1959)

The "Admission Act" *(An Act to Provide for the Admission of the State of Hawaii[17] into the Union [Act of March 18, 1959, Pub L 86-3, 73 Stat 4])* was created to give the impression that Hawaii was to be the 50th State of the American Union of States. This huge deception and fraud, compounds lie upon lie.

In its preamble, *"The Admission Act of 1959 (i.e. Statehood Act)"* states Hawaii *"...is declared admitted into the Union on an equal footing with the other States..."* Unfortunately, the words *"is declared admitted"* are <u>not the same as the words, *"is admitted,"*</u> which were not used in this instance. So what is the distinction? The use of the words *"is declared admitted"* is simply *"a publicly avowed or professed statement"* *(Source: Webster's Unabridged Dictionary)* not necessarily being true or of fact. Just by saying, "Robert <u>is declared admitted</u> into the swimming pool," does not give Robert authority to enter into the pool. It's a shallow *(pardon the pun)*, meaningless statement. If the statement was, "Robert <u>is admitted</u> into the swimming pool," *(Definition: allow to*

---

[17] **STATE OF HAWAII.** (Author's Note) The defacto STATE OF HAWAII was created by Presidential Proclamation No. 3309 of August 21, 1959, 24 F. R. 868, 73 Stat. C74. <u>A Proclamation cannot create a "State of the Union,"</u> but maybe only a limited corporation under Article 1 § 8 of the American Constitution. Only the U.S. <u>National</u> Congress of the Republic in lawful session, not the <u>Federal</u> Congress, can create an American "State" for admission into the American "Union of States". **(America has two (2) Congresses. The <u>National</u> Congress represents "We the People" of the sovereign American Republic, and its Union of States, whereas the <u>Federal</u> Congress represents Washington, D.C. its territories, foreign affairs, etc., as structured under the subsidiary Article 1 § 8 of that same U.S. Constitution. – Author)**

enter, grant or afford entrance into; to give right or permission to enter, etc." Source: *Webster's Unabridged Dictionary)*, I am stating Robert now has authority to enter into the pool.

The usage of *"is declared admitted"* is *"legalese"* word-art and implies something that is not of fact. Either Hawaii <u>is</u> a State of the Union, OR, it <u>is</u> only <u>declared</u> to be a State of the Union. Facts of language *(Dictionary)* word meanings affirm the latter.

The U.S. deliberately misrepresents the truth, which still is, that the so-called *"State of Hawaii"* was never admitted into the American *"Union of States."* It could never have been because from the outset, *the Provisional Government, the Republic of Hawaii* and *the Territory of Hawaii* were each unlawful, de facto governing entities and known to be such by the U.S.

<u>Secondly, only the *"National Congress of the American Republic of States,"* in lawful session, can create a lawful state of the *American Union of States (U.S. Constitution, Article IV, § 3),* which in this case, it did not.</u> There are two U.S. Congresses: *National and Federal.* The lesser one, the *Federal Congress* has no power or authority, constitutionally, to create or add a *"State to the Union,"* yet it was this *Federal Congress* that passed the Admissions Act of 1959.

Without being lawfully empowered to do so, the most that the lesser Federal Congress could do was to create the appearance and impression of having created a *"State"* within the *"American Union of States."*

In *"Section 2"* the de facto STATE OF HAWAII is defined. Please read closely the following:

> **Section 2:** *"The State of Hawaii shall consist of all the islands, together with their appurtenant reefs and territorial waters, <u>included in the Territory of Hawaii</u> on the date of enactment of this Act..."* (Underlined emphasis by Author).

<u>Of importance here is the simple fact that the *"Territory of Hawaii"* did not possess any islands, appurtenant reefs or territorial waters!</u> They did not even have a lawful basis of existence except that created by a fraudulent representation to the populace of *The Hawaiian Islands* and the United States. No documented evidence exists of a transfer of *"sovereign territorial jurisdiction"* of *Hawaiian Kingdom National* assets *(in rem)* and its Islands of the Hawaiian Archipelago to the United States! No evidence is found of a transfer of *Hawaiian Kingdom* land to the United States or any other foreign

government! Therefore, the land is still under its original ownership and title in *Hawaiian National Government* jurisdiction. **"The Kingdom still exists!"** <u>Only a major part of the lawful Hawaiian Kingdom National Citizens are missing!</u>

In *"Section 3"* it states:

> **Section 3:** *"The constitution of the State of Hawaii shall always be* **republican in form**[18] *and shall not be repugnant to the Constitution of the United States and the principles of the Declaration of Independence." (Bold by Author)*

In truth, the State of Hawaii is openly *"repugnant"* and is not *"republican in form"* as required by the <u>u</u>nited *State's Constitution under Article IV, § 4.*

By all my research and observations, *The Hawaiian Kingdom Nation* still exists at law. It is time for constructive, positive, political change!

The continued U.S. effort of injustice and lack of political integrity regarding the Hawaiian Nation and its Hawaiian National People has been and continue to be blights on the moral character of all previous and current Presidents and Congresses of the United States and the American People. It is apparent that the ***in rem***[19] assets of the Hawaiian Kingdom never transferred and still remain in the *"exclusive"* jurisdictional possession of the *Hawaiian National Government (Ko Hawaii Pae Aina – i.e. Hawaiian Kingdom.)*

A good quote is that of U.S. Congressman Neil Abercrombie of Hawaii on February 15, 2008 in Washington D. C.:

> *"No one in the United States of America is above the law, not the president or those who work for the president." "Nor do they get to pick and choose which laws they will obey and which laws they can ignore."*

---

[18] **"Republican in form."** "From the word "republic." 1. a state in which the supreme power rests in the body of citizens entitled to vote and is exercised by representatives chosen directly or indirectly by them. 2. any body of persons viewed as a commonwealth. 3. a state in which the head of government is not a monarch or other hereditary head of state. 4. any of the five periods of republican government in France. Cf. First Republic, Second Republic, Third Republic, Forth Republic, Fifth Republic. Etc." (Source: Webster's Unabridged Dictionary, 2001 Edition)

[19] ***In rem.*** "A technical term used to designate proceedings or actions instituted against the thing in contradistinction to personal actions, which are said to be in personam…" *(Black's Law Dictionary, 6ᵗʰ Ed.)* "against a thing (as a right, status, or property) – used esp. of legal actions, judgments or jurisdiction; compare IN PERSONAM." (Source: Merriam – Webster Collegiate Dictionary, 10ᵗʰ Ed.)

"Can you really believe this or is this typical of all politicians who only use such rhetoric when it appears expedient for political and partisan purposes? It really sounds just like another politician to me because if he did mean what he says, this so-called U.S. Congressman and stickler for the law would apply his convictions to the flagrant violation and corruption of numerous U.S. laws with regard to Hawaii." – Author.

Chapter 2

The United Nations, Genocide[1] and Hawaii

AN AMERICAN NATIONAL CITIZEN'S VIEWPOINT

The United Nations, an international organization, was created in 1946 in San Francisco, California just after the Second World War. It replaced the previous world council known as the League of Nations. The League of Nations was to promote world peace and cooperation among nations and peoples and was created by the Treaty of Versailles in 1919, but collapsed due to the economic crisis of the Great Depression, the rise of Hitler's Germany and the League's total ineffectiveness in averting World War II. The League of Nations was dissolved in April of 1946 with the formation of the United Nations. The member nations of the U.N. are either voting or non-voting members of the General Assembly. Major Powers hold seats on its powerful Security Council.

The United Nations has oversight ability to protect individual nations and peoples from hurt, injury or genocide from larger and more powerful neighbors. Yet, even though the Hawaiian Kingdom Government exists lawfully, in *interregnum*,[2] Hawaiian National rights are not being protected by the United Nations. I believe because of U.S. pressure, the U.N. deliberately ignores the fact that Hawaii, prior to U.S. occupation, existed as an independent nation.

Hawaiian Nationals' voices are still muted by the politically oppressive powers of the de facto State of Hawaii courts and continual U.S. presence ever since the overthrow. The United Nations has ignored the violations and abuse of Hawaiian Nationals because it does not choose to see them. By turning a blind eye to the situation, the United Nations has given tacit approval to the United States' military occupation of this sovereign Hawaiian Nation.

---

[1] *Genocide. "The systematic, planned annihilation of a racial political, or cultural group."* (American Heritage Dictionary 1973 Ed.)

[2] *Interregnum. (in'ter reg'nam) "1. an interval of time between the close of a sovereign's reign and the accession of his or her normal or legitimate successor. 2. any period during which a state has no ruler or only a temporary executive. 3. any period of freedom from the usual authority. 4. any pause or interruption in continuity.*

Presently, The United States stands in violation of *CHAPTER XI, Article 73 of the United Nations' Charter* as well as The United Nations' General Assembly proclamation, *"Declaration on the Granting of Independence to Colonial Countries and Peoples"* (Resolution 1541 [XV]), of 14 December 1960.

It is very interesting to notice that *United Nations' Resolution 1541(XV)* was passed AFTER the United States apparently assured the U.N. nations that Hawaiians had voted for U.S. Statehood, when in fact <u>only U.S. federal citizens with as little as one year's residency in Hawaii were allowed to vote.   Hawaiian Nationals (non U.S. citizens) were excluded from that vote! Hawaiian Nationals (non U.S. citizens) are still not allowed to vote</u> in Hawaii as affirmed on the *State of Hawaii Voter Registration Forms* (See EXHIBIT G).   <u>This document and its exclusion therein affirms that only U.S. citizens can vote in a U.S. election in Hawaii.</u>

It seems that the United Nations is too weak and too intimidated to do what is right according to their Charter and before Almighty God; that is, stand up for the less fortunate and oppressed People of Hawaii.   Perhaps the United Nations is intimidated by the fact that the United States, a major financial contributor to the U.N.'s existence, might withdraw its financial support.

This Author believes that the United Nations has neither the backbone nor desire to stand up against the United States even if it is the right thing to do. The United Nations has been duly notified by *Ke Aupuni O Hawaii Nei (The Hawaiian Government)*, et al, and is aware that the United States in 1893 acted in violation of the *"Law of Nations"* by assisting in the overthrow of the *neutral*, peaceful *National Government of Ko Hawaii Pae Aina* (the Hawaiian Islands) and its Monarch.

The United Nations is aware that the United States has occupied *The Hawaiian Islands* through a de facto chain of puppet governments titled: *The Territory of Hawaii*; then later, *The State of Hawaii*. The U.N. is also aware that when it implemented *Chapter XI - Declaration Regarding Non-Self Governing Territories*, it required major countries after World War II that possessed colonies, to grant independence to those colonies if they desired independence. The United States did not make any such offer to the Hawaiian Islands and its people; it only called for a plebiscite, which was limited to its own U.S. citizens and military living on Hawaiian soil, and with "Statehood" as the only option available.

Most people in Hawaii, the U.S. and the nations of the world are unaware that the United States did not create a lawful "State" of the *"American Union of States"* when it supposedly created and then supposedly admitted the de facto State of Hawaii in 1959 into a questionable "Union." Most nations are unaware that Hawaiian Nationals were not given any right of choice; which was the choice of independence or continued U.S. military occupancy. Not all nations are aware that Hawaiian Nationals were not allowed to vote in the creation of that false statehood, but foreign U.S. Federal citizens and U.S. military families and their dependents with only one year of residence in Hawaii were permitted to vote. Of note is the fact that Hawaiians who gave up their Hawaiian National Citizenship *(birth names and birthrights)* to become *"second-class," "public servant," "immigration status," "U.S. federal citizens"* were allowed to vote *(See Chapter 7, Disenfranchisement).*

Not all people, even Hawaiians are aware that their land has never transferred to the U.S. Government *"exclusive"* jurisdictional ownership. Only the de jure Hawaiian National Government can lawfully transfer its land with approval of its National People! The U.S. occupies the Hawaiian Islands without the U.S. possessing lawful title to any Hawaiian lands! The deed of ownership still exists in the title name of the Hawaiian Government, *Ke Aupuni O Hawaii Nei, Ko Hawaii Pae Aina,* for its people.

History reveals that the United States' primary interest is its military use of the Hawaiian Islands, not to protect the independent, sovereign welfare, customs, culture and traditions of the Hawaiian People.

REGARDING U.S. CONSTITUTIONAL AUTHORITY

The President of the United States does not have the power to create a *State of the Union*, nor, can the President create a *State of the Union* by simply executing a *Proclamation* or *Executive Order*. That right is reserved only for the *united State's Congress of the Republic (National Congress)* functioning under authority of the U.S. Constitution. Not even the lesser, U.S. Federal Congress *(which governs Washington, D.C., etc.; and created under Article 1, Section 8 of that very same Constitution)* has the right to create a lawful State within the American Union of States.

Under the **United States Code** *(Positive law)* **Title 4, Section 1**, the united *State's Flag of the American Union of States* is therein lawfully documented. In that description you will find that the proper American Flag, today, is still the one displaying only 48 Stars! How then do we get 50 Stars on the American Flag of the Republic? Confused? It's really very simple. The President as the Commander-in-Chief of the United States Military simply ordered two stars added to the 48 Star Fringed Military Flag *(under the pretext that they represented Alaska and Hawaii)* and that is the flag of occupation obvious in the U.S. Federal Court and State of Hawaii Courts unlawfully located on *Hawaiian Kingdom* soil, with its usage now spread across the continental u̲nited "States."

The courts in Hawaii fly the Federal United States' 50-Star Military Flag with the *"yellow fringe"* (in violation of 4 USC § 3, by adding a fourth color) around it, openly reflecting that it is a flag of the United States Military. It is not the Flag of the American "Republic" for which I stand. So then, what kind of law do we have being forced over Hawaiians and others who come into these supposedly foreign, federal U.S. courts? Publicly, no one knows. It can be readily assumed that these are military tribunals because of the *Law of the Flag*,[3] but most definitely, they function under what I believe can only be some foreign administrative dictate, not limited to local, de facto Statutes.

THE CRIME OF GENOCIDE AGAINST HAWAIIAN NATIONALS

Under United States Federal Law, specifically, **Title 18, USCr.C Section 1091**, also cited as the **"Genocide Convention Implementation Act of 1987 (the Proxmire Act),"** the United States Federal Government affirms its opposition to *"genocide"* (*"The systematic, planned annihilation of a racial, political, or cultural group."- Amer. Herit. Dict. 1973).* It is very interesting to notice that even though the United States takes this openly righteous position, it does not adhere to it in its own Pacific Ocean back yard.

What I am saying is that the U.S. Government is in direct violation of the very intent of the law it requires of other nations and its own people. I am saying that the United States Federal Government is two-faced! It is extremely tragic when the United States Federal Government says one thing and does another while suppressing the evidence of such actions. Other nations must surely be aware of this travesty and abuse

---

[3] **Law of the Flag.** *"The maritime law, the law of that nation or country whose flag is flown by a particular vessel. A ship owner who sends his vessel into a foreign port gives notice by his flag to all who enter into contracts with the master that he intends the law of that flag to regulate such contracts, and that they must either submit to its operation or not contract with him."* (Source: Black's Law Dictionary 6th Ed., Page 638). See better definition in Bouvier's Law Dictionary (1949 Edition) – Author

of law even though such actions are considered as being internal (within U.S. boundaries when they are not). <u>The Hawaiian Nation and its Nationals are admittedly geographically outside of United States boundaries and not within the jurisdiction or lawful scope of U.S. internal affairs</u>!

Let me be more specific referencing this United States law. In **18 USC § 1091, Genocide, (The Proxmire Act) STATUTE - (a)**, it states:

> *Basic Offense. - Whoever, whether in time of peace or in time of war, in a circumstance described in subsection (d) and with the specific intent to destroy, in whole or in substantial part, a national, ethnic, racial, or religious group as such -*
>
> *(4) subjects the group to conditions of life that are intended to cause the physical destruction of the group in whole or in part;*
>
> *(5) imposes measures intended to prevent births within the group; or*
>
> *(6) transfers by force children of the group to another group; or attempts to do so, shall be punished as provided in subsection (b)*

The *puppet State of Hawaii Government* is deliberately and blatantly violating the above sections in its educational system, political and judicial processes. Land use policies and advocacy of population control (genocide-through-abortion). Hawaiian Nationals are excluded not in just a *"substantial part,"* but in their entirety from all due process rights within State of Hawaii courts. They are not recipients of any benefits to the needy unless they abrogate their citizenship rights as Hawaiian Nationals. Their traditions, customs and religious practices, are being systematically destroyed. They have had their lawful history as a nation removed from the educational system in order to hide the truth. For decades, their native language was ignored and strongly discouraged within and removed from public school systems (i.e. See, *"children," "ethnic group," "national group," "racial group" "religious group," which are defined and are inclusive in "Title 18, Section 1093, Definitions")*. The resulting effect of these anti-Hawaiian U.S. actions on Hawaiian soil is called, GENOCIDE!

Under **18 USCr.C § 1091(d)**, "Required Circumstance for Offenses. - The circumstance referred to in subsections (a) and (c) is that:

> *(1) the offense is committed within the United States; or*

> *(2) the alleged offender is a national of the United States (as defined in section 101 of the Immigration and Nationality Act (8 U.S. C. 1101)."*

Item (1) above, is interesting only in that these offenses must be committed *"within"* the United States. Unfortunately, these crimes have been and are being *"committed"* outside of the United States boundaries on foreign Hawaiian Kingdom National soil. <u>Result</u>: <u>There is no violation of this domestic U.S. law pertaining to Hawaii or Hawaiian Nationals, **but** it is a violation of International Law!</u>

Item (2) above, affirms that <u>the offender must be a *"national"*</u> of the United States, thus <u>omitting and ignoring the offenses of U.S. second-class *"federal citizens"*</u> or members of the U.S. Military who occupy Hawaii. That leaves only one type of person who can be legally guilty, that would be, an *"American, State's born, National Citizen"* of one of the 48 contiguous states, who has not given up his *State's Citizenship*, birthright and birth name to become a *"Washington D. C.," "U.S. immigration status," "second-class federal"* citizen. <u>Again, there can be no United States infraction of this law regarding Hawaii since all citizens in Hawaii that have residence and hold office, and vote, are U. S *"Washington D. C.," "public servant," "federal," "second-class," "immigration status" citizens"*</u>! Is it now getting interesting?

The above law is what this Author calls, *"…speaking out of both sides of its two-faced head!"* The U.S. gives the impression of being in compliance with the law, but not being bound to comply with the law.

WHO HOLDS THE POWER OVER THE HAWAIIAN NATION?

Who is holding the National power yielded conditionally by Queen Liliʻuokalani? Answer: The President of the United States. He possesses the sole authority in trust since 1893 *(See Footnote 10, Chapter 1, "General Background," Page 7.)* Therefore, *the President of the [united] States, also known as the **Commander-in-Chief** (his U.S. Constitutional Article 1 Section 8 federal, Executive title);* issues **Executive Orders** to maintain control and execute power and functions under a Military Flag **(Attorney General's Opinion - 34 Op Atty Gen 483 - 1925)**. The Office of the President (not Congress or the Courts) is presently in control over the Hawaiian People and its Nation.

What has happened to America's character and integrity as a nation? It is obvious to me that the U.S. Federal Government and its Presidency, although facing the truth of their errors, do not want to face the ramifications. The Apology Bill *(Public Law 103-150 of the U.S. Congress, November 23, 1993)* was not offered to Hawaiian Nationals (Hawaiian Citizens of all ethnic backgrounds) and their de jure government, but deliberately, and deviously offered to only "Native Hawaiians" *(as if they were aboriginals, uneducated and stupid).*

It is the Hawaiian Nationals of the Hawaiian Kingdom whom the President and U.S. Government injured in the theft and occupation of their nation! In the *Organic Act of 1900,* the United States Federal Government changed the definition of "Hawaiian" from that meaning "Hawaiian National" (not of a specific racial group) to "native" Hawaiian, characterized by race. The Organic Act says:

> **Hawaiian and native Hawaiian.** *"Hawaiian' and 'native Hawaiian' mean any descendent of the races inhabiting the Hawaiian Islands Prior to 1778."* (The time of Captain Cook's arrival - Author)

This definition of the term Native Hawaiian is restated in USPL 103-150 (The Apology Bill), clearly apologizing only to the aboriginal ancestors of the Hawaiian bloodline of Hawaiian National Citizens. It excludes and discriminates against all other Hawaiian Nationals *(i.e. those of ethnic heritages such as German, Russian, Chinese, Japanese, Portuguese, French, Scottish etc. who are also Hawaiian Nationals)* at the time of the U.S. invasion in support of treason on Hawaiian National soil. The apology, (as do the politicians behind it) lacks integrity and rings hollow, but it is an admission of United States Government guilt, wrongdoing, and flagrant violation of international law.

THE DE JURE HAWAIIAN KINGDOM GOVERNMENT

The forceful unlawful usurpation of the government in 1893 and subsequent occupation of Hawaii by the United States, put the lawful operations of the Hawaiian Kingdom into suspension for *a hundred and three years…* until the *lawful Government, Ke Aupuni O Hawaii* was reclaimed and reactivated; and its laws brought forward by Hawaiian Nationals and their court in August and September of 1996.

That action, under Hawaiian Kingdom laws and the reformation of its *Supreme Court for the Hawaiian Islands* was publicized and noticed *(under the de jure "common-law"*[4] *of the Hawaiian Kingdom).* The **Supreme Court for the Hawaiian Islands** was reactivated with lawful public notices in the Pacific Business News, a local newspaper *(September / October of 1996).* The Hawaiian Nationals who compose the government on Hawaiian Kingdom soil are under the Hawaiian Kingdom common-law and not under the corporately created "Revised Statutes" of the occupier nation's de facto puppet state *(i.e. State of Hawaii).* The *Hawaiian National Government,* as previously mentioned, functions in a state of interregnum.

When the *Hawaiian Kingdom **(Ke Aupuni O Hawaii);** under its "living" de jure laws,* had its Offices restored and activated in 1996 under the de jure *Hawaiian Kingdom Constitution* and Hawaiian Kingdom *"common-law,"* it formally notified the United Nations and United States Government by Registered United States Mail of its reinstatement. The filling of Offices included the de jure **Supreme Court for the Hawaiian Islands**.

The Cabinet Council *(Privy Council of State)* of the Executive Branch has been active since 1996 with various Cabinet Ministers, under Hawaiian Kingdom common-law, and consisting of Hawaiian Nationals functioning under lawful Hawaiian Kingdom Government oaths of Office.

The Hawaiian Kingdom National Government Offices consist of:

The Cabinet Council (Privy Council of State) consists of:

---

[4] **Common-law.** Chapter LVII. An Act To Reorganize the Judiciary Department *(of the Hawaiian Kingdom),* (1892) **Section 5.** *"The common law of England, as ascertained by English and American decisions, is hereby declared to be the common law of the Hawaiian Islands in all cases, except as otherwise expressly provided by the Hawaiian Constitution or laws, or fixed by Hawaiian judicial precedent, or established by Hawaiian national usage, provided however,* that no person shall be subject to criminal proceedings except as provided by the Hawaiian laws."
Author's Note: Under "Hawaii Court Rules," Rule No. 202, "Judicial notice of law" the following is stated:
"**(b) Mandatory judicial notice of law. The court shall take judicial notice of (1) the common law,** (2) the constitutions and statutes of the United States and of every state, territory and other jurisdiction of the United States…" (**Bold** emphasis by Author)
Of interest is the fact that the only "common law" that has ever existed and still exists within the jurisdiction of the lands of the Hawaiian Archipelago, and upon which the **Hawaii Revised Statutes (HRS)** are based, is that of the Hawaiian *common-law.* Specifically, *"Chapter LVII. An Act to Reorganize the Judiciary Department, Section 5."*
If this is in fact true, the judges of these de facto courts are required and bound to respond to and honor the common-law, law requirements of Hawaiian Nationals presently domiciled under their birthright law and Citizenship.
This rule of law is presently blatantly ignored by the de facto Hawaii courts.

The Minister of Foreign Affairs
The Minister of Interior
The Minister of Finance
The Attorney General

The Supreme Court for the Hawaiian Islands (re-activated in 1996) consists of:

The Honorable Chief Justice
The Honorable Associate Justice
The Honorable Associate Justice
The Honorable Associate Justice (vacant)
The Honorable Associate Justice (vacant)

The Government's proper mailing address is as follows:

Ke Aupuni O Hawaii Nei *(The Government of Hawaii)*
Hawaiian Kingdom
General Delivery (Box 62107)
Manoa Station, Island of Oahu
The Hawaiian Islands

(Please do not use a U.S. federal Zip Code)

Chapter 3

Nations, Treaties, Laws and Jurisdiction

A NATION:

In the first book of the Bible, Genesis, Chapter 1, vs. 19, Almighty God tells us that the whole world was populated from the three sons of Noah. In Genesis Chapter 10, verses 20, 31 and 32, God tells us how He differentiated and established the boundaries and confines of "nations" from which our understanding and definitions of peoples and nations are derived. In Genesis, God deals with the sons of Noah who are Shem, Ham and Japheth. These three Sons, with their wives, survived the great flood and are considered the source of all presently existing mankind. Some choose not to believe this basis of origins.

In Genesis Chapter 10, above, we are told that Almighty God has set the parameters and perimeters of just who is called a *"People"* and what is called a *"Nation."* This definition clarifies that a *"People"* is one who is *"...after their families,"* (from family descendants from generation to generation); *"...after their tongues,"* (in the distinct language of one's race); *"...in their lands"* (in a defined, distinct geographical area); *"...after their nations."* Thus "nations" are composed of peoples speaking distinctly different languages living in different geographical areas from each other.

Nation. 1. A large body of people associated with a particular territory, that is sufficiently conscious of its unity to seek or to possess a government peculiarly it own... 4) an aggregation of persons from the same ethnic family often speaking the same language or cognate languages.
(Source: Webster's Encyclopedic Unabridged Dictionary, 2001 Edition)

TREATIES

Treaties are made between and among Nations. These are agreements or contracts (conventions) between national societies for the common-good or welfare of both. Such treaties are most often in the interest of peace and to avoid hostilities, or, more commonly, for commerce between nations.

There is a treaty still in existence between the Hawaiian Kingdom Nation *(i.e. The Hawaiian Islands)* and the united ***States of America***. The U.S. ratified that treaty in 1849 and the Hawaiian Kingdom in 1850. It was ratified by the governments and leaders of both nations and never abrogated *(annulled, cancelled, revoked, repealed or destroyed)*.

NOTE: A lesser, de facto entity (i.e. treasonists) has no authority or power to destroy the lawful contract or treaty created by the greater, de jure authority of a Nation (i.e. the Hawaiian Kingdom). The de jure Hawaiian Kingdom was internationally recognized as evidenced by its treaties. Recognized as a Nation among Nations, only the de jure Hawaiian Kingdom Government can cancel a treaty such as the Treaty of 1850 with the U.S. Likewise, a subsidiary federal authority (lesser federal government created under Article 1 § 8 of the American Constitution) has no authority to cancel a treaty made by that greater authority, the united "**States of America National Congress of the Republic.**"[1] It is my firm belief that this treaty still exists.

JURISDICTION

Jurisdiction[2] is a simple issue. For a court to have jurisdiction it must have authority over the action or crime and the place of the action or crime. That could be

---

[1] Congress is supposed to wear two hats: National and Federal, the latter functioning under the limited authority of Article 1, § 8 and Article 1, § 10 of that very same Constitution.

[2] **Jurisdiction.** *"A term of comprehensive import embracing every kind of judicial action. Federal Land Bank of Louisville, Ky. V. Crombie, 258 Ky. 383, 80 S.W.2d 39, 40. It is the power of the court to decide a matter in controversy and presupposes the existence of a duly constituted court with control over the subject matter and the parties. Pinner v. Pinner, 33 N.C. App. 204, 234 S.E.2d 633. Jurisdiction defines the powers of courts to inquire into facts, apply the law, make decisions, and declare judgment. Police Com'r of Boston v. Municipal Court of Dorchester Dist., 374 Mass. 640, 374 N.E.2d 272, 285. The legal right by which judge's exercise their authority. Max Ams. Inc. v. Barker, 293 Ky. 698, 170 S.W.2d 45, 48. It exists when court has cognizance of class of cases involved, proper parties are present, and point to be decided is within powers of court. United Cemeteries Co. v. Strother 342 Mo. 1155, 119 S.W.2d 762, 765. Power and authority of a court to hear and determine a judicial proceeding; and power to render particular judgment in question. In re De Camillis' Estate, 66 Misc.2d 882, 322 N.Y.S.2d 551, 556. The right and power of a court to adjudicate concerning the subject matter in a given case. Biddinger v. Fletcher, 224 Ga. 501, 162 S.E.2d 414, 416. The term may have different meanings in different contexts. Martin v. Louther, C.A.Ill., 689 F.2d 109, 114.*

Areas of authority; the geographical area in which a court has power or types of cases it has power to hear.

Scope and extent of jurisdiction of federal courts is governed by 28 U.S.C.A. § 1251 et seq...."

limited to a national, state, county, and city, island, territory, military base type of geographical jurisdiction, etc. It must also posse*ss jurisdiction in rem;*[3] *(that is, over the thing or item car, property, land, etc.); jurisdiction in personam:*[4] *(would be jurisdiction over the person or citizen within a courts geographical limitation)*; and, *jurisdiction over the subject matter,*[5] *(the court's ability within its legal and designated limits as to type of case)* in order to execute justice. I will attempt, for the sake of understanding citizenship, to clarify jurisdiction as it pertains to the Hawaiian *National*[6] Citizen.

The *de facto*[7] courts in place in Hawaii are at the present time, courts of incompetent jurisdiction. What is meant by that statement and the use of the word *"incompetent"*?[8] The fact is, none of the U.S. courts on Hawaiian National soil are

---

[3] *Jurisdiction in rem.* *"Power of a court over a thing so that its judgment is valid as against the rights of every person in the thing, e.g. a judgment or decree of registration of title to land. See also In rem; Jurisdiction quasi in rem."*

[4] *Jurisdiction in personam.* *"Power which a court has over the defendant's person and which is required before a court can enter a personal or in personam judgment. Pennoyer v. Neff, 95 U.S. 714, 24 L.Ed. 565. It may be acquired by an act of the defendant within a jurisdiction under a law by which the defendant impliedly consents to the personal jurisdiction of the court, e.g. operation of a motor vehicle on the highways of state confers jurisdiction of operator and owner on courts of state. Hess v. Pawloski, 274 U.S. 352, 47 S.Ct. 632, 71 L.Ed. 1091. A judgment in personam brings about a merger of the original cause of action into the judgment and there after the action is upon the judgment and not on the original cause of action See also in personam; Jurisdiction over person."*
(Source of jurisdictional definitions: Black's Law Dictionary, 6th Edition)

[5] *Jurisdiction of the subject matter.* *"Power of a particular court to hear the type of case that is then before it. Alfaro v. Meagher, 27 Ill.App.3d 292, 326 N.E.2d 545, 548. term refers to jurisdiction of court over class of cases to which particular case belongs, Ferree v. Ferree, 285 Ky. 825, 149 S. w.2d 719, 721; jurisdiction over the nature of the cause of action and relief sought, Mid-City Bank & Trust Co. v. Myers, 343 Pa. 465, 23 A.2d 20, 423; or the amount for which a court of limited jurisdiction is authorized to enter judgment.*

[6] *National.* *"Pertaining or relating to a nation as a whole. Commonly applied in American law to institutions, laws, or affairs of the United States or its government, as opposed to those of the several states. "National" contemplates an activity with a nationwide scope"…. "A person owing permanent allegiance to a state"…. "The term "national" as used in the phrase "national of the United States: is broader than the term "citizen"."* (Source: Black's Law Dict. 6th Ed. Page 1024.)

[7] *De facto court.* *"One established, organized, and exercising its judicial functions under authority of a statute apparently valid, though such statute may be in fact unconstitutional and may be afterwards so adjudged;* **or a court established and acting under the authority of a de facto government.***"* (Bold emphasis by Author)

[8] *Incompetent.* Just the opposite of a court that is "competent" (Author's note)<u>. Court of competent jurisdiction.</u> *"One having power and authority of law at the time of action to do the particular act. One recognized by law as possessing the right to adjudicate a controversy. One having jurisdiction under the Constitution and/or laws to determine the question in controversy." (See* Chapter 6.   Hawaii's Courts: De facto State and U.S. District Court).

lawful, being outside of their national jurisdiction. They function in violation of the Constitution, under *"color of U.S. law."* [9]

"A court is without authority to adjudicate a matter over which it has no jurisdiction even though the court possesses jurisdiction over the parties to the litigation. For example, a court of limited criminal jurisdiction has no power to try a murder indictment and if it did, its judgment would be void and of no effect because it lacks subject matter jurisdiction." (Source: Black's Law Dictionary, 6th Ed. Page 854) *"Color of U.S. law"* is a criminal violation of the United States Criminal Code (USCr.C), Title 18 §§ 241 and 242 *(i.e. conspiracy against rights and deprivation of rights under color of law)*

If you are a Hawaiian National (Citizen) under Hawaiian National Law, properly documented, you are not subject to an unlawful foreign court placed on your land. For instance, if you are stopped while traveling in an automobile in Hawaii, and given a traffic ticket by an *ignorant* [10] de facto "county police officer" for not possessing State of Hawaii plates on your private property (car or truck), they have transgressed jurisdictional lines of law to do so *(These are violations of United States Criminal Code; Title 18 USCr.C §§ 871, 872, 1201, 1342, etc.)*. Yet, under law enforcement of the State of Hawaii, the City and County of Honolulu, and the Counties of Hawaii, Maui and Kauai, we find that the jurisdictional rights of Hawaiian Nationals are usurped by abuse of *police power* [11] in order to control and suppress Hawaiians on their own national

---

[9] **Color of law.** "The appearance or semblance, without the substance, of legal right. Misuse of power, possessed by virtue of state law and made possible only because wrongdoer is clothed with authority of state, is action taken under "color of state law." Akins v. Lanning. D.C.Okl., 415 F.Supp. 186, 188...."
"Color of U.S. law." (Source of definitions: Black's Law Dictionary, 6th Edition, pages 265-266.)

[10] **Ignorant.** *"1. lacking in knowledge or training; unlearned: an ignorant man. 2. lacking knowledge or information as to a particular subject or fact. 3. uninformed; unaware. 4. due to or showing lack of knowledge or training; etc.* (Source: Webster's Encyclopedic Unabridged Dictionary, 2001 Ed.)

[11] **Police Power.** *"An authority conferred by the American constitutional system in the Tenth Amendment, U.S. Const., upon the individual sates, and, in turn, delegated to local governments, through which they are enabled to establish a special department of police; adopt such laws and regulations as tend to prevent the commission of fraud and crime, and secure generally the comfort, safety, morals, health, and prosperity of its citizens by preserving the public order, preventing a conflict of rights in the common intercourse of the citizens, and insuring to each and uninterrupted enjoyment of all the privileges conferred upon him or her by the general laws. The power of the State to place restraints on the personal freedom and property rights of persons for the protection of the public safety, health and morals or the promotion of the public convenience and general prosperity. The police power is subject to limitations of the federal and state constitutions, and especially to the requirement of due process. Police power is the exercise of the sovereign right of a government to promote order, safety, security, health, morals and general welfare within constitutional limits and is a essential attribute of government. Marshall v. Kansas Fity, Mo., 355 S.W.2d 877, 883."* (Source: Black's Law Dictionary, 6th Edition, Page 1156)

land. <u>Unfortunately, as I see it,</u> de facto violations under *"color of U.S. law"* are deliberately perpetrated against Hawaiian Nationals on their own Hawaiian National soil.

<u>Example</u>: A country like Canada cannot make laws for Mexico and then go down there and try to make the Mexican citizens honor those laws, or attempt to enforce those laws upon that foreign people documented within their own sovereign territory of the Mexican Nation, called Mexico. This would be tantamount to an act of war! Therefore, neither can the United States lawfully create legislation for its own country and impose it on the Hawaiian Kingdom Nation. <u>To do so is a blatant violation of the international Law of Nations</u>!

The laws passed regarding Hawaii within the Congress of the Federal United States do not have lawful authority on the foreign, sovereign National Lands of *Ko Hawaii Pae Aina (i.e., Hawaiian Kingdom)* because the U.S. admittedly does not have **"sovereign [territorial] jurisdiction"** by either treaty or conquest over the Hawaiian Islands, nor do they have jurisdiction over the Hawaiian Nationals domiciled under their own National Laws and Flag when on their own land. Yet, these foreign laws with U.S. approval are forcefully imposed upon Hawaiian Nationals by <u>abuse of police power</u>.

All present foreign courts *(U.S. and State)* on Hawaiian Kingdom soil are de facto, lacking lawful jurisdiction *(See Chapter 6, Hawaii's Courts: De facto state and U.S. District Court).* Their judges, as previously mentioned, are judges of *"incompetent jurisdiction."* What most people do not realize is that the judge is the court, not the building! <u>U.S. and State of Hawaii courts are courts of *"incompetent jurisdiction"*</u> because de jure law does not support them *(these judges function under unlawful, modified, oaths of Office; since the overthrow).* These U.S. controlled courts use United States' Laws and de facto State Statutes as an appearance or front for their continued military and administrative control *(by abuse of judicial power from the benches).* Court filings and actions by Hawaiian Nationals that I have recorded over the past twelve plus years confirm these statements. <u>There is no justice in these incompetent, unlawful courts for Hawaiian Nationals living in the *Hawaiian Islands*</u>!

CITIZENSHIP WAIVER OF RIGHTS

LICENSING: If Hawaiians accept State of Hawaii Driver's Licenses or Identification Cards without a "reservation of their rights," they enter into a *posted contract* to become one of the State of Hawaii or U.S. federal jurisdiction's *"corporate, public servant Washington D.C. citizens."*   This is accomplished by changing your birth name to a pseudonym name, which removes you from your inalienable rights; and burdens you with liabilities of debt and obligation *(See Chapter 4, Birth Names and Birthrights).*   This is accomplished by the State giving you a differently spelled name that it owns, which sounds identical to your true name! But by identifying yourself by use of that new fiction name, you thus affirm that you are a *"citizen of Washington D.C."* You further confirm this by affixing your signature (your Seal) on their documents.

Remember, a *"federal public servant"* name is a name that the U.S. Government has created, uses and owns; and, individual *"private citizens"*[12] do not!   When you acquiesce to use their ALL CAPITALIZED NAME, you contract away your God Given birth rights and come voluntarily, or by ignorance, into the U.S. corporate jurisdiction as that public servant citizen (federal) guarantor of a ***foreign debt***[13] that you, as a Hawaiian National, didn't create.   By doing so, you place yourself into bondage to a foreign U.S. jurisdictional law system while domiciled on your own national soil!

This is what jurisdiction is all about.   This is how Hawaiians are bound by adhesive contracts to a foreign state and foreign national government functioning unlawfully on their land! This knowledge and deliberate misapplication of the English language, utilized by the federal U.S. is extremely subtle.

Hawaiians are either *"Hawaiian Nationals"* (not the same as *"Native Hawaiians"*) under their own de jure Hawaiian Kingdom National Laws; or, are Hawaiian Nationals by birth *(coming from our many varied ethnic backgrounds)* that willingly have submitted themselves to a foreign *"color of U.S. law"* legal system on our own soil. One cannot be both!

---

[12] **Private Citizen.** Private. Affecting or belonging to private individuals, as distinct from the public generally. Not official; not clothed with office. *People v. Powell*, 280 Mich. 699, 274 N.W. 372, 373.

Private person. Term sometimes used to refer to person other than those holding public office or in military services. Source: Black's Dictionary of Law, 6th Edition.

[13] **Foreign debt.**   See Chapter 9, The Taxable Corporate Citizens.

If American (*Nationals*) and Hawaiian *(Nationals)* do not understand their citizenship rights <u>and</u> jurisdiction, both will continue to be enslaved. It is time for us, the peaceful and loving Island Peoples of Aloha, to wake up, unify, and exercise our rights <u>as a National People</u>. For Hawaiian Nationals, the issue is not a matter of who is to be king or queen, but that of <u>knowing our citizenship rights and who we are</u> *(See Chapter 4, Birth Names and Birthrights and Chapter 10, Restoring Hawaiians to their Proper Citizenship)*

The choice is yours. <u>You can *(in writing and by public filing)* declare your Hawaiian National citizenship and sever the unrecorded and *implied contracts*[14]</u> that bind you to the foreign corporate state; and federal United States on the basis of fraud!

The Hawaiians have a saying. *"Nou ke koho!"* *(The choice is yours!)*

---

[14] ***Implied Contract.*** *"An implied contract is one not created or evidenced by the explicit agreement of the parties, but inferred by the law, as a matter of reason and justice from their acts or conduct, the circumstances surrounding the transaction making it a reasonable, or even a necessary, assumption that a contract existed between them by tacit understanding."* (Source: Black's Law Dictionary 6th Ed., Page 323)

Chapter 4

BIRTH NAMES, BIRTHRIGHTS AND CITIZENSHIP

TYPE OF CITIZENSHIP BY NAME: BIRTHRIGHT

What are "rights"?

For the purposes of this discussion on citizenship, "Rights" are those inherent entitlements, freedoms, privileges and blessings given by God to every human being. They are Godly attributes expressed in the Bible and, in modern times, by the U.S. Declaration of Independence[1] (1776) and the Hawaiian Declaration of Rights[2] (1839). These documents profess that God alone created living human beings, and God endows each one with certain rights that are inalienable and unalienable, such as the right to "life, liberty and the pursuit of happiness…"

The basic *principle* asserted by these documents is: Since these *rights* were conferred by Almighty God, any attempt to separate, deny or take away these rights from the people *(living human beings)* without their consent, is a violation not only of the people's rights, but of God's order and purposes.

What are birthrights? These are basic rights that, according to the customs of the society, somebody has or is entitled to from birth or because of one's hereditary status. This includes the right of inheritance, like money, real property, and other possessions, as well as social position in a family, tribe or nation.

---

[1] *"We hold these truths to be self evident: That all men are created equal; that they are endowed with certain unalienable rights; that among these are Life, Liberty and the pursuit of happiness…"* **American Declaration of Independence (1776)**

[2] *"God hath made of one blood all nations of men to dwell on the earth, in unity and blessedness. God has also bestowed certain rights alike on all men and all chiefs, and all people of all lands. These are some of the rights which He has given alike to every man and every chief of correct deportment; life, limb, liberty, freedom from oppression; the earnings of his hands and the productions of his mind, not however to those who act in violation of the laws.*

A classic example for our purposes is the issue of birthrights between Esau and Jacob, the sons of Isaac as told in Genesis 25: 27-34. The second son, Jacob, traded[3] for the birthright of his brother Esau, the first born, in order to inherit the abundant worldly possessions of their father and the promise of Spiritual blessings bestowed by God Almighty to their grandfather, Abraham. Esau unwisely and foolishly traded his birthright for a bowl of pottage (stew), not fully realizing the value his birthrights, particularly the value of God's promised inheritance. Esau was more concerned about his immediate carnal need for food.

The centuries-long development of the modern "democratic" societies fueled by the application of Biblical principles and refined in crucibles like England and the American Colonies, gave rise to nations of *free men* such has not been prior known. Citizenship in a free nation entails the most precious birthright of all: one's identity[4] (one's name) and the ability to maintain its integrity.

Just like Esau, most people today are ignorant of the significance and value of their *birthright* and are willing to barter it away for immediate gratification. On the other hand, governments like the United States Federal Government and those of other "developed" nations understand the intrinsic power of birthrights and have set up mechanisms to exploit it to their benefit. They do so by deviously hijacking certain aspects of the birthright: *personal identity* and *citizenship*.

The United States Federal Government knows that if they can get people, whether voluntarily or through trickery, to relinquish their birthrights of *personal identity* and *citizenship*, the government can claim and exploit the inherent blessings that come with those birthrights. This is identity theft!

One of the ways the United States Federal Government does this is through an identity theft scam. As you know, in today's world, if someone can steal your identity, they have the means to steal your assets: your bank accounts, your earnings, and your property. They can even get loans, run up your credit cards and other debts in your name. This in essence is the same trick the United States Federal Government has used to capture your *personal identity* — *your name!* It is identity theft on a grand scale!

---

[3] **Trade.** *"An exchange of somebody or something for another; a deal or transaction; the activity of buying and selling or sometimes bartering goods."*

[4] **Freedom**. *The state of being free; liberty; self determination; absence of restraint; the opposite of slavery. The power of acting, in the character of a moral personality… (Source: Black's Law Dictionary, 8th Edition, Page 664)*

Like other *identity theft* scams, the U.S. government uses your name, to run up all kinds of debt against you and compel you to accept it. How do they do this? And how can they do this without your consent? The United States Federal Government agencies (and their collection contractors like the IRS), take your name (your identity) and subtly change it by utilizing a distinct way of spelling your name, and having you sign documents verifying that it is your name, thus deceiving you into giving them blanket authorization for them to use that new name/identity in any way they desire.

TAKEOVER BY THE FEDERAL UNITED STATES GOVERNMENT

The country known as the united "States of America" is not the same as it was when it was founded. The framers of the U.S. Constitution deliberately intended *"We the People…" (i.e. Private Citizens)* to be in control and the individual states to be essentially autonomous (self-governing) entities *united* together only for certain limited functions such as the *common defense*, standardizing inter-state *commerce*, establishing a *monetary system*, representation in *foreign affairs*, and so forth. The entire mechanism was set up by *"We the People…"* to protect the *rights* of *"We the People…" (i.e. Private Citizens)*.

The right of the individual was paramount. *The right of state government was* next. This made the rights of the individual and the state superior to *federal government*. The federal government was to be limited in power; to serve the common good by performing only those functions specified and allowed by the states for the common interest of the "Union." Thus, *federal citizens* were citizens of Washington, D.C. or were those who served in official federal capacities and/or those living in the jurisdictions of the federal government. The jurisdiction of the federal government only encompassed places such as Washington, D.C., military bases, and other areas that had been set aside specifically for Federal Government usage. Federal jurisdiction also extended over acquired territories not yet developed as states, such as the Louisiana Purchase. In later years, it also included the National Parks and acquired federal territories such as the U.S. Virgin Islands, Puerto Rico, Guam and American Samoa.

The American Civil War drastically changed things. Not only did it emancipate the slaves, but it had the affect of subjugating *"states rights"*[5] to the Federal Government, thus increasing the power of the central government and consequently, reducing the autonomy of the individual states. This trend of redefining the United States of America has continued to the present, virtually obliterating the original sovereignty of individual Private Citizen Americans of the "several states." Today, individual and states rights are entirely subservient to the Federal Government and Federal Laws.

How does this pertain to the theft of one's personal identity?

USE OF THE ALL-CAPITALIZED SPELLING OF NAMES

After the American Civil War, the *Federal* United States began to incorporate the spelling of names in *ALL CAPITALIZED* letters to designate the newly created class of "federal citizens" consisting of former slaves. Soon, the *ALL CAPITALIZED* name was used for those who worked for the Federal Government (public workers, public officials, the military); or lived in Federal districts (Washington D. C., military bases, and other federal installations). The *ALL CAPITALIZED* name was further applied to business entities licensed by the Federal Government (corporations, partnerships, sole proprietorships). The *ALL CAPITALIZED* name was also applied to all those who lived in federal territories such as the U.S. Virgin Islands, Puerto Rico, Guam and American Samoa.

The *ALL CAPITALIZED* name denotes a *Federal United States* "citizen," not a "Private Citizen" of one of the several States of the Union. This *Federal United States citizen* designates a "fictitious"[6] corporate (government created) entity, different from and lacking the lawful status of *"We the People"* (*living, Private Citizen, human beings*) with inherent, inalienable rights. Thus, an *ALL CAPITALIZED* -named-fictitious-corporate-entity, has no rights, either God-given or as enumerated by the *Constitution of the United States.*

---

[5] *States Rights. The doctrine as put forth by the framers of the U.S. Constitution and as expounded upon by the Federalist Papers, that the "several states" of the union maintained their sovereignty and their right to self determination based on a representative form of government.*

[6] *Fictitious. 1.* Created, taken or assumed for the sake of concealment; not genuine; false; fictitious names. 2. Of, pertaining to, or consisting of fiction; imaginatively product of set forth; created by the imagination;... (*Source: Webster's Encyclopedic Unabridged Dictionary – 2001 Edition*)

This *ALL CAPITALIZED* method of spelling the names of *Federal United States* citizens was eventually extended to include <u>every person</u> in the "States," not just those working for the Federal government or living in designated Federal areas. This *ALL CAPITALIZED*-name-identity is now universally applied to all the people living in America, the Private Citizen and federal citizen. This device is also used by most of the governments around the world. Why did this happen? And what is so wrong with the ALL CAPITALIZED name?

WHAT'S WRONG WITH THE ALL-CAPITALIZED SPELLING?

The United States Federal Government uses ALL CAPITALIZED NAMES as a device to convert people *(living human beings)* who are Private American National Citizens, into fictional, *corporate persons* called *Federal U.S.* citizens or *"Taxpayers."*

All Federal United States bureaus, agencies, offices, databases and registers employ the usage of the *ALL CAPITALIZED* names. The *ALL CAPITALIZED* names are used exclusively in all Federal U.S. Courts, State Courts, legislation and virtually every legal document produced in the United States. This *pseudonym*[7] enables the Federal U.S. Government to regard everyone in the U.S. as a *Federal U.S.* citizen, a taxpayer liable for any and all debts or liabilities that the owner *(Federal U.S. Government, IRS, et al)* of this pseudonym title has placed against it

When the natural, *living human being or living soul*, places his signature (his personal seal) next to the corporate *(ALL CAPITALIZED)* pseudonym on a legal document, he affirms that he is that *corporate person*, thus assuming any and all debts or liabilities placed against that *corporate name.* [8]

The natural, Private American National Citizen, *(human being and living soul)* through the seal of his own signature, thus signs away his own birthright (his identity), submits his citizenship rights to the federal jurisdiction (forfeiting State and National

---

[7] **Pseudonym.** *n.* a fictitious name used by an author to conceal his of her identity; pen name. *(Source: Webster's Encyclopedic Unabridged Dictionary – 2001 Edition)*

[8] **Custom and usage.** *(U.C.C. § 1-205 [2[):* "A usage or practice of the people, which, by common adoption and acquiescence, and by long and unvarying habit, has become compulsory, and has acquired the force of law with respect to the Place or subject matter to which it relates. It results from a long series of actions, constantly repeated, which have, by such repetition and by uninterrupted acquiescence, acquired the force of a tacit and common consent…"

Constitutional rights) and becomes *surety*[9] for the portion of the federal debt assigned to him.

Accepting this change of name moves one's citizenship from protection under sovereign State Constitution *(common law)* and <u>united</u> *State's National Constitution of the Republic,* to that of the Federal, military jurisdiction under *Article 1 Section 8* of that same Constitution. The American National citizenship is changed to a U.S. federal citizenship, and comes under military and "Civil Rights" law, <u>not constitutional common law</u>. Over the years since the Civil War, the Federal U.S. Government has gradually reclassified virtually all American National Private Citizens and "captured" them under the Federal jurisdiction.

In order to reverse the process and regain one's freedom and proper identity, one must purposefully rescind the false identity and reclaim the real one. One does this by filing affidavits and notices with the U.S. government, rejecting the *ALL CAPITALIZED* name and all legal adhesions to that name and reasserting ones identity as a natural, *living human being and living soul,* i.e. Private National Citizen.

The *Emancipation Proclamation* and the 13th Amendment to the U.S. Constitution freed the Negro *(today we would say, "Black" or "African-American")* from slavery and guaranteed them citizenship when the North won the Civil War. At that time, the "sovereign" American *(one born to his/her respective, sovereign State of the Union and whose birthright was under his/her* **State's** *"common law"[10])* was primarily of

---

[9] <u>Surety</u>. "One who at the request of another, and for the purpose of securing to him a benefit, becomes responsible for the performance by the latter of some act in favor of a third person, or hypothecates property as security therefore. One who undertakes to pay money or to do any other act in event that his principal fails therein. A person who is primarily liable for payment of debt or performance of obligation of another. Branch Banking and Trust Co. v. Creasy, 301 N.C. 44, 269 S.E.2nd 117, 122. One bound with his principal for the payment of a sum of money or for the performance of some duty or promise and who is entitled to be indemnified by some one who ought to have paid or performed if payment or performance be enforced against him. Term includes a guarantor. U.C.C. § 1-201 (40)." *(Source: Black's Law Dictionary, 6th Edition, Page 1441.)*

[10] *(State's) Common law.* "As distinguished from statutory law created by the enactment of legislatures, the common law comprises the body of those principles and rules of action, relating to the government and security of persons and property, which derive their authority solely from usages and customs of immemorial antiquity, or from the judgments and decrees of the courts recognizing, and affirming, and enforcing such usages and customs; and, in this sense, particularly the ancient unwritten law of England. … In general, it is a body of law that develops and derives through judicial decisions, as distinguished from legislative enactments. The "common law" is all the statutory and case law background of England and the American colonies before the American Revolution." *People v. Rehman, 253 C.A. 2d 119, 61 Cal. Rptr. 65, 85.* "It consists of those principles, usage and rules of action applicable to

Caucasian extraction. The 14th Amendment to the U.S. Constitution was not designed to rectify this limitation, but created a different, lesser standard of federal citizenship regardless of color.

This is what happened. In order to skirt the granting of full citizenship rights (the 14th Amendment) the ALL CAPITALIZED name was deceptively utilized to create a **"government-created chattel person"**[11] possessing a lesser degree of standing, and a type of *federal citizenship* that is distinctly different from that of ***"American, States-***

---

government and security of persons and property, which do not rest for their authority upon any express and positive declaration of the will of the legislature." *Bishop v. U.S., D.C. Tex., 334 F. Supp. 415, 418.* *"As distinguished from ecclesiastical law, it is the system of jurisprudence administered by the purely secular tribunals."*

Comparatively speaking, Calif. Civil Code, Section 22.2, provides that the *"common law of England, so far as it is not repugnant to or inconsistent with the Constitution of the United States, or the Constitution or laws of this State, is the rule of decision in all the courts of this State."*

"In a broad sense, "common law" may designate all that part of the positive law, juristic theory, and ancient custom of any state or nation, which is of general and universal application, thus marking off special or local rules or customs…" *(Source: Black's Law Dictionary, 6th Ed. Page 276)*

[11] Government-created chattel person. *(Author's Opinion) A Fourteenth Amendment "citizenship" created by the united States Congress (1868). The ALL CAPITALIZED name is that of a chattel ("slave," "bondsman," "public servant"), a citizenship created after the Civil War as a separate and distinct federal "citizenship" for Emancipated Black Slaves. It was a new type of* "Federal citizenship" (existing only within the "Federal" side [i.e. Washington D. C. its Territories, Military, etc.] as distinct from the greater in power "National State's Citizen" under the U.S. Constitution – i.e. One born within one of the 48, "contiguous" "several states"). *This federally created* "chattel citizen" or "public servant" *name was, I believe, created to provide Emancipated Slaves a citizenship with a separate, distinct, but lesser identity (using the ALL CAPITALIZED NAME) for Emancipated Black Slaves. This federally created* "chattel citizen" or "public servant" *was, I believe, created by the 14th Amendment to provide Emancipated Slaves citizenship, but* one that was not on par *with that of white Americans of the several States.*

This U.S. Congress-created "Federal citizen" *is, just like the status of a member of the military today— outside of the direct protection of the American Constitution of the Republic and The Bill of Rights. Thus arose the need for* Civil Rights Acts *in 1866, 1957 and 1964 to provide these federally created, limited protection public servant* "citizens" *some rights, similar to those already possessed by State's born* Citizens *under the American Constitution. This secondary, lesser citizenship functions only under the federal government and military jurisdictions created by* **Article 1 Section 8** *(federal limitations) and* **Article 1 Section 10** *(right to contract) of the* U.S. **Constitution.** *This distinction is now evident through* "custom and usage" *of the ALL CAPITALIZED name, as evidenced by its use for that purpose since the Civil War* (and its accelerated usage after the U.S. bankruptcy of 1933 and **War Powers Act, used by President Roosevelt in the 1930's)**. *This fraudulent government citizenship conversion (of moving American* "State's Citizens" *into the lesser of right, federal jurisdiction) was politically accelerated by the bankruptcy, Roosevelt's Public Works Programs and the Second World War* (but most definitely implemented through the people's ignorance, and without their knowledge, awareness or direct consent). ***AUTHOR'S NOTE: Distinction in this text between a "Private Citizen American" with State's Rights and a U.S. Congressional created "thing or lesser in right" Federal U.S.*** "citizen" ***is highlighted by the underlining of the lower case letter,*** "c".

born *"sovereign" National Citizenship."[12]* A different type of slavery or bondage was hence created by this act.

If Blacks *(Emancipated Slaves)* were given full National and State's Right's Citizenship, there would have been a majority of Black citizens in those Southern States. Even to the white majority of the North, this was an unacceptable outcome to the Civil War. Thus, the difficulty confronting the white controlled U.S. Congress was that Blacks, as full citizens, would have the right to vote in State and National elections. So a biased Congress created the new, limited, lesser type of *"Washington D. C.," "public servant citizenship"* with a political maneuver called the *"14th Amendment"* (to the <u>u</u>nited *States Constitution).*

Black slaves were thus not truly emancipated; they were re-categorized into another less-noticeable form of slavery. That type of citizenship, ratified by the white majority, did not provide protection of birthright under the State's common-law Constitution where the Black's *("Emancipated Slaves")* were born.

This newly created 14th Amendment federal citizenship, was originally <u>limited to only the federal jurisdiction</u> *(Article 1 § 8)* as these *"Emancipated Slave federal <u>c</u>itizens"* by law, possessed no protection or rights *unless* individually granted by the several States or Congress. Therefore, discrimination, abuse and even killing of *"Emancipated Slaves"* continued within the several States *(where they were still considered as "things" or "possessions" by many)* and because as 14th Amendment <u>c</u>itizens they possessed no State's Rights protections. Congress was forced into creating <u>Federal</u> Civil Rights Laws in 1866, 1957 and 1964 for their protection under this new citizenship.

<u>NOTE</u>: The Civil Rights laws <u>by design</u> were to provide similar, but definitely not the same rights, as those possessed by White American Nationals. On voter rolls, etc., *"Emancipated Slaves"* of the federal jurisdiction were easily distinguishable. As *"federal <u>c</u>itizens"* they had no guaranteed right to vote in local elections within their respective

---

[12] *American, State's born sovereign Citizen. American Citizens under the American Constitution of the Republic, specifically those born within one of the sovereign States of the American Union of States and that State's "common-law", are "sovereign" as all sovereign rights are vested in the American "sovereign" Citizen and not in the Government or a leader. Our Forefathers determined we would not have a King as our sovereign; therefore, they vested that power into the American (State's) Citizen. The Citizen in the American Republic is empowered and supreme, not the President or Congress. See dictionary definition of "Republic". Capital "C" on "Citizen" (proper noun) denotes an American National, or State's sovereign. A lower-case "<u>c</u>" on "citizen" denotes a lesser entity known as a "federal, Washington D. C. "person".*

States *(their votes could easily be distinguished and discarded).* But as Federal citizens they could vote in local elections if they were domiciled within Federal jurisdictions like Washington D. C. and U. S Territories *(but more than likely, their votes were discarded there as well).*

Eventually this category of *federal citizenship* came to engulf all in America. Today the U.S. Federal Government automatically groups everyone, including those who are supposed to be American National Citizens, as *14th Amendment federal citizens.* And the U.S. Federal Government refuses to acknowledge even the existence of genuine *American, States-born "sovereign" National Citizens.* This contrived and forced designation of *federal citizenship (to Emancipated Slave status)* deviously enslaves all the people to the U.S. Federal Government. Unless one knows this, one remains a second-class citizen slave to the U.S. Federal Government.

Going back to the basic differences in spelling of names, I will try to make that name differentiation and applicable distinction, using my own name, as follows:

"Aran Alton Ardaiz" - The "English language" by traditional and customary usage reveals that this proper English language spelled (printed) name is mine, an American Citizen born within the sovereign State of the Union called, the "California Republic." I am, under God, created as a living soul, a private human being, an American born "Private Citizen," or "sovereign," because of my place of birth. My name when written as my signature is my lawful "Seal." It denotes who I am and that I am protected under my sovereign "State's common-law" (supra), that automatically places me under the protection of not just the Constitution and common-law of my birth State of California, but also the American Constitution of the Republic (united States Constitution).

"ARAN A. ARDAIZ" - This is the ALL CAPITALIZED *"public servant"* name. It is not mine! This type of name can only be printed, not scripted. The Federal United States Government created this type of pseudonym to designate *"14th Amendment Emancipated Slave"* "citizens." As mentioned above, it was not used just for the emancipated black slaves; it was also used for public servants, corporations, the military, fiction entities and government created chattel persons of the limited, federal Washington D. C. jurisdiction. The Federal United States Government now uses it for all citizens whether U.S. Federal or American National.

FOR AMERICAN NATIONALS OF THE UNION OF STATES.

EXTRICATING YOURSELF FROM YOUR SECOND-CLASS U.S. FEDERAL, PUBLIC-SERVANT, WASHINGTON D. C. CITIZENSHIP AND RETURNING TO YOUR "AMERICAN CITIZENSHIP OF THE REPUBLIC" AND "STATE COMMON LAW, BIRTH RIGHTS STATUS" AS AN AMERICAN SOVEREIGN

The identity switch into U.S. Federal citizenship was so deviously achieved that those who should really be Private *(American National) Citizens*,[13] do not know that they have lost their identity along with their inherent rights guaranteed under their Constitutions. They do not know who they really are and what they have been tricked into. They, in ignorance, think they possess a greater type of citizenship rights than they actually have.

To set things right, Americans (currently U.S. Federal "*citizens*") must reverse the process and return to their State's birthright Citizenship as Private *(American National) Citizens*. When <u>u</u>nited *State's Nationals*[14] lawfully leave *(sever the implied, fraudulent contracts that made them federal, public servant, Emancipated Slave, immigration status "citizen")* the corporate state and corporate federal government, <u>their citizenship status changes back to that of their</u> "*sovereign State's right, Private Citizenship of the American Republic and its Union of States*." By declaration and <u>re-claiming one's respective birth State and its *State Constitutional common law*</u>, and, <u>returning to one's properly spelled English language birth name (with new identity cards, etc.)</u>, one automatically again becomes a National '*sovereign*' "*Private Citizen*" of the "*Union of States*" under the covering of the National Government and <u>u</u>nited "*States Constitution of the Republic*"; and, the proper American Flag of 48 Stars *(See: Title 4 United States Code, Section 1)*.

<u>The American Flag as previously mentioned is still by law, 48 Stars, not 50!</u> *(See Chapter 6, "Law of the Flag," Page 109, Footnote 21)* Having severed one-self from the false Federal U.S. citizenship, one would now, as a "*sovereign State's National*," be

---

[13] *Private (American National) Citizens.* Citizens born to their respective sovereign common-law State of the Union who functions only under their proper English-language birth names and who retain their birth rights under the common-law as sovereigns. Not a citizen born to the federal jurisdiction, i.e. Washington, D.C. of U.S. territories. Not a public servant.

[14] <u>u</u>nited *State's Nationals.* Same as sovereign Citizen of one of the contiguous 48 States of the Union (Republic).

protected by the united *"State's Constitution of the Republic"* as a sovereign, <u>Private Citizen</u> under one's birth State's common law, properly documented as a Citizen from your birth State.

As an American-born, State's Citizen or sovereign (i.e. "Private Citizen" "American National," and not a "Washington D. C. federal <u>c</u>itizen") one automatically returns to his respective birth "State of the Union" common-law. The "American Union of States," is a Republic, and not a lesser federal jurisdiction "democracy." Only then are you no longer a U.S. federal second-class, public servant, immigration status "<u>c</u>itizen" under the 14th Amendment! I repeat: When you as an *American National*, are again lawfully restored to the sovereign rights of your American heritage as an American "sovereign," you are again a "Private Citizen," an "American National," confirmed by your birth-State Citizenship standing and how you properly spell your name (your "Seal") in the English language. You place yourself under your respective sovereign birth State's Constitution and its common law!

American citizenship is based upon birth under the varied "common law" of one of the 48 contiguous States of the Union. In order to circumvent this, the attorneys, judges, bankers, politicians and other officials of the federal and corporate state governments unlawfully change the birth names of children on their birth certificates. They substitute the ALL CAPITALIZED NAMES owned by the U.S. Government for proper English-language spelled names given children by their parents. (I find most parents don't even realize the distinction on the birth certificates - Author).

This birth-name switch is just another example of the U.S. Federal Government campaign to capture more Federal U.S. <u>c</u>itizens. Furthermore, by issuing taxpayers Social Security Numbers (SSN) to newborn infants, they can then inventory and number their federal, "Emancipated Slaves" any way they want. This is called numbering the inventory, because in their pseudo, so-called federal, "Democracy," these children are to them just a thing (number), not "Private Citizens," living soul or human beings.

HAWAIIAN CITIZENSHIP ON HAWAIIAN NATIONAL AINA (SOIL)

<u>Your place of birth defines your nationality</u>. You are automatically a Hawaiian National Citizen if born to the Islands. In *Ko Hawaii Pae Aina (The Hawaiian Islands),*

there are also two types of names used to differentiate citizenship but they have a very different effect and impact on the *"Private Hawaiian Citizen,"* a foreigner to the *American Continent* and *The United States.*

"Kawika Kahiapo" – Let's say that my name is *"Kawika Kahiapo."* I was born on the Island of Oahu. My Hawaiian <u>common-law</u> birth name *(as differentiated from the federal government created fiction name)* denotes and assures me *(while in my proper "English-standard" spelling of my Hawaiian name)* that I am within my lawful jurisdictional rights under my <u>Hawaiian Kingdom National "common-law."</u> I am under the National Flag of my Hawaiian Nation; that is, <u>unless</u> I willingly *(with or without knowledge)* enter into the <u>foreign citizenship jurisdiction</u> being imposed upon my people. This name shows me to be a *"Hawaiian National,"* a *"Private Hawaiian Citizen"* under Hawaiian National law.

As mentioned, my proper English-standard spelled name application, when scripted, is my lawful *"Seal,"* even as a Hawaiian. It states who I am. It confirms and affirms my birthrights, as a *"Private Hawaiian National Citizen"* under Hawaiian Kingdom National Law and openly reveals *(by my I. D. Card in my pocket, etc.)* that I am not a U.S. Federal *"citizen"* on my own soil, like many others.

"KAWIKA KAHIAPO" – Just like the U.S. *(ALL CAPITALIZED NAME)* *"citizen,"* this name is <u>not a proper English language spelling for a Private Citizen</u>! This name is not Kawika's; but was created by and is owned by that foreign government called the Federal United States, unlawfully on Hawaiian soil. It is used to deceive Hawaiian Nationals (just like American Citizens) as to their rightful and proper citizenship. It is used in Hawaii by U.S. federal and state agencies, courts and legal systems. **(See: *"Custom and usage"* U.C.C. § 1-205 [2] on Page 45, Footnote 8)**

This U.S. Government-created pseudonym is considered by the de facto U.S. courts on my Hawaiian National soil as a jurisdictional forfeiture of Hawaiian National rights when the Hawaiian National agrees to submit to its use. This also creates **a change in both the law and the flag** that governs the Hawaiian as he subtly becomes an *"Emancipated Slave," "Washington D. C.," "second-class,"* U.S. Federal Government *"public servant" "citizen,"* caught in their deception. By devious use of law and language, the Hawaiian becomes a U.S. Federal *"citizen" (a foreigner)* on his own Hawaiian National homeland.

AUTHOR'S LEGAL NOTE AND CONCERN:

When a Hawaiian National or other private citizen files responses to city, county or state issues, or files complaints, lawsuits, etc. in any of the de facto courts, the courts will change his lawful birth name to the ALL CAPITALIZED NAME owned and used by their authority and jurisdiction. This unauthorized change of name *(a fraudulent conversion)*, if not challenged or protected by a *"reservation"* of rights, automatically locks the person into their U.S. federal jurisdiction by ignorance and acceptance of that change. Judges and clerks have told me *(the Author),* that the name-type does not make a difference. If that was truly the case, then why the necessity to *(without my consent)* change my lawful birth name? *(This Author has not only found these court officials to not be truthful, but unable to distinguish improper usage of a fiction name vs. a proper English language spelled name).*

The Federal U.S. Government does not have any right to change a lawful birth name *(which is one's lawful "Seal")* to that of a fiction or pseudonym name created and owned by the Federal U.S. Government. If one's rightful name is not used for the devious purpose herein described, why violate that person's rights by changing it?

I can find no reasons except those I have given. I firmly believe that the use of this fiction, fabricated, pseudonym name in the Hawaiian Islands places me, a lawfully documented Hawaiian National and Private Hawaiian Citizen, within the corrupt, foreign, intruding legal jurisdiction of that *United States Federal Corporation (i.e. a "puppet government")* called the *"State of Hawaii."*

The Federal U.S. legal system in Hawaii deviously uses this created name to affirm that the person is a guarantor *(captured as their Washington D. C. and State's fictitious, corporate, public servant "person" or "citizen")* willing to pay any debts the Feds attach to that name as well as that portion of a U.S. bankruptcy debt placed upon that fictitious name by the Federal U.S. Government, Internal Revenue Service and others. It is evidence that one becomes *voluntarily or involuntarily (through "fraudulent conversion, constructive fraud" or just plain ignorance),* a willing 14th Amendment, *"Emancipated Slave,"* U.S. federal *"citizen."* I repeat, when a *Hawaiian National Citizen,* allows his name to be changed, he contracts away his Hawaiian Kingdom National birth right and becomes a foreign U.S. *"citizen"* on his very own National Aina. He becomes a second-class, immigration status, naturalized, Washington D. C. Federal public servant *"citizen"* under the *"U.S. Federal Civil Rights Acts"* *(protection)* and becomes subject to the corrupt *Puppet State of Hawaii* courts! **(See Chapter 6. Hawaii's Courts: De facto State and U.S. Court for the Hawaii District)**

Attorneys and judges *(Members of the American and Hawaiian Bar Associations[15])* in their courts admonish us saying, *"Ignorance of the law is no excuse…"* I now believe we now know the truth! It was Jesus the Christ who said, *"And you shall know the truth and the truth shall make you free."* (Source: Holy Scriptures - John 8: 32).

PROOF REGARDING BIRTH NAMES AND BIRTH CERTIFICATES

To prove my point regarding the above texts, please look at my birth certificate **(See EXHIBIT H)** issued on November 4, 1953, a negative printout. I was not provided a copy of the original, that is a positive. Notice the proper English language spelling of my name. I requested a second; **(See EXHIBIT I)** issued on May 28, 1998. My name was changed on this *"Certified Copy"* without my consent to that of a fictional, U.S. Federal citizen. A positive copy *(original)* was also requested **(See EXHIBIT J)**, and issued on May 28, 1998.

NOTICE THE BORDER ON THIS ORIGINAL BIRTH CERTIFICATE. The County of Monterey, in collusion with the CORPORATE STATE OF CALIFORNIA, created a *"Bearer Bond"* document with my birth certificate to commit me as a pledged debtor to a federal U.S. bankruptcy *(debt)* I didn't create. I believe that this *"Bearer Bond"* was unlawfully issued to the U.S. Treasury Department by the State of California as a pledge to pay the bankers for the bankruptcy

---

[15] **Bar Association.** *"An association of members of the legal profession. Such associations have been organized on the national (American Bar Association; Federal Bar Association), state, county, and even on city levels (e.g., New York City Bar Ass'n). The first was established in Mississippi in 1825, but it is not known to have had a continued existence. An association of Grafton and Coos counties in New Hampshire had an existence before 1800, and probably a more or less continuous life since then, having finally merged into a state association. Membership may be either compulsory (integrated bar) or voluntary."* (Source: Black's Law Dictionary, 6th Edition, Page 149.)

of 1933. <u>Note the serial number, which, with my birth date, creates a serial number that cannot be duplicated.</u>

FURTHER PROOF: Please look closely at the lower left corner and you will see in extremely small print *"MIDWEST BANK NOTE COMPANY"* the evidence of a "<u>Bearer Bond</u>;"[16] "<u>Bearer Document</u>;"[17] "<u>Bearer Instrument</u>!"[18] I never gave the County of Monterey or the State of California authority to violate my 'sovereign' rights and freedoms as an American; nor, authority to change my birth name *(Seal)* or that jurisdiction of law *(of my birthplace)* that comes with that birthright.

I am and always will be an American-born *"sovereign."* I am not a *Fourteenth Amendment, Washington D. C., Emancipated Slave, federal immigration status* "citizen" just because someone else wants me to be one. I have State of California common law birthrights and am under my <u>u</u>nited *"State's Constitutional Rights"* as an American.

AUTHOR'S THOUGHTS REGARDING REASONS FOR NAME CHANGES:

The U.S. Federal Government, via the American Bar Association, judges and attorneys, have since the 1960's created the *"Uniform Commercial Code"* to standardize and replace America's individual State's common law (and Hawaii's protective common-law). NOTE: I believe, the international bankers, Federal Reserve, et al, *(controlling since the U.S. bankruptcy of 1933)* have created this trend and deception and have almost fully succeeded in removing we Americans and Hawaiians from our birthrights and into a lesser foreign *(federal)* jurisdiction of law that they can control; by influencing weak, liberal-minded and corrupted politicians who are inept, and function within a corrupted

---

[16] *Bearer bond.* "Bonds payable to the person having possession of them. Such bonds do not require endorsement to transfer ownership but only the transfer of possession." *(Source: Black's Law Dictionary 6th Edition, Page 154.)*

[17] *Bearer document.* "A document that runs to bearer upon issuance or after a blank indorsement, and that is negotiated by delivery alone. U.C.C. §§ 7-501(1) & (2)(a). Anyone in possession of a bearer document is a holder of it. U.C.C. § 1-201(20)." *(Source: Black's Law Dictionary 6th Edition, Page 154.)*

[18] *Bearer instrument.* "An instrument is payable to bearer when by its terms it is payable to (a) bearer or the order of bearer; or (b) a specified person or bearer; or (c) "cash" or the order of "cash", or any other indication which does not purport to designate a specific payee. U.C.C. §§ 3-111, 3-204[2])" *(Source: Black's Law Dictionary 6th Edition, Page 154.)*

government and judiciary. These politicians and bankers have now unlawfully, but legally, created a de facto *"democracy"* of bound, fictitious, federal corporate citizens inhabiting their corporate, fictional *"democracy"*, wherein all *"citizens"* are *"14th Amendment," "Washington D. C.," "Emancipated Slave," "Government created chattel persons" with an "immigration status"* federal citizenship. They are no longer freeborn living souls, Private Citizen American Nationals with Godly Freedoms and Rights.

What these ***unsavory***[19] politicians, judges and attorneys have done is to lower our American standards of citizenship to avoid admitting the truth that they have continually and deliberately fouled up, big time! They have, instead of lifting the *"Emancipated Slaves"* to a proper and dignified level of American, State's Right's and National Citizenship under the *48 Star Flag of the American Republic*; chosen to lower all American's citizenship standards to that of the *"Emancipated Slave"* by removing us from our *"American Republic"* rights to create their de facto federal *"Democracy"* that functions without our 'sovereign State's Private Citizenship rights'... all for the gain of corrupt, international bankers *(i.e. Federal Reserve)* and politicians.

It's time we clean up the acts of devious judges, corrupt attorneys and inept politicians who have literally sold us *(by name change)* into slavery and hold us in bondage to benefit bankers who function without conscience in perpetuating corruption for gain! Their thinking is if they control the money, they can control all of us. Wrong! A fallacy! Script money *(paper money without lawful gold and silver backing i.e. federal notes)* does not control wise and knowledgeable Americans or Hawaiians who find their strength in God. It is the love and concern for each other that gives us strength as a People. As they say, money cannot buy love; it is America's love and generosity for others in the world with a faith in a Living God that is its strength, as a nation.

CONSEQUENCES OF FICTIONAL NAME USE:

Under this fraudulent pseudonym title substituted for our name, we are taken before a judge or magistrate without possessing any constitutional rights *(guilt in their*

---

[19] ***Unsavory.*** *"1. not savory; tasteless or insipid: an unsavory meal. 2. unpleasant in taste or smell; distasteful. 3. unappealing or disagreeable, as a pursuit: Poor teachers can make education unsavory. 4.* **socially or morally objectionable or offensive:** *as unsavory past; an unsavory person..."* (*Highlight in bold to clarify application of Author) (Source: Webster's Encyclopedic Unabridged Dictionary 2001 Ed.)*

jurisdiction is by "presumption") and it is only the degree of guilt or punishment that will be determined against us. We are already deemed guilty as a *"government created chattel person"* or *"federal citizen"* of the corporate State within which we reside *(it only takes an accuser and not two witnesses as required in the Bible and the common-law).*

AMERICAN NATIONALS (i. e. "sovereigns")

Birth citizenship is determined by one or both of two factors: 1) where you are born, and 2) the nationality of your parents. Citizenship in America is based upon birth under your respective State's "common law" *(that is, within one of the 48 contiguous States of the Union).* America is a union made up of *"sovereign"* States. Each State, is a republic, a nation unto itself, under its respective Constitution and common law, and is also committed by its *State Constitution,* to be part of a *"federation"* called, *"The united States of America,"* (also called, *"The American Republic")* and subject to the *United States Constitution.* Attorneys, judges, bankers and politicians as licensed agents of the federal government and state governments desire to *"federalize"* you by unlawfully changing your proper birth name on birth certificates to fictionalize and capture you. It is another justification for the federal government to also issue Social Security Numbers (SSN) to newborn infants who are not even of lawful age to contract in their so-called, federal *"Democracy."*

THREE QUESTIONS FOR THE DEMOCRATIC AND REPUBLICAN PARTIES

Of concern to me is the simple fact that Hawaii is not by law affirmed to be a *"State of the American Union of States, the Republic."*

Since the Apology Bill U.S.P.L. 103-150 of 1993, an admission of wrongdoing signed by President Bill Clinton that recognizes that Hawaii was/is in fact a foreign country violated by the United States and its military, it also affirms that the United States continued control is unlawful and regrettable. Facts of law affirm that the present Hawaiian Kingdom Government is lawful in all respects, which also affirms that all born to the Ko Hawaii Pae Aina (The Hawaiian Islands) are in fact Hawaiian National Citizens foreign to the United States.

Even if Hawaii had been legitimately annexed to the U.S. in 1898, the fact remains that Hawaii is a false state, created by Executive Order, not the National Congress (thus violating the U.S. Constitution), and its federal judges do not meet the same law requirements of real U.S. federal judges. The courts are not as declared in the false State of Hawaii Constitution; the false State possesses no land (by law); the standing of the false State of Hawaii is lawfully repugnant to the U. S. Constitution, and the lawful fact that documentation does not support Hawaiians assenting to U.S. takeover of their land are all further indications of Hawaii's foreign standing.

Whereas the U.S. Constitution (Article 11) requires the President to be a "natural born" to the land, I wonder if the **Democratic Party National Committee** and/or the **Republican Party National Committee** can explain the following:

1) If Presidential Candidate John McCain was born in the Republic of Panama, does this not also create a cloud on his citizenship qualification for President?

2) Since Presidential Candidate, Mr. Barack Obama was born to the foreign land of Ko Hawaii Pae Aina (The Hawaiian Islands) as a land affirmed foreign by U. S. law *(28 USC § 91 [an admission by omission], et cetera)*, then wouldn't that cloud the citizenship of such a foreign born person from being President of the United States according to the U.S. Constitution?

3) If the Governor of California (Mr. Arnold Schwarzenegger) also, a foreign born, is disqualified from being able to run for the Presidency of the United States, does this not also disqualify Mr. Barack Obama and Mr. John McCain?

HAWAIIAN NATIONALS

When Hawaiians execute their lawful separation *(in writing)* from the intruding United States Government functioning unlawfully on their *"Neutral"* Hawaiian National soil *(including the U.S. Puppet Government titled the "State of Hawaii")* they automatically return to their birthright nation, the Hawaiian Kingdom, more appropriately titled, *"Ko Hawaii Pae Aina,"* a Nation in Godly restoration. They again become, *"Hawaiian Nationals!"* There are five (5) types of Hawaiian National Citizenship. **(See Chapter 10. Restoring Hawaiians to their proper Citizenship)**

RESTORING HAWAIIAN NATIONAL CITIZENSHIP (FROM U.S. SECOND - CLASS FEDERAL U.S. PUBLIC-SERVANT CITIZENSHIP STATUS)

WE STILL HAVE CHOICE

The choice is still ours. Which citizenship do you personally prefer? You can stay where you are, or, you can lawfully *(in writing and by public filing)* sever the unrecorded and implied contracts with the de facto corporate state and federal corporate United States that bind you to their jurisdiction and return to that greater birthright, as evidenced herein, under Almighty God. <u>Our rights are affirmed by who we say we are</u> and by the common law of the sovereign State (or nation) domicile of our birth. We can also continue to neglect our rights and stay in bondage.

Again, as Hawaiians say, *"Nou ke koho!"* *(The choice [guess] is yours!)*

Chapter 5

ACTIONS OF A UNITED STATES PUPPET GOVERNMENT

(Acting in Violation of the United States Constitution and International Law [The Law of Nations]).

The de facto STATE OF HAWAII, A PUPPET GOVERNMENT.

The current de facto "State of Hawaii" is a fourth generation puppet[1] government. It is a de facto descendent of the de facto governing entity called the "Provisional Government for the Hawaiian Kingdom," that was initially installed by the "Committee of Safety" a treasonous faction that overthrew the lawful Hawaiian Kingdom Government in a coup executed in 1893. The following year, the U. S recognized the de facto, "Republic of Hawaii" controlled by the same faction of insurrectionists.

These entities were categorically unlawful from inception, having been created by insurrectionists and treasonists acting in violation of *Hawaiian Kingdom National Law,* with military support from the United States. The above entities were created during which time Hawaiian Nationals were denied voice and the seat of government was directly under United States Federal Government influence and military control.

In January of 1893, in violation of the sovereignty of the de jure *Hawaiian Kingdom Government*, the *United States Government* under President Benjamin Harrison, landed armed military onto Hawaiian soil. The United States assisted the Caucasian treasonists and then remained on Hawaiian Kingdom soil until that element *(with its extensive armory of U.S. imported weapons and the United States Military support at the ready)* had secured all the High Offices of the *Hawaiian Kingdom National Government*. It was only then that the United States Military withdrew leaving a substantial number of armed rebels of mostly American, and some of German and English ancestry, etc., in authority. These traitors continued to be supported by the Navy

---

[1] **Puppet (Government):** *"1 a: a small-scale figure (as of a person or animal) usu. With a cloth body and hollow head that fits over and is moved by the hand   b: MARRIONETTE   2: doll   3: one whose acts are controlled by an outside force or influence"* *(Bold emphasis by Author. Source: Merriam-Webster's Collegiate Dictionary, Tenth Edition)*

and Marine personnel aboard a U.S. military gunship anchored in Honolulu Harbor. The *Federal United States Government*, since that time, has simply taken that original treasonous pirate ship of state *(to conceal unlawful U.S. involvement)*, repainted it, ran up another flag and renamed its de facto colonial entity four times, in order to camouflage its corrupt character, insulting knowledgeable Hawaiian Nationals and others!

To its dishonor, the United States, in favor of its new colonial Hawaiian puppet government *(Republic of Hawaii)* did not support the re-institution of the lawful Constitutional Monarchy of the Hawaiian Kingdom Government. The U.S. just stepped back, ignored their violation of a friendly nation's trust, and violation of international law. The U.S. abandoned their Christian moral character and their standing treaties with the Hawaiian Kingdom, and then proceeded to assist in the active dismantling of the *Hawaiian National Government*.

U.S. laws *claiming U.S. interest in Hawaii and the sequence of de facto governments to the present "State of Hawaii Puppet Government,"* are false, making the very existence of the *Puppet State of Hawaii* its laws and agencies patently fraudulent. This means that the entire U.S. imposed judicial system in Hawaii *(including the United States Federal Court for the Hawaii District)* <u>operates in violation of its own United States Federal Laws</u>. **(Please read Chapter 6, "Hawaii's Courts" to understand this Author's position.)** This is a bold statement, but it's the truth.

Consistent violation of U.S. laws and <u>the pretense that the U.S. sustained courts honor federal U.S. laws</u> creates a foreign, corrupting influence on Hawaiian Kingdom soil. It becomes obvious that officials of the *Puppet State of Hawaii* function under *"color of U.S. law"* which is in direct violation of **United States Criminal Laws (USCr.C) Title 18 §§ 241, 242** *(which is applicable to federal citizens in federal jurisdictions like Washington, D.C. etc.)*.

WHO OWNS THE LAND IN HAWAII?

The Hawaiian People and the *Hawaiian Kingdom Government* still possess *"exclusive jurisdiction"* and have never given up any claim or the rights to their land. As Hawaiian Nationals, they are never allowed to participate in U.S. related issues of any kind. Treasonists unlawfully exercised authority in behalf of the Hawaiian People without the consent or approval of the Hawaiian People or that of their *Hawaiian*

National Government. The U.S. never conquered the Hawaiian Nation through warfare nor have the Hawaiian People assented to foreign U.S. intervention <u>on their soil</u>.

<u>The Great Mahele.</u>   (Hawaii's Land Division Under the Monarchy of 1848)

Kamehameha III *("Kauikeaouli") became King on July 14, 1824.* He issued the *"1839 Bill of Rights"* for Hawaiians, et al, followed by Hawaii's First *Constitution* in October 8, 1840, thus providing a written system of law and order for all the people.   In the year 1848, there was devised at the request of Kamehameha III, a lawful and proper manner of land holding system that preceded by almost half a century, any foreign, United States military or de facto *Hawaii Republic* intrusion into government on Hawaiian National soil.

The definitive land holding and division thereof <u>was set in perpetuity</u> for the Hawaiian People and was called *"The Great Mahele"* or just, "Mahele." It consisted of a distribution of the land among the monarchy, the chiefs and people. It replaced the feudal Hawaiian land system previously used by those whom foreigners would ignorantly call, *"aboriginals" (i.e. natives who did not own the land).* Hawaiians were literate, possessed educational systems *(a literacy of over 90%)* and had a great faith in the belief and teachings of Jesus Christ as their Saviour and King. The fact that *"The Great Mahele"* existed then and is still the basis of land ownership today, is fact that the lands of the *Hawaiian Nation* and the *Hawaiian National Government* lawfully existed for the purposes of nationhood and possessed laws appropriate for that purpose, previous to the U.S. Federal Government's illegal intervention.

Islands divided the Hawaiian National lands. The largest land divisions within each island *("mokus")* of that period formed the judicial districts of the present era. Within the Hawaiian Islands the original holdings of the major chiefs were called *"moku."* Each *"moku"* was divided into landholdings known as *"ahupuaa,"* which was ruled by a lesser chief or *"konohiki."* These usually ran from the sea to a point up a valley in the mountains and along a ridge or other designated line on each side. They were of various sizes. Within the *"moku"* was found the *"ili"* or *"ili kupono" (also known as "ili ku").* These were further reduced to *"moo" ("mooaina"); "pauka,"* called *"koele," "poalima"* and *"kihipai"* depending on their agricultural or designated usage.

Possession of the lands was distinctly held in three divisions of ownership. The first was that of the monarchy, the second by the chiefs or *konohiki* and the third by the common people or tenants. The Land Commission was formed in 1846 to register and document, record and affirm the holdings of land and titles of all within the Hawaiian Kingdom under the National Government thereof. The Land Commission completed its work and was disbanded in 1853.

NOTE: Something that the *United States Federal Government* and the *de facto State of Hawaii* are ignoring is that aboriginals do not divide record and document land holdings as has been done within the Hawaiian Nation through **"The Great Mahele."** The land boundaries were later relegated to *"metes and bounds"* measurements for a more accurate clarification of holdings. This is an identical system of boundaries used in most other western civilized countries and nations, including the United States. So how does the United States lawfully claim an interest in Hawaiian National and private Hawaiian lands that are recorded and documented in lawful records as being held in perpetuity for the Hawaiian People? How can it claim or lawfully possess a right to title in Hawaiian National or Hawaiian Private land of any kind? It lawfully cannot!

REGARDING THE OFFICE OF HAWAIIAN AFFAIRS
(OHA – A Subordinate State Agency)

Another present devious action by the *United States Federal Government* through its *Puppet State of Hawaii* is the creating of the *Office of Hawaiian Affairs (OHA)* in order to create an *"Indian Reservation Government"* for only *"Native Hawaiians"*[2] *(those with 50% aboriginal blood as defined by the Organic Act)* who sign up with *"Kau Inoa" through OHA, are forfeiting both their Hawaiian National Citizenship rights AND their inherent claim to the land!* When the U.S. has signed up all the so-called *"Native Hawaiians"* and put them on a limited area of land *(a reservation under a limited, quasi-government —* upon receipt of any kind of payment made by the U.S. to these *"Native Hawaiians"* — these natives will have sold (forfeited) all Kingdom Trust lands and national rights, to the United States!

---

[2] Author's Note: The term "Native Hawaiians" originated with the U.S. Congress-created "Organic Act" of 1900 to create a "Territory of Hawaii" to deliberately separate Hawaiians by blood heritage from all other peoples of the Kingdom (Created a blood bias).

This is the goal of the United States: to obtain Hawaii's land! This is the deliberate maneuver and cunning tactic of a corrupt *United States Federal Congress* led by *U.S. Federal Senators Inouye and Akaka*, et al. These politicians and OHA serve only the interest of the *United States Federal Government* and the *Puppet State of Hawaii*; they do not serve Hawaiian National Citizens or Hawaiian interests. OHA only benefits those Hawaiians who have given away their birthrights and citizenships by affirming they are foreign *"Federal U.S. citizens."* These misinformed leaders of their people are a privileged few. Sincere Hawaiians, who do participate within OHA, do so without the fullness of knowledge as to their rights; and function in ignorance with at least one arm of knowledge being tied behind their backs. **OHA should be disbanded.**

THE LAND IS HAWAIIAN NATIONAL LAND!

The above statement that the land is Hawaiian is affirmed by United States Congressional law *(reflecting the position of the American People)*, which openly admits in **United States Code Title 28 § 91,**[3] by an obvious admission by omission, confirming lack of lawful jurisdictional authority, "exclusive" or otherwise, on and over Hawaiian Kingdom soil and its people. **Fact:** The *United States Court for the Hawaii District* lacks jurisdiction by virtue of its own *"jurisdictional statement"* (**Revealed in 28 USC § 91**) and thus admittedly functions without lawful right on Hawaii's National sovereign soil.

---

[3] 28 U. S. C. § 91: (See Pages 4 - 6 for details) **defines the jurisdiction of the U.S. District Court located on Hawaiian Kingdom National soil.** The quoted jurisdictional statement from Title 28 USC 91 follows:

"Title 28 U. S. C. § 91. **Hawaii** - Hawaii constitutes one judicial district which includes the Midway Islands, Wake Island, Johnston Island, Sand Island, Kingman Reef, Palmyra Island, Baker Island, Howland Island, Jarvis Island, Canton Island, and Enderbury Island: *Provided, That the inclusion of Canton and Enderbury Islands in such judicial district shall in no way be construed to be prejudicial to the claims of the United Kingdom to said Islands in accordance with the agreement of April 6, 1939, between the Governments of the United States and of the United Kingdom to set up a regime for their use in common. Court shall be held at Honolulu."* (It is imperative to note that the term *"Hawaii"* was not defined in this description, nor are the Islands of *Kauai, Niihau, Oahu, Molokai, Lanai, Maui or Hawaii (the Big Island) either mentioned or referenced therein, being omitted therefore from that court's jurisdictional control. Secondly, the use of the word "includes" is very limiting at law therein because the word "Hawaii" was not defined, being ambiguous (i.e. is the "Hawaii" referenced therein an Island? A State? An Archipelago? A Nationality? An Atoll? Therefore the word "includes" only means that territory, which follows the word "includes" is to be considered as that territory contained within the jurisdictional statement. [This is called* **"an admission by omission"** *affirming that the de jure "Hawaiian Kingdom Nation" is still lawfully recognized by the United States Congress as foreign, national soil - Author's Note])*

ATTEMPTED STATE THEFT OF HAWAIIAN LANDS BY TAX DEVIOUSNESS

One method the *Puppet State of Hawaii* uses to claim Hawaiian Land from Hawaiian Nationals is by corrupt State of Hawaii Tax Assessors assigning *"Tax Map Key Numbers"* to exempt, non-taxable Hawaiian Royal Patent, Grant or Kuleana lands, not in de facto State possession. The application of a *Tax Map Key* is a devious method by the State to identify all land as being under their taxing authority, regardless of the rightful jurisdictional holding of that land. The State assesses these private holdings by falsely asserting they are taxable State lands, applying false tax claims, and then, accruing penalties. Usually, after several generations of family, descendents of Hawaiian Nationals who possess the lands are forced to either pay the falsely accrued tax or get suckered into defending *(crossing jurisdictional lines, thus admitting authority of the Puppet State)* in a foreign State Tax Court where they must join the system or loose their lands through forced default and foreclosure. This method of "legal" theft has been ongoing against Hawaiians since the overthrow. Hawaiians (discriminated against by banks for loans unless submitting their ancestral lands as collateral) in most cases do not possess sufficient assets, rights and legal knowledge to defend themselves within the de facto State courts where there is no justice for them.

ABUSIVE POLICE POWER

Both *United States Federal Government* corporations *(State and Federal)* are active on Hawaiian Kingdom soil imposing their *"color of U.S. law"* authority by using armed and hostile abuse of power, to enforce their intents and purposes. Judges utilize and impose this force with or without signed orders, warrants, liens, etc. Directives are blindly followed by *ignorant*[4] police officers that don't know law. They know they function under what is known to them as, *"color of ordinance," "color of statute"* or *"color of law,"* but really don't understand the meanings.

These police officers *(sworn to uphold the U.S. Constitution and laws of the United States)* do not even realize <u>they violate international law every time they cross</u>

---

[4] **Ignorant / Ignorance.** *"The want or absence of knowledge, unaware or uninformed. Ignorance of the law is want of knowledge or acquaintance with the laws of the land in so far as they apply to the act, relation, duty, or matter under consideration. Ignorance of fact is want of knowledge of some fact or facts constituting or relating to the subject matter in hand."* (Source: Black's Law Dictionary 6th Edition, Page 746.)

jurisdictional lines to suppress Hawaiian Nationals who are: under their Hawaiian National Flag; in their proper English-language spelled birth names; within lawful Citizenship; under their Hawaiian National *"common-law;"*[5] and, are domiciled on their own Hawaiian National soil. Some police officers know their actions (enforcing U.S. laws) are unlawful yet still do so knowing they are protected by immunity through a corrupt and protective U.S. judicial system.

Higher-ups in authority use those ignorant in law enforcement to forcefully impose their will to the point of using physical abuse to inflict hurt upon Hawaiian Nationals and others who challenge their authority. I have personally noticed that quite often this abuse appears to be with indifference by some individual police officers *(i.e. threats; shoving Hawaiian's heads against walls; placing handcuffs so tight they cut off circulation, sometimes causing cutting and bleeding; hitting prisoners with batons while held down; denying phone calls after arrest until late at night; denying phone calls after getting a busy signal; denying blankets to cold, elderly prisoners; etc.).* These offensive police officers act above the law and assume that all who do not agree with their limited knowledge, power and authority, are adversarial. **They taint the good officers of these police departments.** Unfortunately, <u>these undesirable officers also cover up for each other</u>. I personally experienced that complaints to officers or to the courts, go unheeded.

A SUMMATION: (Regarding A Grand Criminal Conspiracy)

The *"Puppet State of Hawaii"* functions on Hawaiian Kingdom National soil in behalf of the United States interests and their own personal interests. It functions as an instrument of control, oppression and *genocide*[6] against the Hawaiian National People and any that stand up against it. This Author has personally experienced that on the public rights-of-way where Hawaiian Nationals *(with privately owned automobiles properly registered and licensed under Hawaiian Kingdom law)* are set upon, cited and

---

[5] **Common-law.** That law of Ko Hawaii Pae Aina (The Hawaiian Islands) known as the Hawaiian Kingdom as affirmed under the *1892 Revision of the Judiciary, An Act, Chapter LVII, § 5.* The common-law (superior law) comes from the British and American common-law with Hawaiian traditions and customs incorporated. Common-law is case law in which God Almighty is recognized as Supreme Authority.

[6] **Genocide.** *(Not in Black's Law Dictionary, 6ᵗʰ Ed.) "The deliberate and systematic destruction of a racial, political, or cultural group – Geno-cid-al" Source: Merriam Webster's Collegiate Dictionary, 10th Edition. "The systematic, planned annihilation of a racial, political, or cultural group" (Source: American Heritage Dictionary, 1973 Edition)*

arrested. These Nationals, having previously and lawfully cancelled their *Puppet State of Hawaii Driver's License (an identity/contract)* executed in the process of transferring their citizenship, find the de facto courts determining that they are driving *"without a license," "driving with an expired license,"* or *"driving with a fraudulent license,"* even though properly terminated and the *Puppet State* lawfully noticed.

This Author cannot find a *Puppet State of Hawaii* law requiring that non-state citizens *(even foreign visitors i.e. "tourists")* must possess Hawaii State Driver's Licenses. Therefore the *actions* of the *Puppet State of Hawaii* display a prejudicial presumption that Hawaiian National Citizens, cannot leave the *Puppet State of Hawaii* to move to the *de jure* (lawful) jurisdiction of their birth *(a rightful choice)*. In effect, Hawaiian Nationals are treated as prisoners of the Puppet State! When responses to false charges are made in writing in State courts, which is acceptable at law, they are ignored, stricken from the record; with bench warrants issued and bails forfeited... This happens even with appearances. This Author has experienced these unlawful acts himself.

Documented filings of record made in the *United States (Federal) Court for the Hawaii District* and de facto *State of Hawaii* court records *(copies possessed by Ke Aupuni O Hawaii Nei)* substantiate the above statements, and many more.

THE FOLLOWING AFFIRM THAT HAWAII IS NOT A LAWFUL STATE

First of all, the false *Puppet State of Hawaii* doesn't meet the criteria of the united *State's Constitution* and that required of the other State's within the Union. Let me reflect upon and enumerate some very obvious facts that do not conform to the requirement for Statehood in the American *"Union of States:"*

1)   Queen Liliuokalani, Queen of a Nation titled, **Ko Hawaii Pae Aina** *(The Hawaiian Islands)* while in the midst of foreign intervention (U.S.) and under house arrest by treasonists, to avoid bloodshed of both Hawaiian and American forces, entrusted the *"President of the United States"* with the responsibility to restore the Monarchy to power. She did not relinquish her Hawaiian Kingdom National Government or sovereignty to the U.S. but reserved them *(See Queen Liliuokalani letter of June 17, 1897 to U.S. Secretary of State John Sherman [See EXHIBIT K])*.

2) The President of the United States cannot create a *State of the Union*[7] by a *"Resolution," "Executive Order,"* or *"Proclamation."* The State of Hawaii was supposedly created by the following *Presidential Proclamation*[8] *No. 3309 of August 21, 1959, 24 F. R. 6868, 73 Stat. C74.* The President can only create a limited corporation within the federal jurisdiction under Article 1, § 8 of the American Constitution. <u>Hawaii cannot be a lawful State of the American Union of States under Constitutional law; therefore, it can be only a limited corporation.</u>

3) <u>The President of the United States cannot add stars to the United States Flag of the Republic.</u> Under "Positive Law" of the United States Code, Title 4, § 1, (See EXHIBIT S, [Positive Law] 1st part of Exhibit), it is stated that the <u>President can only *"arrange"* the stars</u>!   How then did the President add stars to the Flag of the Republic (See EXHIBIT S, [Executive Order No. 10834] 2nd **part of Exhibit)** for Hawaii and Alaska?   He couldn't and he didn't!   I believe **he, in violation of 4 USC 1 (Positive Law), added stars to the military flag in order to create the false impression of statehood** by using Paragraphs 2, 3 and 4 of E.O. 10834 as justification under the *Federal Property and Administrative Act of 1949* as his authority *(to add the extra stars and the yellow fringe to the mock 50-star flag over which he is Commander-in-Chief).* As a matter of fact and law, the military also has no authority to add stars to the American Flag <u>which Constitutional right is reserved only to the National Congress</u> *(not the lesser Article 1, Section 8 Federal Congress)!*

4) The *"Statehood Act" (§ 9[a] of The Admission Act) (An Act to Provide for the admission of the State of Hawaii into the Union - Act of March 18, 1959, Pub L 86-3, 73 State 4)* states: *"(a) the United States District Court for the District of Hawaii established by and existing under title 28 of the United States Code shall henceforth be a court of the United States with judicial power derived from*

---

[7] *State of the Union (Hawaii).* *(Author's Note) The de facto STATE OF HAWAII was created by Presidential Proclamation No. 3309 of August 21, 1959, 24 F. R. 868, 73 Stat. C74. A Proclamation cannot create a "State of the Union", but only a limited corporation under Article 1 § 8 of the American Constitution. Only the U.S. <u>National</u> Congress in lawful session, not the <u>Federal</u> Congress, can create an American "State" for admission into the American Union of States.*

[8] Proclamation. *"Something that is proclaimed; a public and official announcement.   2. The act of proclaiming." (Source: Webster's Encyclopedic Unabridged Dictionary 2001 Ed. Page 1543). (Author's Note: A "proclamation" is an announcement; a shouting into the wind.   It is not necessarily of fact and carries no legal impact.   Example: "I proclaim the moon is blue cheese!"... Where are the facts that support my proclamation?   By the way, there are no facts in support of Hawaii as a State of the American Union of States, either.)*

Article III, § 1, of the Constitution of the United States." The Hawaii State Constitution states that the United States Court for the Hawaii District is a United States Constitutional Article III, § 1 Court. It **is not and never was!** Therefore the court is de facto by virtue of law, being only a lesser Article 1 federal court and not the Article III Constitutional Court of the American Republic, stated therein.

5) <u>None of the judges</u> in the U.S. Court for the Hawaii District are under the "Positive Law" required United States Code, Title 28 § 453, oath of Office. <u>Therefore, all judges are by law, incompetent impersonators.</u>

6) The jurisdiction of the *U.S. Federal Court for the Hawaii District* established by the U.S. Congress under the United States Code, Title 28 § 91 (supra) is unique. Yet, when its words are clearly and definitively interpreted, it is in reality, an *"admission by omission"* that the Hawaiian Archipelago is not part of its defined U.S. jurisdiction. *(See Explanation, Chapter 1, Pages 3-5)*

7) <u>Only United States military flags fly in the courtrooms of the *United States Court for the Hawaii District*</u> (Occupation? You bet!). A 50 Star flag is a U.S. Federal Government Military Flag, <u>with or without the military fringe on it</u>. The lawful flag of the <u>u</u>nited *State's, i.e. American Republic* as cited under the Positive Law of **Title 4 § 1** of the **United States Code** is still 48 Stars! **(See EXHIBIT S, Positive Law portion)**

8) <u>The *State of Hawaii* derives its power and authority</u> from the *"Organic Act"*, i.e., *"Territory of Hawaii" "An Act to Provide a Government for the Territory of Hawaii" (Act of April 30, 1900, C 339, 31 Stat 141)* which Act has no lawful power on foreign Hawaiian National soil, being based upon a foreign, U.S. Congressional Resolution of Congress *(i.e. Newlands Resolution – [Resolution No. 55, 2nd Session, 55th Congress, July 7, 1898; 30 Sta. At L. 750; 2 Supp. R. S. 895] See Page 9)* <u>which was not a treaty as falsely claimed by the United States.</u>

9) The U.S. claims the *"Newlands Resolution,"* supra, as their basis of authority and legal right in the creation of the *Organic Act, (i.e. creating the Territory of Hawaii)* as if it were a treaty. It is not! It is nothing more than <u>a resolution that has no legal or lawful affect on foreign soil</u> of the Hawaiian Kingdom Nation. It is a false basis of claim knowingly made (contracted) with treasonists, without any right at law.

10) In the *Organic Act* (Territorial Act), Article 1. General Provision, it shall be noted that *"the laws of Hawaii" ... shall mean the*

constitution and laws of the Republic of Hawaii..." This is very interesting, because the Republic of Hawaii, <u>recognized as de facto by the U.S.</u>, consisted of the treasonists *("The Committee of Safety" who were also the "Republic of Hawaii")* without international right at law, and possessed no lawful right to make or cancel any treaties or conventions. **Therefore, the *Organic Act* is null and void from its inception.**

11)   The *Organic Act* was specifically <u>created for *U.S. Federal "citizens"*</u> and not for <u>u</u>nited *State's Nationals* or *Hawaiian Nationals* **(See: 8 USC § 1405.**[9] Therefore, under this law, if only U.S. Federal *"citizens" (i.e. who are "second-class," "14th Amendment," "naturalized," "immigration status," of Washington D.C.)* have rights <u>on Hawaiian soil</u> and American Nationals did not; **the resulting lawful affect of its discriminatory implementation is that Hawaii cannot be a lawful State of the American Union of States.**

12)   In an attempt to create and legalize a type of citizenship for statehood, the United States <u>granted immunity and citizenship to the treasonists</u> prior to the pseudo statehood (See #8 & #10, above). **The *Organic Act* under Section 4, also granted citizenship to** *"citizens of the Republic of Hawaii as of August twelfth, eighteen hundred and ninety-eight are hereby <u>declared </u>to be citizens of the United States and citizens of the Territory of Hawaii"* **(Bold and underline by Author)**. The word *"declared"* means nothing. It should state, *"...are hereby citizens of the United States..."* but that would not be true. The people here are not United States citizens by declaration, because the declaration rings hollow, lacking the substance of law. There were no <u>u</u>nited *State's National* <u>Citizens</u> created by this Act, only United State's <u>Federal, *"Washington D.C., second-class, immigration status"*</u> citizens, on foreign Hawaiian National soil!

13)   Under *Article 1, § 8, of the Organic Act*, certain offices were abolished. It is interesting to note that the de facto *Organic Act*, made with treasonists, <u>could not and did not abolish the de jure National Offices of *Ke Aupuni O Hawaii Nei*</u>! It stated, *"That the offices of President, minister of foreign affairs, minister of the interior, minister of finance, minister of, public instruction, auditor-general, deputy auditor-general*

---

[9] <u>8 USC § 1405.</u> (Also, *Immigration and Nationality Act; § 305*). I quote: *"<u>A person</u> born in Hawaii on or after August 12, 1898, and before April 30, 1900 is <u>declared </u>to be a citizen of the United States as of April 30, 1900. A person born in Hawaii on or after 1900, is a <u>citizen </u>of the United States at birth. A <u>person</u> who was a citizen of the Republic of Hawaii on the date of August 12, 1898 is declared to be a citizen of the United States as of April 30, 1900."* (Underlining emphasis by Author)

surveyor-general, marshal, and deputy marshal of the Republic of Hawaii are hereby abolished." <u>These were de facto, not Kingdom Offices that were abolished,</u> and this did not apply to the de jure and lawful Offices of the Monarchy and Hawaiian Kingdom National Cabinet Offices, which were re-activated in 1996. Not mentioned are the National Offices of the Hawaiian Kingdom: the Minister of Foreign Affairs; Minister of the Interior; Minister of Finance; Attorney General and Marshal (High-Sheriff)! These Offices still exist and Hawaiian Nationals refilled those Offices, as mentioned, in September of 1996.

14) <u>Only United States military flags fly in the courtrooms of the *Puppet State of Hawaii*.</u> A 50 Star flag is a U.S. Federal <u>Military Flag</u>, with or without the ***yellow fringe***[10] on it. The lawful flag of the <u>united</u> *State's American Republic* is cited under "Positive Law" **Title 4 § 1 of the United States Code** and it is still 48 Stars! This confirms that Hawaii cannot be a lawful state while under a foreign ***military flag***.[11] The courts are in fact considered "vessels" on land so the *"Law of the Flag"* applies <u>within</u> their confines.

15) <u>The *Puppet State of Hawaii* flies a flag that closely resembles the Hawaiian Kingdom flag</u> but upon close examination, the aspects of the dimensions of the lawful Hawaiian Kingdom flag are different from the *Puppet State of Hawaii's flag*.

16) <u>Lawful Constitutional States of the American Union of States have elected County Sheriffs.</u> <u>No State has an appointed "State Sheriff's Office."</u> Lacking elected County Sheriffs means the State of Hawaii is not in compliance with their own phony Puppet State Constitution. **Article 1 § 3 of The Admission Act** *(An Act to Provide for the admission of the State of Hawaii into the Union - Act of March 18, 1959, Pub L 86-3, 73 Stat 4)* requires that the State(sic) government be ***"republican in form"*** and ***"not repugnant to the Constitution of the United States and the principles of the Declaration of***

---

[10] **Yellow fringe.** "The yellow fringe was determined by the **U.S. Attorney General's Opinion in 4 U.S.C.A. § 1, (1925 Footnote); also see, 34 Op Atty Gen 483,** as being symbolic of a military designation under the control of the Commander-in-Chief (Military). The yellow <u>fringe mutilates</u> the Flag of the Republic by adding a fourth color as affirmed by 4 USC § 3." – (Author)

[11] **Law of the flag.** *"The maritime law, the law of that nation or country whose flag is flown by a particular vessel. A ship owner who sends his vessel into a foreign port gives notice by his flag to all who enter into contracts with the master that he intends the law of that flag to regulate such contracts, and that they must either submit to its operation or not contract with him."* (Source: Black's Law Dictionary 6th Ed., Page 638). Recommended reading: Bouvier's Law Dictionary (1946) version of "Law of the Flag."

Independence." <u>By its non-compliance, the State of Hawaii *is* repugnant!</u>

17) Section 19 of the Statehood Act states: *"Nothing contained in this Act shall operate to confer United States nationality, nor to terminate nationality heretofore lawfully acquired, or restored nationality heretofore lost under any law of the United States or under any treaty to which the United states is or was a party."* <u>Section 19, supra, a U.S. Congressional Act (creating supposed Hawaiian Statehood) conflicts with 8 USC § 1405</u> (See Paragraphs #11 and #12, above). <u>This being the case, "Hawaiian Nationals" are still "Hawaiian Nationals"!</u> "Hawaiian Nationals" were never conferred U.S. citizenship, as per Paragraphs #11 and #12, supra.

18) The Admission Act (Statehood Act) § 7(c) states: *"Upon the issuance of said proclamation by the President, the State of Hawaii **shall be deemed admitted** into the Union as provided by section 1 of this Act..."* (Underlining and bold by Author). Again, notice the wording *"shall be deemed admitted,"* which means nothing. This should read "is admitted." <u>This deceptive, misleading use of words also affirms that Hawaii cannot be a lawful State of the American Union of States!</u>

HAWAII'S STATE DEMOCRATIC AND REPUBLICAN PARTIES

The present Democratic Party and its *'Ole Boy Network'* in Hawaii is extremely corrupt and still in power. One simple tactic I am familiar with is a telephone call by the Contractor's License Board to a General Contractor's insurance company and making false statements to cause cancellation of his insurance so the Contractor focused against could not meet insurance requirements of the oppressive State. Once cancelled, the Contractor could not find other insurance. This procedure is called *"blackballing"* and is a very effective method of oppressive control. If the Insurance Company wants to continue to do business in the corrupt *Puppet State of Hawaii*, it is encouraged to drop one or two individuals rather than be terminated from making money here.

Another *'Ole Boy'* tactic is the use of the local office of the Internal Revenue Service (IRS) as a means of harassment and intimidation against those they want to have fall into line, or they seek to destroy. They have unlawfully used computer attachment of bank accounts *(I know of two)* even if no obligation is owed. This is to intimidate, cause financial hurt and place the party designated into a protective mode and defensive, paranoid state-of-mind.

Another tactic is for the IRS to assess a citizen or citizens they've targeted *(someone who does not support the State's corruption or for just being "Hawaiian"),* who do not owe any taxes. They assess and state a phony, invented amount on supposed income earned, and if challenged by the targeted parties, place penalty upon penalty until finally a U.S. federally insured bank, savings and loan, or Federal Credit Union yields to the IRS's unlawful *(preliminary to a valid lien)* "Notice of Lien." The de facto banking institutions function in collusion with the IRS by attaching the targeted citizen's hard-earned retirement money, setting it aside for a short period and then delivering it to the IRS without a judge ever having signed a required *"Perfected Lien."*

Another form of intimidation is to have the *Puppet State of Hawaii* Attorney General's Office call you to say they have a *"Complaint"* against you, but will not reveal the name of the person who supposedly made or filed the complaint *(you have a right to know who your accuser is).* They make false statements of charges that are close to the truth, but are not true, to cause you to respond to error, thus capturing you by your own admission, uncertainty or ignorance. Unfortunately, the Attorney General's Office represents the system of government corruption, rather than the *"Private Citizens or People"* that they are supposed to protect.

Another tactic is the filing of a complaint by one of their cronies, or a *Puppet State* Agency (through the AG's Office) and then letting your case linger for many years with postponement after postponement after postponement, so as to deny justice…. One case I am aware of went for approximately eight and a half years without being heard! This is to place a burden, oppression and control over the head of the falsely accused, regardless of the consequences to the falsely accused or his family.

Another tactic is to file a false claim against you to cause you to have to hire an attorney *(their justice system's ally)* who will cost you hard earned money and then sell you out through settlement, causing further harassment and hurt. I have found that there is no justice in the *Puppet State* judiciary that participates as part of that *"Ole Boy Network."* It goes on, and on, and on!

It seems to me, from approximately thirty-five plus years of political and investigative observation that the *Puppet State* Civil Service ranks appear filled with Democratic Party workers *(the "Ole Boy Network System?").* The Republican Party is too weak to be sufficiently influential and its values are not much better, both functioning in ignorance and supporting the unlawful *Statehood Act*, et al, under *"color of United*

States law" and its judicial abuses. Other political parties do not have a sufficient base to be influential. The corrupt parties in power that see and know lead the blind that follow, perpetuating corruption in blatant fashion.

Really, it is irrelevant which party is supposedly in control. There cannot be a morally lawfully justice system on *Hawaiian Kingdom National soil* as long as these Godless, foreign, corrupt, incompetent *federal citizens* impersonating judges and functioning without lawful oaths of office, are allowed to hold political control over the Hawaiian Kingdom, its People and others.

It is indeed unfortunate and sad that the average person believes that the *Puppet State of Hawaii* justice system and courts are honorable and that justice can be achieved. Until they are accused and have to defend themselves before these courts, and only then, will they understand the depths of corruption testified to herein. Corruption only breeds more corruption, not justice! Justice will only come by having judges with Godly values of righteousness in authority, in abatement of the base values of the mini-god mentality held by present judges.

Justice by the courts may be granted from time to time to give an image of a just, functioning justice system. In situations where control and ultimate U.S. or de facto *Puppet State of Hawaii* power is of concern or threatened, you can be assured that there will not be any quarter given to deny justice if the power of the judiciary and its power base of corruption is the focus! The *Puppet State of Hawaii* and both political parties, Democratic and Republican, can never attain the full respect, influence or support of knowledgeable and honorable people; because the basis of their very existence is built lie upon lie.

<u>Only Hawaiian Nationals of all ethnic backgrounds</u>, by participating in the functioning of their own National Government, can remove these unlawful administrative judges and correct the injustices being executed against Hawaiians, other multi-ethnic People of Hawaii and foreign U.S. citizens living here. These incompetent administrative judges are nothing more than private, second-class U.S. *federal citizens* under contract *(legal but not lawful).* They function without accountability to anyone but themselves and the corrupt superiors they serve that appointed them. <u>It is not surprising that crime is so high in Hawaii</u>, when the "justice" system itself is guilty of *high crimes of oppression, treason and genocide.*

It is time for the President of the United States to face up to the immoral, devastating occupation of the men and women of the Hawaiian Nation, Ko Hawaii Pae Aina (The Hawaiian Kingdom).

It is time to replace both foreign governments *(Puppet State of Hawaii and U.S. Federal)* unlawfully functioning on Hawaiian National soil with the proper National Government of the de jure Hawaiian Nation!

CITIZENSHIP IS VOLUNTARY BUT JUSTICE COMES FROM RIGHTIOUSNESS, AND RIGHTIOUSNESS COMES FROM HONORING OUR LIVING AND LOVING GOD!

CONCLUSION: The de facto, *Puppet State of Hawaii* does not exist at law. It exists because it is maintained by a foreign power and pretends to be something it is not. It is an imposter, a foreign corporation sustained by abusive use of judicial and police power to maintain a tight-fisted control; and, it functions outside of de jure right of law. The *Puppet State of Hawaii,* like the phony *Republic of Hawaii* and the phony *Territory of Hawaii,* is being used as an instrument of suppression, control and genocide against Hawaiian Nationals, et al, contrary to law as has been done since 1893!

Chapter 6

HAWAII'S COURTS

DE FACTO STATE COURTS AND
U.S. (FEDERAL) DISTRICT COURT

Courts in the de facto[1] Puppet[2] State of Hawaii are courts of incompetent[3] jurisdiction presently functioning under color of United States Law.[4] Now that I've said it, can I prove it? Grasping this assertion requires close comprehension of the following historical background presented herein.

On January 17, 1893, led by Hawaiian citizen Lorrin Thurston, a few other *Hawaiian Nationals*, together with *foreign nationals residing in Hawaii*, using their newly formed, *"Committee for Public Safety,"* overthrew the lawful Hawaiian Kingdom National Government. The *Committee of Safety* appointed its members to serve as the *Provisional Government* for the Hawaiian Kingdom, making it Hawaii's first *"de facto"* government. John L. Stevens, the U.S. Foreign Minister to Hawaii, without proper authority, instantly recognized this *de facto* provisional government on behalf of the United States. To this date, that status has not changed. This set the stage for the succeeding *de facto* governments. The fact is, when you read the following, the United States Congress has never taken a position that would indicate that the *Puppet Government of Hawaii* was anything other than *de facto*.

---

[1] **De facto court.** One established, organized, and exercising its judicial functions under authority of a statute apparently valid, though such statute may be in fact unconstitutional and may be afterwards so adjudged; **or a court established and acting under the authority of a** *de facto* **government."** **(Bold emphasis by Author)** (Black's Law Dictionary 6th Ed.)

[2] **Puppet (Government).** *"1 a: a small-scale figure (as of a person or animal) usu. With a cloth body and hollow head that fits over and is moved by the hand b: MARRIONETTE 2: doll **3: one whose acts are controlled by an outside force or influence** –"* (Merriam-Webster's Collegiate Dictionary, Tenth Edition)

[3] **Incompetent.** Just the opposite of a court that is "competent" (Author's note)**. Court of competent jurisdiction.** *"One having power and authority of law at the time of action to do the particular act. One recognized by law as possessing the right to adjudicate a controversy. One having jurisdiction under the Constitution and/or laws to determine the question in controversy."* (Black's Law Dictionary 6th Ed.)

[4] **Color of law.** *"The appearance or semblance, without the substance, of legal right. Misuse of power, possessed by virtue of state law and made possible only because wrongdoer is clothes with authority of state, is action taken under "color of state law. Akins v. Lanning. D.C. Okl., 415 F. Supp. 186, 188...."*"Color of U.S. law." See "Color of law". (Black's Law Dictionary 6th Ed.)

That being the case, the overthrow of the lawful Hawaiian National Government and the failure of the *Provisional Government* to secure immediate annexation to the United States required the treasonists to create some form of government that would have the appearance of a proper government. This necessitated the invention of the *"Republic of Hawaii"* with Sanford B. Dole, the former Chief Justice of the Hawaiian Kingdom, as president. This was the second de facto governing entity. This new entity was also recognized by the United States as a *"de facto"* government to replace the *Provisional Government*, which supplanted the de jure *Hawaiian Kingdom National Government*. These de facto governments required U.S. commitment of military and financial support to cover up and sustain their tainted character and positions.

This unlawful government continued seeking additional, United States support for years after the overthrow, which *(as during the insurrection and treasonous acts of January 16th and 17th of 1893,)* was now directly provided.

The de facto *Republic of Hawaii* existed until the third de facto puppet government; the *"Territory of Hawaii"* was created by the United States in 1900. This U.S. territorial government was designed for the subjugation of Hawaiian National sovereignty and was created without the basis of a lawful treaty, the consent of the de jure *Hawaiian Kingdom National Government,* or the Hawaiian National populace.

So how does this affect the courts? Following the overthrow, the courts were compromised as to just what laws they should honor, the de jure *"common-law"* of the Hawaiian Kingdom, or, those of the new, dictating parties of the de facto government in power. The judges, being appointed by the de facto entities, of course honored de facto authority of law. By this fact, we have had courts of incompetent jurisdiction on Hawaiian Kingdom soil for over 115 years!

This shell game of de facto governing entities started with the United States Government placing sufficient credibility upon the puppet state *"Republic of Hawaii"* in order to accomplish its primary purpose of obtaining, at the expense of Hawaii's sovereignty and America's integrity, military posts such as Pearl Harbor *(as a military coaling station for its Pacific Fleet).* The United States in doing so had now contracted with a known thief (treasonous de facto governments) of its own making.

U.S. DISTRICT COURT FOR HAWAII – JUDGES' OATHS OF OFFICE

As initially stated, the de facto *U.S. Court for the Hawaii District* supposedly issuing *"justice"* is a court of *"incompetent jurisdiction."* This court does not possess judges who are under the required, lawful, United States oath of Office. Judges in all of the United States District Courts are required to be charged with a *duty*[5] and to be sworn into Office under the *United States Code Title 28 Section 453*, (28 USC § 453) oath of Office (**See EXHIBIT L**). That oath was required under the *"Statehood Act" (Act of March 18, 1959, Pub L 86-3, 73 Stat 4, as verified by Sections 12 and 13).* These Sections require conformity to the status of all other U.S. District Judges throughout the United States yet, no judge, as is required by law, seated on the bench of the *United States Federal Court for the Hawaii District* (**See EXHIBIT M**) can prove to be under the above required **Title 28 USC Section 453** oath of Office.

These present judges, along with attorneys were not required to take the *(Section 19)* oath designated in the de facto 1900 *Organic Act, (…to support the Constitution and laws of the United States…")*. So whom do they support? My answer is: *"De facto Republic of Hawaii power!"* The fact is these judges were drawn from within the local *Republic of Hawaii* on land foreign to the U.S. These attorneys and judges have never had any obligation to honor U.S. law, at least until supposed Statehood. Under the *"Statehood Act" (Act of March 18, 1959, Pub L 86-3, 73 Stat 4)* the oaths were required to be United States law, specifically **28 USC § 453**, supra, *(that is, if Hawaii's U.S. court really was a lawful Article III Court of the American Union of States. Added to that partial bastardized oath is the oath for a U.S. Employee (Title 5 Section 16).*

Part of the Title **28 USC § 453** oath that is removed (invalidating the oath) is the following: *"… **under the Constitution and laws of the United States. So help me God.**"* In its place is inserted: *"… **according to the best of my abilities and understanding, agreeably to the Constitution and laws of the United States;**"* This *"…according to the best my abilities and understanding…"* says to me (the Author) that the judges under this modified oath are not bound and have no obligation to honor United States laws on Hawaiian soil, with the *"understanding"* that they represent a de facto, fake government!

---

[5] **Duty**. *"A human action which is exactly conformable to the laws which require us to obey them. Legal or moral obligation. An obligation that one has by law or contract. Obligation to conform to legal standard of reasonable conduct in light of apparent risk…. Obligatory conduct or service. Mandatory obligation to perform… An obligation, recognized by the law, requiring actor to conform to certain standard of conduct for protection of others against unreasonable risks…."* (Source: Black's Law Dictionary 6th Ed., Page 505)

Yet, the fact remains, there cannot be properly seated, competent, U.S. District Court judges on foreign soil *(Hawaiian National land)* functioning under United States law, which could explain their modified, bastard oaths of Office. Therefore, I believe Hawaii, as evidenced by requirements of law not honored, <u>is still recognized by the United States as foreign land</u>, yet, for over a hundred years, has been unlawfully occupied (militarily) and Hawaiians subjugated <u>under extreme duress</u> to abuse of police power by direct and indirect United States Federal Government rule.

FRAUDULENT OATH NOT SUBSTANTIATED BY LAW

Judges of the *United States Court for the Hawaii District* are under a very different, and what I believe to be a fraudulent oath that is a creation of two oaths combined to create a third, bastard oath **(See EXHIBIT M)** that is not substantiated by law. The U.S. has combined a portion of the congressionally approved and required **U.S. Code Title 28, Section 453, judicial oath**; and, a portion of the **Title 5 Section 16 (or Section 3331) Civil Service Oath**. By combining the two, they created a third, fraudulent and foreign, *"Territorial Oath"* lacking a lawful, legislative basis for its creation *(This Author could not find a promulgating[6] law covering, affirming this modified oath).*

This latter fact alone renders all court cases past and present, appellate and original, heard *(and adjudicated)* in the *U.S. District Court for the Hawaii (Federal)* as defective, since that court has been and continues to be operating and functioning outside of law and outside of its supposed U.S. jurisdiction, especially since the Organic Act.

This false *U. S District Court for Hawaii* judiciary is made up of U.S. federal <u>c</u>itizens from within the de facto State and none appear to be from the continent, i.e. foreigners. The court is sustained on *Hawaiian Kingdom National soil* only by abuse of police power. It does so without the lawful approval of the sovereign *Hawaiian National Government* or the Hawaiian People. Because the U.S. President appoints its judges, it is my deduction that the U.S. Military, Judiciary, Justice Department and State Department, et al, function on Hawaiian National soil without positive law or Congressional approval under directives of the Office of the President. On that basis, the *U.S. Federal District*

---

[6] **Promulgate or promulgation.** *"To publish; to announce officially; to make public as important or obli-gatory. The formal act of announcing a statute or rule of court. An administrative order that is given to cause an agency law or regulation to become known and obligatory."* (Black's Law, 6th Edition, Pg. 1214)

Court for Hawaii, by law, <u>would therefore be limited in its function to only U.S. *federal citizens*</u> residing on Hawaiian soil. It <u>possesses no lawful rights over Hawaiian Nationals or Hawaiian National issues, including Hawaiian land issues. Yet the de facto U.S. courts (State and Federal) continue in asserting jurisdiction without lawful right.</u>

Note: Because the President still holds Queen Liliuokalani's temporary "Yield" the President alone possesses the power to unilaterally restore the de jure Hawaiian Kingdom National Government at any time.

UNLAWFUL ACTIONS WITHIN THE U.S. HAWAII DISTRICT COURT

From 1998 through 2004, it is documented that former Court Clerk Walter A. Y. H. Chinn of the *United States Court for the Hawaii District*, refused to accept filings of lawfully documented *Hawaiian Nationals*, or even <u>u</u>nited *State's Nationals (American Nationals, i.e. Private Citizens, as distinct from U.S. <u>federal</u> "<u>c</u>itizens")*. If this District Court is truly an Article III Court or even under *Title 28 Section 91 of the United States Code*, then this supposed federal Clerk was <u>acting in direct violation of his charge and duty of Office.</u> He closed the court, refused to accept filings and honor law, as required of him. He told me that he did what he was told *(by the judges)* stating, *"That's how we do it." "That's what I have been told to do." "I cannot file your papers."*

If this was in fact a de jure or lawful Article III Court, the Clerk under **Title 28 USC § 452** has a lawful duty *(which does not apparently apply on Hawaiian Kingdom National soil)*. I quote that law as follows:

> 28 U.S.C. § 452. *"Courts always open; powers unrestricted by expiration of sessions"*
>
> > *"All courts of the United States shall be deemed always open for the purpose of filing proper papers, issuing and returning process, and making motions and orders."*

The fact is the Office of the Clerk of the *U.S. District Court for the Hawaii* is closed (off limits) to <u>u</u>nited *State's National Citizens* and *Hawaiian National Citizens (both Private Citizens)*. Clerk Chinn did not function separately as a Clerk carrying out his charge and duty as is required of a competent United States District Court Clerk, but willingly participated in collusion and conspiracy with incompetent judges to arbitrarily close the court and deny Private National Citizens their due process. <u>This court is most definitely closed to those who challenge its corruption and lawlessness</u>! This is evidence that this court censors and does not function as a U.S. Federal District Court; therefore, it cannot be a lawful U.S. Federal District Court. It is a court that functions under color of title and color of law.

To further affirm this court's unlawful actions, a U.S. Federal District Court Judge from the North American continent, a Mr. Manuel Real, *(from Los Angeles, California)* proceeded to hold court in Honolulu, bypassing or substituting for the authority of supposed, local *U.S. Federal District Court* judges. He opened his court with a foreign pledge of allegiance *(not the "Pledge of Allegiance to the 48 Star Flag of United States of America," nor was it any other recognizable American pledge)* and then proceeded to hold court. His actions that one-day were to deny this Author and another American National Private Citizen, Pastor Jon Robert Johnson, their rights to file cases in the *United States District Court for Hawaii.* In my whole life, I have never heard of an American Court *(i.e. a United States [supposed American] judge... then again, maybe he isn't),* function under a foreign pledge of allegiance that denies rights to justice *(by selectively closing a U.S. Court)* to American born National Citizens! The judicial system of America (if Hawaii is a State) seems to have strayed from God and the truth, and, apparently it marches to a distant, unknown foreign drummer … or banker (?).

I wondered: If Hawaii is a state of the U.S. and its courts are competent, why do judges *(like this un-American Mr. Manuel Real, supra)* have to come to Hawaii from the U.S. continent to hear United States Government cases or International cases *(Like the Philippines case against Dictator Ferdinand Marcos; also handled by Mr. Real)?* It is, I believe, because these local, incompetent federal judges do not have lawful authority and cannot meet the law requirement standards for *U.S. Federal District Court* judges while serving in Hawaii, which remains as sovereign, Hawaiian National (foreign to U.S.) soil. To this Author, this constitutes more evidence that the so-called *U.S. District Court for Hawaii* cannot meet the same standards of other *U.S. Federal District Courts* located on the North American Continent.

A BRIEF SAMPLING OF U.S. DISTRICT COURT CASES

CASE SAMPLE #1: John and Darcy Ebanez vs. IRS; Aloha Airlines Inc.; Emy Tamanaha and Susan Meredith, Private Parties: **Case No 02-CV-198**; Judge Alan C. Kay, United States District Court for Hawaii (Federal).

In this case, the Complainants *(who are <u>lawfully documented Hawaiian Kingdom Nationals, filing in their lawful birth names</u>)* took dispute with an unlawful and questionable IRS attachment of their compensation for labor. To attach the Ebanez' finances, the IRS had used only an unsigned, *"Notice of Federal Lien,"* not a lawful *perfected lien* that is *required by law to be signed by a judge*. The Court, in violation of its own law and <u>without the consent of the Complainants, changed the Complainant's birth names</u> to a ALL CAPITALIZED FICTION names *(as used by second-class, emancipated slaves and Washington D.C. federal <u>c</u>itizens)* in order to capture jurisdiction over the Complainants, a clear violation of law and right. The Ebanez's thereafter never received anything in their proper names from the Courts through the United States Postal Service regarding notices, filings, court appearances or actions thereafter taken.

The Ebanez' filed their complaint against their former employer (Aloha Airlines) and the IRS for fraud.

The Respondents *(Aloha Airlines, IRS, et al)*, failed to respond within the time established by law, which is thirty-days (30) from date of proper Service of the Complaint. Therefore, by and under law, the <u>Respondents (Aloha) incurred a lawful default</u> by their negligence and failure to timely respond as stipulated by law.

At the time of Complainants filing their *"Notice of Default of Respondents"* and *"Entry of Default – Automatic Judgment"* <u>on the date of March 11, 2002</u>, no response to the Complaint had been filed with the Court Clerk (Walter A. Y. H. Chinn). His immediate responsibility was to enter the Default because the amount of default was calculable by the Clerk as stipulated by law under the **Federal Rules of Civil Procedure, Rule 55 (FRCP § 55 [b][1]).**[7] This being an automatic default, <u>the penalties were simply and clearly computable by the Clerk under</u> Rule 55(b) (1), supra. This type of default does not require a "Judgment" or "Order" by a judge. <u>It was solely the responsibility of the Clerk of the U.S. District Court for Hawaii, to enter an automatic default.</u> *But the clerk refused to accept and file the notice of default, thereby deliberately committing a **Fraud on the Court.**[8]*

---

[7] **Federal Rules of Civil Procedure, Rule 55 (b)(1).** *"Judgment by default may be entered as follows: (1) **By the Clerk.** When the plaintiff's claim against a defendant is for a sum certain or for a sum which can by computation be made certain, the clerk upon request of the plaintiff and upon affidavit of the amount due shall enter judgment for that amount and costs against the defendant, if the defendant has been defaulted for failure to appear and is not an infant or incompetent person."*

[8] **Fraud on Court.** *"A scheme to interfere with judicial machinery performing task of impartial adjudication, as by preventing opposing party from fairly presenting his case or defense. Finding of fraud*

AUTHOR'S NOTE: In the above case, District Court Judge Alan C. Kay also deliberately exercised another "Fraud on Court" action when one of the following had to have happened: 1) <u>Judge Kay ordered</u> Clerk Chinn of the Court to not enter or record the lawful default filings of May 11, 2002 into the Docket Sheet *(The Record of the Court)* (See EXHIBIT N) until May 30, 2002, thus concealing the lawful default filed in order to permit the Internal Revenue Service (IRS), et al, the unlawful opportunity to respond, in violation of the time limit for response, i.e., beyond the thirty-day default period, or,   2) <u>Judge Kay, being aware of the lawful filing of the "Entry of Default," i.e. being privy to the documents filed</u>, endorsed the initial "fraud on court" actions of Clerk Chinn in obstructing justice which is a criminal offense, wherein both parties <u>functioned in collusion and in conspiracy to deny justice and defraud the injured parties</u> of the benefits of their valid default victory while providing corrupt, unethical credibility to the Respondent's default (in their failure to timely respond) as if no default existed.

Proof of criminal wrongdoing is easily confirmed in the above case by simply comparing the Clerk Chinn's Filing Stamp on the "Entry of Default – Automatic Judgment" (See EXHIBIT O) with the Clerk's Docket Sheet (See EXHIBIT N) revealing an entry date of May 30th, which date is <u>after</u> the <u>(Aloha Airlines, IRS, et al) responses were unlawfully permitted to be filed</u> thus violating and unlawfully skirting the Automatic Default of the Complainants. Notice the 5/30/02 entry where Clerk Chinn acts as a judge without a lawful order of the court.

The judge and clerk, both supposedly <u>under United States Government oaths of Office</u> in this case abandoned their *"charge"* and *"duty"* of Office.   The judge and clerk, quite obviously functioning in collusion, did so at the expense of justice. This court cannot be under lawful United States Government authority and function in this manner…or can it? This is yet more evidence that this court is corrupt and does not meet the ethical standards for justice of any *United States (Federal) District Court.*

<u>CASE SAMPLE #2:</u> FIRST HAWAIIAN BANK, fka AMERICAN SECURITY BANK and also fka FIRST INTERSTATE BANK OF HAWAII, vs. JON ROBERT

---

on the court is justified only by most egregious misconduct directed to the court itself such as bribery of a judge or jury to fabrication of evidence by counsel and must be supported by clear, unequivocal and convincing evidence. In re Coordinated Pretrial Proceedings in Antibiotic Antitrust Actions, C. A. Minn, 538 F.2d 180, 195. It consists of conduct so egregious that it undermines the integrity of the judicial process. Stone v. Stone, Alaska, 647 P.2d 582, 586." (Black's Law Dictionary, 6th Edition)

JOHNSON; GERALDINE WONG JOHNSON, (ET AL): Case No 98-0961-02; Chief Judge Samuel P. King, United States District Court for Hawaii (Federal).

In this case, (against Private Citizens Pastor Jon and Geraldine Johnson, who are not *U.S. public servant, immigration status, Washington D.C. federal citizens*, but are lawfully documented Hawaiian Kingdom National and American National Private Citizens possessing dual citizenship) were attacked in a lawsuit regarding Johnson's home, which was filed by First Hawaiian Bank against the fiction "person" (ALL CAPITALIZED NAME) created and owned by the federal government. The fiction names used were not the Private Citizen's lawful names of record showing possession on both the title and mortgage documents. The assets (land and improvements) were properly and lawfully titled, documented and recorded in that of the natural, Private Citizen's, proper English-language, upper and lower case birth names as "Jon and Geraldine Johnson."

Background.

Previous to this U.S. District Court action, First Hawaiian Bank in the lower de facto Puppet State of Hawaii Circuit Court (Case No. 98-0-00861), created out of thin air a non-existent "Promissory Note" that was verbally presented to the court by that bank's Attorney. I was a personal witness to this court session and the so-called "Promissory Note" was never presented nor confirmed in open court to exist as fact, by the judge.

The law firm of Watanabe, Ing & Kawashima did not have to present this false, non-existent document into evidence before Judge Kevin S.C. Chang, the presiding judge (now a judge in the U.S. Court for the Hawaii District). Chang accepted the bank attorney's false statement without review while overruling and ignoring Pastor Johnson's challenge. Judge Chang knows the distinction between a lawful "Mortgage Note" (liabilities stay with and are limited to the "in rem", i.e. property) and that of a "Promissory Note." A Promissory Note attaches to the person(s) and is not just limited to the equity of the land and improvements, as a Mortgage Note is. It follows the debtor until paid in full! Judge Chang (without reviewing the document in the hand of the attorney, who read and falsely presented it as a Promissory Note) instantly granted rights to First Hawaiian Bank on the basis of this open "fraud on court" action. Judge Chang, over Pastor Johnson's verbal court objections, and ruling outside of law, had instantly converted the lawful "Mortgage Note" into a "Promissory Note" creating an unlawful liability and an unlawful, unjustified obligation upon defendant Johnson.

This collusion between the judge and attorneys for First Hawaiian Bank in open court reveals the blatant, back door, "Old Boy" network nature of corrupt judicial practices within the corrupt Puppet State of Hawaii judicial system. Judge Chang took a lawful "Mortgage Note" and converted it into a "Promissory Note" to accommodate First Hawaiian Bank, for whom Judge Chang for years had worked as an attorney and legal counsel (under corporate contract). This blatant conflict of interest is one of the many types of abuse of power and justice, cronyism and favoritism utilized by de facto judges in the sham courts of the Puppet State of Hawaii. Shortly thereafter, Judge Chang was promoted to the position of "Magistrate" in the federal *United States District Court for Hawaii*, obviously for his supposedly commendable judicial achievements.

Back to the Johnson Federal Case Filing (In the U.S. Fed. Dist. Ct. for HI)

On January 30, 1998 Pastor Johnson filed a new case (dealing with the injustices of the lower court) in the higher **U.S. DISTRICT COURT as Civil No. CV 98-00089 SPK**, under a reservation of his rights.

The filing was a *"COMPLAINT IN TORT FOR BAD FAITH, FALSE PRETENSE, FRIVOLOUS CLAIM PERTAINING TO NONEXISTENT LOAN CONTRACT, AND COLLUSION." "VIOLATION OF U.S. CONSTITUTIONAL RIGHTS OF PLAINTIFF"* (within the same de facto jurisdiction) which stipulated damages. On March 9, 1998, Plaintiff amended the Complaint, expanding the number of Defendants.

The Docket Sheet shows that on March 26 and March 31, Respondents (Defendants) filed, yet never responded directly to nor addressed the issues of the Complaint, but instead filed Notice of Motions to dismiss and / or in the alternative, for Summary Judgment.

After thirty (30) days from the amended filing, Johnson elected to file for default, but previous to him filing his *"Request for Entry of Default* and *Entry of Default, By Clerk"* on April 9, 1998, Johnson and this Author discussed with Clerk Chinn as to whether or not any filings had been made by the Respondents (Defendants). Clerk Chinn told us that there had not been any filings prior to 3:00 PM! Review of the Docket Sheet

(The Record of the Court) at that time also revealed no entries to that date. Therefore, Johnson elected to file his *"Request for Entry of Default* and *Entry of Default, By Clerk"*. Quite obviously, Johnson had won his case by default on April 9, 1998.

When Johnson then moved to the counter to file his default, which Chief Clerk Walter A. Y. H. Chinn had not been aware of, Chinn with some degree of noticeable shock left the area to present the default filing to someone beyond his office. He returned ten to fifteen minutes later with instructions to Johnson that the default needed to be modified. Clerk Chinn, without lawful authority and practicing law under obvious judicial directive, refused to file Johnson's *"Request for Entry of Default* and *Entry of Default, By Clerk"* until the word *"Proposed"* was hand-written on the Caption Page, thus modifying the filing. Who in the heck has ever heard of a "Proposed" filing? Either it is or it isn't! Johnson finally got his modified papers filed at 3:25 PM!

Four days later, **after the fact**, Judge King issued an Order and dismissed Johnson's case and default on April 13, 1998, using the following basis *"...because Plaintiff failed to include a short and plain statement indicating the basis for this court's jurisdiction..."* Heck, under the Organic Act, it's the same de facto jurisdiction! It is apparent that the issues of justice or crime are not as important as the opportunities found to impede justice and protect friends and/or corporate financial or special interests. Judge Samuel P. King and Clerk Chinn, functioning in collusion in the higher court, were found to be as corrupt and *egregious*[9] in abuse of law and as blatant and shameless as Judge Chang, et al, was in the lower de facto *Puppet State of Hawaii* court.

Johnson had obviously won his case in the Federal Court by default. Yet, Judge King ruled *"sua sponte"*[10] by creating a document **after** the default deadline for Defendant's response, issuing a highly questionable *Judgment*. Even the stamp that I observed used by Judge King on his original Order was different than that used by the Clerk of the Court. This Author believes **Judge King deliberately backdated the**

---

[9] **Egregious**. "1. extraordinary in some bad way; glaring; flagrant; *an egregious mistake; an egregious liar*. 2. *Archaic*. Distinguished or eminent.[1525-35]; e-gre'gious-ly, adv. – e-gre'gious-ness, n. –Syn. 1. gross, outrageous, notorious. (Source: Webster's encyclopedic Unabridged Dictionary, 2001 Edition, Page 624.)

[10] **Sua sponte**. *"Of his or its own will or motion; voluntarily; without prompting or suggestion."* Black's Law Dictionary, 6th Edition.)

date of filing on his *"sua sponte"* document in attempt to modify the *"Docket Sheet"*, abort justice and kill or nullify *(render to no effect)* Pastor Johnson's Automatic Default.

This is another example of corruption and injustice revealing collusion and further evidence that this cannot be a lawful court of the United States.

AUTHOR'S CONCLUSION:
(REGARDING THE U.S. DISTRICT COURT FOR HAWAII)

The unsubstantiated (by law), <u>fraudulent-oath issue</u> *(of local federal judges)* by itself, makes the *U.S. District Court for Hawaii,* for lack of any better description, a sham court of major, national deception and international embarrassment. This fact is further affirmed by *U.S. Code Title 28 Section 91 (See "Chapter 1, General Background, Pages 3 - 5" for explanation of this jurisdiction law)* that the in rem *(lands and assets)* jurisdiction of the Hawaiian Archipelago are not now and never have been a part of the *"jurisdiction"* of the United States.

As clarified in the *"Chapter 1, General Background"* explaining 28 USC § 91 *(which is the U.S. Congress' jurisdictional description for the U.S. District Court for Hawaii),* <u>all Islands of the Hawaiian Archipelago are deliberately omitted</u>. This means that the *Islands of the Hawaiian Archipelago* still belong to the separate and distinct Hawaiian National Citizens under their de jure *Hawaiian Kingdom National Government, Ke Aupuni O Hawaii Nei* e *Ko Hawaii Pae Aina,* and their national judicial system.

DE FACTO PUPPET STATE OF HAWAII JUDGE'S OATHS

My findings are that <u>corporate judges</u> from within the *federal jurisdiction (corporate [federal] state judges, not "sovereign State Judges under their respective State's common-law)* are all required to be under the same oaths as federal judges. That oath required of all U.S. corporate judges in this instance is found in **28 USC § 453.** I personally know of no other.

Note that all recognition of and obligations to Almighty God have also been removed. The last sentence, *"So help me God."* is eliminated from the federal *Puppet State of Hawaii* judicial oaths of Office (**See EXHIBIT Q**). This is a major modification, deletion, and deliberate changing of the required and approved lawful oath that now makes them unaccountable to God *(i.e., no higher authority).* Unfortunately, this does make them accountable to only those of influence and power over them, honorable or dishonorable, denying or ignoring conscience.

These judges have come out of the *"American Bar Association"* or *"Hawaii State Bar Association"* as men or women of law, but not necessarily as having integrity or any required belief, conscience or respect for or in Almighty God, from whom our western society derives its basis for truth, morality, righteousness ... **and** *law*. Because of that lack, these judges generally put man's imperfect law as supreme over God's Laws. It is no wonder that local judges dismiss juries they don't agree with and also render contrary judgments that we cannot understand or justify as morally right; or, which conflict with what we understand to be the law or that of our Christian Faith. Without a Godly conscience, they do what they want!

FACT: A lesser, subordinate court of the same jurisdiction does not possess a right, power or authority greater than that of its superior and highest court authority. The *U.S. District Court for Hawaii (Federal)* is the appellate court for *Puppet State of Hawaii* appeals. It is the highest court created under the *Organic Act* of 1900. When the higher appellate court is in fact incompetent, unlawful and de facto by reason and fact of law, then all lower and lesser courts of that same *(Federal Hawaii)* jurisdiction are also incompetent. This applies to all de facto *Puppet State of Hawaii* courts functioning under *"color of U.S. law"* within *The State of Hawaii Judiciary (i.e. de facto Puppet State of Hawaii Supreme Court; Circuit Courts and District Courts, and all other courts functioning unlawfully, including legal counsels sworn into practice of law by them*.

These inept, incompetent, administrative *Puppet State of Hawaii* court judges, et al, *(who are all Washington D.C. second-class, federal immigration status "citizens")* function in direct violation of the **United States Criminal Code (18 USCr.C § 241, 242) Title 18 Sections 241 and 242**, et al, the American Constitution, and its Bill of Rights. How? These judges, et al, have assumed a responsibility and duty of Office under ***U.S. oath to honor the Constitution and laws of the United States[11]*** as U.S. federal citizens. The above law applies directly to them, not to

---

[11] If the judge's oaths taken were to support the U.S. Constitution and its laws, they (judge's jurisdiction) would be limited to and not applicable to foreign citizens on that foreign soil, but it would only apply to U.S. Federal "citizens" living thereupon. This would explain why this court excludes united *State's Nationals* and *Hawaiian Nationals*, who should have rights even as foreigners to the jurisdiction of this de facto court. Such was previously the case in U.S. District Courts located in China and the Panama Canal Zone, etc.

American National or *Hawaiian National Private Citizens.* I repeat the above Criminal laws of **Title 18 USCr.C** apply only to U.S. <u>federal</u> (Article 1 Section 8) <u>c</u>itizens of Washington D. C., and <u>incompetent judges *(and attorneys) of the Puppet State of Hawaii* are no exception</u>. If these judges, et al, are not under proper oaths of office *(fraudulent misrepresentation)* and are perpetuating acts of fraud upon the people, then they are subject to the law and civil actions for damages and injury and cannot be exempted from fraud and outright misrepresentation any more than you and me.

BACKGROUND OF THE DE FACTO STATE OF HAWAII COURTS AND CREATION OF THE (PUPPET) STATE OF HAWAII

The questionable and false puppet *State of Hawaii* was created in 1959 by the *"Statehood Act"* *(Act of March 18, 1959, Pub L 86-3, 73 Stat 4).* I quote, Section 1:

> *"Be it enacted by the senate and House of representatives of the United States of America in Congress assembled, That, subject to the provision of this Act, and upon issuance of the proclamation required by section 7 (c) of this Act, the State of Hawaii is **hereby declared to be a State** of the United States of America, **is declared admitted** into the Union on an equal footing with the other States in all respects whatever, and the constitution formed pursuant to the provision of the Act of the Territorial Legislature of Hawaii entitled "An Act to provide for a constitutional convention, the adoption of a State constitution, and the forwarding of same to the Congress of the United States, and appropriating money therefore", approved May 20, 1949 (Act 334, Sessions Laws of Hawaii, 1949), and **adopted by a vote of the people** of Hawaii in the election held on **November 7, 1950,** is hereby found to be **republican in Form** and in conformity with the Constitution of the United States and the principles of the Declaration of Independence, and is hereby accepted, ratified and confirmed." (**Bold highlights by Author**)*

First of all, let's look at the English-standard and the application of words used in this opening Section of the *Statehood Act.* Language is the tool used and misused by politicians, attorneys and judges in authority to confuse and mislead, we, the people.

The first phrase we look at is *"...hereby declared to be a State..."* The English language dictionary meaning of the word *"declared"* is as follows:

> *"**de-clare.** (v) 1. to state officially or formally. 2. To state with emphasis or authority; affirm. 3. To reveal or manifest; prove. 4. To make a full statement of (dutiable goods, for example). 5. Bridge. To designate (a trump suit or no-trump) with the final bid of a hand. – intr. 1. To make a declaration. 2. to proclaim one's choice, opinion, or resolution; to act. Used with for or against (**Source: The American Heritage Dict. 1973 Ed.**)*

When we look into Black's Law Dictionary, 6th Edition, Page 409, we find the following definition for that same word. This latter definition has the intended meaning:

> "*Declare. To make known, manifest, or clear. To signify, to show in any manner either by words or acts. To publish; to utter, to announce clearly some opinion or resolution. To solemnly assert a fact before witnesses, e.g., where a testator declares a paper signed by him to be his last will and testament.*"

Of confusion to this Author is the lack of clarity and the fact that what is missing is the absolute requirement for Hawaii to really be what it is supposed to be in this paragraph and phrase. Nowhere in this enabling, empowering and definitive Act does it state "...Hawaii *is* a State..." or "...Hawaii *"is"* admitted into the Union on an equal footing with the other states..."

When we remove the verb *"declared"* and *"declared admitted,"* we find a completely different meaning to this First Section. Let's look at the *Webster's Encyclopedic Unabridged Dictionary* regarding the present tense verb, *"is"*:

Is. (iz,) v. 1. 3rd person, sing. pres. indic. of be. 2. as is..."

What this says, is that *"is"* is a <u>verb, singular and present tense</u>. If Hawaii was in fact a "State," then why didn't the United States use the <u>present tense verb</u>, *"is"* instead of the verb *"declare"*? To *"declare"* in this application is like a shouting into the wind, it having no meaning or appropriate application to connect like the present tense, *"is."* Example: "I '*declare*' the moon is blue cheese!" This statement does not make the moon blue cheese. If I state, "The moon '*is*' blue cheese!" I am asserting a fact, supposedly of knowledge based upon some known truth. That does not appear to be the case in *Section 1* of *The Admission Act*. Either Hawaii "is," admitted into the Union of States or it ISN'T! <u>I do not find by proper language usage that a *"State of Hawaii"* lawfully exists.</u>

Fallacy: *Section 2* of the *Admissions Act* states all land of the *"State of Hawaii"* is that land *"...included in the Territory of Hawaii..."* <u>The *Territory of Hawaii* possessed no land</u>, as affirmed by the *Newland's Resolution* (supra) and *Organic Act* (supra) which derived their unfounded claim from the occupied lands of the *Hawaiian National Government* occupied militarily and controlled by an armed, U.S.-recognized de facto, *Republic of Hawaii!*

Therefore, based upon the above knowledge, we find that the judicial system cannot be *de jure* and is most definitely *de facto* because the *Puppet State of Hawaii* is not a State of the American *Union of States* as is being misrepresented by the United States.

Fact: <u>A foundational land claim and jurisdictional basis for lawful statehood does not exist.</u>

ARREST AND INCARCERATION TACTICS OF THE PUPPET COURTS

The *Puppet State of Hawaii* courts, evidenced as being under *color of U.S. law,* are not obligated to honor United States laws or Hawaii State Statutes or even the <u>u</u>nited *"State's Constitution."* I have observed that local judges see themselves as immune and above the law by granting each other immunity and giving immunity to those who protect their positions of power, *(i.e. law enforcement personnel and other parties).* All evidence reveals that the titled *"State of Hawaii"* is nothing more than a subordinate, de facto, foreign U.S. corporation i.e. *"Puppet government,"* functioning unlawfully on the foreign soil of the *Hawaiian Kingdom Nation.*

Having first hand exposure, I find that these courts victimize Hawaiian Nationals. One of the tactics of the State of Hawaii Judiciary is to brand as many Hawaiian Nationals as is possible with a court record primarily exercised through the traffic division of the District Courts. If a <u>Hawaiian National</u> *(a foreigner to State jurisdiction)* does not show up for a court appearance, for even a non-moving violation, he or she will be held in *"contempt"* of court, a *"criminal traffic"* offense for which one is arrested and jailed! These courts even ignore written appearances *(for non-moving violations)* in lieu of personal appearance even though such written pleas are lawful. The judges' excessive and abusive use of the *"contempt of court"* rulings <u>automatically brand the falsely accused Private Citizen in their records as a *"criminal"*</u> because these incompetent judges feel, whether guilty or not, the cited parties have flaunted their unrighteous authority and questionable, inept court's integrity *(which is nothing more than to have to stand before a judge who is not even under a lawful oath of office).* This and the enforcement in the field are the basic levels used in their abuse of police power. This is how judges intimidate and impinge upon one's character in order to create a negative, oppressive traffic record (**Example: See this Author's Judicial Record, EXHIBIT R**).

Excessive financial penalties *("Appearance Bails" of up to $2,000.00, or more)* are applied to Hawaiians. These courts also have a record of not returning *"Appearance Bails"* even when personal appearances have been made! Other damaging consequences to Hawaiians is the assessing of insurance *"Points"* resulting in abusive premiums as well as the *Puppet State of Hawaii* maintaining falsified, records (See EXHIBIT R).

Other tactics used to cause intimidation and create hardship for Hawaiians is holding back a *bench warrant* or *penal summons* and then executing it on a Friday afternoon or evening, pretty much guaranteeing that the whole weekend will be spent in jail before bail can be posted.

Another is to not issue the bench warrant until months or even years later when the Private Citizen, always in the public arena, listed in the telephone book and not hiding, is stopped for some minor traffic offense and then arrested (without the warrant). After the arrest by a *City and County of Honolulu* Police Officer, the often rubber-stamped and unsigned warrant *(requiring a judge's signature to be lawful, and which was not in the officer's possession)* is then sought from the *Puppet State of Hawaii* courthouse. The intent is to hold you in a cell for the entire weekend to cause you and your family financial hurt and family inconvenience *(The Law requires under your <u>due process rights</u> that you be taken before a magistrate within 24 - 48 hours from arrest. That is not possible under these obstructive, deliberately contrived circumstances).*

Another tactic I personally experienced when unlawfully arrested is that *City and County of Honolulu Police Department* officers deny Hawaiian Nationals reasonable access to a telephone, magistrate or judge. One time after a false arrest, an officer only permitted a phone call three to four hours after incarceration. The line was busy and the officer would not permit another call. His comment, *"You made your call, that's all you get!"* and placed me back into the cell, and only after hours of complaining of that fact to passing officers monitoring the prisoners, was I permitted a very late night telephone call.

These actions by the *City and County of Honolulu Police Department*, et al, reflect a discriminatory and extremely biased attitude towards Hawaiians *(Note: Hawaiians Nationals under the Organic Act or Statehood Act are omitted from U.S. and State of Hawaii jurisdictional authority)*. Another tactic used is, after being falsely arrested and incarcerated; the judges set a time for court appearance (The *"Pleading"* of guilty or innocent only) before a District Court judge as much as four (4) days after the false arrest and not within the 24 – 48 hours required by law. This delayed pleading scenario has even been extended for days to those unlawfully arrested on a Monday! In many instances, these incompetent judges have refused to permit bail on non-moving violations and have held some Hawaiian National Private Citizens for weeks, without charges.

Hawaiian Nationals, when possessing lawful identification and rights at law *(as separate and distinct, lawful, non-State of Hawaii, non-U.S. citizens)* while stopped for driving without a *Puppet State of Hawaii* Driver's License or without *State of Hawaii* vehicle plates on their private property *(upon their own national soil)* are always arrested. Yet, if requiring a *Puppet State of Hawaii* Driver's License and/or having a *Puppet State of Hawaii* licensed automobile are in fact laws required to drive on *Hawaiian Kingdom National soil*, then all out-of-state vacationers (visitors) to Hawaii and those possessing out of state plates must also be immediately arrested, even upon renting a motor vehicle or when stopped by *City and County of Honolulu* Police Officers, et al. Yet, they are not! This reflects a most definite bias and prejudice against Hawaiian Nationals.

This Author was falsely arrested at least four or five times on trumped-up charges, all for non-moving violations. I have experienced *City and County of Honolulu* Police Officers unlawfully crossing jurisdictional lines of authority and exercising an arrest, without a lawful warrant or a warrant in hand.

One lawfully documented Hawaiian National, Mr. Ross Huitt Myers, a Private Citizen, was incarcerated for 21 days in the *Oahu Community Correctional Center (OCCC)* without charges and without trial for not having a *de facto* State Driver's License *(he wasn't their public servant, immigration status Washington D.C. citizen, i.e. a citizen of their jurisdiction)*. He was unlawfully held without charges or a finding of guilt because he would not change his name to that of their fiction person! He eventually was just let go but not without his first suffering loss of time and incurring financial injury.

Another Hawaiian National was incarcerated in the same prison, held down on his back on the floor by guards and beaten on the soles of his feet with a towel wrapped baton because he would not sign a false document to give the de facto *Puppet State of Hawaii* jurisdiction over him! Evil, evil, evil!

Such are the cruel and constantly applied tactics carried out by the *Puppet State of Hawaii Sheriff's Department (i.e. supposed "State" Sheriff Deputies) "City and County of Honolulu Police Department Officers,"* and *"State Security Guards"* within the State's prison system *(By the way, who has ever heard of "State Sheriff" in a "republican" form of government which by the way is not acknowledged, affirmed or permitted under the*

Statehood Act? <u>*The sheriff is supposed to be an elected official!*</u>). This above type of demeaning, malicious and oppressive effort is <u>exercised with the full knowledge of the judges of the courts</u> and with approval of the past and present Chiefs of Police and other higher in authority *City and County of Honolulu* and *Puppet State of Hawaii Government* law enforcement authorities, their Executive Branch and the U.S. Federal Government.

The Federal United States Government has shamefully condoned, for over a hundred years, the above type of abusive and unlawful actions by the *City and County of Honolulu Police Department*, the other counties' Police Departments, the de facto *Puppet State of Hawaii* courts, State Attorney General's Office, County Prosecutors, State Department of Public Safety *(i.e. by the way*, ***there is no Sheriff*** *in the State Sheriff's Department; only a politically appointed administrator who does not carry that title)*, and others in positions of authority in the *de facto* State. Shameful!

REGARDING   TRIALS:

In preparation for trials, the *Puppet State of Hawaii Attorney General's Office* unlawfully changes citizen's names and denies a fundamental right by not allowing Hawaiians to defend themselves. They are required to obtain a *"Public Defender,"* supra, which along with the unlawful name change, <u>automatically moves them</u> into the *de facto State of Hawaii* jurisdiction and outside the protection of their proper Hawaiian National Private Citizenship jurisdiction.

When Hawaiian's do defend themselves, their ***due process rights***[12] are deliberately violated. Every person when charged with a crime has the basic right to file requests for facts of law and the right to ascertain the truth for trial via a questioning process *called,* ***"Interrogatories."***[13]   This due process right is provided in order to

---

[12] **Due process clause.** *"Two such clauses are found in the U.S. Constitution, one in the 5th Amendment pertaining to the federal government, the other in the 14th Amendment which protects persons from state actions. There are two aspects: procedural, in which a person guaranteed fair procedures and substantive, which protects a person's property from unfair governmental interference or taking. Similar clauses are in most state constitutions."* (Black's Law Dictionary, 6th Edition, Page 500.)

[13] Interrogatories. *"A set or series of written questions drawn up for the purpose of being propounded to a party, witness, or other person having information of interest in the case. A pretrial discovery device consisting of written questions about the case submitted by one party to the other party or witness. The answers to the interrogatories are usually given under oath, i.e., the person answering the questions signs a sworn a statement that the answers are true. Fed.R.Civil P. 33. The court may submit to the jury, together with appropriate forms for a general verdict, written interrogatories upon one or more issues of fact the decision of which is necessary to a verdict. See Fed.R. Civil P. 49. "* (Source: Black's Law Dictionary, 6th Edition, Page 818.)

build a proper and lawful defense or prosecution. The *Puppet State of Hawaii*, through its Attorney General's Office via their Deputy Attorneys General *(and/or City and County of Honolulu Prosecutors also acting without authority in these lower State Courts, and who lack a written Attorney General's 'Certificate of Assignment' as required under §§ 806-A and 806-4 of the Hawaii Revised Statutes [HRS])* abuse and violate their own supposed laws. These unassigned (without *Certificate's of Assignment, supra*) Deputy Attorneys General or Deputy City and County Prosecutors in these courts file verbal or written objections and motions to *"strike"*[14] (remove) any and all due process defense efforts of Hawaiian National <u>Respondents</u> (improperly classified as "defendants") and any other respondent filings. This leaves Hawaiian Nationals with no defense at trial *(Author's Note: On appeal [if permitted], only that which was admitted into the record at lower trial is permitted to be heard and argued in the higher, appellate court. So one can never enter arguments that may be pertinent to one's defense. So where is justice?)*

The corrupt *Puppet State of Hawaii* judiciary system allows biases of the judges and State officials deliberately violating United States Federal and *de facto* State Laws. These judges actively participate in a conspiracy of denying the *"inalienable rights"* and *"unalienable rights"* guaranteed to not just each American National, but primarily to Hawaiian Nationals functioning under their own National Constitution *(and the ratified "Treaty of 1850" between the United States and the Hawaiian Kingdom)*. Contemptible and biased judges refuse to *"recuse"* themselves in court when challenged verbally and/or in writing. They even rule on their own fraudulent or inappropriate biases or prejudicial actions (exercised in open court) that are filed against them.

THE UNLAWFUL, FRAUDULENT LABELING OF HAWAIIAN NATIONALS.

Hawaiian Nationals are not "immigration status, Washington D.C. public servants or government-created corporate, fiction" "<u>c</u>itizens," of the federalized U.S. or Puppet State of Hawaii jurisdiction. **They are Private Citizens.** They are foreign to the above jurisdictions and as "Hawaiian Nationals," i.e. "Private Citizens;" they function under their proper English language spelled birth names; under their own National Flag; under their own national common-law; while domiciled upon their own Hawaiian

---

[14] **Motion to Strike.** *"On motion of either party, the court may order stricken from any pleading an insufficient defense, or any redundant, immaterial, impertinent or scandalous matter. Fed.R.Civil P. 12(f)."* (Source: Black's Law Dictionary, 6th Edition, Page 1014.)

Kingdom National Land. Yet, the *de facto* State of Hawaii and unlawful U.S. Federal courts *kidnap*[15] lawfully documented Hawaiian Nationals, as if Hawaiians were criminals, and treats them as such, without rights, supra.

The above and the following is an affirmation of the long-standing policy of *Puppet State of Hawaii* abuses of lawfully documented Hawaiian Kingdom Nationals under separate and foreign, privately owned automobile registrations, licensing and identifications. In the next case, I will be using my own *Puppet State of Hawaii* public court record to not cause harm or reflection upon other Hawaiian National Citizens in identical situations.

The following information confirms that in the *Puppet State of Hawaii* there is no freedom of citizenship choice for *Hawaiian Nationals*, on their own land (which is foreign to the U.S.). The Puppet State of Hawaii Government imposes as mandatory upon *Hawaiian Nationals*, the "Emancipated Slave," "Washington D.C.," "public servant," "immigration-status," "second-class" "U.S. federal citizenship," whether desired or not desired. It is also a mandatory policy of the United States Government, enforced by their judicial systems and local law enforcement. Hawaiian Nationals are in fact, prisoners on their own national land and are not lawfully recognized for whom they are, as affirmed by the documentation provided within this declaration.

Upon obtaining access to the **"State of Hawaii Criminal conviction databases"** at **"eCrim.Ehawaii.gov"** and **"www.courts.state.hi.us"** (Click **'Court Connect' link, Free to browse')** we find the following information on others and myself.

BACKGROUND:

Let us begin with the lawful separation in 1996 of my citizenship in the de facto State of Hawaii and Federal (not National) United States. A lawful document (**No. 96-021786**) titled the *"CONTRACT AND DECLARATION OF CITIZENSHIP"* was filed on February 16, 1996 in the *Hawaiian Kingdom National Bureau of Records (Presently known as the de facto, Puppet State of Hawaii "Bureau of Conveyances"*

---

[15] The forcible abduction or stealing and carrying away of a person from their own country to another's jurisdiction - a **violation of United States Criminal Code Title 18 Section 1201 (Ch. 11 pages 150-151 and 168-170)**

[Public Records]). This filing was a termination of *adhesive citizenship*[16] and *un-filed "power of attorney"* assumed by the de facto *Puppet State of Hawaii* and the Federal United States *(severing my identity and contract as a subordinate, Washington D.C. public servant, emancipated slave, immigration status or corporate fiction U.S. Federal citizen).*

Lawful notices were served by *United States Postal Service Certified Mail* to all necessary agencies including the Internal Revenue Service and the U.S. Secretary of State. Additionally, a formal declaration *("AFFIDAVIT AND DECLARATION OF HAWAIIAN DENIZEN CITIZENSHIP")* for Hawaiian National Citizenship was also filed under the *Hawaiian Kingdom National 'common-law'* on October 23, 1996 (Document No. 96-152274). Again, all pertinent and affected agencies of the de facto *Puppet State of Hawaii* and *U.S. Federal Government* were similarly and lawfully notified by certified U.S. mail service reflecting my lawful change back to my proper birth name and corrected American as well as Hawaiian National Citizenship *(dual citizenship).*

Citizenship is voluntary. If not, we are by unlawful actions, prisoners of government, whether despotic or supposedly *"Democratic,"*as in this case. These actions were taken by me in an open freedom of choice decision of citizenship that every *"Private Citizen,"* living soul or human being is entitled to exercise without hindrance, coercion, oppression, imprisonment or violence by their own government. That has not been the case in this instance.

Upon lawful claiming and filing of denizen *(a special form of Dual Citizenship)* status within the *Hawaiian Nation* under its *common-law (which even the Puppet State of Hawaii affirms as being the basis for their "Revised Statutes")* this free, Private Citizen returned to the de facto *Puppet State of Hawaii* all its adhesive documents[17] such as *"driver's license," "motor vehicle registration,"* etc. The same was done with the *Federal United States Government*, thus clearing the way of lawful separation and transition.

As a *Hawaiian Kingdom National (of Denizen Citizenship status),* there was issued to me by the *Hawaiian Kingdom National Government*, a new *"private automobile"* registration, plates, Motorist *(Driver's)* Certificate and Citizenship

---

[16] **Adhesive citizenship.** A citizenship not desired, but required by superior police power (Author)

[17] **Adhesive documents.** Any document that binds one by contract away from one's primary citizenship to a required, undesirable, imposed citizenship. (Author)

Identification. As a documented Hawaiian National, I was already residing in the nation to which the superior *'common law'* of the *Hawaiian Kingdom National Government* applied.

Now we come face to face with the ugly issue of failure of the *Puppet State of Hawaii* and *U.S. Federal Government* to honor de jure law, International Law and their own *Organic Act, Admission Act, Statehood Act* and supposedly lawful Constitutions. Their actions are at the expense of my dual citizenship (American National and Hawaiian National) Constitutional due process rights and freedoms.

Now, let's look at my supposed *"Criminal"* record as reflected by the biased, unlawful *Puppet State of Hawaii Judiciary.*

All of the data (See EXHIBIT R) was publicly supplied by the de facto, *Puppet State of Hawaii,* and when accessed and viewed, implies an extensive *"Criminal"* record of immense and shocking proportion.

First impression is that I have a real criminal record of one hundred and ninety-two violations and convictions! That is really not the case. This is to give anyone who searches this system an outright bias and impression that this Private Citizen (Aran Alton Ardaiz) is not a law-abiding citizen. Secondly, please notice that the record immediately shows a name as *"Alton, Aran,"* an alias. As a God fearing, Christian man, I have never used an alias of any kind. This site reveals 64 violations under that unlawful, fraudulent name created by the State of Hawaii judiciary. This takes you to Page 4 of the *"Person/Case Type Search Results."*

Upon further review of Page 4, we find another alias created by and being used by the State judiciary titled, *"Alton, Ardaiz,"* a fraudulent name that I also have never used at any time for any reason. This is a duplication of the first and second identical listings of supposed offenses. We find here being revealed, yet another false, fraudulent attempt to defame and libel me. This falsified, fraudulent listing goes from Page 4 to Page 7 of their public, published judicial criminal record.

On Page 7, the judiciary finally used my lawful, English language spelled birth name *(a first),* surprisingly not in the ALL CAPITALIZED FICTION NAME used in their court and court records. This latter proper name listing runs from Page 7 to the end at Page 10! Wow! Ten full pages of violations! What an ugly, horrible criminal I must be!

The immediate impact of such an extensive, falsified record of supposed wrongs, which was automatically and <u>deliberately tripled</u> through the falsification of the records, openly implies I use aliases, which I never have. They have created two additional false, pseudonym names never before used by this private, **American National Citizen**. They have labeled and libeled me in the eyes of the general public and before the average person who does not understand the extensive corruption and lawless character of the *Puppet State of Hawaii* judicial system. Let's now continue deeper into this Record of the corrupt *Puppet State of Hawaii* Court system.

<u>Upon opening up the last four supposed violations on</u> **Page 10 of EXHIBIT R**, above, we can get a better understanding of just what the *Puppet State of Hawaii* is doing to Hawaiian Nationals and American Nationals who are not their fictitious, *Washington D.C. public servant, immigration status, federal 14th Amendment "<u>c</u>itizens."* Let's look more closely at these four traffic citations.

<u>Case ID: 5528289MO (Traffic Citation No.), DATED MAY 30, 2003:</u> Notice that the Violation says, *"NO MOTOR VEH DRIVER'S LICENSE."* A lawful Hawaiian Kingdom *"Motorist Certificate" (acknowledgment of one's ability to drive an automobile)* issued by the *National Government of the Hawaiian Kingdom* was presented to the officer affirming my ability and right to drive my *"privately owned"* automobile. It was obvious to *City and County of Honolulu* Police Officer Rick Sung Yong Yi, I.D. No. 101100344, that this car was not under law of the *Puppet State of Hawaii*, but was under *Hawaiian National "common-law,"* it being lawfully displayed upon the automobile on plates that replaced the *Puppet State of Hawaii* plates, which had been properly returned. <u>Jurisdiction was openly and lawfully stated during such unlawful stops.</u> Yet, this driver was arrested with great display by no less than a dozen local police officers in at least seven or more police cars and scooters as if I was a murder, rapist or seller of drugs, handcuffed and stuffed into a police car and hauled to jail.

Please note: As previously mentioned, there is no law requiring a foreign licensed person to have a de facto *"State of Hawaii Driver's License."* Therefore, why the necessity to arrest on this basis? I had made a lawful, proper response in writing, as permitted by law, which was filed with the Clerk but totally ignored by JUDGE

KOYANAGI who issued a *"Penal Summons"* (PS) on July 15th, 2003 for my arrest on this falsified and trumped up charge.

<u>Case ID: 5528290 MO (Traffic Citation No.), DATED MAY 30, 2003:</u> Notice that the Violation says, *"NO SAFETY CHECK."* That is a requirement of the *Puppet State of Hawaii* vehicle code system, but this car was not within that jurisdiction as lawfully declared, noticed and documented. The car met all safety requirements under the de jure *'common-law'* of the *Hawaiian National Government* lawfully functioning on its own sovereign *Hawaiian Kingdom National soil*. So how can the *Puppet State of Hawaii* lawfully reach across jurisdictional lines in violation of U.S. Law *(this is kidnapping under 18 U.S.C. Section 1201)* and impose a Statute that does not apply to a foreigner who is not a <u>c</u>itizen of their corrupt jurisdiction or in any way contractually obligated to comply? Answer: <u>You are a prisoner of their system</u>. They do so by abuse of police power, and systematic falsification of names and documents within their judiciary and law enforcement systems. Lawful response had been made in writing and totally ignored by JUDGE KOYANAGI and a *"Penal Summons"* (PS) was issued for arrest.

<u>Case ID: 5528291 MO (Traffic Citation No.), DATED MAY 30, 2003:</u> Notice what the Citation reads under Violation, "DELIQUENT MOTOR VEHICLE TAX."

ARGUMENT: How does the *Puppet State of Hawaii* lawfully tax an automobile lawfully registered and documented since 1996 (for a period of eight years) as being outside of their jurisdiction and attempt to impose a *"Delinquent motor vehicle tax"* when the automobile *(my private possession)* had been lawfully transferred out of their jurisdiction? I personally and privately owned that car. Can I ship this car to any other state including foreign countries and discontinue paying a tax to the *Puppet State of Hawaii* when the automobile is in fact within that foreign jurisdiction under the laws of that foreign state? Yes I can. But in this particular case of a car owned by me, a Hawaiian National, I cannot. This is yet another imposition upon and attempt to unlawfully suppress Hawaiian Nationals lawfully documented under their own superior laws by the foreign use and abuse of judicial and police power. <u>The *Puppet State of Hawaii* is saying that this car that I paid for, in full, is not mine. What they are also saying is that they own my private property</u> (car) under some fraudulent and misleading pretense. That would be usury, deceit and a fraud upon me, an honest Private Citizen of dual *American National Hawaiian* and *Hawaiian National Citizenship* on land acknowledged and documented within U.S. law as still being that of the lawful *Hawaiian Kingdom Nation.* JUDGE KOYANAGE issued yet another *"Penal Summons"* (PS) for my arrest.

Case ID: 5528292 MO (Traffic Citation No.), DATED MAY 30, 2003: Notice that under Violation, it states, *"NO MOTOR VEH INSURANCE."* Under Kingdom common-law, I am lawfully *"Bonded"* and personally responsible for any and all damages or bodily harm caused another. Insurance is presently not required under *Hawaiian National common-law* on private owned property. I personally carry that liability and responsibility. The above, argument *(of do I own my car),* applies in this matter. Again, this was lawfully responded to in written form and ignored by the judge, who issued still another *"Penal Summons"* (PS) for my arrest.

Case ID: 5528293 MO (Traffic Citation No.), DATED MAY 30, 2003: Notice on this particular citation the Violation states: *"FRAUD USE VEH PLATES, EMBL, DECL."* There was no fraud! The *Puppet State of Hawaii* plates were properly returned and terminated via U.S. Postal Certified Mail to their Motor Vehicle Department, and they were lawfully notified therein, and sent samples of the new, proper plates being applied to this car. This car when stopped had *Hawaiian Kingdom National* automobile plates that were openly displayed and properly recorded *(by U.S. Postal Certified Mail)* with the *Puppet State of Hawaii* and also publicly recorded for open review in their *Puppet State of Hawaii Bureau of Conveyances* in 1996! Everything was done openly and honestly before Almighty God and man, and according to law. So then, why do we now have a falsely generated claim of fraud by the de facto *Puppet State*? This car since 1996, had Kingdom plates openly displayed and was properly registered under *Hawaiian Kingdom National 'common law,'* and was not in the pseudo jurisdiction of the *Puppet State of Hawaii*, which was now falsely claiming a jurisdictional right not possessed. JUDGE KOYANAGI issued yet another *"Penal Summons"* (PS) for my arrest.

Are we are starting to get the impression here that Hawaiian Nationals who hold up their heads get them chopped off? The false *Puppet State of Hawaii* is functioning with unlawful, militant, despotic type oppression, labeling, libeling and imprisoning Hawaiians *(of all ethnic backgrounds)* who do not cower against this abuse of police power. Yes, that is the case. The *Puppet State of Hawaii* uses its *City and County of Honolulu Police Department (and the police departments of the other counties)* and the repugnant and unlawful *State of Hawaii Sheriff's Department (not a County Sheriff as required by law under their own "republican in form" Puppet State of Hawaii Constitution)* to do their dirty work. These particular enforcement officers have taken oath to honor law under the Constitution of the United States yet do not even honor their own State Constitution, as affirmed by their limitations within the *Organic Act* and *Admissions Act.* These enforcement officers simply follow the directives that are handed down from above *(like any other job)*, perhaps not realizing … or just not knowing what is right and what is lawful. Like the judges, they too are subject to civil actions *(by Hawaiian Nationals)* for their offenses.

At this time, if I am caught by the police of the de facto *Puppet State of Hawaii* while driving on the roads of this Hawaiian Nation, they will arrest and imprison me and deny me my rights, and deny my voice to be raised in my own defense. *Consider the sham, **kangaroo court**,[18] Puppet State of Hawaii Souza Case [#3, following]; wherein this Hawaiian Respondent's due process defense and interrogatory filings were removed before they let him get to trial so that he did not have a due process defense in writing of any kind of record; making it fruitless to appeal. <u>Being stripped of the right to enter evidence and all lawful defense in the original trial, he was therefore incapacitated in any appeal (supra) because only issues permitted by the judge into the record of the original trial, are considered in an appeal</u>).*

I could easily wind up being held in prison *(like in the Sousa Case)* without freedom to file protective motions in my own behalf, or, until I hire one of their *"incompetent Hawaii Bar Association Attorneys"* which automatically places me into their jurisdiction of law. The judge controls the actions of the attorney who is hired *(collusion)* and dictates his will to the attorney... a practice I've been exposed to many times. Most likely I would be framed and go to jail, or, due to financial hardship, be forced to compromise my values by a *"settlement" (which is an admission of guilt)*, or both, with a sweet legal bill to boot. No! Under Almighty God, I cannot and would not submit to this corrupt system, regardless.

There is no defense provided for the *Hawaiian National Private Citizen* in this tainted, U.S. Government sustained, corrupt, kangaroo court judicial system. These *Puppet State of Hawaii "kangaroo courts"* have power and authority because we, the people, <u>in our blind obedience and great ignorance, presume they are just</u>. We give them

---

[18] **Kangaroo Court.** *"Term descriptive of a sham legal proceeding in which a person's rights are totally disregarded and in which the result is a foregone conclusion because of the bias of the court or other tribunal."* (Source: Black's Law Dictionary, 6th Edition, Page 868.)

blank authority and power instead of reserving it to ourselves, requiring them to be honest and true to their own *Organic Act, Admission Act, State of Hawaii Constitution* and international law *(not to mention the U.S. Constitution, U.S. law and God's Law).*

A good example of the *"kangaroo court"* character of the judiciary of the *Puppet State of Hawaii* courts follows:

<u>CASE SAMPLE #3:</u> STATE OF HAWAII VS JOHN PHILIP SOUZA AND/OR JOHN P. SOUZA *(Not against John Philip Souza, Private Citizen, Hawaiian National Citizen),* Case No CR 03-1-2024; Chief Judge Michael D. Wilson, Hawaii Circuit Court of the First District.

(LAWFUL NOTE: Of issue in this case is: Does a lawfully documented, foreign national Citizen, domiciled on his birth soil, in his lawful birth name, under the laws of his birth nation, owe taxes to a foreign corporation, foreign government, or "puppet government" that cannot prove it is lawful and de jure.)

"John Philip Souza," a Private Hawaiian National Citizen, and living soul, is a Christian man born to Ko Hawaii Pae Aina, *(The Hawaiian Islands) (a foreign Citizen to the state of the forum de facto State of Hawaii Government).* Souza had elected to, declared and reclaimed his lawful, proper birth name and Hawaiian National Citizenship <u>birthright</u> in 1996, lawfully notifying both State and Federal Governments of that proper birth name and birthright citizenship. His choice was made because <u>Souza knew that his lawful birth Nation *(Ko Hawaii Pae Aina)* defined his proper citizenship</u> and also the fact that <u>citizenship is voluntary, not mandatory</u>.

Souza had no previous criminal record or court actions against him and is an upstanding Hawaiian Citizen of good moral character.

Mr. Souza's employer (First Insurance Company [hereinafter, "employer"] licensed by the de facto State) was the cause of this unwarranted legal action. The employer had been notified by Mr. Souza of his new citizenship status and was instructed in writing to stop withholding from his personal earnings, the customary Puppet State of Hawaii income tax withholdings, as it no longer applied to him.

The employer <u>dishonored the written instructions by Souza</u> and improperly and without consent, elected to take responsibility for payment of Souza's supposed Puppet State of Hawaii personal tax obligation, and, without Souza's consent removed his "compensation for labor" (Under the IRS Code, "compensation for labor" is not taxable) from Souza's paycheck and gave it to the Puppet State of Hawaii Tax Office. Without written authority to do so, the employer's actions constituted collusion and an unauthorized assumed power of attorney depriving Mr. Souza of a portion of his compensation for labor.

After his retirement, Souza, applied to the State for a refund of all those funds that had been improperly (and illegally) withheld. The Puppet State tax officials (experts in the field) then refunded Souza's "compensation for labor" that it had improperly received from his employer. When Souza deposited the refund into his bank account, he was arrested for theft of State funds.

In this particular case, the *Puppet State of Hawaii Tax Office* filed a "**Four Count**" **action**[19] against the fiction person (the ALL CAPITALIZED NAME owned by

---

[19] "Four count action." *Two original charges of "False and Fraudulent Statements" (HRS 231.36[a]) and two charges of "Theft in the 2ⁿᵈ Degree" (HRS 708-830; HRS 708-831[b]) HRS 231.36(a) This Section states that "Any person who wilfully (sic) makes and subscribes any return, statement, or other documents required to be made under **title 14, except chapter 238**, which contains or is verified by a written declaration that is true and correct as to every material matter, and which the person does not believe to be true and correct as to every material matter, shall be guilty of a class C felony and, upon conviction, shall be subject to one or any combination of the following: 1) A fine of not more than $100,000.00. 2) Imprisonment of not more than three years, or 3) Probation.... (Subject moves to corporations - Author)"*

Author's Note: *Under Title 14 Chapter 238 [supra] (which defines a "person" and "taxpayer") Souza, who is not a U.S. Federal "citizen" of the de facto State of Hawaii jurisdiction, is exempt. The above Title cannot and does not apply and therefore, the charges against Souza, being foreign to the state of the forum, is not obligated to pay a tax to a foreign entity to which he has no allegiance. This is. the unlawful reasoning of the de facto State of Hawaii Circuit Court refusing to address the issue of jurisdiction and birthrights.*

HRS 708-831[b]. Section [b] states: *"criminal charges may be instituted by written information for a felony when the charge is a class B felony under ...(HRS section 708-830 reveals for) "theft in the First Degree." These charges do not apply in Souza's case.* One must be a *"federal citizen"* or *"corporate entity,"* domiciled within that jurisdiction. Souza did not and does not meet those qualifications or requirements of de facto law, which pertains only to U.S. Federal *"citizens"* of the de facto State. HRS 708-830. "Felonies for which criminal charges maybe instituted by written information." This Statute pertains only to U.S. Federal "citizens" of the de facto State of Hawaii. Souza is not a "State" "citizen" nor a U.S. Federal "citizen," but a Private Hawaiian National Citizen who is foreign to that jurisdiction of law, lawfully domiciled on his national birth soil under his lawful and proper birth name since 1996 (prior to the filing of the falsified charges [supra]).

Under "General Provision Section 231-1 Definitions." We find the following definition for "Person" (This is the entity or name under which Mr. Souza was falsely charged in this case.)

Person. *"Person as used in sections 231-34, 231-35, and 231-36 includes an officer or employee of a corporation, a partner or employee of a partnership, a trustee of a trust, a fiduciary of an estate, or a member, employee, or principal of any other entity who as such officer, employee, partner, trustee,*

the U.S. Government) and not against the Living Soul, Private Hawaiian National Citizen known as "John Philip Souza," which is his lawful birth name (his proper English spelled name as documented in all records, his birth certificate and church records). Souza had previously and lawfully terminated his citizenship in 1996 with the de facto Puppet State of Hawaii and U.S. Federal Government when he withdrew as a guarantor of debts unlawfully placed upon the fiction name (a pseudonym) and returned to his lawful and proper English language spelled birth name and his rights under the common-law of his birth country.

Souza (supra) was a foreigner by law to the de facto Puppet State of Hawaii jurisdiction. The reason for this undeserved attack is because Souza had a program on public television dealing with tax issues and citizenship. Souza, <u>by lawful notice and declaration</u>, was no longer a United States "second-class" "emancipated slave" "federal <u>c</u>itizen" living as a foreigner on his birth soil; nor did he function as a U.S. "public servant <u>c</u>itizen" or "person" ("person", i.e. a corporate entity) under a U.S. "second-class immigration status," ALL CAPITALIZED fiction name.

Without prior notification or even a courtesy phone call giving awareness of an error or mistake either by the Tax Office or by Souza, the Puppet State Tax Office through the Office of the Attorney General indicted Souza. The State had quietly sought an "indictment" and filed a "criminal" action against Souza seeking repayment and return of his "compensation for labor" that the Puppet State Tax "officials" had approved refund for, but now claim was "stolen." The indictment asked for the "stolen" Puppet State money (actually Souza's) to be returned along with penalties.

From the beginning of this case, Souza not only questioned the basis of the indictment for theft, but also challenged the jurisdiction of the *Puppet State*, which had filed the action, and the court, which was to hear the case. Souza also had filed with the court an *Affirmation* of his publicly recorded foreign, Hawaiian National citizenship, with lawful exhibits affirming that foreign citizenship. <u>At no time would the court respond or address citizenship or jurisdiction</u>, which is the basis of determining whether or not the court has jurisdiction over the person,

---

fiduciary, member, or principal is under a duty to perform and is principally responsible for performing the act in respect of which the violation occurs." (Bold Emphasis by Author)

Please take note of the word "includes" <u>is a limiting word and limits obligation to only those titles that follow</u> in the sentence. Nowhere can we find the application of this Act or Statute applying to a *"private person," "Private Citizen"* or *"living soul"* (one who is not a corporation or obligated by duty to perform a function or act under a creation of government, i.e. corporation, etc.).

thing or issue. The judge only verbalized in the courtroom, *"We have jurisdiction,"* which is contrary to law, because when challenged, jurisdiction must be proven *(in writing)*! Jurisdiction in this case has never been proven by this judge or the corrupt *Puppet State of Hawaii* judiciary, as is required at law.

The State also falsely claimed there was no distinction between the two types of names and yet, the court would only address Mr. Souza in the *Washington D.C., "public servant," "emancipated slave," "immigration status,"* ALL CAPITALIZED *"fiction name"* and would not address Souza in his proper, lawful birth name wherein his rights are lawfully and rightfully reserved as a Hawaiian National Citizen under *Hawaiian Kingdom National common-law.*

This sham, *"kangaroo court"* continued to address Souza as one who was *"Pro se" (representing himself as an attorney)* when in fact all of Souza's documents filed, affirm that he was representing himself *"in Propria persona" (as the proper Private Citizen, as one's natural self).* This twisting of facts and misrepresentation by the court is in itself a travesty and abuse of justice, a defrauding and denial of the due process rights and those unalienable rights guaranteed not to just Souza and Hawaiian Nationals under the Hawaiian Kingdom Constitution, but also guaranteed under the Organic Act, *Puppet State of Hawaii* and America's united *State's Constitutions* as well.

This is absolute corruption!

Denial of a Defense.

When Souza filed his first "Interrogatory" with the court (questions asked of witnesses, et al, upon which to base a defense), the Attorney General's Office filed a Motion to Strike the Interrogatory from the record, denying Souza a right to build a defense, which is a constitutional due process right. Souza filed a second Interrogatory only to have it also stricken from the record. It is apparent the Puppet State did not want Souza to be able to build any kind of a defense for his case and position. This is a grave travesty and abuse of justice. All this was blatantly done with the consent of the judge working in collusion with the State of Hawaii Attorney General and powers that be, which reflects a lack of the separation of powers (i.e. Executive, Judicial, Legislative). The State courts exercise this violation of due process rights with impunity in violation of both their Puppet State and United States Government laws and respective Constitutions.

When Souza filed a Motion for "Summary Judgment" for termination of the case for fraud on court, collusion, want of jurisdiction and other infractions of the court, the Circuit Court Judge sitting on the bench, Michael D. Wilson, who had created the infractions, <u>refused to recuse</u>[20] himself, and elected to hear the Summary Judgment to recuse filed against him. <u>Judge Wilson refused to address all points of the filing, primarily that of citizenship and jurisdiction.</u> Ignoring the claims of impropriety against himself, he elected to dismiss the Summary Judgment, *sua sponte*. Souza filed another Motion to Recuse Judge Michael D. Wilson for a second fraud on court action, which, against all propriety and right of law, he again elected to hear and dismiss. <u>Wilson's actions were abominable, an insult to justice and apparently encouraged by the Puppet State of Hawaii judiciary reflecting in this case a total abuse of power and disregard for justice by reflecting unquestionable judicial bias and a complete lack of impartiality.</u>

This case was heard at trial on June 28, 2004. Souza in this case was denied the right to any defense (violation of due process rights) by a system of blatant, judicial corruption of the worst type. He was wrongly convicted of fraud and theft for requesting back his own money, which the Puppet State judiciary would not address. The Puppet State prosecuted Souza as having "stolen" their money, <u>without the Puppet State ever stating any specific law as having been violated.</u>

At the time of this writing, Souza is serving time in prison on these trumped up, unlawful and corrupt actions utilized collusively by the Puppet State of Hawaii Tax Office, Attorney General's Office and biased Judge Michael D. Wilson. Souza was denied release on two subsequent appeals after Wilson's biased judgment and Order and has been forced to put his third appeal on the back burner. Perhaps you might see a little clearer how this corrupt *Puppet State of Hawaii* suppresses Hawaiian Nationals and decent citizens who stand up against them.

(Note: Mr. Souza was released from prison on Thursday, October 6, 2005 after one year in prison on the trumped-up and falsified charges originating through the Puppet State of Hawaii Tax Office.)

---

[20] **Recuse / Recusal.** *"The process by which a judge is disqualified on objection of either party (or disqualifies himself or herself) from hearing a lawsuit because of self-interest, bias or prejudice."* (Source: Black's Law Dictionary, 6th Edition)

LAW OF THE FLAG IN THE PUPPET STATE OF HAWAII COURTS

The U.S. Military Flag.

You may have noticed (then again, you may not have noticed) that <u>only United States Military Flags fly in all the courtrooms of the false, *Puppet State of Hawaii*.</u> I will confirm this statement that the flags that I address in the first sentence are really military flags and not flags of the American Republic *(American National Flag)* by having you do the following: Go to **Title 4, Section 1 (Positive Law-1949) of the United States Code (4 USC § 1) (See EXHIBIT S)** and read the footnote about the *"fringe"* upon the American flag. You will find <u>the 1925 United States Attorney General Opinion No. 34,</u> regarding military flag use *(4 U.S.C. § 1 (1925 footnote) 34 Op Atty Gen 483)*. (Also, See 4 USCA §§ 1, 2).

What you need to understand is that under the ***"law of the flag"***[21] the vessel on or in which you operate, sit or stand *(i.e. boat, ship <u>or even a courtroom</u>),* is governed by the laws of the country whose flag flies above it. So, if a court flies a military flag, the court operates under military law or military rule. If it flies a civil flag, the court operates under civil law.

The courts of *Puppet State of Hawaii* fly the *United States Government Military Flag (and Puppet State of Hawaii flag)* as evidenced by the fringes around them. These courts operate under military authority, therefore, anyone who is tried there is presumably tried under Military or Admiralty/Maritime law, which primarily applies to occupied territories or vessels at sea, but regardless, <u>it also applies to any individual under which a trial or infraction is charged and heard beneath that specific flag.</u>

Example: If you are a U.S. Private Citizen, your U.S. rights at law are forfeited when you submit to a foreign flag or a foreign country's jurisdiction.

The Puppet State of Hawaii Flag.

Although at a glance they look the same, <u>the flag of the de facto, *Puppet State of Hawaii* is not the same flag as the *Hawaiian Kingdom flag.*</u> The de facto, *Puppet State of Hawaii* uses a standardized type of U.S. flag size (2:3 or 3:5 or 5:8). These U.S. flag

---

[21] **Law of the Flag:** *"In maritime law, the law of that nation or country whose flag is flown by a particular vessel. A ship owner who sends his vessel into a foreign port gives notice by his flag to all who enter into contracts with the master that he intends the law of that flag to regulate such contracts, and that they must either submit to its operation or not contract with him."* (Black's Law Dictionary, 6th Ed.)

aspects are considerably disproportionate to the Hawaiian Kingdom Flag and therefore, do not represent the *Hawaiian Kingdom National Government*. It does represent the laws and government of the *U.S. de facto, Puppet State of Hawaii*. <u>Hawaiians who fly this modified Puppet State flag need to know the difference</u>.

The Hawaiian Kingdom National Flag.

The Hawaiian Kingdom National Flag is simple dimensionally, being one by two (1:2) in ratio; or, three feet by six feet, etc. which is its lawful aspect by custom and tradition. This Author could find no Hawaiian National Government Sessions Law pertaining to the standard size used for the "Hawaiian National Flag." Thus, the dimensions of the Hawaiian National Flag appear to be affirmed by custom, tradition, and historical usage.

AUTHOR'S CONCLUSION.

AFFIRMATION OF HAWAII'S COURTS AS COURTS OF INCOMPETENT JURISDICTION: (Inability of Judges to Provide Evidence of Lawful Oaths of Office)

In the month of December 1999, Civil Case No. 99-00690 was filed <u>under a reservation of rights</u> in the United States Court for the Hawaii District (Federal). The Complainant halted that case in order to affirm the lawful competency of the judges of that court. A second filing was made <u>asking for lawful confirmation of oaths of Office</u> of both the magistrate and judge set for hearing of the case to affirm competency. <u>A proper time was set for lawful and courteous response</u> by all judges of the court to which <u>there was no response-affirming competency</u> of any judge possessing a supposed lawful oath of Office. On March 13, 2000, a "common law" Acquiescence by Estoppel (acknowledgment by silence) was filed by Complainant, <u>affirming at law the unlawful standing of this United States Court for the Hawaii District (Federal) and the incompetence of its judges;</u> automatically affirming as well, the incompetence of the <u>lesser, federalized corporate courts</u> of the false Puppet State of Hawaii.

WHAT JUSTICE IS TO ME, THE AUTHOR

To me, justice is determined by the goodness of rules as set down and established by a Righteous, Loving, and Just God *(God's Law)*. Justice to me is that moral standard and order set forth and established for living in peaceful harmony with each other in a just society. The following are from Black's Law Dictionary.

> *Justice.* (v) *"To do justice, to see justice done; to summon one to do justice."*
>
> **Justice.** (n) *"The title given to judges, particularly to judges of U.S. and state supreme courts, and as well to judges of appellate courts. The U.S. supreme court, and most state supreme courts are composed of a chief justice and several associate justices.*
>
> *Proper administration of laws. In jurisprudence, the constant and perpetual disposition of legal matters or disputes to render every man his due."* **Source: Black's Law Dictionary, 6th Ed., Page 864**

We find a more appropriate and complete meaning for the word "justice" in Webster's Encyclopedic Unabridged Dictionary (Deluxe Edition, 2001):

> *"1. the quality of being just; righteousness, equitableness, or moral rightness: to uphold the justice of a cause. 2. rightfulness or lawfulness, as of a claim or title; justness of ground or reason: to complain with justice. 3. the moral principle determining just conduct. 4. conformity to this principle, as manifested in conduct; just conduct, dealing, or treatment. 5. the administering of deserved punishment or reward. 6. the maintenance or administration of what is just by law, as by judicial or other proceedings: a court of justice. 7. judgment or persons or causes by judicial process: to administer justice in a community. 8. a judicial officer; a judge or magistrate.*

Justice today is not founded upon God's moral principles, but man's values. God's Truth is not found in the courts of the false Puppet State of Hawaii or in the "color of U.S. law" federal court titled the, United States Court for the Hawaii District. God's Truth hasn't changed; the system of law has redefined "truth" as being something relative, even presumptive, but definitely not absolute! There is no reflection of God in either of Hawaii's de facto judicial systems.

CONCLUSION: These attorneys, judges, and law advocates, in the Puppet State of Hawaii are an embarrassment to us all, and should also be to the American People. It's time to remove these lying, mini-god scoundrels from power and authority over decent people. It is time to file civil actions against them and have them tried before lawful, competent judges, for their unlawful impersonations and injuries caused to an innocent and un-deserving people who have sought justice and found ineptness, corruption, abuse, hurt and injury. Need I say more?

A very prominent jurist and expert in "common law," and a Judge in the One Supreme Court of the United States once said, *"State interference is an evil where it cannot be shown to be good."* His name was Oliver Wendell Holmes, Jr. (b.1841-1935) who served as a Supreme Court Justice from 1902 to 1931.

Chapter 7

DISENFRANCHISEMENT

AMERICAN NATIONAL'S LOSS OF THEIR RIGHT TO VOTE

Author's Note: In this Section, I address those who think of themselves as American Citizens.

It is an interesting time in American History. American National[1] Citizens, also known as united "States Nationals" or "sovereigns" (they are one and the same), who love their Country, honor and respect their birth names in their proper English language spelling, and respect and honor their National 48 Star Flag; are denied their right to vote in any election unless they are willing to become second-class U.S. Federal citizens. They are disenfranchised. By registering, they forfeit their inalienable and unalienable sovereign State of birth Citizenship and their National Constitutional rights.

To vote in the United States, "American Nationals" must submit, admit and yield to the fact that they are the "Washington D.C.," "public servant," "Emancipated Slave," "immigration status," "federal government created chattel person" type "citizen" as discussed in Chapter 4 (Birth Names and Birthrights - Types of Citizenship by Name). Yes, America's State "sovereigns" can only vote in America as "Fourteenth Amendment Emancipated Slaves," "second-class," "federal citizens;" which is the same citizenship given "Freed Black American Slaves," also known as an "immigration status" federal citizenship given to foreigners who are naturalized. This is wrong! Who gave politicians the right to deviously take away our rights to vote or through the actions of our courts, force an inferior type of federal, bondage citizenship upon us? I didn't, did you?

---

[1] **National.** *(Definition from Webster's Encyclopedic Unabridged Dictionary, 2001) 1. of, pertaining to, or maintained by a nation as an organized whole or independent political unit:* national *affairs.* **2.** *owned, preserved or maintained by the federal government: a* national *wildlife refuge.* **3.** *particular or common to the whole people of a country:* national *customs.* **4.** *devoted to one's own nation, its interests, etc.; patriotic: to stir up* national *pride.* **5.** *Nationalist.* **6.** *concerning or encompassing an entire nation:* a"...national *radio network.* **7.** *limited to one nation. -n.* **8.** *a citizen or subject of a particular nation who is entitled to its protection:* U.S. nationals *living abroad.* 9. Often, nationals. a national competition, *tournament, or the like:* We're invited to Minneapolis for the nationals. **10.** *a national company or organization..."* (Bold emphasis by Author)

ONLY U.S. FEDERAL CITIZENS ARE ALLOWED TO VOTE IN HAWAII

When a U.S. Citizen registers to vote in the U.S., he is required to have a U.S. Federal Government Social Security Number (SEE: "VOTER REGISTRATION FORM," EXHIBIT G) *(NOTE: Social Security registration acknowledges your citizenship as being within the Federal, not National jurisdiction of America's U.S. Constitution).* Registrars do not permit a person registering to properly spell and/or retain his lawful birth name. Automatically, and without the person's consent, they fraudulently convert your proper name to the ALL CAPITALIZED fiction. Should the person choose to register under that pseudonym name, he is in fact recognizing that fiction name and confirming his citizenship being as that of a second-class U.S. Federal, 14th Amendment Emancipated Slave *"citizen."* One cannot be both persons. One is either an American State's 'sovereign' Private Citizen *(National)* with State's rights under his proper English language birth name and his birth State's common law; or through the eyes of the federal government; he is a second-class federal *"citizen."* Should one decide to not honor their federal *"Washington D.C."* fiction name, he will not be allowed to register to vote. He is disenfranchised!

If you look at **EXHIBIT G**, on line Item 10[a], you will see the following:

"a. I am a citizen of the United States of America (Non-U.S. citizens including U.S. Nationals do not qualify.)"

(Author's Clarification: Please notice the Author's English language distinction between the spelling of the word "citizen" and "Citizen" which separates your "State's 'sovereign' private Citizen" of the American Republic from that of the second-class, immigration status federal "citizen." This right to vote is limited to only U.S. Federal second-class "citizens." American National "Citizens" of the Republic and Hawaiian National Citizens on their own soil are denied any right to vote. Doesn't this ring of bias and corruption? This is most definitely a planned disenfranchisement even if Hawaii was a lawful "State of the Union" OR, rightfully affirms that Hawaii has never been and presently is not, a lawful State of the American "Union of States.")

Now, what do you think about being an American National with no right to vote? Have you ever wondered why so many Americans do not vote? Are the Federal Government politicians, the federal judiciary and its corporate State legal systems anti-American, anti-State's 'sovereign' American National Citizenship? Are they anti-

"American National;" anti-American "Union of States;" and, against the 'Republic, for which *our 48 Star National Flag* stands'? The facts speak for themselves! <u>Justification</u>: Evidence and facts provide me that conclusion.

When one restores himself to his proper American *State's right, English-standard birth name* he also restores himself to his State and U.S. Constitutional *due process rights* as an American National and State's right 'sovereign.' Did you know that even with your rightful, restored State's birthright American National Citizenship, you will still be denied your right to vote in any U.S. Federal or State election?

American Nationals like me, have severed the adhesive, binding contract with the *Federal U.S. Social Security Administration* and no longer have use of, nor desire to use, their Social Security Number issued unlawfully and fraudulently contracted. This *Social Security Administration System Number* binds us to the federal jurisdiction through the unlawful, implied, adhesive contract. This American National *(Author)* gave lawful notice in 1996 of severance and cancellation of my signature as the *"surety"* for the titled, *"Washington D.C. public servant," "legal fiction," "14th Amendment Emancipated Slave," "immigration status," "government created chattel person"* type federal *"citizen."*

My implied contract with the *Social Security Administration* initiated when I was a minor, was implemented without my parents' consent or lawful counsel present. *My father had died and out of necessity I had to go to work part-time.* As a 14-year-old (1953) American Citizen, I was told by government authorities, *"You cannot get a job without a Social Security Number." (Which wasn't true).* The legal age at that time for lawful contract in California was 21 years of age! The *U.S. Federal Government* age of consent was also 21 years of age! Since I was under-aged, this implied, adhesive and bondage *contract* was <u>fraudulent from the very beginning,</u> based upon the existing laws of my *U.S. Government* and my sovereign birth *State of California.*

Why is this fraudulent, unethical, unlawful government process still going on today? *(It is now providing Social Security Numbers to newborn infants!)* It's because we lack the knowledge to pay attention to protecting our rights. Our rights are no longer there like we assumed they were. This method of capturing children and literally brain washing them from birth to adulthood is morally very, very wrong and is legal entrapment by a fraudulent conversion of their name and rights. We are dealing here with a socialist mentality of conspiring people *(i.e. politicians, government officials and public servants who are supposed to be our American and Hawaiian public servants*) but who instead, have become public servant mini-gods unto themselves.

A POSSIBLE JUSTIFICATION FOR PERMITTING ONLY U.S. FEDERAL CITIZENS, NOT AMERICAN *STATE'S NATIONALS*, THE RIGHT TO VOTE

I believe the reason for this *refusal* to permit American Nationals under their birth names and birthrights the right to vote is, very simply, they do not want us as *"American Nationals" (sovereigns)* of the *"American Republic"* and its *"Union of States"* to exercise our rights! They do not want *"American Nationals" (those born to one of the contiguous 48 States of the Union)* to be free!

This lesser-of-right U.S. Constitution, Article 1 Section 8, Washington, D.C. federal government jurisdiction has deviously and deliberately over-extended its *citizenship jurisdiction* beyond its limitation as restricted and limited under *Paragraph 17, Article 1 § 8 of the U.S. Constitution.* Like an octopus, with bankers as the head; and politicians, attorneys and judges as its tentacles, it has overextended itself beyond its authorized jurisdiction of restricted Constitutional control. It has deceitfully captured sovereign, *State's born, American National "Citizens"* domiciled outside of Washington D.C., et al, to be their financial beasts of burden, reined in and controlled as their own federal *"citizens."* Yet, these American State's right Nationals are domiciled within the sovereign 48 States, beyond the federal Constitutional jurisdiction. This is why, by devious, federal political ploy and design, *"American Nationals"* are now foreign, disenfranchised electors in their own American communities.

FOREIGN VOTERS IN HAWAII

The de facto United States and the *Puppet State of Hawaii* encourage the movement of foreign U.S. citizens onto Hawaiian National soil *(requiring only a one-year residency)* in order to build a larger voter base of Federal United States second-class "citizens." Likewise, disenfranchisement of *"Hawaiian Nationals"* is accomplished by limiting State of Hawaii voters to only U.S. Federal, 14th Amendment *"citizens" (ALL CAPITALIZED or fiction named persons only).* It is not that *"Hawaiian Nationals"* desire to vote in the occupier's elections, or that *"American Nationals"* desire to vote in the lawful *National Hawaiian Kingdom* jurisdiction. It is the desire of Hawaiians to vote under their own Hawaiian National laws without being hindered by the occupier's deprivation of their rights to do so. <u>American Nationals and U.S. Federal citizens, as previously mentioned, also have no right to vote in Hawaiian National elections on Hawaiian soil</u>.

The limited jurisdiction, federal government's denying the right to vote to constitutionally protected American and Hawaiian Nationals is totally wrong! It is yet another affirmation of an unlawful jurisdictionally over-extended and corrupt *United States Federal Government* policy of depriving both national peoples of their inalienable rights to vote.

What happened to the *"...Republic for which we stand..."* and that *"American Democracy"* of our *"Republic"* and our *"Union of States"* <u>in which we *Americans* all had the right to vote</u>? Answer. We *Americans* have, through ignorance and deceit, become a *Federal United States of America* supposed democracy with all Americans deviously transitioned into being *"immigration-status, second-class federal ̲citizens"* and residents of Washington D.C.; which jurisdiction is limited by **Article 1 § 8** of the American Constitution, and have jurisdictionally removed us from our sovereign State's rights so we can be emancipated slaves.

American Nationals and Hawaiian Nationals must restore their proper rights to vote within their respective countries, counties, cities and communities. American Nationals and Hawaiian Nationals must restore their respective governments, to be lawful and intact, as they should, can and must be.

"American National Citizens" are *"Private Citizens"* and have rights but need to unify. They must exercise their inalienable rights as *American Nationals'* under their Constitutional rights as *"State's Citizens of the Republic"* within the *"Union of States"* *under their 48 Star American Flag!* They need to cause the lawful right to vote to be reopened to them.

<u>Hawaiian Nationals are also Private Citizens and also need to come together in unity as a single voice and People; and must put away their petty differences and claims for individual power and majesty</u>. Both nations need to elect decent, moral and Godly representatives to their respective governments who would not be driven by the corrupting monetary influence of bankers and big business, ego and greed.

It is time to take our governments back and restore them to health through truth, decency and righteousness by removing all those in authority who do not respect our God and our Constitutional Citizenship Rights as American and Hawaiian Nationals.

SOLUTION: Force the opening of voter registration to *American Nationals* in all 48 American States, counties, cities and communities; and, in Hawaii acknowledge *"Hawaiian Nationals"* right to vote in Hawaiian Kingdom elections.

(NOTE: Federal c̲itizens have the right to vote in Washington D.C. and within designated federal jurisdictions. They should vote there. Federal c̲itizens voting rights are specifically limited under the u̲nited "State's Constitution" to their federal jurisdictions (i.e. Washington D.C. and its federal territories like the former Panama Canal Zone, Puerto Rico, Guam, etc.).

It's time for Americans to once again look at the *"Word of God" (Bible)* for guidance; educate themselves about government and reclaim their birthrights and sovereign Citizenship that made America *("The States")* great. At one time, America possessed a Godly dignity *(as well as a powerful military)* that carried the respect and envy of peoples all around the world. Unfortunately, that is not the case today. It is time to restore the American *"Union of States"* and our *"American Republic"* as a Godly Nation. If not, we only condemn ourselves and shall fall from God's Grace by our missing the mark (Sin)!

I conclude this Chapter with the following statement made by Queen Liliuokalani in 1897, which subject matter of concern is still applicable today.

> *"After the overthrow of the monarchy, these people had no representation at home or abroad, and such is their condition to this day [1897]. Comprising four-fifths of the legally qualified voters, they are voiceless, save those few who, for the purpose of obtaining the necessaries of life, have sworn allegiance to the present government. In this connection, the following statement, which is sent to me from Honolulu, may be of interest as showing how few now assume to govern a nation of 109,000 persons. The registered voters in 1890, under the monarchy, numbered 13,593 persons.*
>
> *The registered voters in 1894, under the Provisional Government, for delegation to the so-called constitutional Convention, numbered 4,477.*

The actual voters in 1896, under the so-called Republic, numbered, for Senators, 2047, and for Representatives, 3,196. In other words, there were qualified to vote for Senators and Representatives 2,017 persons, and for Representatives only 1,179. From figures already in, it is doubtful whether the total vote to be cast in September next will exceed 2,000."

Chapter 8

THE BISHOP TRUST

THE WILL OF BERNICE PAUAHI BISHOP[1]
(A Private, Common-Law,[2] Pure Trust)

On October 31, A.D. 1883 Princess Bernice Pauahi Bishop created a *Hawaiian Kingdom National common-law, Private, Pure Trust* called the **Bernice Pauahi Bishop Trust**. The Princess stipulated that the assets of her Trust were to be used to provide children of Hawaiian ancestry with educational opportunities.

Princess Bernice Pauahi Bishop died on the Sixteenth Day of October A.D. 1884. Her Will was probated by Supreme Court Justice, L. Mc Cully of the *Supreme Court for the Hawaiian Islands* (the Supreme Court of the Hawaiian Kingdom) as Probate No. 2425, dated December 2, A. D. 1884.

The assets of the Trust constitute nearly ten percent of all the privately held lands in Hawaii, making the Trust the largest privately land owner in Hawaii. The value of the properties of the **Bernice Pauahi Bishop Trust** (today also known as *Kamehameha Schools Bishop Estate* and more recently, simply *Kamehameha Schools*) constitutes one of the largest endowments in the world for a private school.

The existence of the **Bernice Pauahi Bishop Trust** is acknowledged by the *Hawaiian National Government* (re-activated in 1996), the de facto *Puppet State of Hawaii* and even the *Federal U.S. Government*.

Because of its sheer size, the endowment and the operations of the Trust has been a major factor in the political and economic landscape of Hawaii. As a result, right after the lawful Government of the Hawaiian Kingdom was usurped in 1893; the integrity of Pure Trust has been repeatedly violated and abused by the various governments and

---

[1] Bernice Pauahi Bishop Trust is EXHIBIT T

[2] "Chapter LVII. An Act To Reorganize the Judiciary Department (of the Hawaiian Kingdom, 1892) § 5. *The common law of England, as ascertained by English and American decisions, is hereby declared to be the common law of the Hawaiian Islands in all cases, except as otherwise expressly provided by the Hawaiian Constitution or laws, or fixed by Hawaiian judicial precedent, or established by Hawaiian national usage, provided however, that no person shall be subject to criminal proceedings except as provided by the Hawaiian laws.*"

judicial systems of the *Republic of Hawaii*, the *Puppet Territory of Hawaii*, the *Puppet State of Hawaii* and the *Federal U.S. Government*. Add to that, *U.S. Internal Revenue Service*, and other *jurisdictions of law foreign to that law under which the Trust was created*. These foreign jurisdictions deliberately and with impunity controlled and mutilated the Trust, contrary to the specific, protective dictates of the Trust.

In recent years, this effort appears to be accelerated to further diminish, and possibly even extinguish the Trust, to eventually seize its land and assets. This latter statement is based upon evidence of actions I have observed over the past thirty plus years of watching the *Puppet State of Hawaii* judiciary function contrary to and in violation of the Trust and the interests of its beneficiaries, Hawaiian children. For all intents and purposes, what is now seen as *Kamehameha Schools Bishop Estate* is not the original intact Trust, but a fabricated *U.S. non-profit corporation* with the assets of the Trust, but functioning under the dictates of U.S. laws and IRS regulations.

Under the original and still applicable conditions of the Trust, it is the **Chief Justice of the Supreme Court for the Hawaiian Islands** *(that of the Hawaiian Kingdom, not the Puppet State of Hawaii)* that is to exercise the **"Protector"** requirements to preserve this Living, Pure Trust and, in particular *(with a majority of the Justices of the Supreme Court for the Hawaiian Islands)*, the responsibility to appoint or remove Trustees of the Trust. The *Protector* has the right to do what is necessary to preserve the integrity and intent of *Bernice Pauahi Bishop's Private Trust Estate*, as stipulated within the Trust Document itself.

This Trust's lawful intent and procedure has been most recently violated and modified by the *Supreme Court* of the *Puppet State of Hawaii*, a fourth generation, de facto pirate entity, asserting unlawful and corrupted influence as a *"pseudo Protector,"* which it then abandoned in recent years to a lesser *Circuit Court Judge* functioning as a *Probate Court* in yet another violation of the conditions of the Will and Trust.

I quote the Trust:

> **(Thirteenth)** *"I also direct that my said trustees shall annually make a full and complete report of all receipts and expenditures and of the condition of said schools to the Chief Justice of the Supreme Court, or other highest judicial officer in this country;[3] and shall also file before him annually an inventory of the*

---

[3] **Author's clarification:** The "country" is, Ko Hawaii Pae Aina - The Hawaiian Islands, under which laws this Private Pure Trust was created

property in their hands and how invested, and to publish the same in some Newspaper published in said Honolulu; I also direct my said trustees to keep said school buildings insured in good Companies, and in case of loss to expend the amounts recovered in replacing or repairing said buildings. I also direct that the teachers of said schools shall forever be persons of the Protestant religion, but I do not intend that the choice should be restricted to persons of any particular sect of Protestants."

(Fourteenth*)* *"...I further direct that the number of my said trustees shall be kept at five; and that vacancies shall be filled by the choice of a majority of the Justices of the Supreme Court, the selection to be made from persons of the Protestant religion."[4],*

The acting *Puppet State of Hawaii's Supreme Court Chief Justice*, in lieu of his claimed duty as a pseudo *"third-party[5] interloper"[6]* or pseudo *"Protector"* abandoned his duty, and contrary to the condition of the Trust, permitted the appointment of a private attorney *"Special Master"* from the *"State Probate Court." **This was not a Supreme Court Justice from the <u>Supreme Court for the Hawaiian Islands (the Hawaiian Kingdom)</u> as required by the Trust**.* This constituted another direct, blatant violation and abrogation of the *"interloper"* Chief Justice's duty and charge under the Trust.

Even the de facto U.S. (Federal) District Court Judge Samuel P. King, having no authority or right of involvement, either public or private in the matter, became publicly involved in the issue in 1997 <u>while serving as a judge in the *United States Court for the Hawaii District (Federal)*</u>. I would say that this reflects U.S. Federal judicial bias. The *Puppet State of Hawaii's* lower Circuit Court and Probate Court had no lawful right of involvement in or over the Trust.

The initial take-over of the *Bernice Pauahi Bishop Trust* by courts of improper jurisdiction occurred when the "Supreme Court" of the de facto *Republic of Hawaii* "assumed" the responsibility of *Protector* for the Trust, particularly the duty of appointing

---

[4] **Author's clarification:** The court being referred to is the Supreme Court of The Hawaiian Islands (the independent nation), not the de facto, Puppet State of Hawaii Supreme Court"

[5] **Third Party.** *"One not a party to an agreement, a transaction, or an action but who may have rights therein."* (Source: Black's Law Dict. 6th Ed.)

[6] **Interloper.** *"Persons who interfere or intermeddle into business to which they have no right. Persons who enter a country or place to trade without license. One who meddles in affairs which are none of his business and for which he has no responsibility; an intruder; an intermeddler. Encroachment on rights of others."* (Source: Black's Law Dictionary, 6th Ed.)

the Trustees. From the initial pirate-government entity, the *Republic of Hawaii,* the stolen mantle was passed on to the "Supreme Courts" of succeeding pirate entities, the *Territory of Hawaii* and the *State of Hawaii.* The most recent and arguably the most egregious actions against the Trust occurred from 1997-1999 when the Governor and the Attorney General for the Puppet State of Hawaii invaded the sanctity of the Trust and stripped it of any remaining vestige of autonomy as a Private Pure Trust.

Margery Bronster, the Attorney General for the State of Hawaii at the time, had absolutely no authority to conduct an investigation of the Trust, much less make recommendations as to reorganizing its operations. Likewise, Benjamin Cayetano, Governor of the State of Hawaii, and the (U.S.) Internal Revenue Service had absolutely no lawful authority to take over control of the Trust or appoint new trustees to this private, *Hawaiian National common-law Pure Trust,* which is a judicial function.

Unfortunately, the Trust, having its autonomy and integrity compromised and eroded for over 100 years, had no lawfully competent counselors that understood or were willing to advise the Trust to assert and stand on its proper and lawful rights as a Hawaiian Kingdom *Private Pure Trust.* In its ignorance and folly, rather than telling the Puppet State of Hawaii interlopers to step aside, as they could have, and should have done, the Trust complied with the unlawful dictates of the officials from the de facto State of Hawaii. *(In this Author's personal opinion)*

Even though the Trustees at the time had been appointed by an improper *Protector* (the Supreme Court of the State of Hawaii) these Trustees still had moral and fiduciary responsibilities to the Trust and the Trust's beneficiaries.

Instead, the Trustees reacted blindly and subjected themselves to the corrupt de facto State of Hawaii and U.S. legal system by hiring *Puppet State of Hawaii Bar Association* attorneys *(trained in U.S. federal schools of law).* By doing so, they ignorantly (or deliberately) subjugated this lawful, private, *Hawaiian Kingdom National Pure Trust* to foreign U.S. interests on Hawaiian National soil; a violation of the Trustee's fiduciary duty under *Hawaiian Kingdom National law* to without reservation, or excuse, protect the *Hawaiian National Beneficiaries.* The Trustees do not know their responsibilities and strengths and with poor legal advice are incurring a fuliginous legal character, which is compromising the true intent of the Trust and its purpose.

VIOLATION OF TRUST CONDITIONS BY THE DE FACTO STATE

The participation and fraudulent actions by an unlawful *"third-party interloper"* *the Puppet State of Hawaii,* through its *Supreme Court Chief Justice* and its lesser *"Probate Court"* had no lawful authority to intervene and were in direct violation of the intent and conditions of the Trust.

According to the dictates of the Trust, *the Chief Justice of the Supreme Court for the Hawaiian Islands (the Hawaiian Kingdom), which had already been re-activated by that time,* is the only lawful authority to make decision over the affairs of the Trust, such as behavior and actions of the Trustees in question.

The Board of Trustees, advised by foreign, U.S. federal-trained attorneys, failed to avail itself of the jurisdiction of the *Hawaiian Kingdom National Court,* and neglected to consult with the Hawaiian Kingdom Supreme Court Chief Justice *(the lawful and designated "Protector" of Bernice Pauahi Bishop's Pure Trust),* even though their legal counsels were made aware of the opportunity to do so in 1996 and 1997. It is apparent to this Author that in 1996, the *Puppet State of Hawaii* legal counsels retained by the Trustees had deliberately ignored the information provided regarding notices of the re-activated, de jure *Hawaiian Kingdom National Court* and the existence of the Trust's lawful *"Protector."*

The Hawaiian National system of law was in fact properly and lawfully restored in September and October of 1996 *(Notices were published locally three times in the Pacific Business News)* informing the general Hawaiian business public and private sectors of its existence. Therefore, the participation and actions of the de facto *Puppet State of Hawaii Probate Court* were and are, unlawful.

The *Puppet State of Hawaii* was also informed that the lawful **Supreme Court for the Hawaiian Islands** was in fact, reactivated at that time. At law, since the lawful publication of the *Supreme Court for the Hawaiian Islands,* all actions pertaining to the Trust of Princess Bernice Pauahi Bishop by the *Puppet State of Hawaii* Court system are in fact, ***void ab initio.***[7]

---

[7] **Void ab initio.** *"A contract is null from the beginning if it seriously offends law or public policy in contrast to a contract which is merely voidable at the election of one of the parties to the contract."* (Source: Black's Law Dictionary, 6th Edition, Page 1574.)

(*BACKGROUND: The former Hawaiian Kingdom Supreme Court Chief Justice Sanford B. Dole was a prominent participant in the usurpation of the Hawaiian National Government in 1893 and by his actions was an initial detractor leading to removing the protection of the Trust [as its Protector] from the lawful jurisdiction of the Hawaiian Kingdom. The Bishop Trust since its creation is unchanged; it still exists as a de jure Hawaiian Kingdom common-law jurisdictional document and has no de facto status or character.*)

VIOLATIONS OF THE BISHOP TRUST BY TRUSTEES

Since the overthrow of the *Hawaiian National Government* in 1893, the actions of the Trustees have, *ipso jure*,[8] been functioning unlawfully with United States Federal *"citizens"* (foreigners) on Hawaiian Kingdom soil monitoring and operating the Trust as if they possessed proper authority. Although it presumably was the intent of Bernice Bishop that all Trustees be Hawaiian Nationals, the Trust itself does not limit Trustees to being only Hawaiian Nationals, which fact shall be determined by the **Chief Justice of the Supreme Court for the Hawaiian Islands,** its lawful **Protector.**

It is this Author's opinion, based upon the intent of the Trust, that it would be in the best interest of the Hawaiian People that at least three of the five Trustees be Hawaiian Nationals to assure the proper intent and purpose of the Trust be sustained. Secondly, the U.S. federal *"citizen"* Trustees, ignorant of judicial standing and citizenship rights, have hired foreign attorneys that only know and practice *"U.S. color of law"* (which is not law) and who do not honor the de jure Hawaiian Kingdom National *"common-law"* and Sessions Laws of the Kingdom. This latter fact is also a violation of the conditions of the Trust by the Trustees as created and structured under the *Hawaiian Kingdom National common-law,* of 1883.

The *Bernice Pauahi Bishop Pure Trust Document* is still a viable and powerful instrument of authority and requires within its formation and intent the right to be sustained according to the *"common-law"* of the *Hawaiian Kingdom Nation.* Otherwise, the Trust would be null and void as it stands. The Trust has been recognized and permitted to stand today as a lawful Hawaiian Kingdom entity by both the de facto State and Federal U.S. This is an admission under the common-law that the de facto State

---

[8] *ipso jure.* *"By the law itself; by the mere operation of law." (Source: Black's Law Dictionary, 6th Edition, Page 828)*

does not really have lawful jurisdiction over the Trust, that is, unless they foolishly continue to listen to de facto attorneys who are compromising the Trust and its intent, and grant it to them. The Trust is under continued and deliberate erosive legal attack by both foreign entities.

By law, the de facto *Puppet State of Hawaii* does not have jurisdiction over the Trust <u>or its Trustees,</u> unless those Trustees, misdirected by their U.S. federal and State hired attorneys, yield themselves foolishly to the de facto *Puppet State of Hawaii Government.*

That in fact is what was happening in 1997, when the Trustees yielded to a lesser, unlawful *Puppet State* probate court decision, rather than demanding and instructing that the de facto, interloper, *Puppet State of Hawaii Supreme Court Chief Justice (pseudo responsible Protector)* back off or administer properly as a pseudo Protector, or, seek the de jure *Chief Justice of the Supreme Court for the Hawaiian Islands.*

The present Trustees were appointed by an incompetent Circuit Court Judge *(Kevin C. K. Chang)* of questionable standing, posturing as a Probate Judge. Rightfully, as mentioned above, these Trustees should be communicating with the *Chief Justice of the Supreme Court for the Hawaiian Islands*, their proper, lawful, Pure Trust **Protector**, who is available to them. <u>At the present time, this Pure Trust is functioning in an unlawful manner,</u> without the rightful Protector as designated and required by the Trust Document.

CONCLUSION: It is time for the present *Bernice Pauahi Bishop Estate Trustees* to open their minds to understanding their rights in behalf of the Trust and its beneficiaries! This Pure Trust was established by Bernice Pauahi Bishop, <u>a Hawaiian National</u> for Hawaiian children; and, was created under the common-law of the *Hawaiian Kingdom National Government.* As a *Hawaiian National common-law Pure Trust*, it is not a *Puppet State of Hawaii* or *United States Federal Government* created trust and has neither relationship nor obligation under *Hawaiian Kingdom National law* to the foreign *Internal Revenue Service (IRS)* or the foreign, *Federal United States Government* on *Hawaiian National soil.*

Chapter 9

The IRS and the Federal Reserve

Note: In this Chapter the Author is speaking as an American Citizen to other American and U.S. Federal Citizens

THE TAXABLE CORPORATE CITIZENS OF THE INTERNAL REVENUE SERVICE (IRS) AND NON-TAXABLE "NON-RESIDENT ALIENS"

United States "federal citizens" (i.e. U.S. federal public servants, citizens of Washington D.C., 14th Amendment emancipated slaves, or any Constitutional "citizens" under Article 1 Section 8, including U.S. territories and the military) are obligated to pay an income tax to the Office of the Internal Revenue Service (IRS) because they are assumed to be "residents" within that jurisdiction. But how can this be applied if the united "States Constitution" says there is not to be a direct tax on the "American National Citizen" (i.e. State's rights "sovereign") (Article 1, Section 9 of the U.S. Constitution)?

The American National "sovereign,"[1] a "Private Citizen" (also titled a "nonresident alien" in the Title 26 Internal Revenue Code), is one born to one of the "48 contiguous States" of the "Union of States" (i.e. American Republic), is not to be taxed. He is exempt. In contrast, those who are corporations, identified as a "corporate fiction," "U.S. Federal citizen," "public servant" etc. of the federal jurisdiction, found to be citizens of Washington D.C., are taxed.

So, how then are we found to be a "federal citizen" of Washington D.C.? It is because we have been registered as one of "their federal citizens" by actions of our County and State Governments who, without our consent, pledged us financially, our earning power and our abilities as a financial security to the Federal United States

---

1 **American born sovereign.** American Private Citizens under the American Constitution of the Republic, specifically those born within one of the sovereign States of the American Union of States and that State's "common law", are "sovereign" in that all sovereign rights (power to change) are vested in the American Citizen (not Federal citizen who does not have those rights). Our Forefathers determined we would not have a King as sovereign; therefore, they vested that power for change in the American Citizen. The Citizen in the American Republic is supreme, not the President. **See dictionary definition of "Republic."**

Government, for a federal bankruptcy debt obligation owed private bankers. Our proper birth certificate can be found in Washington D.C. as security on a "Bearer Bond"[2] document **(See EXHIBIT J)** filed in the U.S. Treasury Department (which just happens to be in Washington D.C.) affirming us to be a citizen of that Washington D.C. jurisdiction.

The questionable transfer of our citizenship and pledge of our birth document accomplished this citizenship maneuver and our acceptance of their new ALL CAPITALIZED corporate name as their federal citizen provided them (our lying politicians and bankers) control over us from within their Washington D.C. jurisdiction (a fraudulent conversion of our name and citizenship).

THE TAXABLE AND NON-TAXABLE CITIZENS

As mentioned previously in this book, there are two (2) types of American citizenships.

First, there is the ***American State's born "sovereign,"*** *a private Citizen,* by virtue of his *"common law"* birth right within one of the 48 contiguous *"sovereign"* States. He is protected by the *"common law"* of his birth State and its Constitution, and, the united *"State's Constitution of the Republic,"* i.e., as an *"American National,"* and "sovereign."

Second, there is the **"created chattel citizenship"**[3] (i.e. "public servant" or "immigration status citizenship," "Washington D.C. resident,") created by the U.S.

---

[2] Bearer Bond. See Footnote, Chapter 4, Page 50

[3] **"Created chattel citizenship,"** I believe the ALL CAPITALIZED name, a chattel (slave, bondsman), was created by the United States Federal Government after the Civil War to create a separate identity, a "Federal citizenship" separate and distinct from that of a "sovereign State's National Citizenship" (a Private Citizen of one of the sovereign States of the American Republic and its Union of States) from hence our common law birth rights originate.

Author's Clarification. This Congressionally created "chattel citizen" was created by the 14th Amendment to provide Emancipated Slaves after the Civil War a citizenship that was not on par with that of white Americans of the Republic; and was in fact, just as is our military today, outside of the direct protection of the sovereign State's and National Constitutions, and, our Bill of Rights. Therefore, there was need for Civil Right's Acts in the 1860's and 1960's to provide these federal, limited protection federal citizens rights similar to those possessed by State's Citizens under their State and National Constitutions. This secondary citizenship exists only under the corporate and military authority of Article 1 § 8 and Article 1 § 10 of the Constitution. This distinction, supra, of the ALL CAPITALIZED name designates a citizenship of Washington D.C., now affirmed by custom and usage. This secondary, limited jurisdiction citizenship has been used for that purpose since the Civil War and through two World Wars to transfer American Citizens into the federal / military jurisdiction without their knowledge or awareness.

Federal Congress by the **14th Amendment** to the U.S. Constitution after the Civil War for the Emancipated Slaves which promised citizenship is "federal," not State. It is a lesser, second-class (limited) type of national citizenship.

This congressionally created "public servant" "citizen" with the "corporate," ALL CAPITALIZED NAME reveals that this "government created" "person" or "corporate thing" exists without any sovereign State constitutional or federal constitutional protection or rights. That is why the U.S. Government (our politicians) created the **Civil Rights Acts** (just after the Civil War and again, in the 1960's) to provide this limited, so-called second-class "federal citizen" some right of protection (**Title 42 U.S. Code, Civil Rights**).

Starting to get the picture? I hope so. The government created, corporate, ALL CAPITALIZED NAMED U.S. Federal "citizen" does not possess the same rights at law that State's right's "American Nationals" *("sovereigns")* possess. This knowledgeable distinction in the two types of citizenship is extremely important and invaluable. This differentiation has been ignored for decades and is no longer taught in our school systems. Important: We must know who we are, and if we don't know, we must find out!

The *Federal United States Government* and its judiciary permits and encourages its agencies to change birth names on our Birth Certificates, Driver's Licenses, Social Security Act Identification Cards, etc, to the corporate fiction name to provide them an implied control.

The *Social Security Administration* and *Internal Revenue Service (IRS)* also change our birth name to the ALL CAPITALIZED LEGAL FICTION just like the State, county and local governments. This is done without our explicit consent and is a fraudulent conversion (identity theft) of our birth name and rights. The City, County, State or Federal Governments give us an identity using the ALL CAPITALIZED NAME and we ignorantly place our seal *(which is our lawful signature)* of approval upon the document. In doing so, we acknowledge that we are a federal guarantor of any debt placed upon or against that fictitious, U.S. corporately created name which they own. By our own ignorance and signature, we are captured by this adhesive recognition to be that foreign, federal government created *"corporate person"* registered as a *"second-class federal citizen"* and *"resident of Washington D.C."* We then become their limited jurisdiction *"federal citizen."* In ignorance, we bit the bait of corruption and we got hooked.

The issue <u>is</u> jurisdiction <u>and</u> our Private Citizenship rights. They both go together. The *Internal Revenue Service (IRS)*, as mentioned, does not have lawful authority over *American National* sovereigns *(titled, "<u>non-resident aliens</u>" as defined within their own Title 26 IRS Code)* but <u>they do have a right to tax those identified as U.S. federal citizens</u> or citizens within their federal enclave *(under Article 1 Section 8)*, military jurisdiction and rule *(i.e. residents of Washington D.C., its U.S. Territories, etc.)*. They have the weight of a corrupted Federal *(not National)* U.S. Congress and judiciary to exercise that right. Unfortunately, the IRS <u>unlawfully and forcefully imposes taxes</u> upon those who are also sovereign *American Nationals* because these weak <u>tax-crazy politicians</u> in Congress and their politically appointed judges do not and will not enforce the lawful limitations imposed upon the corrupt, dishonest IRS as set forth in Title 26 *(Internal Revenue Code)*.

Of interest is the fact that City, County and State governments are following Federal practice <u>by changing birth names on birth certificates</u> in order to capture a child at birth *(as one who is a resident of Washington D.C., a second-class, corporate, U.S. Federal citizen)* <u>without obtaining the consent of the birth parents.</u> Our State Governments *(politicians we have elected)* refuse to protect us — maybe they are just plain ignorant. The *Federal U.S. Government* is assigning Social Security Numbers to newborn infants and the parents and hospital staff members believe it is proper and right. Parents, through their ignorance, do not realize that the government is capturing their children, literally making children *"captives"* who are *"ignorant of law and citizenship rights"* within their pseudo-State in this subordinate federalized system *(i. e. creating a federal citizen <u>with no sovereign State's right's</u> or rights of due process in the courts)*. This enslaving system is designed so that when this child grows up *(lacking knowledge of the truth)* the child will not know the distinction between *State's birthright citizenship rights* and that of the Emancipated Slave, second-class, limited corporate citizenship created by Congressional politicians and supported by their corrupted court systems *(i. e. judges)*. By design, the child grows up, mentally conditioned, deliberately entrapped and indoctrinated to believe that the only true *(American)* citizenship is the second-class *"U.S. federal Washington D.C. citizen."* This is wrong!

Hopefully, we now understand more clearly the true distinctions between the American *"National"* State's right Private Citizen *(sovereign)* and the *U.S. Federal* *("Washington D.C.," "public servant," "14th Amendment emancipated slave," "debtor," "corporate," "created chattel") citizen*, and can proceed into the issue of the Federal Reserve and the Internal Revenue Service systems.

BACKGROUND OF THE FEDERAL RESERVE BANK AND THE INTERNAL REVENUE SERVICE POWER BASE[4]

It is important to understand some background regarding the 1913 creation of the *Federal Reserve Bank Act*, the creation of America's central banking system; and, the Internal Revenue Service (IRS) *(the collection system for the Federal Reserve)* and how they impact us today.

The Federal Reserve is a private, non-judicial *(not subject to the courts)* entity called a *Common-law Pure Trust* held by private and international banking interests. The collection agency for the Federal Reserve was formed on July 11, 1917 as the *"INTERNAL REVENUE TAX AND AUDIT SERVICE, INC."* in New York and then filed in the State of Delaware as a taxing and collection entity **(See EXHIBIT U).** My knowledge shows it is presently titled, *"The Internal Revenue Service (IRS)."* (See Chapter, *"Background of the IRS,"* which follows)

THE COMING TO POWER OF THE FEDERAL RESERVE BANKS

The measure the U.S. Congress used to create the basis for the individual income tax came during urgency to raise funds for the United States participation in World War I, "The War to End All Wars." Because the *Constitution for these united States* prohibited the levying of taxes based on a person's income, some means had to be found to overcome the Constitutional prohibition and to enable such a tax. This situation meant amending the Constitution; thus, the 16th Amendment. Although the 16th Amendment passed both houses of Congress, it fell far short of being ratified by the required two thirds of the States of the Union. However, like several other key digressions (violations) of the Constitutional process (e.g. the 1898 "annexation" of Hawaii) the 16th Amendment was put into effect as if it had been ratified, and the Government began collecting income

---

[4] **Source:** *"The First New Deal"* by Raymond Moley, First Addition, Published in 1966 by Harcourt, Brace & World, Inc. Mr. Moley was personal Advisor to President Franklin D. Roosevelt and was the creator of the 1932 *"Brains Trust"* which advised Roosevelt on policies and speeches assuring his first election. Moley was instrumental in the creation and implementation of Roosevelt's "New Deal" for depression torn America and reviving public confidence impacting the newly reformed banking system under the Federal Reserve (Federal Reserve Act).

tax to fund the war effort. This set the precedence and put the modern-day income tax collection scheme into motion.

In order to deal with the crisis of the Great Depression caused by the "*shaky foundations*" and the collapse of many of thousands of private and State banks under the Central Bank System, President Franklin Delano Roosevelt invoked the *War Powers Act* and the *Trading With the Enemy Act*, giving himself as President, martial law authority to re-organize America's banking system. Americans became Roosevelt's enemy and were treated as such!

In 1933, the U.S. Treasury was bankrupt and no longer able to support the monetary system with the required gold and silver deposits. So Roosevelt, encouraged by his financial advisors, invoked the *Trading With the Enemy Act (Oct. 6, 1917, ch. 106. 40 stat. 41 [Title 50] Trading with the Enemy Act.)* and removed the U.S. currency from the international gold standard (money backed by the real value of gold and silver) and put America on a system based on borrowed money. The currency in circulation was changed from gold and silver certificates to a system of "*script*" currency[5] or "*Federal Reserve Notes*" that looked like lawful currency but in reality wasn't. These Federal Reserve Notes are actually bank notes, a printed piece of paper signifying money that the United States had borrowed from the Federal Reserve (which incidentally is a private banking entity, not the U.S. Treasury).

This concept was the idea of Roosevelt's Secretary of the Treasury, William H. Woodin, who at that time was a Director of the New York Federal Reserve Bank, President of American Car and Foundry Company and a major contributor to FDR's political campaign. He was a direct participant regarding the creation and issuance of Federal Reserve bank notes. Mr. Woodin stated, and I quote:

> *"We don't have to issue script. Those bankers have hypnotized themselves. The Federal Reserve Act permits us (the U.S. Treasury) to print all the money we need".* It won't frighten people. It will be money (script) that looks like money."*
> (Secretary of the Treasury William H. Woodin)
> (Source: "The First New Deal"- Page 172).

---

[5] (**Source, supra**) *"The First New Deal"* by Raymond Moley, First Addition, Published in 1966 by Harcourt, Brace & World, Inc.

This questionable solution created provision for the *"script"* type *"bank note currency"* known as, *"Federal Reserve Notes."* The availability of these so-called *"Federal Reserve Notes"* (in reality *"debt note currency")* renewed a public confidence (through deception) in this new banking system, in President Roosevelt, and in his administration. What the American public did not realize at the time (and most still don't realize today) was that they became guarantors of the debt owed to the Federal Reserve. Like all other debts, it accrues interest and other service charges that has been compounding since the 1930s. The American public (known to the Government as "Taxpayers") through the Income Tax pays for this debt service.

The whole monetary and tax system built by the Roosevelt administration and carried forward since then by the U.S. Federal Government is an enormous fraud that enslaves the American people to a tremendous debt to which they never consented and can never repay. It is the root of the debilitating debtor society that America has become.

In February and March of 1933, both then President Herbert Hoover and President-elect Roosevelt *(Inaugurated on March 4, 1933)* were fully aware of the run on America's banking system taking place in most States. This panic demand for withdrawal of gold deposits was draining the National Reserve Banks and other banks *(5,938 national banks, not including 4,000 State banks)* of their silver and gold reserves. Smaller banks not able to meet the withdrawal demands of their customers were forced to close their doors, causing many States to initiate emergency procedures *(cooling off periods)* called *"Bank Holidays."*

The desire was to create a solution to the problem during these closed periods. All this activity was taking place during and after Roosevelt's election and within the period of thirty days of Roosevelt's First Inauguration. The major right to create a national banking holiday was the responsibility of then President Hoover who had set up the mechanics, but was not desirous of doing so without President-elect Roosevelt's public support prior to his taking Office. This lack of action reflected negatively against the *"lame duck"* administration of President Hoover. Roosevelt would not cooperate and his uncooperativeness only created a much greater problem and panic in the general public and private sectors.

The solution *(the using of script, debt note paper)* was supposed to be a temporary one. President Roosevelt, when asked by a reporter, *"Is it still the desire of the United*

States to go back on the international gold standard?" Roosevelt's answer was, *"Absolutely…"* (Source: Roosevelt, *Public Papers*, II, Page 140). Obviously, he lied (?)

Section 5(b) of the October 6, 1917 <u>Trading with the Enemy Act</u>[6] had been passed during World War 1, and was a very questionable justification for the *"Executive Order"* to close all banks nationally (assuming that the Governors of each State participated) and allowing for the issuance of *"…money (script) that looks like money…"* <u>While president, Hoover refused to implement this</u> *Trading with the Enemy Act* <u>against Americans</u> *(under Section 5[b] supra)* because he <u>questioned the legality and authority of the Act</u> empowering him to exercise such power. He also didn't feel it was necessary to close all the banks just to control withdrawals of gold and currency; hence President Hoover's requirement for President-elect Roosevelt's open public support before his doing anything.

NOTICE: Since its unlawful implementation against Americans by President Roosevelt in 1933 (outlawing gold and taking America off the Gold Standard) the act has never been revoked and every U.S. Congress and President has renewed this infamous Trading with the Enemy Act.

It was Hoover's Attorney General William D. Mitchell who said (but would not put into writing) that there existed a *"…sufficient color of authority to justify issuance of executive order…" (Though questionable)* under which Section 5(b) could be

---

[6] The *(Oct. 6, 1917, ch.106. 40 stat. 41 [Title 50] Trading with the Enemy Act.)* Provision of <u>Section 5(b)</u> *"War Powers Act" of World War 1* was cited as authority: *"That the President may investigate, regulate, or prohibit, under such rules and regulations as he may prescribe, by means of licenses or otherwise, any transactions in foreign exchange, and the export, hoarding, [melting?], or earmarking of gold or silver coin or bullion or currency."* (Misquoted and quoted in part: Author) This provision was created by *"Milton C. Elliott, the first General Counsel of the Federal Reserve Board, (who) had drafted the original Trading with the Enemy Act, and in 1918 he was asked to draft certain amendments. While he was doing so, the late Paul M. Warburg, one of the original members of the Federal Reserve Board, suggested that, if the powers granted under Sec. 5(b) to prohibit the exporting or hoarding of gold, silver or currency, etc. could be made permanent, instead of expiring with the termination of the war, it might be a great help in some future emergency…" (Source: Pages 157, 158 Footnotes, "The First New Deal")* (Author: Warburg reflects a true banker's mentality.)

(Author's Note) Here, we have the instrument, or weapon, used by the bankers against the American public as if they were a *"foreign enemy"* to outlaw gold, silver, or, gold and silver backed currency. The Federal Reserve Board hereby created a means of applying a war time Act <u>created for use against America's war enemies on U.S. soil</u>, to prevent Americans from possessing their rightful gold, silver, or, gold and silver backed currency. This war (enemy) Act is now being applied directly against American Nationals! This definitely was then, and still presently is, unlawful and shameful!

implemented. As mentioned, President Hoover, *supra*, could have also implemented the Bank Holiday but refused to do so without full public support from President-elect Roosevelt. On March 6, 1933 immediately after taking Office, President Roosevelt issued **Proclamation 19 F. R. Bull. 113-114**.

This Bulletin issuance was followed by Roosevelt's implementation of the "*Bank Holiday*" as well as the House of Representatives passage of **H. R. 1491 (The Emergency Banking Act) on March 9th.** The Senate also approved it on March 9th. This required the phased opening of banks in three classes, "*sound,*" "*unsound*" and "*doubtful*" for licensing under the new *"Federal Reserve Bank."* This included both State and National Federal Reserve Banks. It was resolved that the District Federal Reserve Banks would approve which banks were to be licensed within their federal jurisdiction; the Chief National Bank Examiner would recommend to the Comptroller's Office, who would make recommendation to the Treasury. The Secretary of the Treasury would then issue the banking licenses. **The new Federal Reserve Bank now controls America's money.** *(As I understand it, the Federal Reserve Bank is a private, common law Pure Trust of Bankers, et al)*

It is also noteworthy that the *Emergency Banking Act* gave much greater power to the private Federal Reserve Bank System than the previous system. When the majority of banks reopened and when the influx of gold, silver and currency *(gold and silver backed)* was collected and re-deposited by the public and private sectors, the amount was substantial. Public and private confidence was restored. The emergency and panic subsided and Roosevelt then issued his highly controversial **Executive Order,** *"Forbidding the Hoarding of Gold and Gold Certificates"* on April 5, 1933. I believe *(from what my parents told me)* that it was deception, and *"...a slap in the face"* of all Americans.

A new, deficit, script, monetary system was now in place that did not require the backing of the lawful standard of currency *(i.e. gold and silver, which is our real currency or money)*. The United States now has a legal debt note system *(like fake Monopoly money - "script")* based solely on the confidence of the American People and the expectation that the American People will, *through their future earning (the compensation Americans receive from their labor)*, honor and repay the debts incurred and amassed by the these devious and corrupted politicians and bankers.

This required an ignorant, blind confidence by the average American in the system itself. Unfortunately that blind confidence was forthcoming, which enabled the creation of the IRS and empowered it to collect increasingly burdensome taxes to service that infinite, non-payable future debt.

(Author's Note: America is now off the Gold Standard but it is facing real problems in its future because it cannot pay the (bankruptcy) debt in real money [gold and silver] to the Private and International Bankers. The U.S. can only use its federal debt notes [paper, debt obligation "script" with no real value]. Interest would continue to rise on the obligation with no means to fulfill it except with assets, like land and federal slave labor, etc. Since the U.S. has no gold or silver reserves, it must rely on these other "assets.")

This I believe, is when the fairly conservative President Roosevelt found that Americans' confidence and security was in America's People and that if *they* were the security one wouldn't need gold, and with the unlimited printing of deficit monetary notes, he could now "afford" to implement all kinds of liberal back-to-work programs in a totally irresponsible spending spree. Since it was only the federal jurisdiction of the government that went into debt, he also had to find a way to cure that debt by providing security *(i.e. federal "citizens" of Washington D.C.)* for that debt; and, that was found by transferring Americans from their *State's right's 'sovereign'* and National citizenship to that of the federal, *"Washington D.C. public servant," "14ᵗʰ Amendment Emancipated Slave," "created chattel people," "corporate fiction"* citizenship, where, through the fiction name, the national debt could be assigned to each American as income taxes *(a lawful tax meant for a specific group, but improperly and fraudulently applied to everyone)* to satisfy the bankers behind the debt.

The transition of American National Citizens from the National jurisdiction *(of the Republic)* to the Federal jurisdiction (as *"Washington D.C. federal citizens"*) was activated in the late 30's via the federal public works programs *(CCC, WPA, TVA etc.)* and during the early 40's with the outbreak of World War II. With a great number of Americans working in government projects, the war effort or serving directly in the military, all payrolls were simply converted to the ALL CAPITALIZED corporate fiction name and Americans, distracted by the war effort, and being unaware of the fraudulent conversion and transition of their identity and citizenship into the federal jurisdiction, continued on in ignorance.

I believe that by *"custom and usage"*[7] this has become the basis for the Federal Government's present U.C.C. application and usage of the pseudonym *"corporate"* name application to recognize Private Citizen American sovereigns as converted second-class *"Federal U.S. citizens."*

A TEMPORARY FIX HAS BECOME A MAJOR NATIONAL DECEPTION – AUTHOR'S COMMENTARY

The 1933 banking emergency required a temporary fix, but the fix has become a permanent, negative, destructive force. It's like the little white lie that requires another lie to cover it and then more lies to create cover for the continual lies; while functioning in deception and defrauding the American and Hawaiian People.

The *United States Federal Government (Not the National Government of our Republic - Remember* **"America's Pledge of Allegiance?" "... and to the Republic for which we stand...?"***)*, presently has a deficit banking system imposed upon it that is not backed by gold and silver *(substance)*, but by a massive *"promissory note"* *(promises)* for which every *"U.S. Federal citizen"* *(i.e. resident of Washington D.C.)* is a direct guarantor. The U.S. Federal Government *(not our National Government of the American Republic)* now exists in an atmosphere of great, unchecked, overextended, unlimited, deficit spending that is irresponsible and not backed by anything <u>except the future labors of you, its citizens!</u> **ONLY YOU AND I <u>AS AMERICAN NATIONALS</u> CAN FIX IT!** Under the present system of *"Debt Note Currency,"* the federal deficit can never be balanced. America is still bankrupt!

BACKGROUND OF THE IRS

To the best of my knowledge, the present Internal Revenue Service (IRS) was created in New York City on July 11, 1933 under the name, **"INTERNAL REVENUE TAX AND AUDIT SERVICE, INC"** **(See EXHIBIT U).** This was just a few months

---

[7] **Custom and usage.** Uniform Commercial Code (U.C.C. § 1-205 [2[): *"A usage or practice of the people, which, by common adoption and acquiescence, and by long and unvarying habit, has become compulsory, and has acquired the force of law with respect to the Place or subject matter to which it relates. It results from a long series of actions, constantly repeated, which have, by such repetition and by uninterrupted acquiescence, acquired the force of a tacit and common consent. Louisville & N. R. Co. v. Reverman, 243 Ky. 702, 49 S.W.2d 558, 560. An habitual or customary practice, more or less widespread, which prevails within a geographical or sociological area; usage is a course of conduct based on a series of actual occurrences. Corbin-Dykes elect. Co. v. Burr, 18 Ariz. App. 101, 500 P.2d 632 634."*

after Franklin Delano Roosevelt assumed the Office of the Presidency, which happens to be a few months after Roosevelt's creation of the *Federal Reserve Act* and the *Federal Reserve Bank System (run by private bankers)*. The incorporation documents creating the entity were signed by E. Clifton Barton, Helen E'dele Barton and a Laurence Echevarria *(private parties whom I can only assume represented other interests)*. The **"Certificate of Incorporation"** was then filed as an affiliate of the **"Corporate Trust Company of Delaware"** within the *Division of Corporations Agency of the State of Delaware*. The Division of Corporations of the State of Delaware would not provide this Author with any additional information after several phone calls and letters.

It is my awareness and experience that the Internal Revenue System *(IRS)* is an extortion entity that collects *(by whatever means it can)* those assets of the American and Hawaiian People *(with the help of the supporting federal judiciary, which doesn't differentiate or discriminate between U.S. Federal citizens and State's rights American Citizens "sovereigns" of the National Republic)*. This is done to sustain, protect and profit the unscrupulous Federal Reserve and their Trust Beneficiaries *(Bankers)* and the inflationary, deficit congressional spending practices of incompetent politician's of the federal jurisdiction.

Unfortunately, when the federal debt gets heavy enough and the people *(surety[8] and guarantors of the debt)* are all fully mortgaged, borrowed to the hilt and in bondage to insurmountable government debt, unable to pay taxes to sustain this corrupt, ballooning, inflationary federal system and unable to feed and support their loved ones; maybe then we shall see change. The United States Federal Government will again most definitely collapse financially into a much greater *"Great Depression"* or even revolution if this issue is not corrected and immediately resolved. The danger we face as a people is indeed very great and very real. Our American National financial security or insecurity will impact the entire world.

---

[8] **Surety.** *"One who at the request of another, and for the purpose of securing to him a benefit, becomes responsible for the performance by the latter of some act in favor of a third person, or hypothecates property as security therefore. One who undertakes to pay money or to do any other act in event that his principal fails therein. A person who is primarily liable for payment of debt or performance of obligation of another. Branch Banking and Trust Co. v. Creasy, 301 N.C. 44, 269 S.E.2nd 117, 122. One bound with his principal for the payment of a sum of money or for the performance of some duty or promise and who is entitled to be indemnified by some one who ought to have paid or performed if payment or performance be enforced against him. Term includes a guarantor. U.C.C. § 1-201 (40)."* (Source: Black's Law Dictionary, 6th Ed.)

QUESTIONS FOR THE IRS DIRECTOR (2007)

Congress created the "IRS Restructuring and Reform Act" (Public Law 105-206) and establishing the "Internal Revenue Service Oversight Board" (Section 7802 of Title 26), after the 1998 "Abuse Hearings" held before the Senate Finance Committee. Yet, nothing has changed regarding improper and unlawful procedures against those in Hawaii who are documented as both "federal taxpayers" and Hawaiian Nationals. The IRS penalizes documented Hawaiian Nationals that are not "taxpayers" being these Hawaiians are exempt while domiciled upon their own national soil under their own national government and national flag. **Fact:** Your tax collection procedures are lawfully limited and apply only to U.S federal citizens, i.e. "taxpayers." **Question:** Why is this Congressional Act not applied to those of your collection staff here in Hawaii (foreign soil) who consistently abuse and violate the law?

Please, Mr. Director, correct me if I am wrong. Presently, it has been said that the IRS (in 2006) received over *"2.2 Trillion Dollars"* from approximately *"200 million Tax Returns."*[9] This amounts to approximately $11,000.00 per Tax Return *(an average, including business and personal returns combined)*! My understanding is that the money collected is distributed in the following manner. Please clarify and correct the following and respond to the following questions:

1)	Social Security Administration (Whose?)	21%
2)	National Defense (Whose?)	21%
3)	Income Security (Whose?)	13%
4)	Medicare (Whose?)	12%
5)	Health (Whose?)	10%
6)	Net Interest (Whose?)	09%
7)	Education Employment and Social Services (Whose?)	03%
8)	Transportation (Whose?)	03%
9)	Veteran's Benefits and Services (Whose?)	03%
10)	Other Services (Such as what?)	05%

Americans (i.e. federal taxpaying citizens) have a right to know where their tax dollars go! I ask the above questions of *"Whose"* agencies receive these funds because I find it personally very difficult to justify the inappropriate and devious use of the term

---

[9] **Tax Returns.** Source: **"H & R Block,"** as publicized on the **"History Channel"** in April, 2007.

"Department of the Treasury" on the IRS envelopes and letterheads, without any clarification as to *"Whose?"* treasury is being alluded to. Is the *"Department of the Treasury"* referencing your *IRS "Treasury" or that of the Private Federal Reserve?* Is it that of the *United States "National" Government* or *United States "Federal" Government "Department of the Treasury,"* both of which are located in Washington D.C.? Please clarify.

<u>I have many other questions that I would very much appreciate answers to, like</u>:

1. Do IRS employees pay IRS Taxes, or are they exempt? Explain.

2. Are our United States Senators and Congressmen exempt from paying IRS taxes?" Explain.

3. Are our Supreme Court and Federal Court judges exempt from IRS taxes? Explain.

4. Are there others in the Federal Government systems that are also exempt from IRS taxes? Explain.

5. Why do so-called, *"Whistleblowers,"* receive a 10-15% commission of up to $2,000,000 just for being, or acting the same as IRS Tax Collectors? Explain.

6. Do IRS *"Tax Collectors"* also get a 10-15% or higher commission on money collected in the field <u>above their basic salaries</u>? Explain.

7. Do IRS Agents get <u>any kind of commission</u>? From what and how much? Explain.

8. Why is there no law requiring an *"American National Citizen"* or a second-class *"U.S. Federal citizen"* to fill out and file a *"1040 Tax Form?"* Explain.

9. Because the *"1040 Tax Form"* has a signature line for only the citizen filing, not the person or agency receiving, <u>does this mean that this is a voluntary monetary offering</u> (like an IOU?) to the IRS that requires its acceptance to become a legal, lawful or binding contract obligation? Explain.

10. Simply, why does the IRS refuse to give honest, direct answers to questions but <u>penalizes any citizen questioning them</u> when that citizen is just seeking reasonable understanding of questionable IRS practices? Explain.

11. Why does the IRS make false *(these are called "lies")* statements and assessments that it refuses to prove? Explain.

12. Why does the IRS use these false statements and assessments to intimidate and attack undeserving *Private Senior Citizens* and any who question the IRS' unethical practices? Explain.

13. Why does the IRS use *"Notices of Liens" (which are not lawful "Liens" since "Liens" by law are required to be signed by a lawful, competent judge)* to steal money from bank accounts, businesses, *American National Citizens, Hawaiian Senior Citizens* and others undeserving of such destructive, devious and cruel tactics? Explain.

14. Does the IRS use the *"Notice of Lien"* to falsely attach private assets because all federal *"citizens"* are considered to be *"federal corporations"*, *"federal civil servants"* or similar *(i.e. like military)*, and their due process rights waived under that specific ALL CAPITALIZED NAME usage? Explain.

15. Why is the IRS so inconsiderate, merciless *(heartless)* in its methods and ways against average Americans who are basically honest, and not the devious crooks that the IRS treats all of them to be? Explain.

16. Why does the IRS seek to oppress and suppress any American Citizen who does not agree with them? Explain.

17. Why does the IRS presume it **owns** the average American Citizen and treats them as if they are slaves *(not even as "Emancipated Slaves")* without due process or Constitutional rights? Explain.

18. Why is the IRS not forthright, but devious and secretive regarding the exemption from income taxes of *American Nationals* known in their Code as, **"nonresident alien"** *Citizens*? Explain.

19. Could you show me under your **Title 26 USC** and the laws of the *American Union of States* and *America's National Congress* that *American Nationals* are obligated to pay an *"income tax?"* Explain.

20. Could you show me the law that gives you and your agency a right to change my lawful American, proper English-language spelled birth name *(that of a "State's birthright, American National")* to a legal fiction *(the federal owned ALL CAPITALIZED NAME "citizen")* which is a fraudulent conversion of my proper English-standard birth name and my jurisdictional rights at law, exercised without my explicit, written consent? Explain.

21. Why is there a *"disclaimer"* in the **Title 26 United States Code (IRS Code) in Section 7806. Construction of Title, Paragraphs (a) and (b)?** Doesn't this *"disclaimer"* imply that the IRS Code is not *"Positive law?"* Explain.

22. If *Title 26 of the U.S. Code* is not *"Positive law,"* doesn't this mean that the IRS Code is only suggestion? Explain.

23. Was **Title 26 USC** ever read into the *"Congressional Record"* of the *"National Congress"* to make it *"Positive law?"* *(As an "American National,"*

I am aware that I am bound to the honoring of "Positive law", not suggestion!) Explain.

24. Am I, as an *"American National"* (not being a federal *"citizen"* and <u>having no contract, written or implied, with the IRS or federal jurisdiction</u>), an American *"sovereign"* domiciled within the *"American Republic"* and its *"Union of States,"* (not a resident of Washington D.C.), and functioning under the American National; *"48 Star"* American Flag of the Republic; using only my lawfully given English-language birth name *(as differentiated from that of the ALL CAPITALIZED legal fiction name owned by the U.S. Federal Government)*; while functioning within my inherent birth rights *(lawfully identified by my "Seal" i.e. written signature – <u>not by a Social Security Number</u>)*; under my *"sovereign"* Birth State *"common-law"* Citizenship *(not a Washington D.C. resident or within that jurisdiction)*; <u>exempt from U.S. Federal Income Taxes</u>?????? I will answer this last question for you.... "You bet I am!"

AN IRS COLLECTION AGAINST HAWAIIAN NATIONALS LIVING ON HAWAIIAN CROWN LAND

One of the most unnecessary, despicable and criminal IRS efforts to create income for their agency and possible commissions for their IRS Collection Agents comes out of the IRS Office located at 300 Ala Moana Boulevard (RO GROUP 35, M/S H212), Honolulu, Hawaii.

Hawaiian National George Haui'onalani Victor (Born July 11, 1929, now deceased), had retired from this work from the City and County of Honolulu as a heavy equipment operator, and his wife, Lily Pauliaokekomohana Kawelo Victor, also a Hawaiian National, had retired from the State of Hawaii Department of Education, as a cook. Both were on fixed pensions and without any other source of sustenance. Their domicile is on land documented as: *"Heirs of Royal Patent of Kuleana Land; Royal Patent No. 2926; Kuleana Helu No. 6105; Land Commission Awards Survey No. 172-1; Nakane'elua Land Grant; Kingdom of Hawaii, de jure."*

The Victor's problem started in December of 1995, just after retirement, with a claim by the IRS for $4,774.00. The knowledge of such supposed tax was claimed by the IRS to be *"...from your bank, your employer or other sources."* The Victors were shocked at a claim of supposed taxable income that of which they had never received knowledge. They had not sold any personal items in the tens of thousands of dollars; or, received any money from any source that would have justified or given cause to be flagged as a bank account tax source of information for that year. They were now on retirement income and there was no *"employer"* source for income for either party that could be determined. <u>When they asked the IRS for confirmation of the "other source" that was claimed as IRS justification for the additional IRS tax claim, they were fined, penalized for being *"tax protestors"* and ignored.</u>

The IRS claim is based upon a questionable 1995 tax filing which seemingly permitted the duplication of Social Security Retirement Benefits and what appears to this Author to possibly be a preparation error by the Tax Preparer. When asked by the Victors, the IRS did not respond to the basis of their tax claim, nor could the Victors find any IRS response addressing the new claim. The IRS simply continued their assumption that there was no error and no needed justification for the Victors' voicing a legitimate concern that the IRS claim was not justifiable.

J. R. Reed, Chief, Automated Collection Branch, notifying of an "Intent to Levy" in the amount of $6,404.70 on December 9, 1998, started IRS collection actions. Others acting in behalf of the IRS were Deborah S. Decker, Director, Ogden Service Center; Paul Beene, District Director, Pacific-North-west District (via letter dated April 27, 1998); Donald Williams, Representative of the Pacific-Northwest District Director; a Regina Duffy, Technical Staff (Letter to Congresswoman Patsy T. Mink on December 31, 1995).

They took action against two very loving, honest, trusting, frustrated and retired Hawaiian Nationals in their late seventies. Other IRS Agents and parties to this action are: Gwen Kai, Employee I. D. No. 99-00429 (or is it the other I. D. used, 99-20022?), Marilyn Williams and Donald Williams of Taxpayer Advocate – Hawaii (I. D. No. 99-00028, letter of August 22, 2002 in response to a letter from Senator Daniel K. Inouye dated August 14, 2002. In his letter to Senator Inouye, William's states the following:

"The Fourteenth Amendment of the United States Constitution defines the basis for United States citizenship, stating that "[a]ll (NOTE: Deliberate error known as "word art" – Author) persons born or naturalized in the United States, and subject to the jurisdiction thereof, are citizens of the United States and of the State wherein they reside. The Fourteenth Amendment therefore established simultaneous state and federal citizenship."

(AUTHOR'S NOTE: Please take notice that Williams in his above statement does not address "American National" or "Hawaiian National" Citizens, whose standings and rights are superior to the Article 1, Section 8 "federal <u>c</u>itizen." American Nationals (defined, as "non-resident aliens" in Title 26 of the IRS Tax Code; and, the documented and lawful Hawaiian Nationals [foreigners to the U.S. federal state of the forum jurisdiction] are exempt from IRS taxation as per the Organic [Territorial] Act of 1900. The latter two "National" citizenships, by law, are exempt from U.S. Federal Income Tax.)

Of repetitive, but great interest here is the fact that the United States under its own jurisdictional law, specifically **United States Code, Title 28, § 91**, affirms that it does not possess the lands of the Hawaiian Archipelago by virtue of its own legal description of jurisdiction as described in its undefined (un-clarified and obscure) "Hawaii" jurisdictional statement. That being the case, the lands are still Hawaiian National lands and its Citizen's, Hawaiian Nationals except for those foreign U.S. federal <u>c</u>itizens (taxpayers) unlawfully living on Hawaiian National Lands.

The Victor's are born to the land, they are by virtue of their births, Hawaiian Nationals, and by law, cannot be forced to be U.S. *"federal <u>c</u>itizens"* against their will as is falsely claimed and exercised by the IRS. To affirm this fact, when we look at the State of Hawaii Constitution, we find obvious fraud by the United States Government in that the State of Hawaii does not possess any land... and, the President of the United States, under the Constitution of the United States, cannot create (by a declaration) a *"State of the Union"* nor can the President add stars to the Positive Law 48 Star American Flag as affirmed by **Title 4 USC § 1!** Therefore, how can the Victors be United States *"<u>c</u>itizens"* when in fact they steadfastly claimed, documented and filed their Hawaiian National Citizenship under the "living" Hawaiian Kingdom laws of the Hawaiian Archipelago, which even United State's law admits is still foreign land! Someone's lying here and the IRS is overextending its authority!

Upon receipt of this questionable claim for taxable income that was never received, nor substantiated in any way to the Victors by the IRS, with what appears to be an incorrect 1995 tax year filing as its basis, the Victors contacted Senator Inouye and Senator Akaka asking for assistance. They asked Congresswoman Patsy Mink (now deceased) and Congressman Neil Abercrombie also for assistance. The only impacting response was from Congresswoman Patsy Mink (Letter of July 14, 1998) reflecting incorrect and inaccurate law, jurisdiction, citizenship and even <u>the non-ratified Sixteenth</u>

Amendment to the U.S. Constitution as a justification for IRS actions against the Victors. The result was that the Victors were left with no relief in the form of intervention from U.S. politicians from Hawaii.

After approximately two years of no communication, the Victors were again threatened in 2002 by the IRS for the initial $6,404.70 by a false and modified *"Notice of Lien" (not a "Perfected Lien" with the signature of a judge of a court of record, as required by law)* and the IRS seized the retirement savings and income of George Victor, who at the time was suffering from terminal cancer, leaving the Victors in dire financial hardship. The Victors since the 1995 frustration had refused to file Form 1040's because of what they felt was a fraud being perpetrated upon them by the IRS and because they found that there was no protection or options left open to them except their rights as Hawaiian Nationals.

The result of the Victor's failure to file Form 1040's incurred additional assessments and penalties by the IRS against the Victors. The IRS on their own proceeded to file Form 1040's for the Victors for the years 2000, 2001, 2002 and 2003, without their signatures, approval or facts of law being met. The new penalties and assessments based upon these fabricated additional filings of Form 1040's now amount to an additional $11,091.02 as of July 19, 2007. Another false and modified *"Notice of Lien"* was then filed on August 8, 2007 by Gwen Kai of the IRS in Honolulu against Lily Victor, age 78, and by now a widow.

At the present time, Lily Victor is living in a house without a roof (**covered only with tarps See Photo EXHIBIT V**). She had been setting aside her pension checks for ten years so she could put a proper roof on her single-wall leaking home. The IRS has now seized that money. Now she can no longer afford to cover her house with a roof or even protect her belongings in a manner acceptable to any other deserving family or Citizen. She is being rendered destitute by corrupt IRS actions, sustained by Hawaii's politicians who do not even know the law or ignore the law (or both) as it pertains to Hawaii and its Hawaiian National Citizens.

In the latest *"Notice of Lien"* claim by the IRS, the IRS exceeded the proper amount that could be seized even under a lawful claim, by seizing over $15,000. They seized $11,091 dollars from **Bank of Hawaii** (plus institutional charges for handling the false IRS seizure) and another $4,300 plus dollars from **HawaiiUSA Federal Credit Union- Honolulu** (plus institutional charges for handling the false IRS seizure). This total exceeds by thousands of dollars what was claimed by the IRS and far above what could and should have been seized by law IF this was in fact a proper and rightful claim, which is wasn't!

Both financial institutions, the Bank of Hawaii and the HawaiiUSA Federal Credit Union, participated collusively in this criminal fraud after being noticed that the claim by the IRS was fraudulent as affirmed by letter sent by U.S. Certified Mail to both institutions on August 28, 2007 **(See EXHIBIT W)**. They were notified that Lily Victor was not **(as affirmed by their own Title 26, Section 6331 [a])** a *"person"* subject to seizure being she was not *"...any officer, employee, or elected official, of the United States, the District of Columbia, or any agency or instrumentality of the United States of the District of Columbia..."* as required for such a seizure. The basis for the fraudulent and criminal IRS claim against this innocent, unprotected widow has proceeded without concern or compassion for the reality, consequences or impact upon her, and most definitely without respect for law.

Whatever happened to those politicians who are supposed to represent and protect the people? Do they pay income taxes? I don't think so. Whatever happened to the judges in our courts of record that are supposed to function with integrity and honesty? As interpreters and sustainers of the law they are supposed to honor, respect and distinguish between the types of citizenship when it comes to who is rightfully under their laws and who is not obligated to pay income taxes (*i.e. American National Citizen [a Private Person] or U.S. Federal citizen [a Debtor or Bond Servant]; a Hawaiian National Citizen [a foreign Citizen to the U.S. living on his or her own land,] or, the U.S. Federal citizen of Hawaiian birth [just another debtor or bond servant who gave his Hawaiian birthright away])?* It seems like these judges and politicians are all getting a free ride at the expense poor little widows like Lily Victor who suffer for these public servants and political wonder's indifference and sins. It is time for change.

BACK TO OUR GREAT AMERICAN NATION
(Speaking as an American to other Americans and captured Americans)

America is a great nation of very generous and wonderful People, a nation founded on Judeo-Christian values and principles. Unfortunately much of that has been judicially stripped away and corrupted.

The present oppressive and deviously devised income tax, its collection procedures, and the pressures unlawfully placed upon our *"State's Rights Citizens" (i.e. American National "sovereigns"),* was never the intent of our nation's founders. Politicians and judges, who condone and perpetuate this corruption, <u>need to be immediately removed from office</u> and prosecuted to stop the corrupt, abusive IRS practices. I address those who do not protect us when the IRS comes against our Citizens with their unethical practices of unlawful and falsified claims of debt. Therefore, we should hold them accountable for their unlawful acts *(politicians, attorneys, judges, IRS agents and personnel)* and not protect or sustain or reward or compensate them for their ineptness, cowardice and corruption.

The judges of our shameful U.S. <u>federal</u> judiciary system *(and State courts)* ignore the law and condone abuse by the IRS against the very Citizens they are under oath to protect and who pay their salaries. Perhaps these judges who ignore our laws, and politicians who represent us, are immoral, bought off, lack backbone, are afraid *(cowards)*, or just do not believe in who we are as a free *(well, we used to be)*, American People. Maybe they make money and benefits on the sly… maybe they just, not knowing Our God, do not know right from wrong, otherwise, they surely would honor justice and protect us *(this is presumption on my part).*

It's quite obvious they lack the integrity, character, truthfulness and strength necessary to stand up righteously against the evil and oppressive actions of the IRS, which is a deadly destructive element nationally, and a cancer created and supported by bankers.

These judges, like the politicians, no longer represent *"We, the People…"* but themselves and a corrupted federal government, while giving us lip service and refusing to reign in not just the IRS, et al, but their own abusive U.S. Justice Department. They assume that we are their enemy, just like President Roosevelt *(and all Presidents since)* using the *War Powers Act* against Americans. Maybe it's because they do not honor or cannot honor, <u>but dishonor the lawful</u> **48 Star Flag of the American Republic** (Positive Law) while preferring to function under the lesser jurisdiction, military federal flag of 50 stars.

America's Elected Politicians

Americans must also replace inept politicians that exercise and encourage irresponsible and unlimited state and federal spending *(i.e. the "Pork Barrel Boys")*. These politicians, overtaxing all Americans, assure us of the eventual complete and total loss of our confidence in government that can only result in a complete monetary collapse and the destruction of our American way of life. Americans cannot continue to be ignorant slaves of a corrupted *United States Federal Government (Which is not the "National" Government)*. Theirs is a programmed system of human bondage, loss of our rights and freedoms as a People to sustain a false and corrupt economy of corrupt and devious, self-serving public servants.

These judges, attorneys, politicians, IRS agents and civil personnel should and must be held accountable, even jailed.

HELPFUL DEFINITIONS AND CLARIFICATIONS - For purpose of a better understanding.

Custom and usage. (U.C.C. § 1-205 [2]): *"A usage or practice of the people, which, by common adoption and acquiescence, and by long and unvarying habit, has become compulsory, and has acquired the force of law with respect to the Place or subject matter to which it relates. It results from a long series of actions, constantly repeated, which have, by such repetition and by uninterrupted acquiescence, acquired the force of a tacit and common consent…"*

Surety. *"One who at the request of another, and for the purpose of securing to him a benefit, becomes responsible for the performance by the latter of some act in favor of a third person, or hypothecates property as security therefore. One who undertakes to pay money or to do any other act in event that his principal fails therein. A person who is primarily liable for payment of debt or performance of obligation of another. Branch Banking and Trust Co. v. Creasy, 301 N.C. 44, 269 S.E.2nd 117, 122. One bound with his principal for the payment of a sum of money or for the performance of some duty or promise and who is entitled to be indemnified by some one who ought to have paid or performed if payment or performance be enforced against him. Term includes a guarantor."* U.C.C. § 1-201 (40). (Source: Black's Law Dictionary, 6th Ed.)

Constructive Fraud. *"Exists where conduct, though not actually fraudulent, has all actual consequences and all legal effects of actual fraud. Afair Inc. v. Shaeffer, 232 Cal. App. 2d 513, 42 Cal. Reptr. 883, 886. Breach of legal or equitable duty which, irrespective of moral guild, is declared by law to be fraudulent because of its tendency to deceive others or violate confidence. Daves v. Lawyers Sur. Corp., Tex. Civ. App., 459 S.W. 2d 655, 657."* (Source: Black's Law Dict. 6th Ed.

Birth name. The proper spelling of one's name in the language of that nation as bestowed or given him or her by the natural parents as established by time, usage, custom and tradition through the ages in contrast with that of the government created legal fiction, ALL CAPITALIZED federal name.

Common-law. *"As distinguished from statutory law created by the enactment of legislatures, the common law comprises the body of those principles and rules of action, relating to the government and security of persons and property, which derive their authority solely from usages and customs of immemorial antiquity, or from the judgments and decrees of the courts recognizing, affirming, and enforcing such usages and customs; and, in this sense, particularly the ancient unwritten law of England. In general, it is a body of law that develops and derives through judicial decisions, as distinguished from legislative enactments. The "common law" is all the statutory and case law background of England and the American colonies before the American Revolution. People v. Rehman, 253 C.A. 2d 119, 61 Cal. Rptr. 65, 85. It consists of those principles, usage and rules of action applicable to government and security of persons and property, which do not rest for their authority upon any express and positive declaration of the will of the legislature. Bishop v. U.S., D.C. Tex., 334 F. Supp. 415, 418."*

"As distinguished from ecclesiastical law, it is the system of jurisprudence administered by the purely secular tribunals."

Calif. Civil Code, § 22.2, provides that the *"common law of England, so far as it is not repugnant to or inconsistent with the Constitution of the United States, or the Constitution or laws of this State, is the rule of decision in all the courts of this State."*

"In a broad sense, "common law" may designate all that part of the positive law, juristic theory, and ancient custom of any state or nation, which is of general and universal application, thus marking off special or local rules or customs... (Source: Black's Law Dict. 6th Ed.)"

(Author's Insert: National Hawaiian Kingdom common law, is positive law, as stated in the National Sessions Laws of 1892, Chapter LVII, Section 5, and I quote: "The common law of England as ascertained by English and American decisions is hereby declared to be the common law of the Hawai'ian Islands in all cases, except as otherwise provided by the Hawai'ian Constitution or laws...")

Chapter 10

Restoring Hawaiian Citizenship

RESTORING HAWAIIANS TO THEIR PROPER NATIONAL CITIZENSHIP

Like the people of the United States, all but a few Hawaiians eventually submitted to being made into second-class U.S. Federal citizens. This was accomplished by the deceptive practice of concealing the truth from the people of U.S. occupied Hawaii and making it appear that U.S. Federal citizenship was the only option available.

The *Organic Act of 1900*, imposed the governing mechanism for the newly "annexed" *Territory of Hawaii*, and utilized a blanket change of citizenship by stating that, because the Republic of Hawaii became a supposed "territory" of the United States, all Republic of Hawaii citizens were henceforth treated as Federal United States citizens.

The truth is during its four-year existence; relatively few people were actually citizens of the Republic of Hawaii because the vast majority of the population had been vehemently opposed to the illegal overthrow, the illegal Republic and illegal annexation. The conspirator/leaders, who controlled the commerce and government of the Republic of Hawaii with force of arms, could not allow the general suffrage required of a democratic form of government because their rebel government would have been quickly voted out.

Eventually, through 60 years of coercion by the police/military occupation power of the U.S.; through the distortion of Hawaii's history, involvement in two World Wars as supposed Americans, persistent (U.S.) patriotic propaganda, intense cultural indoctrination by the American educational system, and abject economic subjugation, the Hawaiian people living in the *Territory of Hawaii* came to regard and identify themselves as *State of Hawaii, Federal U.S. citizens.*

The Statehood Act of 1959 then "transferred" citizenship from the *Territory of Hawaii* into the *State of Hawaii,* and the U.S. indoctrination and assimilation of Hawaiians increased exponentially, overwhelming and almost obliterating any notion of Hawaii being anything other than the 50th State of the U.S. But over the past 30 years, to those honestly searching the historical and legal record, it grew apparent that the Federal U.S. Government was perpetrating a terrible fraud on the People of Hawaii.

Even though the *de facto Territorial* and *State of Hawaii citizenships* (both are forms of *Federal U.S. citizenship*) were imposed fraudulently through the mechanisms of the *Federal U.S. Government,* it is *presumed* that *consent* was given by the people when they affixed their lawful seals (signatures) to the many forms and documents (voter registration, tax returns, applications for social security, passports, drivers licenses, and so forth) acknowledging and accepting the imposed *ALL CAPITALIZED* Federal U.S. citizenship identity and its so-called "privileges."

However, this fraud can be reversed. There are fundamental common laws that invalidate contracts attained by fraud, and because these *consents* to *State of Hawaii, Federal U.S. citizenship* were exacted through fraud, the People of Hawaii have the lawful right to utilize positive procedures to lawfully rescind and annul the fraudulent *citizenship* of the *State of Hawaii* and *Federal U.S.* Furthermore, because in a free society *citizenship* is a matter of choice, the People of Hawaii have the right to lawfully reclaim their proper identities as Hawaiian Private Citizens (a.k.a. Hawaiian Nationals).

FALSIFYING AND CHANGING OF HAWAIIAN'S BIRTH NAMES

Since the passage of pseudo statehood, the *Puppet State of Hawaii Government* has been registering the names on the birth certificates of newborn children in ALL CAPITALIZED letters. This is in keeping with the system of the *Federal U.S. Government. (Chapter 4: Birth names and Birthrights).*

This improper change in the spelling of the birth name automatically removes from the child, what is rightfully his/her Hawaiian National birthright. It removes the child from the protection of the common-law of the Hawaiian Kingdom, and makes the child into chattel, ultimately responsible for U.S. debt and taxes attached to that child's fictitious corporate U.S. name. Because it looks and sounds like the child's name, and they don't know the significance of the legal nuances, unsuspecting parents sign off on the ALL CAPITALIZED name and subject their child to the imposed identity.

Thus, when a person answers affirmatively to that ALL CAPITALIZED name, or uses it in everyday transactions, he affirms that he is that fiction and he becomes the guarantor of the U.S.' debts and accepts the enslaving obligations imposed upon that name. A person, who doesn't know the difference, loses. This is called in law, *"constructive fraud"* or *"fraud by conversion"* because it is a deliberate, planned deception on a grand criminal scale to steal people's birthrights, citizenships and freedoms (i.e. identity theft by constructive fraud).

We, the People of Hawaii, by surrendering to a foreign jurisdiction and its imposed foreign statutory law, also abandon our Hawaiian Kingdom National Flag and our National "common-law," inalienable rights, even while domiciled on our own National birth soil. Without knowing (by ignorance) we become captured by the controlling foreign law; are assigned and issued a Social Security Number with its accompanying (foreign) tax debt (federal U.S. bankruptcy). Instead of being free, we become a *"Washington D.C.," "foreign," "second-class," "immigration status"* U.S. Federal *"citizen"* on our own soil, owned by bankers. As stated, we have in fact by acceptance, contracted to use their pseudonym name, thus becoming *by an implied power of attorney*, legally captured; transferring our citizenship to a foreign jurisdiction of law from that of our birth!

Hawaiians need to unite to restore their "living" National Government without interference from the de facto *Puppet State of Hawaii* and *Federal United States Government*.

So, who is a Hawaiian? Simple answer: *1) All who are born in the Hawaiian Islands regardless of blood, race or ethnicity; 2) All those naturalized under Hawaiian Kingdom National law; and, 3) All those born anywhere else in the world and of Hawaiian (by birth or naturalized) parentage.*

TYPES OF HAWAIIAN CITIZENSHIP

There are five (5) types of Hawaiian Kingdom Citizens under Hawaiian Kingdom Law *(which is, Hawaiian National common-law[1])*. These five are as follows:

---

[1] **The Hawaiian Kingdom National "common-law."** Hawaiian Kingdom National common-law is clarified under the **National Sessions Laws of 1892**, more specifically, **Chapter LVII, § 5.** It is quoted as follows*: "The common-law of England as ascertained by English and American decisions is hereby declared to be the common-law of the Hawaiian Islands in all cases, except as otherwise provided by the Hawaiian Constitution or laws…"*

1. <u>Hawaiian aboriginals</u>. <u>This Hawaiian National citizenship includes all those Hawaiians of Hawaiian bloodline (koko)</u>. *(kanaka maoli, "native Hawaiians" of the koko [blood])* born anywhere in the archipelago or in the world. These are the original or earliest known, indigenous people of Hawaii. Having Native Hawaiian blood is important because of certain provisions for them regarding land tenure and stewardship.

2. <u>Hawaiians born in Hawaii (regardless of ethnic heritage)</u>. This pertains to all ethnic heritages such as the Portuguese, Italian, French, German, English, Chinese, Japanese, Filipino, etc. who were lawful citizens of the Hawaiian Kingdom *preceding* the overthrow of 1893 as well as all those presently born within the boundaries or jurisdiction of the Hawaiian Islands.

3. <u>Hawaiians born abroad to a parent who is a Hawaiian National</u>. These children have a choice of claiming their Hawaiian Citizenship through their parent's Hawaiian Nationality, as Hawaiians *(of the parent's country of birth)*. Such a decision is normally made at or after the legal age of consent and affirmed under oath in a Hawaiian Kingdom National Circuit Court of record.

4. <u>Naturalized Hawaiians</u> *(Foreign citizens who willingly give up their foreign citizenship to become Hawaiian National Subjects/Citizens)* This foreign immigrant, after having been resident in Hawaii for at least three years, is "naturalized" by the taking of an oath accepting the responsibilities of citizenship in the Hawaiian Kingdom. Naturalization requires the person to abandon their former foreign country citizenship.

5. <u>Denizen Hawaiians.</u> (Dual Citizenship) These are foreign citizens, who, are deemed to provide a particular service to the Government of Hawaii; and after being domiciled three years in the Nation, attest under lawful oath to uphold the Monarchy, Constitution and laws of the Hawaiian Nation. They are not required to give up their foreign citizenship, so enjoy <u>a form of *"Dual Citizenship*."</u>

<u>Citizenship begins with birthrights i.e. where you were born!</u> Today, most people who were born in Hawaii think they were born within the United States, when they were actually born in *The Hawaiian Islands (Ko Hawaii Pae Aina)*.

APPLICATION FOR HAWAIIAN NATIONAL CITIZENSHIP:

Restoration of Hawaiian's National People begins with knowledge and understanding of truth; and returning to Hawaiian National citizenship. Restoring the sovereign nation, *the Hawaiian Kingdom,* begins with Hawaiians acting wisely, and intelligently, to *restore their birthrights, proper birth names* and *citizenship* under their *Hawaiian Kingdom National Government "common-law"* wherein the rights, and the social and political structures are preserved to a lawful people and nation.

Because of the complications created by the imposition of the fraudulent citizenships in *Puppet State of Hawaii* and *Federal U.S.*, the People of Hawaii desiring Hawaiian National citizenship have to take positive action to sever their former adhesions to the U.S. governing system and clearly assert their identities as Hawaiian Citizens (a.k.a. Hawaiian Nationals).

Those desiring citizenship in the **Hawaiian Kingdom** need to fill out and submit the attached **Form #C-77, Application for Citizenship.**

To qualify for citizenship you must present proof that you: **a)** were born to the Hawaiian Islands, OR, **b)** have been domiciled in the Hawaiian Islands for at least three years, OR, **c)** are able to confirm that at least one of your of parents was born to the Hawaiian Islands OR, d) at least one of your parents is/was a Hawaiian National (born or naturalized).

(ATTACHED ARE THE FIRST TWO PAGES OF THE CITIZENSHIP APPLICATION FORM – See EXHIBIT X)

Mail to:

> Office of the Ministry of the Finance
> The Hawaiian Kingdom
> General Delivery (Box 62107)
> Manoa Station, Island of Oahu
> The Hawaiian Islands

TO PROCESS (If you have met the above qualifications): Include a $35.00 Postal Money Order processing fee and two (2) Passport Photos. Make out the Postal Money Order to "Minister of Finance" and retain your receipt.

Also include photocopies of your driver's license and birth certificate, OR, your State I.D. and birth certificate; OR, your Birth certificate and a copy of your Passport *(inside pages)* showing your photo and signature therein. If you do not possess a driver's license or State of Hawaii I.D., submit your birth certificate with a notarized affidavit signed by two witnesses, affirming your proper identity.

Chapter 11

RESTORING KE AUPUNI

THE HAWAIIAN KINGDOM STILL EXISTS

The *Hawaiian Kingdom National Government (Ke Aupuni O Hawaii)* is the lawful government for the archipelago and sovereign nation known as *The Hawaiian Islands (Ko Hawaii Pae Aina)*. The Hawaiian Islands continues to exist as a sovereign nation despite the 1893 unlawful seizure of Hawaii by a treasonous group of white businessmen (aided by the U.S. military); and despite the more than a century-long illegal occupation by the United States of America.

The de jure *Hawaiian Kingdom* is lawfully documented as having served proper, lawful written notices on the *Federal United States Government* of its 1996 reactivation. The Minister of Foreign Affairs also served written notice upon the Government of the United States in August of 2003, and previous to that, on its President, Attorney General and Secretary of State by proper declaration asserting the Hawaiian Nation's de juré (lawful) right to exist, and as further affirmed by United States Criminal Code (USCrC) Title 18 Section 11[1] *(See Footnote below and Definitions and Clarifications on Pages 168 through 170, following.).* The "living" Hawaiian Kingdom Constitution, Civil, Penal and Sessions Laws that support the separated and distinct Hawaiian Kingdom National Citizens bind Ke Aupuni O Hawaii Nei.

BRIEF BACKGROUND

King Kamehameha the Great, through a campaign of conquest and statesmanship, united the islands in 1795 as an absolute monarch. In 1810 he formally proclaimed the

---

[1] Title 18, U. S. Criminal Code, Chapter 1, General Provisions, Section 11. "Foreign Government defined," is as follows: The term 'foreign government,' as used in this title except in section 112, 878, 970, 1116, and 1201 includes any government, faction, or body of insurgents within a country with which the United States is at peace, irrespective of recognition by the United States (June 25, 1948, c. 645, 62 Stat. 686; Oct. 8, 1976, Pub. L. 94-467, § 11, 90 Stat. 2001) (Source: 1999Ed., Federal Criminal Code and Rules)" (Bold emphasis by Author). See, "Definition of words used in Title 18 § 11, USCr.C" on Pages 168-170, following.

establishment the Hawaiian Kingdom Government as an Absolute Monarchy. It continued as such until 1840 when, during Hawaii's transformation to Christianity, King Kamehameha III, promulgated a *Constitution for the Hawaiian Islands.*

The adoption of the Constitution changed Hawaii's civil government from an Absolute Monarchy into that of a Constitutional Monarchy. The Constitution also acknowledges *"the laws of Jehovah God"* (Biblical Law) as the supreme authority to which all the laws of Hawaii are to conform. The Kingdom adopted the English and American common law as the format for the Hawaiian judicial system. The Hawaiian national Constitution provides for a Legislative Branch, a Judicial Branch and an Executive Branch with distinct separation of powers and appropriate checks and balances.

Under the Constitution, the bi-cameral Legislature (House of Representatives and House of Nobles) created, adopted and periodically revised the laws of the land, embodied in the Organic Laws, Sessions Laws, Civil Codes and Penal Codes, etc., for the Hawaiian Kingdom.

Under the Constitution, the apex of the judicial system is the *Supreme Court for the Hawaiian Islands* with its Chief Justice and Associate Justices. The lesser courts are the Circuit and District or Police (also called, Justice) Courts, along with magistrates, the Attorney General's Office, Marshal, deputies and other law enforcement personnel.

REVIVAL OF THE HAWAIIAN KINGDOM GOVERNMENT

Lawful Reactivation

The *Hawaiian Kingdom National Government* lay in a state of dormancy (alive, but asleep) for a hundred years, until the 1993 formal apology by the United States admitting their unlawful role in the 1893 overthrow. The apology triggered activity by various *Hawaiian Nationals* (a.k.a. *Private Citizens* or *Subjects*) and Hawaiian patriotic entities to initiate lawful filings and notices declaring the reactivation of the Hawaiian Kingdom, and began efforts to reassert the independent, self-governing Hawaiian National Government. Various potential monarchs, privy councils and other components of governing entities arose, including what is now known as *Ke Aupuni O Hawaii.* This sovereign *Hawaiian Kingdom National Government* was reactivated with proper foundation of Kingdom common-law, legal public notices, announcements, and filings from 1994 through 1996.

Unlike the other Hawaiian entities, *Ke Aupuni O Hawaii*, in October 1996, reactivated the Supreme Court for the Hawaiian Islands, thus reactivating the *National Judicial System of the Kingdom Government* as affirmed under the *1892 Revision of the Judiciary, An Act of the Sessions* under Hawaiian National "*common-law.*" Thus, the mechanism and authority to administrate and execute the laws of Hawaii's National Government was revived, providing the proper authority upon which the Hawaiian Kingdom and its people could again function as a lawful national society.

Ke Aupuni O Hawaii, the lawful Government of Hawaii, unlike other Hawaiian claimants, operates under Biblical authority ("*the laws of Jehovah God*"). It also is the sole entity possessing Courts that function under de juré judicial authority in accordance with and subject to, the Constitution and civil and penal laws of the Hawaiian Kingdom.

The reactivated Government of the Hawaiian Kingdom, functions in exigency[2] (emergency), as closely as possible in accordance to the Hawaiian Kingdom Constitution and Laws that existed prior to the 1893 illegal seizure of Hawaii. Despite the occupying presence of the United States, these laws of the Hawaiian Kingdom and Nation are still alive today. Over the past decade, notifications were duly served upon the various agencies of the foreign occupying, *de facto* governing entities, the general public and the international community, that the *National Government of the Hawaiian Kingdom, Ke Aupuni O Hawaii*, is *de juré* (lawful) and functioning under the Constitution and laws of the Hawaiian Kingdom... a nation at peace with all nations. In addition, this *Hawaiian Kingdom National Government* can affirm that the numerous treaties, covenants and conventions enacted between the Hawaiian Nation and foreign nations were never abrogated, and thus, remain valid and in force.

Executive Branch – Cabinet Council Activated

The initial part of government reactivated by the Hawaiian People was the **Cabinet Council** constituting of the Offices of the **Ministry of the Interior**; the

---

[2] **Exigency.** "n. 1. exigent state or character, urgency. 2. usually exigencies. the need, demand or requirement intrinsic to a circumstance, condition, etc.; the exigencies of city life. 3. a case or situation that demands prompt action or remedy; emergency: He promised help in any exigency... crisis, contingency, plight, strait, predicament, fix, pinch." (Source: Webster's Encyclopedic Unabridged Dictionary – 2001)

Ministry of Finance; the **Ministry of Foreign Affairs** and the **Attorney General**. According to the Constitution, in the event of a vacancy (as has existed over the past 115 years) of the seat of the Monarch (the Chief Executive and Head of State), the Cabinet Council acts as the **Regent of State**, until such time that the vacancy can be lawfully filled.

All who presently serve in government offices, through *pro tempore* are Hawaiian National Citizens, under proper, lawful Oaths of Office, and under the binding authority of the *Constitution for the Hawaiian Islands*, and the national statutory laws. There are also current, lawfully appointed deputies and agency personnel. The Monarch may also form a broader advisory group called the Privy Council of State, which includes, ex officio, the Members of the Cabinet Council. At the present time, this government functions in a lawful state of *interregnum*.[3] Other ministry office may be added at the discretion of the Monarch and with legislative approval.

Judicial Branch – *Supreme Court for the Hawaiian Islands* Activated

The *Supreme Court for the Hawaiian Islands*, the judicial branch of the Hawaiian National government was formally reactivated in October of 1996 (supra) with a Chief Justice of the Court appointed and sworn into Office. With the Supreme Court for the Hawaiian Islands reactivated as the authentic and proper court of jurisdiction for the archipelago, all the laws of the Kingdom Nation once again apply within that jurisdiction. The Office of the Chief Justice has been continuously maintained to this date.

This *Supreme Court for the Hawaiian Islands*, supra, has heard limited cases between Hawaiian Nationals (lawfully separated from the de facto, puppet state of Hawaii and Federal United States jurisdictions).

Legislative Branch – Pending Activation

Currently the government is functioning lawfully in exigency, without the Legislative Branch. Once the roster of National (confirmed) Citizens is of a sufficient

---

[3] **Interregnum.** (in'ter reg'nam) "1. an interval of time between the close of a sovereign's reign and the accession of his or her normal or legitimate successor. 2. any period during which a state has no ruler or only a temporary executive. 3. any period of freedom from the usual authority. 4. any pause or interruption in continuity.

size, elections will be lawfully held and the Legislature seated. At this point, the Legislature will resume conducting its law-making duties in behalf of the Nation's Citizens, choosing the Monarch, confirming appointments and so forth, within the lawful processes proscribed by the Hawaiian Constitution.

Hawaiian Kingdom National Citizens (Nationals)

The most crucial ingredient of a nation is its people. Without a distinct people, a nation cannot exist. Since 1993, through various means, thousands of Hawaiians (Private Citizens) have made formal declarations of their citizenship within the Hawaiian Kingdom. These are **Hawaiian Nationals**. Many more have not taken formal action but still consider their nationality as Hawaiian.

Nationality, under international standards (See God's Definition in Chapter 3, Page 31) is determined by the country to which one is born or belongs, not by one's race or ethnicity, political or religious persuasion. Thus *Hawaiian Nationals* (a.k.a. *Hawaiian Private Citizens* or *Hawaiian Subjects*) become such in one of three ways: 1) by **birth** (one born in the Hawaiian Islands or to Hawaiian National parents(s) living abroad; 2) by **naturalization** (an adult who has taken the legal steps to renounce nationality to his former country to become a Hawaiian National); or in special cases, 3) by becoming a **denizen** (dual citizenship) (an adult who chooses to retain his prior citizenship and under Oath, to also become a Hawaiian National). Hawaiian nationals are domiciled under the de juré, Hawaiian National Laws, their lawful birth names and birthrights. Furthermore, Hawaiian Nationals (except for Denizens) have lawfully separated themselves from citizenship in – and other contractual adhesions or allegiances to – foreign countries *(including the United States Federal Government that currently and unlawfully occupies the Hawaiian Islands)*.

Goals and Objectives

Independence

The government's primary objective is to achieve full restoration of the *Hawaiian Kingdom National Government* as an independent, "neutral" nation, as it existed previously, operating for the benefit of the People of Hawaii. This requires that the

Hawaiian Kingdom National Government build its citizenship base and the mechanisms necessary to govern and provide lawful order, peace and security for its people.

Infrastructure

The infrastructure for day-to-day operations already exists in the *de facto State of Hawaii*. Numerous state departments are already in place to deliver vital public services like roadways, water systems, building codes, harbors and airports, public education, corrections facilities, taxation, and so forth. The transition from the *State of Hawaii* to the *Hawaiian Kingdom National Government* can bring these public services under the control, management and jurisdiction of the Hawaiian National Government.

The most challenging problem that will need to be addressed will be land titles. Because of the many layers of improper and even fraudulent transfers of land ownership under illegal jurisdictions, this problem will take much time, patience and extraordinary wisdom to sort out and clarify in a manner that would be just and equitable for those with legitimate claims and those who were innocent victims of U.S. and State of Hawaii fraud.

International Affairs

To achieve the restoration of Hawaii as an independent nation, the Ministry of Foreign Affairs can work to persuade the United States that it would be in its best interest to gracefully relinquish its unlawful and morally bankrupt claim to Hawaii, and set conditions and timetables for the U.S. to begin making a peaceful, orderly withdrawal and reparations. As a sovereign nation, the *Hawaiian Kingdom National Government* can once again conduct foreign relations in the world community, maintaining friendly reciprocal agreements with all other nations including the United States.

National Finances

The *Hawaiian Kingdom National Government* can develop entrepreneurial systems to provide revenues to support its government operations so that the fiscal reliance can be on proceeds from trade and commerce rather than individual income taxes. To achieve this, the Hawaiian Kingdom can develop business-friendly policies and support mini and micro entrepreneurship, as well as developing Hawaii as a Pacific Trade

Center, including a Pacific stock exchange and central and clearinghouse international banking services.

Government Activities and Campaigns

The first priority for Ke Aupuni's activities is to rebuild the Hawaiian Nation. To achieve this, the various components of government have been active in the following ways:

Ministry of the Interior – The largest ministry. At this time, the primary task of this ministry is rebuilding the people-base of the nation. This *Ministry of the Interior* has been involved in educating the public, providing citizenship information and assisting people in claiming their citizenship and providing proper documentation to register them as Hawaiian Nationals. Interior also provides registration of automobiles, trucks, vessels, business, etc. issuing various certificates, business licensing and documentations. The *Ministry of the Interior* is also in the process of re-establishing physical control over the lands and seas of the Hawaiian Archipelago.

Ministry of Finance – The Ministry of Finance is primarily involved in devising strategies to reactivate the fiscal means for the nation and the Citizens of Hawaii to operate; namely: reviving the *Treasury of the Hawaiian Kingdom* and *Hawaii Postal Savings Bank*; the financial services for the government and the general public; reviving the tax system and creating enterprises to provide a revenue flow into the Hawaiian kingdom. Reparations for the century-long illegal occupation will play a large role in the financial operations of the Hawaiian Kingdom National Government.

Attorney General – this Office provides counsel to the government. It also has the primary duty to provide counsel, filings and legal strategies to protect the Hawaiian National Citizens who are being wrongfully persecuted in unlawful foreign jurisdictions. The *Attorney General* produces documents consistent with Hawaiian Kingdom National Laws in issuing lawful notices and filings to de facto State and U.S. Federal Agencies and their representatives, in the assertion of Hawaiian Kingdom National jurisdiction. The *Attorney General* is preparing to try in the Hawaiian Kingdom Courts the wrongful persecution of Hawaiian Nationals by U.S. / State of Hawaii courts, etcetera. There also exists within the *Office of the Attorney General*, a law enforcement division titled the *Office of the Marshal (High-Sheriff)*.

Ministry of Foreign Affairs – The *Ministry of Foreign Affairs* has been pursing diplomatic relations with other nations, particularly renewing those that have existing treaties with the Hawaiian Kingdom. This ministry maintains foreign correspondence, negotiates trade agreements and other activities on behalf of the Hawaiian Kingdom. The ministry issues documentation (passports, etc.), oversees protocols for foreign legations in Hawaii and establishes Hawaiian legations overseas. The *Ministry of Foreign Affairs* is the lead agency in charge of developing and executing a plan for the peaceful withdrawal of the U.S. from the Hawaiian Islands and for reparations that stem from the illegal occupation.

National Supreme Court – The Supreme Court, titled, *"The Supreme Court for the Hawaiian Islands"* provides the proper venue to exercise the lawful authority of the *Hawaiian Kingdom National Constitution* and the Kingdom laws and asserts the jurisdiction of the Hawaiian Kingdom National Government as required by law. The court is in the process of rebuilding the judiciary system by recruiting, qualifying and educating competent judges, court clerks, officers and staff that populate the various courts, etcetera. The *Supreme Court for the Hawaiian Islands* is in the process of reviewing and validating actions taken by various Kukupa Councils, tribunals and other courts operating in exigency on behalf of the Peoples of the Hawaiian Kingdom. Preparations are being made to adjudicate land cases and so forth, in the Hawaiian Kingdom National Courts.

<u>Caveat:</u>

Currently, the hostile occupation of Hawaii by the United States and its puppet corporate construct, the de facto STATE OF HAWAII, makes it troublesome and dangerous for many to live openly and fully as Hawaiian kingdom Nationals. The U.S. and State of Hawaii have adopted illegal policies to forcibly suppress the assertion of Hawaiian independence by using U. S. law enforcement agencies and its courts to arrest, prosecute and punish (through the use of fines, prison, torture, confiscation of property, criminalization, defamation of character...) those Hawaiian National Citizens who choose to abide by the laws of the Hawaiian Kingdom Government, not the laws of the occupiers. This policy of suppression is expected to continue until the United States admits to its unlawful occupation status in Hawaii, and agrees to peaceful and orderly withdrawal from the Hawaiian Islands.

Summary:

The Hawaiian Kingdom is actually a *theocracy* established in Hawaii through the covenant embraced in the hearts of the people during *Hawaii's Great Awakening* and as declared in the *1840 Constitution for the Hawaiian Islands,* placing *God's laws and the Spirit of God's laws* as the standard over all the laws of the Hawaiian Islands. This covenant is the spiritual and moral authority upon which this *Hawaiian Kingdom Government (Ke Aupuni O Hawaii Nei)* stands and continues through today.

The United States' occupation of Hawaiian national territory is categorically unlawful. Therefore, despite the 115 plus years of insurgent usurpation and foreign occupation, the sovereignty of the Hawaiian Nation has never been extinguished. Thus, by international standards, the Hawaiian Kingdom is in *continuity* (still in existence), as a sovereign, independent *nation-state.*

Ke Aupuni o Hawaii (the National Government of the Hawaiian Kingdom) is the lawful government, reactivated through lawful means, to govern this sovereign, peaceful, neutral nation-state-in-continuity called, **Ko Hawaii Pae Aina** (The Hawaiian Islands).

The Executive Branch was reactivated through the installation of a *pro tem Cabinet Council of State* whose constitutional powers and duties are to administer the country in the absence of the Monarch (the Chief Executive and Head of State).

The Judicial Branch was reactivated both through lawful notices and filings; and through actual court proceedings, operating under the *Hawaiian Kingdom National Constitution* and laws.

The lawful reactivation, by the people, of the *Legislative Branch* and full empowerment of the other branches, is pending the attainment of a larger National Citizen body politic.

The reinstatement of the *Monarch* is awaiting the lawful activation of the Legislature of the Kingdom, which has the constitutional authority to elect someone to fill the vacancy.

The remedy to the problem of the United States' occupation will be found by applying God's principles and provision for reconciliation: ho'oponopono. The strategy is to reach an amicable, peaceful agreement that provides the United States the means to withdraw in a graceful and orderly fashion, and provides Hawaii with the means to transition into full self-governance.

DEFINITIONS: Definitions of words used in Title 18 Section 11, USCr.C that define a foreign government entity.

The following are definitions of words used in **USCr.C Title 18 Section 11** (U.S. Criminal code). (Source: Black's Law Dictionary, 6th Edition)

1. **Foreign Government.** "The term 'foreign government,' as used in this title except in section 112, 878, 970. 1116, and 1201, includes any government, faction, or body of insurgents within a country with which the United States is at peace, irrespective of recognition by the United States. (June 25, 1948, c. 645, 62 Stat. 686; Oct. 8, 1976, Pub. L. 94-467, § 11, 90 Stat. 2001.) (Source; 1999 Ed. Federal Criminal Code and Rules)"

2. **Foreign.** "Belonging to another nation or country; belonging or attached to another jurisdiction; made, done or rendered in another state or jurisdiction; subject to another jurisdiction; operating or solvable in another territory; extrinsic; outside; extraordinary. Nonresident person, corporation, executor, etc."

3. **Government.** "*From the Latin gubernaculum.* Signifies the instrument, the helm, whereby the ship to which the state is compared, was guided on its course by the "gubernator" or Helmsman, and in that view, the government is but an agency of the state, distinguished as it must be in accurate thought from its scheme and machinery of government."

In the United States, government consists of the executive, legislative and judicial branches in addition to administrative agencies. In a broader sense, it includes the federal government and all its agencies, bureaus, state and county governments, and city and township governments.

The system of polity in a state; that form of fundamental rules and principles by which a nation or state is governed, or by which individual members of a body politic are to regulate their social actions. A constitution, either written or unwritten, by which the rights and duties of citizens and public officers are prescribed and defined, as a monarchical government, a republican government, etc. The sovereign or supreme power in a state or nation. The machinery by which the sovereign power in a state expresses its will and exercises its functions; or the framework of political institutions, departments, and offices, by means of which the executive, judicial, legislative, and administrative business of state is carried on.

The whole class of body of officeholders or functionaries considered in the aggregate, upon whom devolves the executive, judicial, legislative, qnde administrative business of state.

In a colloquial sense, the United States or its representatives, considered as the prosecutor in a criminal action; as in the phase, "the government objects to the witness"

The regulation, restraint, supervision, or control which is exercised upon the individual members of an organized jural society by those invested with authority; or the act of exercising supreme political power or control." *(And more)*

In a colloquial sense, the United States or its representatives, considered as the prosecutor in a criminal action; as in the phase, "the government objects to the witness"

The regulation, restraint, supervision, or control which is exercised upon the individual members of an organized jural society by whose invested with authority; or the act of exercising supreme political power of control." *(And more)*

4. <u>Faction</u>. *(Not defined in Black's Law Dictionary. Webster's Definition follows:)* "1: a party or group (as within a government) that is often contentious or self seeking; CLIQUE 2: party spirit exp. When marked by dissension – factional – factionalism – factionally. (Merriam-Webster's Collegiate Dictionary, 10th Edition 1997)

5. <u>Body.</u> "A person. Used of a natural body, or of an artificial one created by law, as a corporation. Body in the broad sense is the main central or principal part of anything as distinguished from subordinate parts.

6. <u>Insurgents.</u> "One who participates in an insurrections; one who opposes the execution of law by force of arms, or who rises in revolt against the constituted authorities. An enemy."

7. <u>Country.</u> "The territory occupied by an independent nation or people, or the inhabitants of such territory. In the primary meaning 'country' denotes the population, the nation, the state, or the government, having possession and dominion over a territory."

8. <u>Irrespective.</u> (Merriam-Webster's Dictionary; not in Black's Law Dictionary) same as, *"Regardless of"*

9. <u>United States.</u> This term has several meanings. It may be merely the name of a sovereign occupying the position analogous to that of other sovereigns in the family of nations, it may designate territory over which sovereignty of the United States extends, or it may be collective name of the states that are united by and under the Constitution. (or, it may mean the Federal United States Government) Hooven & Allison Co. v. Evatt, U. S. Ohio, 324 U. s. 652, 65 S. Ct. 879, 880, 89, L. Ed. 1252.

Chapter 12

THE KINGDOM IS!

AUTHOR'S CAPSULATION AND COMMENTARY FOR HAWAIIANS (with a real personal bias)

This document was not written to just point out past and present abuses, but to hopefully rectify the future and to establish righteousness. It is to provide the basis for the peaceful and righteous restoration of the lawful Hawaiian Kingdom, a nation and a government that will stand for the protection of its Nationals that rightfully deserve their way of life, with the preservation of their customs and traditions, and the elimination of foreign occupation and genocide.

The truth will always prevail over the lie. Yet, the lies from abroad for over a hundred years have created confusion and conflict within the ranks of the Hawaiian People of all ethnicities. It's that old political divide and conquer thing. This confusion needs to be corrected by proper, truthful information so that the Hawaiian People of all ethnic backgrounds can come together in peace and unity to determine their own government and their place among the nations of the world.

The truth is, the de jure *Hawaiian Kingdom National Government's laws* have been *"alive"* and in continuity since 1840. How can that be? It is very simple. De jure law cannot be replaced by de facto lawlessness pretending or imposing itself to be law *(i.e. "color of law")*. A false government cannot replace a true government and be maintained as lawful. Therefore, the U.S. sustained de facto *Puppet State of Hawaii* and its *"Revised Statutes" (also, "color of law" – admittedly created by a treasonous entity)* are indeed not lawful and cannot be binding particularly upon Hawaiian Nationals who are domiciled in Hawaii, under their own laws created by their own *nation*.

The existing *U. S* and *Puppet State of Hawaii Governments* have sought to hide and replace Hawaii's National laws by deception and suppression. Those in authority in the de facto State have been hiding Hawaiian national history in a concerted attempt to keep the Hawaiian People ignorant of their history and rights. This was effectively accomplished through the systematic indoctrination of three generations by: deviously distorting the historical record; denying the Hawaiian language to be spoken in the schools; demeaning the Hawaiian people and their culture; forcibly making everyone U.S. citizens; imposing strict economic and social controls; and by not permitting the full history of Hawaii to be revealed and taught in the U.S. administered State of Hawaii schools or America's schools.

Hawaiians have been denied their rich, colorful and wonderful history (which they should be able to openly and truthfully share); as well as their proper citizenship and jurisdictional rights as a sovereign *People*. The Hawaiian people have been misled through the denial of truth as to who they really are, so that they are ignorant of their lawful birth names, citizenship rights, culture, traditions and freedoms!   Generations after the overthrow they have become federalized, *brain washed chattel* from birth. Many Hawaiian adults today still believe and are trapped by these foreign misrepresentations!

There is no need for *Hawaiian Nationals* to use force or get angry toward those politicians, lawyers and judges who have, through lies and deception, violated their rights and put them all into bondage. No need to "throw stones." No need to destroy. No need to be angry for anger's sake and call names or to falsify names like the occupier has done.

It is the Truth that will make us free and will restore the *National Government* of *Ko Hawaii Pae Aina* to its rightful place within the world community of nations.

Therefore, let all the Hawaiian People unite, pray and labor to rebuild their Government in a peaceful and mature manner and with a character that is reflective of a Peaceful and Loving God and of a patient, loving Hawaiian People.

God's Truth is more than sufficient! We have *Ke Akua* and the law to protect us. God's Truth is more powerful than the laws of the adversary and those corrupt parties in power who are abusing Hawaii and America's National peoples. Everything will work out for the common good if we keep our focus and do what is honorable and right before Almighty God *(Ke Akua Mana Loa)*.

THE HAWAIIAN KINGDOM IS

I say, *"The Hawaiian Kingdom is,"* because it is. It is still here, even though it has been pushed back and hidden from sight and awareness by corrupt and evil people desiring to conceal the truth of its existence. That is no longer the case. Yes, the Kingdom is, but it will not be what it should and can be, without applying the truth, wisdom and guidance of Almighty God to help us.

TREATY OF 1849/50 *(Applicable)*

The **Treaty of 1850 (See EXHIBIT C)** *(See Chapter 3, Nations, Laws, Treaties and Jurisdiction)* between the United States of America and the *Hawaiian Kingdom* was <u>ratified on August 19, 1850</u>. It is a valid and lawful Treaty of *"Perpetual Friendship," "Peace"* and *"Commerce"* between two distinct and sovereign nations, executed before Almighty God and the entire world. This Treaty between lawful nations, also met all lawful constitutional requirements of <u>both</u> national governments.

<u>This Treaty is still valid and in lawful existence</u> between the two lawful parties. It could not have been lawfully cancelled by third parties such as the *"Federalized"* United States Congress *(which does not represent the "Union of States" of the "American Republic" through its proper National Congress)* or by the men of treason and insurrection that comprised the de facto *Republic of Hawaii, and subsequent de facto governments*. These subsequent *<u>de facto governments</u> <u>possess no lawful authority</u>* to activate or cancel anything lawful.

Therefore, because there has been no proper action by either lawful party of the Treaty to terminate the Treaty, this Treaty (and others) still exists and is in effect guaranteeing mutual protections to the Nationals of both countries as specified in the treaty.

Therefore, **"The Kingdom is."**

THE NEWLANDS RESOLUTION
(Not Applicable to Hawaiians on Hawaiian Soil)

The so-called *"Newlands Resolution"* (See **EXHIBIT F**) *(Joint Resolution No. 55, 2nd Session, July 7, 1898, Sta. At L. 750; 2 Supp. R. S. 895 "To Provide for Annexing the Hawaiian Islands to the United States.")* was a resolution designed to supposedly *"Annex"* the Hawaiian Kingdom and was approved by both houses of Congress, signed by the Speaker of the U.S. House of Representatives, the Vice-President of the United States (as President of the Senate) and by President William McKinle<u>y. However, a legal and lawful problem exists in that this Resolution is a domestic directive only applicable to the people of the U.S. jurisdiction within which it was initiated. It would have no</u>

lawful effect upon a foreign nation such as the Hawaiian Kingdom or its People (Hawaiian Nationals).

Please take note that this U.S. Congressional Resolution is the document and basis upon which the United States gave its political and military support to insurrectionists and treasonists, who initially *(after the overthrow)* maintained private control with hundreds of imported U.S. Winchester Repeating Rifles *(latest technology of that era)* and direct U.S. military power.

The *Newlands Resolution* pretended to cancel all lawful *Hawaiian Kingdom* Treaties with other nations. But the Resolution, lacking lawful authority on foreign soil, could not and did not cancel any treaties. It would be akin to the United States canceling France's, Japan's, Brazil's, South Africa's, England's, or any other nation's treaties by passing a domestic U.S. Resolution. Get the point?

The *Newlands Resolution* refers to having cancelled treaties of the *"Hawaiian Islands,"* which is another deception and misrepresentation. The *Republic of Hawaii (treasonous usurping entity)* could not assume nor abrogate lawful International Treaties because it never made them. To begin with as a lesser in right, de facto, treasonous, unlawfully implemented and installed (with direct military intervention of a foreign government - i.e. the Federal United States) de facto rebel government, it possessed no right at law. Therefore, the *Hawaiian Kingdom's International Treaties* still exist at law.

Therefore, **"The Kingdom is.**

NO CONQUEST OF HAWAIIAN ISLANDS BY WARFARE
(Applicable)

Under international law, there are two ways in which the sovereignty of a nation can be transferred — by choice or by conquest.

The National Government of the Citizens of the Hawaiian Kingdom never chose by a referendum or other indication of approval, to transfer their sovereignty to the United States or to be annexed to the U.S. or anyone else. There is no proof of consensual right of possession or lawful control justifying a United States foreign political presence on Hawaiian National soil.

Hawaii and the United States have never been at war *(or any kind of military conflict or hostility)* against each other, so there cannot be a claim of U.S. military conquest of Hawaii. There is no military action justifying a United States foreign <u>military presence</u> on Hawaiian National soil.

Therefore, **"The Kingdom is."**

NO CEDING OF THE HAWAIIAN ISLANDS TO THE U.S. *(Applicable)*

There is not now nor has there ever been a treaty ceding *the Hawaiian Islands* to the United States by the de jure *Government of the Hawaiian Kingdom*! U.S. laws affirm, proving that point.[1] In the 1890's and early 1900's Queen Liliuokalani filed several actions in U.S. courts and with the U.S. Congress emphasizing the fact that no titles were ever transferred to the United States.

Therefore, **"The Kingdom is."**

DE FACTO RECOGNITION OF HAWAIIAN NATIONALS *(Applicable)*

There never was a vote of consent by either the *Hawaiian Kingdom Government* or *Hawaiian Nationals* for the United States to take over Hawaii. And there never was a vote of consent from the Hawaiian Kingdom to cede any of its land to the U.S.

Even though Hawaiian Nationals are the lawful citizens of the Hawaiian Islands, they have been totally disregarded by the United States' foreign occupation, which exerts firm controls over Hawaii's political, economic, social and cultural spheres. All political and economic activities are conducted within the de facto authority of the *U.S. Federal* occupation and its *Puppet State of Hawaii* government. Thus, Hawaiian Nationals are excluded from any decision making within their own country.

Since 1900, *Voter Registration Forms* **(See EXHIBIT G)** for both the *Territory of Hawaii* and *State of Hawaii stipulated* that only "U.S. <u>c</u>itizens" are allowed to participate in elections in Hawaii. Thus, all actions, including the "ratification" of

---

[1] Author refers you to: USC Title 28, Section 91 (Jurisdiction of U.S. District Court for Hawaii).

Statehood were voted on not by _lawful Hawaiian National Citizens_ but by _de facto U.S. citizens_ on Hawaiian National soil.

This deliberate exclusion of Hawaiian Nationals from voting is evidence that the governments of the de facto _Puppet State of Hawaii_ and _Federal United States_ know that Hawaiian Nationals exist within this Island Nation. This is obvious recognition of Hawaiian National existence!

Therefore, **"The Kingdom is."**

UNITED STATES ADMISSION OF WRONGDOING INTERNATIONALLY (Applicable)

Trying to appear to clear its sinful national conscience, the _United States Federal Government_ passed the _"Apology Bill," Public Law 103-150 of November 23, 1993,_ (See **EXHIBIT A**) acknowledging the unlawful U.S. Military invasion and intervention in support of treason and insurrection. They assisted in arming the rebels and then utilized its U.S. military power in a blatant, unlawful, foreign nation power-grab. This U.S. Apology Law is an admission and confession of an unlawful and deliberate act of United States international wrongdoing... further proof that; the _Hawaiian Kingdom National Government of The Hawaiian Islands_ is _"pono" (just, right morally, legal, good, etc.)_!

Therefore, **"The Kingdom is."**

AUTHOR'S CONCLUSION: "THE KINGDOM IS!"

I believe it is appropriate to conclude this matter _(prior to my own personal biases of the following Chapter 13)_ in the following way by quoting Queen Liliuokalani, the last reigning _Monarch of the Hawaiian Kingdom._ Her 1897 prayer, statement, petition to America is as follows:

"Oh, honest Americans, as Christians hear me for my down-trodden people! Their form of government is as dear to them as yours is precious to you. Quite as warily as you love your *country, so they love theirs. With all your goodly possessions, covering a territory so immense that there yet remains parts unexplored, possessing islands that, although near at hand, had to be neutral ground in time of war, do not covet the little vineyard of Naboth's, so far from your shores, lest the punishment of Ahab fall upon you, if not in your day, in that of your children, for "be not deceived, God is not mocked." The people to whom your fathers told of the living God, and taught to call "Father," and whom the sons now seek to despoil and destroy, are crying aloud to Him in their time of trouble; and He will keep His promise, and will listen to the voices of His Hawaiian children lamenting for their homes.*

It is for them that I would give the last drop of my blood; it is for them that I would spend, nay, am spending, everything belonging to me. Will it be in vain? It is for the American people and their representatives in Congress to answer these questions. As they deal with me and my people, kindly, generously, and justly, so may the Great Ruler of all nations deal with the grand and glorious nation of the United States of America."

Chapter 13

AUTHOR'S MANY MORE BIASED, CONCLUDING OPINIONS / CRITIQUE

ABOUT CRIME AND THE COMPLACENT CHRISTIAN CHURCHES OF AMERICA

In my personal opinion, America is heading for disaster! Around the world, it is no longer respected as a Godly Nation or as one that honors its word. It is only known for flexing its military and economic might.

As the institution entrusted to be the Godly standard for society; governing its morality and promoting virtue and wholesomeness, America's Christian churches must carry much of the blame for America's precipitous decline.

What has happened to that great, wonderful country? It is presently immersed in crime, killing of its unborn babies, and abusing its children, and children killing other children in its schools. Its people today are more dedicated to saving the trees, whale, turtle, dog, cat, etc., than upholding the righteousness of God's laws in their families.

America has become a country where sodomites and other perverts are not even prosecuted and where murderers and rapists are just slapped on the wrist and released from prison on parole to murder and rape again and again, because these have been *"socially deprived," "didn't mean to do it"* or, *"were raised in a dysfunctional family"*! Hogwash! All of them know right from wrong! They made deliberate choices. Modern American societal acceptance of this deviate kind of thinking is grievous and foolish!

Today, criminals do not see their actions as repulsive and sinful before Almighty God. They do not fear punishment or even the death penalty, because we, as a society, don't want to appear to be too harsh. Our politicians and courts, because of their weaknesses and vacillation to the death penalty, encourage the worst criminals in their aberrant activities. Sadly, many of these politicians and judges in desiring to be *"politically correct"* ignore or refuse to take action against those in our society who promote morally repulsive, unacceptable and destructive behaviors.

This supposedly civilized, Christian country is one that allows mothers to kill by the millions, their babies while they are still within the womb, and say, *"It's the law, I can do what I want with my body!"* These women actually believe that lie that it's okay to kill innocent babies because the law says they have the so-called "right" to privacy! Our politicians and judges in the courts support this mass murder of the Innocents. God doesn't!

These are just some of today's ungodly behaviors that are not being directly confronted by our churches, en masse; in order to preserve and protect our children and society. As a society, we have turned from God and become an uncaring people of indifference, creating a breeding ground within which values have been degraded and deviate minds operate relatively unchecked, without fear of consequences.

The reason we have such deplorable crime conditions is because our more liberal lawmakers, judges and attorneys think they know better than God on how to maintain order in our society, while the majority of our Pastors and Ministers sit back, passively observing this moral decay and do little or nothing to stand against the tide of evil.

Christians are obligated to *"...render unto Caesar that which is Caesar's,"* but our Shepherds have foolishly gone beyond that and given *everything* they have to Caesar: their Pastorates, their Pulpits, their denominations. So as not to offend the sinners, they sanitize their speech from the pulpits and do not face sin directly, doing a disservice to their flock, not to mention their first priority of respect and honor owed Almighty God and Our Lord Jesus Christ!

I observe many of those who call themselves *"Christians"* in our churches who only attend for ritual's sake, or out of guilt, and do not have a personal, meaningful relationship with Our Lord. They do not feel any obligation beyond the doors of the church to Honor Him in righteousness. After church, they return to their un-Godly, non-edifying businesses and ways of life of lying, deceiving, using profane and abusive language, satisfying only their own selfish ways. This too is repulsive. Perhaps it was rightfully said to me by my older brother, *"We (Christians) are blind in one eye and cannot see out of the other."*

ABOUT RIGHTEOUSNESS IN THE HOME.

Righteousness and moral values start in the home.

Let's start by having our marriages sanctified *"Under God"*... not in the public offices of the subordinate, local government system requiring our marrying couples to be *"licensed"* as if God's Word and God's Witnesses to such a union are not sufficient! Marriage under Almighty God and the superior *"common law" (the law of America derived from God's Laws and that recognizes Almighty God)* was our way of marriage in America until the late nineteen forties and early fifties. Surely, it is still good enough today! Why subordinate God's Union and Sanctity of Marriage to that of man's licensing when man's way is improperly used to diminish that sanctity and value of commitment?

When these unions in marriage produce children, let's encourage the parents to dedicate them to the Lord and let's hold the parents accountable for raising the children in the admonition of the Lord to the age of consent. Let's allow these children to be baptized *(at the child's desire when at the age of consent)* by immersion in water *(God's way)* when they make their own decision to accept Jesus Christ as their Lord and Savior.

Let's not forget to tell them about that <u>second baptism</u> *(the infilling of the "Holy Spirit" equipping them for service in the Body of Christ – Luke 11:13; John 14:26)* that Our Lord Jesus gives to each of us so we can stand strong in Him and help build His Church. We are the church!

Only with Christ's Truth and Preeminence prevailing in our churches, will Righteousness be restored to us as a People and to the character of our National Government. Let's not forget that God alone created government (Isaiah 33:22); the judicial, legislative and executive.

CHRISTIAN CHURCHES AND THEIR SUBJUGATION TO THE IRS.

<u>God submits Himself to no government and to no man</u>! He alone created government (Isaiah 33: 22; the judicial, legislative and executive).

Today's church needs to decide: a) if the state is God under IRS Title 26 Section 501(c)(3), with a corporate board of directors, or b) if Almighty God is God under a body of Holy Spirit filled Elders as ordained by the Holy Scriptures. The reason today's churches in America, in Hawaii, in "Western" civilization, are compromised is because they have come to hold the state in higher esteem than Almighty God.

America's Christian Churches have unwittingly subjugated (voluntarily submitted) themselves to the U.S. Federal Government and the **Internal Revenue Service Code as "non-profit religious organizations" under Section 8, of Title 26, USC - U.S. Federal Government,** thus placing the Government between themselves and God. The American churches that are supposed to be submitted to Almighty God have abandoned their spiritual authority and have become IRS-controlled, non-profit corporations, ultimately answerable to the corrupt IRS (man's laws), and not Almighty God.

Unlike God, the IRS uses intimidation, threat and abuse of law without conscience, against individuals and businesses. This is fact. Therefore, my opinion is that churches need to terminate their corporate contracts with the IRS and replace their corporate "Board of Directors" with Godly "Elders" as God has so ordained in His Word.

If Ministers, Pastors or Shepherds claim to be "Called" by God, but through ignorance have placed their flocks under the U.S. Federal Government non-profit laws, and they realize it was wrong, they must repent, correct their thinking, then re-educate and re-direct their flocks for whom God has given them spiritual responsibility.

In the Bible the Greek word used and interpreted in the New Testament as "repent," is *"metanoia,"* which in Greek simply means, "Change your thought patterns" or "Change your way of thinking." I wonder about America as a Nation. Can Americans change their way of thinking? Can we, as Servants of the Most High God, help others to do likewise? Is Almighty God really the first priority in our own lives?

Ministers in our churches should be aware that **United States Code Title 26** (the "Internal Revenue Code") is not "Positive law!" Read **Title 26, Section 7806 of the United States Code**. It states that nothing within Title 26 is to be considered law until enacted into "Positive law" by Congress.

Since Title 26 has never been read into the Congressional (Record) Register, as required by law, it is not "Positive law." Therefore, it is not law, but only suggestion. So why does the church obey and honor that which extorts and does evil against the people? The reasons? … Blind ignorance, entrapment and plain old fear! Yet fear is not from Our Loving God *(Read the Holy Scriptures, 1ˢᵗ John, Chapter 4, Verse 18).*

What I also do not understand is: why do we encourage and require God's Children in our flocks to honor this unlawful and corrupt authority functioning in hostility to God? By doing so, we voluntarily bind others and ourselves to a subordinate, worldly corporate authority outside of God's Will. We abandon and violate God's Trust. As Christian Ministers and leaders, we must honor God first, not man!

Let's get right with Almighty God! As a step of proper understanding of God's authority, we need to remove from our sanctuaries of worship, *any* government flags and other such symbols of secular authority.

It's time for our Christian Shepherds and Leaders to get right with God!

ABOUT GOD AND OUR POLITICIANS, LAWYERS, ATTORNEYS AND JUDGES

Those attempting to remove God and a moral consciousness from our society are doing so through the actions of ungodly parties *(primarily attorneys, judges, legislatures)* practicing the art of law, and making *"law"* their god. Based on flawed secular moral standards, these men and women ignorantly attempt to create and enforce a process of law *without Godly compassion, knowledge, wisdom or reason.*

Judges who take oaths today omit any obligation to Almighty God and have no accountability to anyone but their own egos and those who appoint them. The result is that they, along with our own abdication of responsibility, are creating a deficient, godless and immoral society of conflicting values of judgment because there are no Godly absolutes in their system of law. The substitution of a legally legislated secular-law-generated morality is in direct conflict with the Godly conscience of the Christian Believer and falls very far short of Almighty God's absolutes.

The Christian Believer in his loving, personal relationship and responsibility to God functions in the Grace of that Greater Power of Almighty God. Those who err and live by a double standard have not learned the Scripture of the Lord, which says:

> *"Thou shall not have in thy bag different weights, a great and a small. Thou shalt not have in thine house different measures, a great and a small. But thou shalt have a perfect and just weight; a perfect and just measure shall thou have, that their days may be lengthened in the land which the lord thy God giveth thee. For all who do such things, and all who do unrighteously, are an abomination unto the Lord thy God."* (Source: Deuteronomy 25:13-16, New Scofield Reference Bible)

The above Scripture also applies to the inconsistent standard of justice exercised in our courts by godless judges and attorneys. God has not changed His ways of justice, we have tried to change His.

Is it possible that we do these foolish things (like submission to wrongful authority) because we do not know right from wrong or because others do it? Is it possible that we have misplaced our belief and faith by putting trust in politicians, attorneys, and judges, et al, who do not know or honor Almighty God or God's Law's and do not understand God's Grace? Are we too intimidated to act righteously against them?

I have found that the legalistic minds under man's law are committed to their own created law as their first priority (their god) and not to Almighty God! It is time for us to correct them!

It is true today that our politicians, attorneys at law and judges *(who are also attorneys)* have encouraged and brought about fulfillment of the following Scripture by putting man's civil and criminal laws above God's Law and God's Justice:

> *"None calls for justice, nor any pleads for truth; they trust in vanity, and speak lies; they conceive mischief, and bring forth iniquity"* (Isaiah 59:4).

ABOUT CHRISTIANS AND SHEPHERDS FALLING SHORT OF THE MARK

Our Pastors and Ministers do not realize the condition of our court systems today! Our Pastors and Ministers do nothing to stop those who administer foolish laws that conflict with our Christian Faith and allow the ungodly to be appointed as judges over us.

In Hawaii's courts there is great inconsistency in the judgments rendered and penalties requested by the corrupt *Puppet State of Hawaii* and *U.S. Federal Prosecutors.* In some cases there are excessive, inapplicable charges filed to intimidate, which are then diminished or dropped, if a *"plea" (of guilt)* is entered into. Also, *"Plea Bargaining"* is constantly used to escape proper punishment or to waive the proper execution of law and judgment for major criminal offenses committed.

The <u>more you know</u> about the law in the *Puppet State of Hawaii*, the greater the corruption you will see in its courts. The iniquities that I have witnessed are reflected by these *Puppet State of Hawaii* and *Federal United States Government* justice systems.

Unfortunately, these corrupt politicians, attorneys and judges, who are supposed to be public servants, reflect negatively upon those who do serve honorably within these systems today.

God's Prophet, Isaiah, said something that is so appropriate for this moment for both nations, *the united "States of America"* and the *Hawaiian Kingdom*. I quote:

> *"The way of peace they know not and there is no justice in their goings; they have made them crooked paths; whosoever goes in them shall not know peace. Therefore is justice far from us, neither does righteousness overtake us. We wait for light, but behold obscurity; for brightness, but we walk in darkness." "In transgressing and lying against the Lord, and departing from our God, speaking oppression and revolt, conceiving and uttering from the heart words of falsehood. And justice is turned away backward, and righteousness stands afar off; for truth is fallen into the street, and equity cannot enter"* (Isaiah 59: 8, 9, 13, 14).

Have you as Pastors and Ministers ever stopped to wonder why we have problems in government? It is really quite simple. When we take the absolute values of Almighty God out of our government and our oaths of Office, and, our so-called Christian church leaders permit replacement of Him by individuals in government authority who defy God and do not know Him, we condemn ourselves as a people. Overall, we Christian's have not uniformly stood up publicly for righteousness, as we should against ungodly people and ungodly actions of Government. We've elected compromisers, liars and thieves to office. We have compromised ourselves by becoming followers, not leaders, submitting ourselves to government's negative and suppressive influences as being superior and in substitution for Almighty God as the Ultimate Authority. We compromise and then re-compromise again and again to a dilution and dissolution of truth.

It is time for us Christians who know Him to stand up and do what is right in His sight. It is also time for non-Christians who know and have Godly values to stand up and do what is right. Speaking of this, it is we, the Christian Body of Believers who have failed to do our work in standing up against evil and corruption. We justified ourselves improperly saying, *"Render to Caesar what is Caesars"* and then we foolishly *" render to Caesar what is God's."* Let's keep God's laws above man's law and cause man's law to honor God! As a people, we are told to study in order to show ourselves approved of God. Don't let Caesar rule!!

ABOUT A COUNTRY OF COMPROMISING NATIONAL VALUES AND THE FEDERAL ACCEPTANCE OF GODLESS FAITHS
(continuing to speak as an American National Citizen)

"American Citizens" and the immigration status, second-class *"Federal U.S. citizens"* have for many decades ignored and definitely have not protected the values that had made America great. I have in my lifetime of awareness since World War II, watched America degenerate; abandon its *National Government*, and its moral values.

We Americans have become a nation of ignorant people, deep in debt, who do not know our State and National rights as Citizens, our Judeo-Christian values upon which our Nations were founded, our basic laws, those military conflicts and sacrifices that gave us and preserved our freedoms and liberties as a people, or even our own proper English language names. We Americans, educationally, have become ignorant, or should I say, just plain dumb! We don't even know what real money is... and we accept it and strive and destroy people and lives for it!

Having been taken over by the U.S. and made into Federal U.S. citizens, most of the People of Hawaii have also been enmeshed in the civic ignorance and the degenerate values that pulled down the once great American nation.

ABOUT HAWAII'S DE FACTO, U.S. SENATE AND CONGRESSIONALLY ELECTED FEDERAL OFFICIALS.

[NOTE: Since Hawaii's elected officials were voted into office in the Federal U.S. system, by *Federal U.S. citizens*, it cannot be expected that these elected officials would do anything other than to serve the interests of their country (the United States) and their constituents (*Federal U.S. citizens* residing in Hawaii) whom they are sworn to serve. They are under no legal obligation to serve the interests of lawful Hawaiian Nationals or the interests of the Hawaiian Kingdom, the lawful government of the Hawaiian Islands.]

Presently, the vast majority of the people residing in the Hawaiian Islands are illegal aliens *(Federal U.S. citizens)*, and those who participate in civic matters, such as voting, do so as *Federal U.S. citizens*. Yet even these U.S. voters in U.S. elections are unaware of the rampant corruption throughout their own U.S. governing system, including the U.S. Congress.

For example, inappropriate U.S. Congressional procedures are practiced by these elected politicians, using various devious tactics to control the outcome of their bills such as: meeting in closed-door sessions, stifling opposition voices, collusion with the press, and excluding the public's input. Improper methods such as these point to a continuing, systemic corruption.

A case in point is the present method used by the *Democratic Party* and the *Democratic Senators from Hawaii, Mr. Akaka and Mr. Inouye, (along with their rubber-stamp Congressional Representatives from Hawaii)* who are attempting, through a measure called the *"Akaka Bill"[1]* to create an *"Indian Reservation type of Government"* for those of Hawaiian ancestry in order to take Hawaiian land!

These politicians have repeatedly revised the Akaka Bill *(without open public hearings)*, to the extent that it reveals by their devious methodology their ugly intentions to attain their ends at the expense of the Hawaiian People. These politicians have refused to hold *public hearings* in Hawaii, deliberately excluding Hawaiians from participating in the determination of their own future. Through this devious legislative ploy *(and by lying)* they seek to finally consummate the theft of the *Hawaiian National Lands, an objective that despite their political smoke and mirrors, has remained uncompleted and dangling since the 1893 overthrow and the 1898 "annexation."*

Perhaps these local U.S. "public officials" also hope to attain some distorted measure of personal pride in their attempted land theft, suppression of Hawaiian Nationals, and perhaps behind-the-scenes monetary gain.

Are these politicians selling out their own Hawaiian People? Where is that integrity, truth and honesty of these *U.S. Federal officials* placed into U.S. public authority and power *(who call themselves "Americans"* but born in Hawaii, and functioning as *Federal U.S. citizens)*? I cannot find it! Where is the church on this issue?

---

[1] *Akaka Bill. Formally titled the "Native Hawaiian Government Reorganization Act," this bill first introduced in 1999 by U.S. Senator Daniel K. Akaka, seeks Federal (Congressional) recognition of Native Hawaiians as an indigenous people of America. This is designed to mimic the tribal status of Native Americans, in effect creating a new American Indian tribe called "Native Hawaiians," to be administered by the U.S. Department of the Interior (Bureau of Indian Affairs). The bill proposes to allow Native Hawaiians to form their own still-to-be-negotiated "governing entity" with still-to-be-negotiated powers and still-to-be-negotiated jurisdiction. The danger this bill poses to Hawaiians is that, just entering into negotiations would be a concession by Hawaiians that the United States possesses jurisdiction over their lands to begin with. It accepts the lie perpetrated by the U.S. The bill is based on the presumption of U.S. ownership of the lands of Hawaii and, therefore, complete U.S. discretion in the disposition of those lands.*

AND ON WE GO WITH MORE OF THE SAME

Unfortunately in America, politicians, attorneys and federal judges *(all members of the ABA)*[2] have been allowed to take away from our laws and justice systems, the truthful and absolute values of a Righteousness God, and have instituted the compromise of America's Christian values in order to please men and other religions of foreign peoples admitted onto this land.

America appeases those who have come from distressed and oppressed foreign lands, whose gods are failures and who themselves are anti-God and anti-Christ. These demand their "*freedom of religion*" and our godless politicians, attorneys and judges strive to grant it while suppressing the truthful and rightful Judeo-Christian foundational values *(which is a way of life, not a religion)* that created and provided those personal freedoms within the *"sovereign"* united *"State's of America"* and in the Hawaiian Nation!

These godless politicians, judges and attorneys are delusional, thinking that our Christian faith is a religion and not a way of life! These *(all the above)* are the ones who without conscience *(Godless)*, consent to and encourage the murder *(by legal abortion)* of millions of babies who are within or partially removed from their mother's womb. This Federal U.S. policy, when applied to Hawaii, has been the cause of death for approximately 60% of all unborn babies of Native Hawaiian ancestry! This latter statistic, my friends, is evidence of *"genocide."*

Truly, the U.S. representative assemblies and courts are saturated with Godless men and women of varied and distorted *"religious"* values and non-religious values *(as distinct from Christian-Judeo values)*. They seek to take Americans away from our faith in God, Our Lord and Saviour Jesus Christ, and the sensitive leading of His Holy Spirit that guides us as a People and made our nations great!

These faithless-in-God public servants want us to follow their man-created laws that conflict with God's Word, God's Will and God's Spirit. They grant the minority a voice greater than they deserve, while seeking to please all people at the expense of God's Righteousness, Justice and People. More folly!

---

[2] **ABA. American Bar Association** *is a legal profession and fellowship of attorneys, lawyers and judges who practice within certain parameters as stipulated by the Association. Some States require that all who practice before their courts must be members, and some States do not.*

It is a time to take issue with the unrighteousness of these self-appointed gods of those minorities who serve foreign gods in our systems of law! These are the godless ones who declare and proclaim *"...separation of church and state..."* a statement that does not exist in the American Constitution and laws. These godless politicians, attorneys and judges are so ignorant that they don't know the difference. **They deliberately or inadvertently apply this false and misleading statement to our Christian Faith, which, as mentioned previously, is a way of life not a religion!**

Religion is man created and man ordained to satisfy their own selfish and self-righteous effort to reach and please God and not God's ordained way. Belief and faith in the Living God through Jesus Christ is, *"The Way, the Truth and the Life!"*

It is time to take back all that belongs to America and its People in order to preserve a great Nation. It does not mean destroying anyone or anything, but it does require the removal of unethical, unjust, sinful politicians, attorneys, judges, judicial parties and public officials in authority, who only see money and people-pleasing as power and who do not possess the Godly values that made America great. What it was in the past, it can be again, with respect as a people, not just as a military power.

MORE ABOUT AMERICA'S GOVERNMENT CIVIL SERVICE SERVANTS

This very biased and opinionated document was not written just for the Christian community and Private Citizens, but also for those many Civil Service public servants *(i.e. "federal citizens")*, who function with indifference in government positions without concern for God's righteous moral values.

I address those who act without conscience and are more concerned for their jobs while attempting to justify misguided, distorted and unrighteous actions by saying; *"Well, it's my job."* or, *"I'm just doing what I am told."* while hurting and injuring others. Isn't this type of thinking similar to that which existed during the Nazi reign of terror during World War II? We have offered blind, purchased obedience to deception at the expense of our integrity, righteousness and good Godly character.

Does any job really mean so much that we are willing to sear and abandon our conscience *(and hurt our family and fellow man in the process)* by refusing to do what is right as a public servant? Can we look at the people we hurt and justify it because, *"The law is the law"* or, *"I'm just doing what I am paid to do!"* Is it worth taking a bribe and knowing we have sold our integrity and diminished our character for a lousy, phony buck? It is never too late for us to change as a people and correct our thinking and our actions. As public servants, we don't have to lie, cheat, steal and do evil. We can and should act righteously and sleep well at night.

MORE ABOUT THIS WHOLE HAWAIIAN ISSUE

It is sad, yet very interesting to read the documents the United States Government utilized to tell the world and its own people how Hawaii was created as a supposed *United States Territory* and later, a supposed *"State of the Union."* It is and has been a bold and on-going deception and deliberate misrepresentation *(God would call it lie upon lie)!*

The lands of the *Nation,* **Ko Hawaii Pae Aina** *(The Hawaiian Islands)* not only have never transferred to U.S. ownership, they could not have been! The Hawaiian Kingdom lands still belong to the Hawaiian Kingdom and its People. It is time for the United States Federal Government to own up to this fact and make things right.

The United States Federal Government maintains authority over Hawaii by using a puppet government and military control, not by right, but by deception and abuse of police power, to utilize Hawaiian land for commercial and military purposes. So whom does this federal United States Government serve?

Does it really reflect *"We, The People..."? No!*

Does it really reflect Our God? *No!*

Does the U.S. have any jurisdiction in Hawaii? *No!*

Are U.S. public officials our masters? *No!*

The U.S. Federal Government and legal systems in Hawaii, are corrupt, and not as they represent themselves to be. Instead of upholding law, they condone and exercise lawlessness. But we can clean up that too!

Wake up Hawaiians! Wake up Americans! Take interest in who governs us because it is we, in our ignorance that has allowed them to steal our citizenship rights!

At this time, I bear witness that the *United States Federal Government* does not honor the Will and Righteousness of Almighty God; thus, I find from my studies that the god they do serve is *"The god of lies!"*

MORE ABOUT HAWAII: THE TRUTH SHALL PREVAIL

It is quite apparent that the words and the intents of two Presidents of the united "States," Benjamin Harrison and William McKinley, were without honor when it came to the friendly and loving *Peoples of Hawaii,* living within their own Nation, *Ko Hawaii Pae Aina.* While President Grover Cleveland recognized the U.S. role in the overthrow of the Hawaiian Kingdom Government as patently unlawful, he did not act to rectify the wrong.

Each of these Presidents *(and all who have served since)* as *Commander-in-Chief of the Armed Forces* of the united "States," had the ability and power to immediately correct the unlawful international violation of law committed against the Hawaiian Kingdom and its people. These Presidents *and all since, presumably for reasons of political expediency,* have chosen to ignore their fiduciary duty placed upon them by Almighty God, International Law, the Treaty of 1850, the American Constitution, et cetera. These supposedly Christian Presidents all in turn neglected their moral obligations to respond honestly and truthfully regarding the *conditional yield* by Queen Liliuokalani.

At the time, Queen Liliuokalani was <u>under extreme duress</u> caused by treasonist acts being supported by fully armed U.S. Marines and Navy forces unlawfully discharged on Hawaii's National *(foreign)* soil. Not wanting to shed innocent blood and provoke armed hostilities she put her trust in a just and lawful diplomatic resolution to the affair. Thus, she submitted to the presumed integrity of the President of the united "States" and the American People to act honorably and justly by restoring Hawaii's Government. They did not!

<u>Since 1893, the **Hawaiian Islands** has been under U.S. Military occupation by an undeclared, but admitted **"act of war"**</u>[3] perpetrated by the United States Government in violation of a recognized friendly, *"neutral"* nation, while at peace! There was no conquest! There was no war! There was only treachery in the violation of a small and feeble foreign nation by military invasion! There was a great, sinful violation of trust!

---

[3] **"act of war"** See President Grover Cleveland's address to Congress; Partial quotation can be found in Chapter 1, Pages 2, 3.

There was and still is a determined political conspiracy *(U.S.)* to continue usurping the lands of an innocent people; to destroy their values, customs and traditions by suppressing their rights to govern themselves as a free people. All this for economic and military gain and contrary to everything decent and right! Hawaiians who fight in the military conflicts of the Federal United States are considered to be expendable!

History shows that there has been open support of treason, conspiracy, piracy and deception conceived and resulting from an undeclared *"act of war"* by a greater nation *(Federal United States)* lacking morality, against a peaceful *"neutral"* nation *(The Hawaiian Kingdom)* with no standing army, only a Home Guard *(Palace Guard)*!

To date, there has been no condemnation or reprisal from the People of the United States or the world community against the perpetrators *(treasonists)* of the overthrow; only an ignoring and covering up of the truth and facts by the *United States Federal Government*. It was and is politically expedient for the *Federal United States Government* to ignore the lawful claims of a *"neutral"* government and its tormented and innocent people, who are clearly today, facing genocide.

The Hawaiian Kingdom, as a *neutral* nation without a standing army, could not resist the powerful United States' military actions fueled by *"Manifest Destiny" (greed)* of the United States, acting as an opportunistic colonial power against the peaceful *Hawaiian Island Nation*. At that time the United States, using gunboat diplomacy, was fast becoming the most powerful nation in the world. That military might went on world display *(i.e. "Great White Fleet")* and it could not be overcome by the *"neutral"* and peaceful Hawaiian People not possessing any sufficient means of resistance. So then, is might right? No, of course not! The U.S. threatened other nations from interceding on behalf of the *Hawaiian Nation*. Was that right? No, of course it wasn't. U.S. foreign policy today does not appear to have changed.

Hawaii is a political embarrassment to the *United States Government* due to the continued unlawful and abusive actions of their chain of occupying puppet governments and the United States military, which refuses to honor Hawaiian National laws while on Hawaiian land. <u>My birth country's fraud is an embarrassment to me.</u> The U.S. continuously supports these corrupt politicians and judiciaries in Hawaii who are of questionable character and who support distorted and corrupted U.S. values.

Hawaii's de jure National Government was re-activated in 1996; and, the Hawaiian National People despite 115 years of occupation are not going away! The

Hawaiian Kingdom Nation and its People are here for eternity as is the embarrassment created by the ongoing unauthorized and unlawful U.S. military occupation and its Puppet Government presence on Hawaiian National soil. The U.S. presence in Hawaii is evidence of a continuing blight on the character and integrity of the American People.

ABOUT THE NEWS MEDIA

It is very interesting to monitor the American news media, which these days, thrives on sensationalism and distortion, instead of proper reporting of the truth. I find in particular they do not research major issues in depth, such as brought forth in this text. They tend to skim over major issues and slant their attention toward minor concerns while neglecting the major priorities of balance, truth and honesty.

A good example is the issue of the Pilipo Souza case (See Chapter 6), another, the Montez Salamasina Ottley case, wherein the media sided with the government without investigating the truth and the facts. Another is the slanted reporting favoring the State of Hawaii's attacks on Bishop Estate (Kamehameha Schools), leading to the state's unlawful intervention and attempted dismantling and encroachment into this private trust.

By comparison, I would like to quote an article from the San Francisco Chronicle of Monday, September 5, 1887, which is still appropriate for today:

> *"The government of the sandwich Islands appears to have passed from the hands of the King into the hands of a military oligarchy that is more domineering than Kalakaua ever was. Before the recent revolt of the Europeans (Actually Americans) in Honolulu, the press of the city was very plain-spoken. It printed unadorned truths about the king, and the later made no effort to suppress such unpleasant utterances. Now, under the new regime, the newspapers are kept in check with military thoroughness. It seems incredible, but is an actual fact, that not one of the Honolulu journals dared to reprint the comments of the American press on the so-called revolution, although such comment would have been very interesting reading to all Hawaiians. Even the reports of court proceedings are dry and matter-of-fact records, very different from the ordinary accounts. In a word, the freedom of the press of Honolulu is a myth under the reform party (Republic of Hawaii), and the man who looks for the facts in the Honolulu journals will not find them."*

So it is today!

It is indeed unfortunate that the media *(both broadcast and print)* often do not look deeply into the stories they present, failing to substantiate the underlying facts prior to reporting to the people. Maybe this godless, liberal media does so deliberately in order to please the established economic and political system. I find that they will accept the word of self-serving attorneys and judges without questioning the facts to determine the truth before presenting them to the public and private sectors as fact.

The controlled and inappropriate use of the media is a trick of the legal system utilized in Hawaii by the Federal U.S. Justice Department, State Attorney General's Office and City and County of Honolulu Prosecutor's Office as well as the local law enforcement system *(i.e. their "Public Notice")* to imply immediate guilt long before a trial or before any ability of the accused to defend himself. <u>I wonder if the media really understands that in this corrupt system, it only takes accusations, not any proof of guilt, to be imprisoned</u>!

ABOUT A CHALLENGE FOR AMERICANS

What has happened to America? Have its people changed? Yes, its people have changed. Have its values changed? Yes, its values have changed. Its character is tarnished and its name is not what it used to be. Why? It is all very simple. The successful life of any nation, just as that of a natural person or family, comes from Righteousness. <u>Righteousness comes from honoring the living, Almighty God</u>. A nation outwardly reflects the values of its people. So what has happened to America?

The answer is you and me! If we wonder why judges are corrupt, it's because we permit it. If we wonder why we work so hard and are left with so little, it's because we consent to it. If we wonder why our child does not learn, it's because many schools no longer teach truth or with authority, but baby-sit *(if that)* and we condone it. We lose because we consent to these diminished values! <u>We have waived our birthrights and birth names and blindly placed ourselves into bondage</u> by consenting to a banker controlled, godless government, under laws that are abusive and that places people into bondage. So there! You may not like what I've said in this book, but I've said it. Let's restore America's dignity and honor. Let's once again honor Almighty God!

It is time for the *Government of the United States* to take its dirtied hands off the Hawaiian Kingdom, and allow its re-activated (1996) *Ke Aupuni O Hawaii Nei* and its

Hawaiian Kingdom National Judiciary and *Hawaiian Kingdom Laws* to replace the judicial corruption that the U.S. has propagated *(for over 115 years of military rule and control)* using *"color of U.S. law"*!

It is time for the United States to consider restitution and reparations to **Ke Aupuni O Hawaii Nei, Ko Hawaii Pae Aina,** and its People for the international trespass and intrusion upon their foreign neutral and sovereign land. I speak of not just the Hawaiians of the blood *(koko)*, but also of <u>Hawaiian Nationals of all ethnic backgrounds</u> that love their Islands and their Country!

A RIGHTEOUS CHALLENGE FOR AMERICANS

Hey America! In America let's get our *"republican form of government"* and justice system back... we cannot survive without it. Let's honor America's sovereign *"Union of States."* It's time to resurrect and preserve the *"Union."* Let's honor God Almighty and walk the straight and narrow where His Righteousness makes us aware of the right to an honorable and just government system and peace in the communities in which we live. Let's be God pleasers, not people pleasers. Let's be pleasers of God, not pleasers of corruption in Government.

A RIGHTEOUS CHALLENGE FOR HAWAIIANS

I say to you *Hawaiians Nationals*; you must unite as *Hawaiian Nationals*. Remember, *"Citizenship is Voluntary"* and your citizenship rights are yours alone! <u>As *"Native Hawaiians"* you do not own the land</u>, but as *"Hawaiian Nationals,"* you do! <u>As *"Native Hawaiians"* you do not have rights</u>, but as *"Hawaiian Nationals,"* you do! That is why the U.S. wants you to be *"Native Hawaiian,"* ignorant, subordinated and controlled under a de facto *reservation-style "Reorganized Native Hawaiian Governing Entity"* administered by their *Puppet State of Hawaii, Office of Hawaiian Affairs (OHA).*

Do you really want to be in the same status as the American Indian on a reservation? Is that what you want? You have three options here.

1. You can lawfully come home to your own Hawaiian Kingdom National laws and Constitution as a Hawaiian National (Private Citizen; <u>or,</u>

2. remain a foreigner on your own land as a *"Washington D. C., "immigration status, second-class, fiction, or public servant U.S. Federal citizen"* on the military and public servant side of the American Constitution *(Under Article 1, Section 8. Most of you are already there)*, and must pay them IRS Taxes, <u>or,</u>

3. you can submit to OHA *and Kau Inoa* as an aboriginal *("Native Hawaiian"),* forfeit your Hawaiian lands to a foreign nation *(U.S.)* and become a *"Native Hawaiian"* on a Reservation.

You have already and unknowingly transferred your citizenship to a foreign corporate government *(U.S.)* unlawfully functioning on our soil. <u>To get it back, you have to lawfully and publicly cancel those implied adhesions that bind you to that foreign jurisdiction of law.</u> You have to properly and lawfully cancel that *un-recorded and implied power of attorney* and binding foreign adhesive citizenship contract!

If we are truthful, honorable Private Citizens and love our ohana and want to do what is right, then we must come home to our rightful place as a National People. It is my hope we will all find Ke Akua's Peace and Freedom. We will most definitely find *"Aloha."*

The lie cannot prevail forever, but truth always does. Where do you stand? The Hawaiian Kingdom is! Are you in or out? Think before acting on what will change the rest of your entire life. Here is a chance to stand up for the Righteousness and the Truth of Almighty God. It is a free choice, but not without its costs. Don't be like those who are weak and walk in fear, being afraid to stand up for what is honorable and just. Also, we do not have to be like those who are angry, profane and destructive. Peace comes from knowing Iesu Kristo, and He is if we honor Him, Our Victory!

Ke Aupuni O Hawaii Nei o **Ko Hawaii Pae Aina** awaits you. It is time to become a *"Hawaiian National"* under your own national laws on your own land… ***nou ke koho*** *(the choice is yours)*. Freedom and rights are given freely by Almighty God, but must be sustained by sincere determination to do what is right, and that sacrifice comes at a price. Freedom belongs to each of us who seeks to preserve righteousness and justice.

Have courage to abide by the motto of the Hawaiian Kingdom, Ua Mau Ke Ea O Ka Aina I Ka Pono O Iesu Kristo. *(The Sovereignty of the land is perpetuated in the righteousness of Jesus Christ)*

The following statement made by Almighty God to his people can sum it up:

"Obey my voice, and I will be your God and ye shall be my people; and walk in all the ways that I have commanded you, that it may be well unto you." (Jeremiah 7:23)
Aloha Ke Akua.

EXHIBIT A

Apology Law U.S. PL 103-150

PUBLIC LAW 103-150—NOV. 23, 1993

100TH ANNIVERSARY OF THE OVERTHROW OF THE HAWAIIAN KINGDOM

PUBLIC LAW 103-150

S. J. Res. 19

One Hundred Third Congress
of the
United States of America

AT THE FIRST SESSION

Begun and held at the City of Washington on Tuesday,
the fifth day of January, one thousand nine hundred and ninety-three

Joint Resolution

107 STAT. 1510   PUBLIC LAW 103-150—NOV. 23, 1993

Public Law 103-150
103d Congress

Joint Resolution

Nov. 23, 1993
[S.J. Res. 19]

To acknowledge the 100th anniversary of the January 17, 1893 overthrow of the Kingdom of Hawaii, and to offer an apology to Native Hawaiians on behalf of the United States for the overthrow of the Kingdom of Hawaii.

Whereas, prior to the arrival of the first Europeans in 1778, the Native Hawaiian people lived in a highly organized, self-sufficient, subsistent social system based on communal land tenure with a sophisticated language, culture, and religion;

Whereas a unified monarchical government of the Hawaiian Islands was established in 1810 under Kamehameha I, the first King of Hawaii;

Whereas, from 1826 until 1893, the United States recognized the independence of the Kingdom of Hawaii, extended full and complete diplomatic recognition to the Hawaiian Government, and entered into treaties and conventions with the Hawaiian monarchs to govern commerce and navigation in 1826, 1842, 1849, 1875, and 1887;

Whereas the Congregational Church (now known as the United Church of Christ), through its American Board of Commissioners for Foreign Missions, sponsored and sent more than 100 missionaries to the Kingdom of Hawaii between 1820 and 1850;

Whereas, on January 14, 1893, John L. Stevens (hereafter referred to in this Resolution as the "United States Minister"), the United States Minister assigned to the sovereign and independent Kingdom of Hawaii conspired with a small group of non-Hawaiian residents of the Kingdom of Hawaii, including citizens of the United States, to overthrow the indigenous and lawful Government of Hawaii;

Whereas, in pursuance of the conspiracy to overthrow the Government of Hawaii, the United States Minister and the naval representatives of the United States caused armed naval forces of the United States to invade the sovereign Hawaiian nation on January 16, 1893, and to position themselves near the Hawaiian Government buildings and the Iolani Palace to intimidate Queen Liliuokalani and her Government;

Whereas, on the afternoon of January 17, 1893, a Committee of Safety that represented the American and European sugar planters, descendents of missionaries, and financiers deposed the Hawaiian monarchy and proclaimed the establishment of a Provisional Government;

Whereas the United States Minister thereupon extended diplomatic recognition to the Provisional Government that was formed by the conspirators without the consent of the Native Hawaiian people or the lawful Government of Hawaii and in violation of treaties between the two nations and of international law;

Whereas, soon thereafter, when informed of the risk of bloodshed with resistance, Queen Liliuokalani issued the following statement yielding her authority to the United States Government rather than to the Provisional Government:

"I Liliuokalani, by the Grace of God and under the Constitution of the Hawaiian Kingdom, Queen, do hereby solemnly protest against any and all acts done against myself and the Constitutional Government of the Hawaiian Kingdom by certain persons claiming to have established a Provisional Government of and for this Kingdom.

"That I yield to the superior force of the United States of America whose Minister Plenipotentiary, His Excellency John L. Stevens, has caused United States troops to be landed at Honolulu and declared that he would support the Provisional Government.

"Now to avoid any collision of armed forces, and perhaps the loss of life, I do this under protest and impelled by said force yield my authority until such time as the Government of the United States shall, upon facts being presented to it, undo the action of its representatives and reinstate me in the authority which I claim as the Constitutional Sovereign of the Hawaiian Islands.".

Done at Honolulu this 17th day of January, A.D. 1893.;

Whereas, without the active support and intervention by the United States diplomatic and military representatives, the insurrection against the Government of Queen Liliuokalani would have failed for lack of popular support and insufficient arms;

Whereas, on February 1, 1893, the United States Minister raised the American flag and proclaimed Hawaii to be a protectorate of the United States;

Whereas the report of a Presidentially established investigation conducted by former Congressman James Blount into the events surrounding the insurrection and overthrow of January 17, 1893, concluded that the United States diplomatic and military representatives had abused their authority and were responsible for the change in government;

Whereas, as a result of this investigation, the United States Minister to Hawaii was recalled from his diplomatic post and the military commander of the United States armed forces stationed in Hawaii was disciplined and forced to resign his commission;

Whereas, in a message to Congress on December 18, 1893, President Grover Cleveland reported fully and accurately on the illegal acts of the conspirators, described such acts as an "act of war, committed with the participation of a diplomatic representative of the United States and without authority of Congress", and acknowledged that by such acts the government of a peaceful and friendly people was overthrown;

Whereas President Cleveland further concluded that a "substantial wrong has thus been done which a due regard for our national character as well as the rights of the injured people requires we should endeavor to repair" and called for the restoration of the Hawaiian monarchy;

Whereas the Provisional Government protested President Cleveland's call for the restoration of the monarchy and continued to hold state power and pursue annexation to the United States;

Whereas the Provisional Government successfully lobbied the Committee on Foreign Relations of the Senate (hereafter referred to in this Resolution as the "Committee") to conduct a new investigation into the events surrounding the overthrow of the monarchy;

Whereas the Committee and its chairman, Senator John Morgan, conducted hearings in Washington, D.C., from December 27, 1893, through February 26, 1894, in which members of the Provisional Government justified and condoned the actions of the United States Minister and recommended annexation of Hawaii;

Whereas, although the Provisional Government was able to obscure the role of the United States in the illegal overthrow of the Hawaiian monarchy, it was unable to rally the support from two-thirds of the Senate needed to ratify a treaty of annexation;

Whereas, on July 4, 1894, the Provisional Government declared itself to be the Republic of Hawaii;

Whereas, on January 24, 1895, while imprisoned in Iolani Palace, Queen Liliuokalani was forced by representatives of the Republic of Hawaii to officially abdicate her throne;

Whereas, in the 1896 United States Presidential election, William McKinley replaced Grover Cleveland;

Whereas, on July 7, 1898, as a consequence of the Spanish-American War, President McKinley signed the Newlands Joint Resolution that provided for the annexation of Hawaii;

Whereas, through the Newlands Resolution, the self-declared Republic of Hawaii ceded sovereignty over the Hawaiian Islands to the United States;

Whereas the Republic of Hawaii also ceded 1,800,000 acres of crown, government and public lands of the Kingdom of Hawaii, without the consent of or compensation to the Native Hawaiian people of Hawaii or their sovereign government;

Whereas the Congress, through the Newlands Resolution, ratified the cession, annexed Hawaii as part of the United States, and vested title to the lands in Hawaii in the United States;

Whereas the Newlands Resolution also specified that treaties existing between Hawaii and foreign nations were to immediately cease and be replaced by United States treaties with such nations;

Whereas the Newlands Resolution effected the transaction between the Republic of Hawaii and the United States Government;

Whereas the indigenous Hawaiian people never directly relinquished their claims to their inherent sovereignty as a people or over their national lands to the United States, either through their monarchy or through a plebiscite or referendum;

Whereas, on April 30, 1900, President McKinley signed the Organic Act that provided a government for the territory of Hawaii and defined the political structure and powers of the newly established Territorial Government and its relationship to the United States;

Whereas, on August 21, 1959, Hawaii became the 50th State of the United States;

Whereas the health and well-being of the Native Hawaiian people is intrinsically tied to their deep feelings and attachment to the land;

Whereas the long-range economic and social changes in Hawaii over the nineteenth and early twentieth centuries have been devastating to the population and to the health and well-being of the Hawaiian people;

Whereas the Native Hawaiian people are determined to preserve, develop and transmit to future generations their ancestral territory, and their cultural identity in accordance with their own

PUBLIC LAW 103-150—NOV. 23, 1993   107 STAT. 151:

spiritual and traditional beliefs, customs, practices, language, and social institutions;

Whereas, in order to promote racial harmony and cultural understanding, the Legislature of the State of Hawaii has determined that the year 1993 should serve Hawaii as a year of special reflection on the rights and dignities of the Native Hawaiians in the Hawaiian and the American societies;

Whereas the Eighteenth General Synod of the United Church of Christ in recognition of the denomination's historical complicity in the illegal overthrow of the Kingdom of Hawaii in 1893 directed the Office of the President of the United Church of Christ to offer a public apology to the Native Hawaiian people and to initiate the process of reconciliation between the United Church of Christ and the Native Hawaiians; and

Whereas it is proper and timely for the Congress on the occasion of the impending one hundredth anniversary of the event, to acknowledge the historic significance of the illegal overthrow of the Kingdom of Hawaii, to express its deep regret to the Native Hawaiian people, and to support the reconciliation efforts of the State of Hawaii and the United Church of Christ with Native Hawaiians: Now, therefore, be it

Resolved by the Senate and House of Representatives of the United States of America in Congress assembled,

SECTION 1. ACKNOWLEDGMENT AND APOLOGY.

The Congress—

(1) on the occasion of the 100th anniversary of the illegal overthrow of the Kingdom of Hawaii on January 17, 1893, acknowledges the historical significance of this event which resulted in the suppression of the inherent sovereignty of the Native Hawaiian people;

(2) recognizes and commends efforts of reconciliation initiated by the State of Hawaii and the United Church of Christ with Native Hawaiians;

(3) apologizes to Native Hawaiians on behalf of the people of the United States for the overthrow of the Kingdom of Hawaii on January 17, 1893 with the participation of agents and citizens of the United States, and the deprivation of the rights of Native Hawaiians to self-determination;

(4) expresses its commitment to acknowledge the ramifications of the overthrow of the Kingdom of Hawaii, in order to provide a proper foundation for reconciliation between the United States and the Native Hawaiian people; and

(5) urges the President of the United States to also acknowledge the ramifications of the overthrow of the Kingdom of Hawaii and to support reconciliation efforts between the United States and the Native Hawaiian people.

SEC. 2. DEFINITIONS.

As used in this Joint Resolution, the term "Native Hawaiian" means any individual who is a descendent of the aboriginal people who, prior to 1778, occupied and exercised sovereignty in the area that now constitutes the State of Hawaii.

107 STAT. 1514   PUBLIC LAW 103-150—NOV. 23, 1993

SEC. 3. DISCLAIMER.

    Nothing in this Joint Resolution is intended to serve as a settlement of any claims against the United States.

    Approved November 23, 1993.

Speaker of the House of Representatives.

_~~Vice President of the United States and~~
President of the Senate pro tempore._

APPROVED

NOV 23 1993

LEGISLATIVE HISTORY—S.J. Res. 19:

SENATE REPORTS: No. 103-126 (Select Comm. on Indian Affairs).
CONGRESSIONAL RECORD, Vol. 139 (1993):
    Oct. 27, considered and passed Senate.
    Nov. 15, considered and passed House.

EXHIBIT B

Acceptance of Apology by the People of God of Hawaii

FRIDAY, NOVEMBER 17, 2000

Aloha Kākou

On November 23, 1993 President William J. Clinton and the 103rd Congress of the United States issued U.S. Public Law 103-150, apologizing for the United States' role in the overthrow of the Hawaiian Kingdom, a friendly, neutral, sovereign nation.

The Apology was a righteous act done on behalf of the People of the United States. Admitting the commission of a wrong and apologizing for that wrong, is a righteous act. It requires a righteous response.

This message publicly accepts the United States' apology, allowing for reconciliation to proceed on a level above that of personal, ethnic, national or other temporal issues or interests. The objective is to make things right—before God—between the two parties.

In the process of ho'oponopono (making things right before God, between two disputing parties), the motivation, intent or circumstances are not relevant, only the virtuous desire to make things right (pono) before God. Therefore, the dispute is given to God to resolve.

Through this message we thank President Clinton, the members of Congress and the people of the United States for the gift of making the first step in ho'oponopono. We gratefully accept the apology as the gift that it is and we commit this matter into God's hands.

Ua mau ke eā o ka 'āina
I ka pono o Iesū Kristo.

Aloha ke Akua

Richard Basuel
Leon Siu
David Kiiupileokalani Kahiapo
William Ko'omealani Amona
Lydia Miller Amona
Allison Sanae Goto
Derek Tamura
KeAloha Aiu
John Phillip Souza
Ross Huirt Myers
Aran Alton Ardaiz
Jon Robert Johnson
Kalani N. Poomaihealani
and others.

Publication of this message was paid for by:

Lāhui Pono
1748 Hite Street,
Kalihi Kai, O'ahu,
Hawaii nei
For more information:
www.LahuiPono.
homepage.com

A Message from People of God
ACCEPTING YOUR APOLOGY, OFFERED FOR VALUE

To: Mr. William J. Clinton, PRESIDENT and COMMANDER-IN-CHIEF of the UNITED STATES; and All incumbents serving as the UNITED STATES CONGRESS

Greetings and salutations from our Sovereign Lord and Savior, Iesu, the Christ, and ourselves by visitation to exercise His Ministerial powers of accepting for value those virtues of the apology offered for the theft of a nation in your U.S. Public Law 103-150, 103rd Congress, 107 Stat. 1510, Nov. 23, 1993 (Apology Law).

It is God's will that we settle disputes peaceably with our adversaries.

For it is written, "Agree with thine adversarie quickly, whiles thou art in the way with him: least at any time the adversarie deliuer thee to the iudge, and the iudge deliuer thee to the officer, and thou be cast into prison. Verily I say unto thee, thou shalt by no meanes come out thence, till thou hast payd the uttermost farthing." THE GOSPEL ACORDING To S. Matthew. CHAP. V V. 25-26

God's laws never change and they are always in force.

And it is written again, "Thinke not that I am come to destroy the lawe or the Prophets. I am not come to destroy, but to fulfill. For verily I say unto you, Till heauen and earth passe, one iote or one title, shall in no wise passe from the law, till all be fulfilled. Whosoeuer therfore shall breake one of these least commaundements, and shall teach men so, he shall be called the least in the kingdome of heauen: but whosoeuer shall due, and teach them, the same, shall be called great in the kingdome of heauen." THE GOSPEL ACORDING To S. Matthew. CHAP. V V. 17-19

For it is written, "Thou shalt not couet thy neighbours house, thou shalt not couet thy neighbours wife, nor his man seruant, nor his maid seruant, nor his oxe, nor his asse, nor any thing that is thy neighbors." THE SECOND BOOKE OF Moses, called Exodus. CHAP. XX. V. 17

An Apology is an acknowledgement of a sin.

For it is written again, "ANd the Lord spake unto Moses, saying, If a soule sinne, and commit a trespasse against the Lord, and lie unto his neighbour in that which was deliuered him to keepe, or in fellowship, or in a thing taken away by violence, or hath deceiued his neighbour: Or haue found that which was lost, and lieth concerning it, and sweareth falsly: in any of these that a man doth, sinning therein: Then it shall be, because he hath sinned, and is guiltie, that hee shall restore that which he tooke violently away, or the thing which he hath deceitfully gotten, or that which was deliuered him to keepe, or the lost thing which he found: Or all that about which hee hath sworne falsly: hee shall euen restore it in the principall, and shall adde the fift part more thereto, and giue it unto him to whom I appertaineth, in the day of his trespasse offering." THE THIRD BOOKE OF Moses, called Leuiticus. CHAP. VI. V. 1-5

Therefore, in His Name and pursuant to His will, we the undersigned, do gratefully accept For Value, those virtues of your apology for the theft of a nation, looking Forward to the day When same is principally and Fully restored. May repentant Friendship become common to us in this journey we share.

We accept your apology as an act of service and honor to our Lord.

"Now when Iesus was in Bethanie, in the house of Simon the leper, There came unto him a woman, hauing an alabaster boxe of very precious ointment, and powred it on his head, as he sate at meat. But when his disciples saw it, they had indignation, saying, To what purpose is this waste? For this ointment might haue bin sold for much, and giuen to the poore. When Iesus understood it, he said unto them, Why trouble ye the woman? For she hath wrought a good worke upon me. For ye haue the poore alwayes with you, but me ye haue not alwayes. For in that she hath powred this ointment on my body, shee did it for my buriall. Verely I say unto you, Wheresoeuer this Gospel shall be preached in the whole world, there shall also be this, that this woman hath done, be told for a memorial of her." THE GOSPEL ACORDING To S. Matthew. CHAP. XXVI. V. 6-13

For it is written again, "So likewise ye, when ye shal haue done all those things which are commanded you, say, Wee are Vnprofitable seruants: wee haue done that which was our duety to doe." THE GOSPEL ACORDING To S. Luke. CHAP. XVII V. 10

We the undersigned, knowing the penalty for bearing false witness, with knowledge of the above, do know the same to be true and correct.

It is written in your law that the testimony of two men is true. I am one who bears witness of myself. My Sovereign Lord and Savior, Iesu, the Christ, in whom I live and move and have my being, bears witness of me. Our Father which art in heaven bears witness of Him.

Done by the Direct act of Iesu, the Christ, upon our hands, this Eleventh day of the Eleventh Month, in the Year Two Thousand of Our Sovereign Lord and Savior, Iesu, the Christ.

208

EXHIBIT C

**Treaty of 1850 between
Hawaiian Kingdom and U.S.**

BENJAMIN J. CAYETANO
GOVERNOR

SAM CALLEJO
COMPTROLLER

MARY PATRICIA WATERHOUSE
DEPUTY COMPTROLLER

STATE OF HAWAII
DEPARTMENT OF ACCOUNTING
AND GENERAL SERVICES

ARCHIVES DIVISION
Hawai'i State Archives
'Iolani Palace Grounds
Honolulu, Hawai'i 96813

I, JOLYN G. TAMURA, State Archivist of the State of Hawai'i, do hereby

certify that the attached document is a true and exact xerographic copy of

Treaty of Friendship, Commerce and Navigation between the United States of

America and the King of the Hawaiian Islands, concluded on December 20, 1849,

with Ratification signed by Zachary Taylor, President of the United States of

America on February 4, 1850, from the records of the Foreign Office and

Executive,

on file in the STATE ARCHIVES, at Honolulu, State of Hawai'i.

WITNESS my hand and seal this 24th day of November A.D., 1997, at

Honolulu, State of Hawai'i.

JOLYN G. TAMURA, STATE ARCHIVIST

Zachary Taylor,

President of the United States of America

To all to whom these presents shall come

Greeting:

Know Ye, that whereas, a Treaty of Friendship, Commerce, and Navigation between the United States of America and His Majesty, the King of the Hawaiian Islands, was concluded and signed by their Plenipotentiaries, in the City of Washington, on the twentieth day of December, last; which Treaty is word for word as follows:

The United States of America and His Majesty the King of the Hawaiian Islands equally animated with the desire of maintaining the relations of good understanding which have hitherto so happily subsisted between their respective states, and consolidating the commercial intercourse between them have agreed to enter into negotiations for the conclusion of a Treaty of Friendship, Commerce and Navigation, for which purpose they have appointed Plenipotentiaries, that is to say:

The President of the United States of America John M. Clayton Secretary of State of the United States; and His Majesty the King of the Hawaiian Islands James Jackson Jarves, accredited as his special Commissioner to the Government of the United States; who after having exchanged

their full powers, found in good and due form, have

concluded and signed the following articles:

Article I.

There shall be perpetual peace and amity between

the United States and the King of the Hawaiian

Islands, his heirs and his successors.

Article II.

There shall be reciprocal liberty of commerce

and navigation between the United States of

America and the Hawaiian Islands.

No duty of customs, or other impost, shall be

charged upon any goods, the produce or manufac-

ture of one country, upon importation from such

country into the other, other or higher than the

duty or impost charged upon goods of the same

kind; the produce or manufacture of, or imported from any other country; and the United
States of America and His Majesty the King
of the Hawaiian Islands do hereby engage, that
the subjects or citizens of any other state shall
not enjoy any favor, privilege, or immunity, whatever, in matters of commerce and navigation,
which shall not also at the same time, be
extended to the subjects or citizens of the other
contracting party gratuitously, if the concession in
favor of that other State shall have been gratui-
tous; and in return for a compensation, as nearly
as possible of proportionate value and effect, to be
adjusted by mutual agreement, if the concession shall have been conditional.

Article III.

All articles the produce or manufacture of either country which can legally be imported into either country from the other, in ships of that other country, and thence coming, shall, when so imported, be subject to the same duties, and enjoy the same privileges, whether imported in ships of the one country, or in ships of the other; and in like manner, all goods which can legally be exported or re-exported from either country to the other, in ships of that other country, shall, when so exported or re-exported, be subject to the same duties, and be entitled to the same privileges, drawbacks, bounties, and allowances, whether exported in ships of the one country, or in ships of the other; and all goods and articles, of whatever description

not being of the produce or manufacture of the
United States, which can be legally imported into
the Sandwich Islands, shall when so imported
in vessels of the United States pay no other or
higher duties, imposts, or charges than shall be
payable upon the like goods, and articles, when
imported in the vessels of the most favored foreign nation other than the nation of which the
said goods and articles are the produce or
manufacture.

Article IV.

No duties of tonnage, harbor, light-houses, pilota-
ge, quarantine, or other similar duties, of whatever
nature, or under whatever denomination, shall be
imposed in either country upon the vessels of the
other, in respect of voyages between the United

States of America and the Hawaiian Islands, if laden, or in respect of any voyage, if in ballast, which shall not be equally imposed in the like cases on national vessels.

Article V.

It is hereby declared, that the stipulations of the present treaty are not to be understood as applying to the navigation and carrying trade between one port and another situated in the States of either contracting party, such navigation and trade being reserved exclusively to national vessels.

Article VI.

Steam vessels of the United States which may be employed by the Government of the said States, in the carrying of their Public Mails across the

Pacific Ocean, or from one port in that ocean to another, shall have free access to the ports of the Sandwich Islands, with the privilege of stopping therein to refit, to refresh, to land passengers and their baggage, and for the transaction of any business pertaining to the public Mail service of the United States, and shall be subject in such ports to no duties of tonnage, harbor, lighthouses, quarantine, or other similar duties of whatever nature or under whatever denomination.

Article VII.

The Whaleships of the United States shall have access to the ports of Hilo, Kealakekua and Hanalei in the Sandwich Islands, for the purposes of refitment and refreshment, as well as to the ports of Honolulu and Lahaina which only are ports of entry for all Merchant vessels, and in all the above named ports they shall be permitted to trade or barter their supplies or goods, excepting spiritous liquors to the amount of two hundred dollars *ad valorem* for each vessel, without paying any charge for tonnage or harbor dues of any description, or any duties or imposts whatever upon the goods or articles so traded or bartered. They shall also be permitted, with the like exemption from all charges for tonnage and harbor dues, further to trade or barter, with the same exception as to spiritous liquors, to the additional amount of one thousand dollars *ad valorem*, for each vessel, paying upon the additional goods, and articles so traded and bartered, no other or higher duties, than are payable on like goods, and articles, when imported in the vessels and by the citizens or subjects of the most favored foreign nation. They shall also be permitted to pass from port to port of the Sandwich Islands for the purpose of procuring refreshments, but they shall not discharge their seamen or land their passengers in the said Islands, except at Lahaina and Honolulu, and, in all the ports named in this article, the whale-ships of the United States shall enjoy in all respects, whatsoever, all the rights, privileges and immunities, which are enjoyed by, or shall be granted to, the whaleships of the most favored foreign nation. The like privilege of frequenting the three ports of the Sandwich Islands, above named in this Article, not being ports of entry for merchant ves-sels, is also guaranteed to all the public armed vessels of the United States. But nothing in this article shall be construed as authorising any vessel of the United States, having on board any disease usually regarded as requiring quarantine, to enter during the continuance of such disease on board, any port of the Sandwich Islands, other than Lahaina or Honolulu.

Article VIII.

The contracting parties engage, in regard to the personal privileges that the citizens of the United States of America shall enjoy in the dominions of his Majesty the King of the Hawaiian Islands, and the subjects of his said Majesty in the United States of America; that they shall have free and undoubted right to travel and to reside in the states of the two high contracting parties, subject to the same precautions of police which are practiced towards the subjects or citizens of the most favored nations. They shall be entitled to occupy dwellings and warehouses, and to dispose of their personal property of every kind and description, by sale, gift, exchange, will, or in any other way whatever, without the smallest hinderance or obstacle; and their heirs or representatives, being subjects or citizens of the other contracting party, shall succeed to their personal goods, whether by testament or ab intestato; and may take possession thereof, either by themselves or by others acting for them, and dispose of the same at will; paying to the profit of the respective governments such dues only as the inhabitants of the country wherein the said goods are, shall be subject to pay in like cases. And in case of the absence of the heirs and representative, such care shall be taken of the said goods as would be taken of the goods of a native of the same country in like case, until the lawful owner may take measures for receiving them. And if a question should arise among several claimants as to which of them said goods belong, the same shall be decided finally by the laws and judges of the land wherein the said goods are. Where on the decease of any person holding real estate within the territories of one party, such real estate would, by the laws of the land, descend on a citizen or subject of the other, were he not disqualified by alienage, such citizen or subject shall be allowed a reasonable time to sell the same, and to withdraw the proceeds without

molestation, and exempt from all duties of detraction
on the part of the government of the respective
States. The citizens or subjects of the contracting
parties shall not be obliged to pay, under any
pretence whatever, any taxes or impositions, other or
greater than those which are paid, or may hereafter
be paid, by the subjects or citizens of the most
favored nations, in the respective states of the high
contracting parties. They shall be exempt from all
military service, whether by land or by sea; from
forced loans, and from every extraordinary contribution not general and by law established. Their
dwellings, warehouses and all premises appertaining
thereto, destined for the purposes of commerce or
residence, shall be respected. No arbitrary search
of, or visit to, their houses, and no arbitrary examina-

tion or inspection whatever of the books, papers, or accounts of their trade shall be made; but such measure shall be executed only in conformity with the legal sentence of a competent tribunal; and each of the two contracting parties engages that the citizens or subjects of the other residing in their respectives states shall enjoy their property and personal security, in as full and ample manner as their own citizens or subjects, or the subjects or citizens of the most favored nation, but subject always to the laws and statutes of the two contries respectively.

Article IX.

The citizens and subjects of each of the two contracting parties shall be free in the States of the other to manage their own affairs themselves or to commit those affairs to the management

of any persons whom they may appoint as their
broker, factor or agent, nor shall the citizens and
subjects of the two contracting parties be restrained
in their choice of persons to act in such capacities, nor shall they be called upon to pay any
salary or remuneration to any person whom they
shall not choose to employ. Absolute freedom
shall be given in all cases to the buyer and seller
to bargain together and to fix the price of any
goods or merchandise imported into, or to be exported from the states and dominions of the two
contracting parties; save and accept generally
such cases wherein the laws and usages of the
country may require the intervention of any
special agents in the states and dominions of
the contracting parties. But nothing contained

in this or any other article of the present Treaty shall be construed to authorize the sale of spiritous liquors to the natives of the Sandwich Islands further than such sale may be allowed by the Hawaiian laws.

Article X.

Each of the two contracting parties may have in the ports of the other, consuls, vice consuls, and commercial agents of their own appointment, who shall enjoy the same privileges and powers with those of the most favored nations; but if any such consuls shall exercise commerce, they shall be subject to the same laws and usages to which the private individuals of their nation are subject in the same place. The said Consuls, vice consuls, and commercial agents are authorized to require

the assistance of the local authorities for the search,
arrest, detention, and imprisonment of the deserters
from the ships of war and merchant vessels of
their country. For this purpose, they shall apply
to the competent tribunals, judges and officers,
and shall in writing demand the said deserters
proving, by the exhibition of the registers of the vessels, the rolls of the crews, or by other official documents
that such individuals formed part of the crews;
and this reclamation being thus substantiated, the
surrender shall not be refused. Such deserters
when arrested shall be placed at the disposal of
the said consuls, vice consuls, or commercial agents,
and may be confined in the public prisons, at the
request and cost of those who shall claim them,
in order to be detained until the time when they

shall be restored to the vessel to which they belonged,

or sent back to their own country by a vessel of the same

nation or any other vessel whatsoever. The agents, owners

or masters of vessels on account of whom the deserters

have been apprehended, upon requisition of the local

authorities shall be required to take or send away

such deserters from the states and dominions of the

contracting parties, or give such security for their

good conduct as the law may require. But if not

sent back nor reclaimed within six months from

the day of their arrest; or if all the expenses of such

imprisonment are not defrayed by the party causing

such arrest and imprisonment, they shall be set at

liberty and shall not be again arrested for the same

cause. However, if the deserters should be found

to have committed any crime or offence, their surrender

may be delayed until the tribunal before which their case shall be depending, shall have pronounced its sentence, and such sentence shall have been carried into effect.

Article XI.

It is agreed that perfect and entire liberty of conscience shall be enjoyed by the citizens and subjects of both the contracting parties, in the countries of the one and the other, without their being liable to be disturbed or molested on account of their religious beliefs. But nothing contained in this article shall be construed to interfere with the exclusive right of the Hawaiian Government to regulate for itself the Schools which it may establish or support within its jurisdiction.

Article XII.

If any ships of war or other vessels, be wrecked on the coasts of the States or territories of either of the contracting parties such ships or vessels, or any parts thereof, and all furniture and appurtenances belonging thereunto and all goods and merchandize which shall be saved therefrom, or the produce thereof, if sold shall be faithfully restored with the least possible delay to the proprietors upon being claimed by them, or by their duly authorized factors; and if there are no such proprietors or factors on the spot, then the said goods and merchandize, or the proceeds thereof, as well as all the papers found on board such wrecked ships or vessels shall be delivered to the American or Hawaiian Consul, or vice consul in whose district the wreck may have taken place.

and such Consul vice consul, proprietors or factors,
shall pay only the expenses incurred in the preservation of the property, together with the rate of salvage
and expenses of quarantine which would have been
payable in the like case of a wreck of a national
vessel; and the goods and merchandize saved from
the wreck shall not be subject to duties unless entered for consumption; it being understood that
in case of any legal claim upon such wreck,
goods or merchandize, the same shall be referred
for decision to the competent tribunals of the country.

Article XIII.

The vessels of either of the two contracting parties
which may be forced by stress of weather or other
cause into one of the ports of the other shall be
exempt from all duties of port or navigation paid

for the benefit of the state, if the motives which led to their seeking refuge be real and evident, and if no cargo be discharged or taken on board, save such as may relate to the subsistence of the crew, or be necessary for the repair of the vessels, and if they do not stay in port beyond the time necessary, keeping in view the cause which led to their seeking refuge.

Article XIV.

The contracting parties mutually agree to surrender, upon official requisition, to the authorities of each, all persons who, being charged with the crimes of murder, piracy, arson, robbery, forgery, or the utterance of forged paper, committed within the jurisdiction of either, shall be found within the territories of the other; provided that this shall only be done upon such evidence of criminality as, according to the laws of the place where the person so charged shall be found, would justify his apprehension and commitment for trial if the crime had there been committed: and the respective judges and other magistrates of the two Governments, shall have authority, upon complaint made under oath, to issue a warrant for the apprehension of the person so charged, that he may be brought before such judges or other magistrates respectively, to the end that the evidence of criminality may be heard and considered; and if, on such hearing, the evidence be deemed sufficient to sustain the charge, it shall be the duty of the examining judge or magistrate to certify the same to the proper Executive authority, that a warrant may issue for the surrender of such fugitive. The expense of such apprehension and delivery shall be borne and defrayed by the party who makes the requisition and receives the fugitive.

Article XV.

So soon as Steam or other Mail Packets under the flag of either of the contracting parties shall have commenced running between their respective ports of entry, the contracting parties agree to receive at the post offices of those ports all mailable matter, and to forward it as directed, the destination being to some regular post office of either country; charging thereupon the regular postal rates as established by law in the territories of either party receiving said mailable matter, in addition to the original postage of the office whence the mail was sent. Mails for the United States shall be made up at regular intervals at the Hawaiian Post Office, and despatched to ports of the United States, the postmasters at which ports shall open the same, and forward the enclosed matter as directed, crediting the Hawaiian Government with their postages as established by law and stamped upon each manuscript or printed sheet.

All mailable matter destined for the Hawaiian Islands shall be received at the several post offices in the United States and forwarded to San Francisco or other ports on the Pacific coast of the United States, whence the postmasters shall despatch it by the regular mail packets to Honolulu, the Hawaiian government agreeing on their part to receive and collect for and credit the Post Office Department of the United States with the United States rates charged thereupon. It shall be optional to prepay the postage on letters in either country, but postage on printed sheets and newspapers shall in all cases be pre-paid. The respective post office Departments of the contracting parties shall in their accounts, which are to be adjusted annually, be credited with all dead letters returned.

Article XVI.

The present treaty shall be in force from the date of the exchange of the ratifications for the term of ten years, and further, until the end of twelve months after either of the contracting parties shall have given notice to the other of its intention to terminate the same, each of the said contracting parties reserving to itself the right of giving such

notice at the end of the said term of ten years, or
at any subsequent term.

Any citizen or subject of either party
infringing the articles of this treaty shall be held
responsible for the same and the harmony and
good correspondence between the two Governments
shall not be interrupted thereby, each party en-
gaging in no way to protect the offender or
sanction such violation.

Article XVII.

The present treaty shall be ratified by the
President of the United States of America, by
and with the advice and consent of the Senate
of the said States, and by His Majesty the
King of the Hawaiian Islands, by and with
the advice of his Privy Council of State, and

the ratifications shall be exchanged at Honolulu within eighteen months from the date of its signature, or sooner if possible.

In witness whereof, the respective Plenipotentiaries have signed the same in triplicate, and have thereto affixed their seals. Done at Washington in the English language the twentieth day of December, in the year one thousand eight hundred and forty nine

John M. Clayton.   (Seal)

James Jackson Jarves   (seal)

And whereas the Senate of the United States, by their Resolution of the fourteenth of last month, two thirds of the Senators then present concurring, did advise and consent to the ratification of the said Treaty:

Now therefore, be it known, that I, Zachary Taylor, President of the United States of America, having seen and considered the said Treaty, do hereby, in pursuance of the aforesaid advice and consent of the Senate, ratify and confirm the same and every article and clause thereof.

In witness whereof, I have caused the seal of the United States to be hereunto affixed. Given under my hand at the City of Washington the fourth day of February, in the year of our Lord one thousand eight hundred and fifty, and in the seventy fourth year of the Independence of the United States.

Z. Taylor

By the President,
John M. Clayton, Secretary of State.

The undersigned, Charles Bunker, Consul of the United States for Lahaina and Robert Crichton Wyllie, having been authorised by our respective governments to exchange the Ratifications of the Treaty of Friendship, Commerce and Navigation between the United States and His Hawaiian Majesty Concluded and signed at Washington, on the twentieth day of December, One Thousand Eight Hundred and Forty Nine, certify. That we have this day met for that purpose, and after comparing the said ratifications, each with the other, and both with the original of the said Treaty, have effected the exchange accordingly.

In witness whereof we have signed this certificate at Honolulu, this Twenty Fourth day of August, 1850, and have thereunto affixed our respective seals.

Charles Bunker

R. C. Wyllie

EXHIBIT D

Apostille

Aran Alton: Ardaiz*, Apostille,
by Special Appearance, a Spiritual
Man and Breathing Human Being,
and Hawaiian Kingdom Subject
C/o: General Delivery (Box 62107)
    Manoa Station
    Manoa, Oahu, Hawaii Nei
    Ko Hawaii Pae Aina
    (U. S. P. Z. Exempt – 96839)
    (808) 947-2449

FILED IN THE
UNITED STATES DISTRICT COURT
DISTRICT OF HAWAII

APR 2 1 2005

at ⎵ o'clock and ⎵ min. ⎵M
WALTER A. Y. H. CHINN, CLERK

IN THE UNITED STATES COURT

FOR THE HAWAII DISTRICT

HG

MISC. NO: _____   **BMK**

ACTUAL NOTICE TO THE JUDICIARY)
OF THE UNITED STATES AND THE)
DE FACTO STATE OF HAWAII,)
　)
　)
　)
from,)
　)
Aran Alton: Ardaiz, a natural Born)
Human Being and Hawaiian Kingdom)
Denizen, under his lawful birth name,)
　)
　)
Apostille, Declarant*.)
　)
　)
　)
　)
　)
　)
_____)

APOSTILLE AND DECLARATION OF FOREIGN STATUS: (NOT RECOGNITION OF THIS COURT'S JURISDICTION BY THIS AMERICAN CITIZEN)

ACTUAL NOTICE: By Aran Alton Ardaiz, Apostille, American sovereign, AND PROTECTED FOREIGN INTERNATIONAL HUMAN BEING OUTSIDE OF THE JURISDICTION OF THE DE FACTO STATE OF HAWAII (18 U. S. Cr. C. § 11); EXHIBIT 'A', APOSTILLE (AFFIRMED COPY)

MEMORANDUM IN SUPPORT OF NOTICE TO THE JUDICIARY OF FOREIGN STATUS

* Aran Alton: Ardaiz, by "special appearance," the natural born human being and a lawful Hawaiian Kingdom Subject of Ko Hawaii Pae Aina, and not a "corporate person" or a "14th Amendment" United States created Federal citizen.

"Now we know that the law is good, if a man use it lawfully, knowing this, that the law is not made for a righteous man but for the lawless and disobedient, for the ungodly and for sinners... for kidnappers, for liars, for perjured persons..." (1 Timothy 8-10)

APOSTILLE AND DECLARATION OF FOREIGN STATUS:
ACTUAL NOTICE BY Aran Alton: Ardaiz, Apostille, American sovereign,
AND PROTECTED FOREIGN INTERNATIONAL BEING OUTSIDE OF THE
JURISDICTION OF THE DE FACTO STATE OF HAWAII (18 U. S. C. § 11)

1

DECLARATION OF APOSTILLE / CITIZENSHIP

Comes now the undersigned *"Apostille-Declarant"*, Aran Alton: Ardaiz, **internationally registered and documented Apostille and protected "foreign official" and member of a lawful and peaceful **"faction" (18 U. S. Cr. C. § 11, see EXHIBIT 'A')**; and, a Minister and Teacher of the Gospel of Jesus Christ, appearing herein by *"special appearance,"* providing actual notice to the UNITED STATES GOVERNMENT and DE FACTO STATE OF HAWAII as a Spiritual Man under the Lordship of Jesus the Christ, solely to deny, object, refute and challenge the courts alleged claim of jurisdiction to charge, try, claim him and/or convict him as the Federal United States Government created fiction *("artificial")* person known as ARDAIZ, ARAN ALTON. **Apostille / Declarant shall be judged by Almighty God.** Whereas *"Citizenship is voluntary, not mandatory"* this Apostille-Declarant, the natural, breathing spiritual person described herein, does not waive his God given, inalienable and *"fundamental"* rights as **a sovereign, American born Citizen of the California Republic** and as a lawfully documented, *"denizen"* subject of *Ko Hawaii Pae Aina* within the Kingdom of Hawaii Government *"faction"* known as, *Ke Aupuni O Hawaii Nei*. Apostille-Declarant does not have any lawful or adhesive contracts with either the DE FACTO STATE OF HAWAII or the FEDERAL UNITED STATES jurisdictions.

Apostille-Declarant, having reserved his lawful rights under International Law, the **Constitution of Ko Hawaii Pae Aina**, and the lawful Hawaiian Kingdom Government known as **Ke Aupuni O Hawaii Nei** of Ko Hawaii Pae Aina, does now notify the JUDICIARY OF THE U. S. COURT FOR THE HAWAII DISTRICT of violations of law by said DE FACTO STATE OF HAWAII JUDICIARY and of unwarranted

---

**Faction. (Not in Black's Law Dictionary, 6th Ed.) Merriam Webster's Collegiate Dictionary, 10th Ed. defines "faction" as follows: *"1: a party or group (as within a government) that is often contentious or self-seeking; CLIQUE 2: PART SPIRIT ESP. WHENMARKED BY DISSENSION- factional – factionalism, factionally."*

2

and deliberate violations against Apostille-Declarant's person, family and property. Apostille-Declarant, under extreme duress and constant threat of kidnapping by the de facto State, which functions **in violation of 18 U. S. Cr. C. §§ 112, 878, 970 and 1201, and 18 USCr.C 241 & 242,** has been constantly harassed through re-arrest and re-imprisonment on falsified charges exercised against the *"artificial"* U. S. Government created person, **which Apostille-Declarant is not.** **Apostille-Declarant** respectfully notifies this foreign U. S. District Court on Hawaiian Aina of the DE FACTO STATE OF HAWAII'S want of jurisdiction, and their erroneous and fraudulent charges within the lower (District and Circuit) courts of the de facto State against the *"artificial"* person and the *"falsified"* **charges being maliciously applied** against Apostille-Declarant (the Spiritual and breathing natural human being) who is protected by the **United Nations Treaty on Apostille, specifically Article 7, The Hague Convention on *"Apostille,"* 1961 [1981, U. S. signatured].** Apostille-Declarant is also a *"secured party"* with a private lien under the **Uniform Commercial Code** against the fiction *"debtor"* *"person"* known as ARDAIZ, ARAN ALTON.

MEMORANDUM IN SUPPORT OF NOTICE TO THE JUDICIARY OF FOREIGN STATUS

Apostille-Declarant, a registered and lawful member of a foreign *"faction"* at *"peace,"* supra, with the United States hereby notices this court that this U. S. COURT FOR THE HAWAII DISTRICT and the courts of the DE FACTO STATE OF HAWAII lack both "subject matter" and "in personam" jurisdiction over said *"Internationally Protected Citizen."* The power of a court to decide a matter in controversy presupposes the existence of a *"duly constituted court with control over the subject matter and the parties"* (Black's Law Dictionary, 6th Edition, Page 853). In the year 1996, Public Record Filing No. 96-152274, Apostille-Declarant lawfully severed his corporate United States federal citizenship by lawful and actual notice, and, at that time notified the U. S. Government, the DE FACTO STATE OF HAWAII and DE

3

FACTO CITY AND COUNTY OF HONOLULU (Via U. S. Certified Mail) of said lawful separation and returned all adhesive documents belonging to said named parties (driver's license, license plates, registration, social security card number, etc.).

Under the DE FACTO STATE OF HAWAII **Rules of Penal Procedure (HRPP) 12 (2)**, Apostille-Declarant can raise the issue of jurisdiction of the court at any time and the court must prove that it has jurisdiction to decide the issues presented. The Courts of the de facto State for over ten years have REFUSED TO, AND HAVE NEVER HONORED, this "Penal" law, even with proof requested in writing:

1.   Apostille-Declarant alleges as fact that the courts, supra, have neither Spiritual Authority under Almighty God, nor *"subject matter"* jurisdiction nor "in personam" or *"personal jurisdiction"* over the Apostille-Declarant in the following respects:

   a) Apostille-Declarant is a lawfully registered *"foreign official"* with the United States Government as a part of a lawful foreign *"faction"* and is not a "U. S. created artificial corporate citizen." Apostille-Declarant's citizenship since 1996 was duly recorded **(file number 96-152274)** in the Bureau of Records of the Hawaiian Kingdom (known today as the Bureau of Conveyances of the DE FACTO STATE OF HAWAII;

   b) Apostille-Declarant under International Law is a *"foreign official,"* under a lawful oath of Office and a government officer **(18 U. S. C. § 1116 [b][4][B])** of **Ko Hawaii Pae Aina**, the lawful and de jure, Hawaiian Kingdom Government *"faction"* titled **Ke Aupuni O Hawaii Nei**, which is a separate and distinct governmental *"faction."* **Ke Aupuni O Hawaii Nei** functions exclusively under the authority of the Living and Almighty God and the de jure non-abrogated, common-law of the Hawaiian Kingdom as established and affirmed by non-abrogated Sessions Law **(An Act to Revise the Judiciary)** of the Hawaiian Kingdom, in **the year 1892, Chapter LVII, Section 5**, thereof;

   c) On October 20, 2000 a *"Declaration"* of *"foreign official"* status (affirmed by **18 U. S. C. § 1116 [b][3][B] and 18 U. S. Cr. C § 11**), was filed by registry through the United States

Postal Service with the Government of the Federal United States of America, specifically the Offices of the Secretary of State and Attorney General, said filing affirming Declarant's *"foreign official"* status as a member of a lawful and peaceful *"faction," supra;*

d) The term *"foreign government"* is defined (within **Title 18 United States Criminal Code, Section 11 and 18 U. S. C. 1116 [b][2]**), to wit:

> *"The term "foreign government," as used in this title*
> *except in section 112, 878, 970, 1116 and 1201,*
> *includes any government, faction, or body of insurgents*
> *within a country with which the United States is at peace,*
> *irrespective of recognition by the United States. (June 25*
> *1948, c. 645, 62 Stat. 686; Oct. 8, 1976, Pub. L. 94-467,*
> *§ 11, 90 Stat. 2001)"* (Source: 1999 Edition, Federal
> Criminal Code and Rules)

e) The meaning of the word *"except"* as used in 18 U. S. Cr. C. § 11 is defined in Black's Law Dictionary, Sixth Edition as follows:

> **"Except.** *But for; only for; not including; other*
> *than; otherwise than; to leave out of account*
> *or consideration".* (underline emphasis by Declarant)

Therefore, the term *"except"* as used and applied in this text is inclusive of the other sections quoted therein, specifically **Sections 112, 878, 970, 1116 and 1201**, whose titles are as follows:

> **§ 112.** **Protection of foreign officials, official guests, and internationally protected persons;**
> **§ 878.** **Threats and extortion against foreign officials, official guests, or internationally protected persons;**
> **§ 970.** **Protection of property occupied by foreign governments;**
> **§ 1116.** **Murder or manslaughter of foreign officials, official guests, or internationally protected persons.**

2. Apostille-Declarant, as defined in the registry filing of October 20, 2000, is a lawful internationally protected citizen of a lawful *"faction"* (being a breathing human being) as is affirmed by the *"declaration"* permitted within United States laws, specifically, **Title 18 U. S. Cr. C. Section 11**, et al.

5

3.   Apostille-Declarant declares that the DE FACTO STATE OF HAWAII is also in violation of private party lien interests in that Apostille-Declarant is a *"secured party"* against the assets of the U. S. Government created *"debtor"* ARDAIZ, ARAN ALTON, and is secured under the Uniform Commercial Code U. C. C. – 1 filing of August 7, 2000; having notified the United States Government, Secretary of the Treasury as affirmed by the Hawaii Bureau of Records (Filing No. 2000 109008) against the *"debtor"* party identified by Employer I. D. No. 558 48 5106.

4.   The President, acting as Commander-in-Chief, and the Federal Congress of the United States on behalf of the People of America, through **U. S. Public Law 103-150 (the Apology Law)** made implicit admission that the *"neutral"* Kingdom of Hawaii existed at *"peace"* at the time of the U. S. military intervention in this foreign nation and at time of their alleged *"annexation."* It is not Apostille-Declarant's intention nor is it Apostille-Declarant's burden to prove that the DE FACTO STATE OF HAWAII <u>does not have jurisdiction</u>; it is Apostille-Declarant's right to insist that the de facto state has the sole burden to prove its legitimacy and jurisdiction, which it cannot.

5.   In <u>**State v. Lorenzo, 77 Haw 219, 221 Footnote 2 (App 1994)**</u>, this court noted that in the light of international law, the following:

> *"A state has an obligation not to recognize or treat as a state any entity*
> *that has attained the qualifications for statehood as a result of a threat or use*
> *of armed force in violation of the United Nations Charter.*
>
> <u>*Restatement (Third) of the Foreign Relations Law of the United States. § 202(2)*</u>
>
> *"The illegal overthrow leaves open the question whether the present governance*
> *system should be recognized, even though the illegal overthrow pre-dated the*
> *United Nations Charter."*

6

6.   Apostille-Declarant further declares that the U. S. COURT FOR THE HAWAII DISTRICT and de facto State judiciaries function unlawfully under a foreign, military flag not in conformity with United States Law but <u>in violation of</u> **Title 4, Section 1 of the U. S. Code, as affirmed by the 1925 U. S. Attorney General's Opinion** *34 Op Atty Gen 483*, that the flags flown in the courts, supra, are in fact military flags signifying that **Ko Hawaii Pae Aina** is under the unlawful military rule of the federal United States Government in violation of international law.

7.   Apostille-Declarant declares that the courts, supra, lacking jurisdiction, also lack judges of proper or competent oaths of Office and exist as courts of incompetent jurisdiction while functioning under *"color of U. S. law,"* in violation of U. S. law. A Judge cannot hear any case or issue of a foreign citizen under International Law or **United States Criminal Law (Title 18)**, which can only be heard by United States Federal Judges under lawful **Title 28 Section 453 (U. S. Code)** oaths of Office, <u>which U. S. District Court Judges, et al, in Hawaii are not</u>.

8.   Apostille-Declarant declares that the aforementioned courts are not capable of lawfully meeting any of the requirements for lawful proof of jurisdiction, as required by law.

<u>PRAYER:</u>

Apostille-Declarant prays that this **Federal U. S. District Court for Hawaii**, on foreign soil, respect de jure **Hawaiian Kingdom Laws**, laws of the United States and International laws, <u>as is required by U. S. Federal Courts of competent jurisdiction</u>. **This truth of want of jurisdiction at law is <u>affirmed by the Congress of the United States in Title 28 Section 91 of the United States Code</u>, which is an *"admission by omission,"* that the Islands of the Hawaiian Archipelago are not a part of the lawful jurisdiction of**

7

the *U. S. District Court for the District of Hawaii* or de facto Hawaii State Courts.

Respectfully submitted before Our Lord and Saviour Jesus the Christ, on this date, April 21, 2005 A. D.

Aran Alton: Ardaiz, Apostille-Declarant and Internationally
Protected Human Being and lawful Hawaiian Kingdom Subject

Attachment: **EXHIBIT 'A', APOSTILLE**

Cc: **United Nations, New York, N.Y.**
        President of the United States
        U. S. Attorney General Gonzales
        U. S. Secretary of State Rice
        Director, Federal Bureau of Investigation
        Governor Lingle of the de facto State of Hawaii
        Lt. Governor Aiona of the de facto State of Hawaii
        Chief Justice Moon, Hawaii State Supreme Court
        Chief of Police, City and County of Honolulu Police Department
        Administrator, State of Hawaii Sheriff's Department

8

Dated: April 21, 2005

AFFIRMATION OF APOSTILLE COPY:

I, Aran Alton Ardaiz, affirm before Almighty God that the attached document titled

"Apostille" is a true and accurate copy of the "Original" maintained by this Apostille / Declarant.

Aran Alton Ardaiz, Apostille / Declarant

STATE OF HAWAII
Office of the Lieutenant Governor

No. 0 9 7 8 5 6

Honolulu, Hawaii .... 1/28 .... 20 02

Received from .... *Aran Alton Ardig* ....

For ....

No.	M.O. / Check # 9034578/372 Cash _____	Realization	Postage
	SALE OF LAW BOOKS: 0781		
	HAWAII REVISED STATUES		
	.... Session Laws		
	.... Supplement		
	.... Replacement Index to HRS		
	.... House Journal		
	.... Senate Journal		
	Other		
	CHANGE OF NAME: 0783		
	SALE OF DOCUMENTS: 0784		
	_____ certification / apostille	1 00	
	_____ acts		
	_____ admin rules / HRS		
	_____ photocopying		
	Subtotal		
	Total	1 00	

.... *R. Matsumura* ....
For Lt. Governor of Hawaii

OFFICE OF THE LIEUTENANT GOVERNOR
State Capitol, Fifth Floor
Honolulu, Hawaii 96813
Phone: (808)586-0255
Fax: (808)586-0231
email: ltgov@exec.state.hi.us
www.state.hi.us/ltgov

MAZIE K. HIRONO
LIEUTENANT GOVERNOR

APOSTILLE
(Convention de La Hague du 5 octobre 1961)

1.   Country: United States of America

THIS PUBLIC DOCUMENT

2.   has been signed by   BRUCE ISHIBASHI

3.   acting in the capacity of NOTARY PUBLIC

4.   bears the seal/stamp of   BRUCE ISHIBASHI

NOTARY PUBLIC STATE OF HAWAII

CERTIFIED

5.   at Honolulu, Hawaii   6. the 28TH day of JANUARY, 2002.

7.   by **MAZIE K. HIRONO, LIEUTENANT GOVERNOR, STATE OF HAWAII**

8.   No. 02- 0075

9.   Seal/stamp: 10. Signature:

MAZIE K. HIRONO
Lieutenant Governor

254

* *

Space above for recording purposes only:

<u>Actual Notice of "Apostille"</u> (The Hague, Treaties and Conventions): To United States Government (automatically inclusive of STATE OF HAWAII) <u>a Signature Party to Article 7, The Hague Convention on "Apostille" ([1961] 1981)</u>.

Kingdom of the Power of the Powers,)	Scilicet: (To Wit)
)	
on the sovereign soil of the de jure)	Declaration of Mission Statement by
)	Foreign Neutral under the Absolute
Hawaiian Kingdom.)	Law's of the Living Father and The
_____)	Highest Power, God Almighty.

KNOW THE PEOPLE BY THESE PRESENTS, GREETINGS:

      KNOW ALL MEN BY THESE PRESENTS: Under the authority of Declaration, for the Trust Written and Recorded in Chapter 9, Verses 15 through 21, and at Chapter 8, Verses 7 through 13, Book of the Hebrews, the undersigned Affiant, Declarant, and Trustee of said Torah Trust accepts and succeeds the appointment and Office of "Trustee", droit, Dominium Jura in re, as "Foreign Neutral", thereof the Kingdom of the Power of Powers, Almighty God, and for the Kingdom of Hawaii, de jure, The United States of America and territories or insular possessions, The Netherlands, as a Neutral *in intinere, ab initio*, **Aran Alton: of the Family, Ardaiz, born March 21, 1939 A. D, I. D. No. HA 96-152274**, in oneness with his wife, **Sandra Jane Saleeby Ardaiz, born May 9, 1944 A. D.**, Genesis 2:24; Matthew 19: 4,5, 6; Galatians 3: 28; <u>recognized by the receiving state</u> Under authority, To Wit:

The Ancient and Holy Scriptures.

1

The Ordinance of the Territory North and West of the River Ohio, 1 Stat. 51, 52, July 13, 1787.

The 1814 Treaty of Ghent.

Treaty of Friendship, Commerce And Navigation of 19 August 1850 (Ratified and non-abrogated), by and between the de jure Kingdom of Hawaii and the United States of America (Republic); sealed by John M. Clayton, James Jackson Jarvis, President Zachary Taylor and King Kamehameha III.

International Organizations Immunities Act, 9 December 1945.

The Convention on Rights and Duties of States, 49 Stat. 3097, T. S. 881, 165 I. N. T. S. 19, 3 Bevans 145, done at Montevideo, Uruguay, 26 December 1934 @ Art. 2-3 id est. "sovereign ecclesiastical State".

Vienna Convention, 18 April 1961, U. N. T. S. Nos. 7310-7312, Vol. 500, pp. 95-239.

Vienna Convention on Consular Relations and Optional Protocols, Vienna 24 April 1963, U. N. T. S. Nos. 8638-8640, Vol. 596, pp. 262-512.

The Convention of the Hague, 5 October 1961.

The Vienna Convention on the Law of Treaties, and, *Hague Convention Abolishing the Requirement of Legalization for Foreign Public Documents*, U. N. Doc. A / Conf. 39/27 (1969), 63 A. J. I. L. 875 (1969) at Article 2 ¶¶ I (a), (b) and (g), and Article II for "limited accession" per T. I. A. S. 10072; 33 U. S. T. 883, 527 U. N. T. S. 189; 28 U. S. C. A., appended to Rule 44; U. S. Senate Executive L., 94th Cong., 2d Sess. (1976)

Vienna Convention on the Law of Treaties, signed at Vienna, 23 May 1969, U. N. T. S., entry into Force: 27 January 1980.

Convention on the Conflict of Laws Relating to the Form of Testamentary Dispositions, concluded 5 October 1961, #11, et. Seq., Conflict of Law (1993).

Primary Duties are: Keep the commandment Laws of the Living Father and, secondarily, perpetuate the Testator's Will and Living Trust, in violate.

Secondary duties include: Establish and maintain the "mission" and "mission post" for and on behalf of the "mission head" in representative capacity and provide for the maintenance and good Order of the families, staff, and other public servants there unto belonging: with absolute respect for and utmost integrity of Testator's Living Will and Trust, in absentia.

"Domicile" is established by virtue of Chapter Nineteen (19), Verse Five (5), of the Book of Exodus, and legal estate thereof with absolute allegiance and fidelity, excluding others.

Any and all family and friends domiciled with the Foreign Neutral are neutrals "opposed to war in any form" and non-resident aliens to the "receiving state" afore said. Affiant-Trustee acknowledges that as Trustee and Individually, he is neither a citizen, nor subject of the receiving state by imprescription and the term "imprescriptibility" is operative herein duly recognized in the cases of *Rabang v. I. N. S. (CA 9 1994)*, 35 F. 3d 1449 @ n4, of *United States v. Wong Kim Ark*, 169 U. S. 649, 18 S. Ct. 456, 483, 42 L. Ed. 890 (1898), and *Udny v. Udny*, L. R. 1, H. L. Sc. 457.

Affiant-Trustee is not a "legal entity" created by, for, nor on behalf of any other person, group, association, nor corporation for political or commercial purpose and is not a surety therefore, nor assumes culpability on behalf thereof as *"civiliter mortuus"*, to the receiving state aforesaid.

Inclusio unius est exclusio alterius

NOTICE TO PRINCIPAL IS NOTICE TO AGENT; NOTICE TO AGENT IS NOTICE TO PRINCIPAL.

"Succession" is "special" for which presumption must yield to Truth.

The undersigned Affiant-Trustee, succeeding to the appointment and Office aforesaid, specially, authorizes the foregoing in Official capacity according to the express exceptions, stipulations, and reservations above set out verbatim and those referenced in the authorities set out above, as attests My Hand and Seal in Faithful Witness thereof, the same being entirely true, correct, certain and complete, according to the Laws of the Kingdom and Commonwealth aforesaid, so help Me Almighty God and Power, Power of the Powers.

The Official Seal of the Foreign Neutral, annexed below, is the only required seal affixed upon Official Documents, charge d' affaires, and other correspondences appertaining to the Trustee's Lawful

3

peaceful mission, held exclusively in the custody, possession and control of Affiant-Trustee-Declarant, unless otherwise expressly assigned or transferred, as set forth and heretofore, and not for any other unauthorized "use" nor "purpose".

LAWFUL NOTIFICATION:

PUBLIC, DE JURE AFFIRMATION OF PRIVATE MINISTRY UNDER ALMIGHTY GOD:

PUBLIC NOTICE: The United States Federal Government has made lawful and public acknowledgement of separation and distinction of powers and jurisdiction of the Kingdom of Hawaii, its in rem assets and People by a United States Public Apology, more specifically, **U. S. P. L. 103-150 of November 23, 1993.** Said "apology" was for its international military violation and invasion of a "Neutral" nation under International Treaty (1850), supra, while at peace, and without a declaration of war, and participating with treasonous and unlawful parties in the overthrow of a de jure government. The President of the United States received a temporary "living trust" of power (1893) from Queen Liliuokalani after the overthrow "until restored to power" and has since failed to honor or return said "trust", and has blatantly abused its intent. This now amounts to a continued abuse of military power on Hawaii Kingdom's Sovereign National soil. The U. S. Government has maintained de facto power since that time by unlawful, military occupational rule through abusive de facto police power and color of law agencies, but, has acknowledged its unlawful nature, and, has also clearly and definitively affirmed no lawful jurisdiction over the de jure lands of the Hawaiian People as clearly defined in United States Law. **Clearly, Title 28 Section 91 of the United States Code (28 U. S. C. § 91, makes no claim of jurisdiction over the Hawaiian Islands), which is an admission by omission.** *Ke Aupuni o Hawaii nei* of the Hawaiian Kingdom, being de jure and a Government "at peace" "with the United States" is a lawfully affirmed Government under lawful notice to the Government of the United States as documented by **18 U. S. Cr. C. § 11.** This de jure Government affirms its lawful Citizen's Godly Ministry, by affirmation hereunder.

4

DATED: On the Seventeenth Day of January in the Year of Our Lord, 2002, in Honolulu, Oahu, Hawaii nei.

Foreign Neutral:

Government Affirmation of Trustee-Declarant:
Private Certificate No: HA 96-152274-02

(L. S.) _____

Affiant-Trustee, but not Individually (Kingdom)
Aran Alton: of the Family, Ardaiz.
I.D. No. HA 96-152274

C/o: 3419 Ala Ilima Street
Moanalua, Oahu, Hawaii nei
(U. S. P. Z. Exempt)

Minister of Foreign Affairs, Leon Siu
Ke Aupuni o Hawaii nei (Documented with the United States Government under 18 USCr.C § 11)
Hawaiian Kingdom, de jure
General Delivery (Box 62107)
Manoa, Oahu, Hawaii nei
(U. S. P. Z. Exempt)

(L. S.) _____

Affiant-Trustee, but not Individually (STATE NOTARY)
Aran Alton: of the Family, Ardaiz.
I.D. No. HA 96-152274

Affirmation of Ministry: Matthew 18:16, and, II Corinthians 13:1: "…in the mouth of two or three witnesses…"

_____
Signature of Witness: Date: 1/17/02

_____
Signature of Witness: Date: January 17, 2000

_____
Signature of Witness: Date: 17 January 2002

(Apostille Form) A Private Declaration by de jure Hawaiian Kingdom Government (Public) Affirmation of Ministry Status

5

EVIDENCE OF NOTARIZATION <u>FOR PUBLIC FILING</u>: (IF REQUIRED)

Kingdom of Hawaii, de jure   )
)   Scilicet:

Island of Oahu, Hawaii nei   )

On this _____17TH_____ day of __January__, in the Year of Our Lord Jesus the Christ, A. D. 2002, before me personally _____Aran Alton: Ardaiz_____ known to me to be the Living Soul described herein and who executed the foregoing instrument and I do further acknowledge that he did so of his own free act and deed.

My Commission Expires 31st December '04 A.D.   (L. S.) _Ross Huitt : Myers_

               Notary Public, _Ross Huitt : Myers_
                      Kingdom of Hawaii, de jure

*   *   *   *   *   *   *   *   *   *   *   *   *   *   *   *

<u>NOTARIZATION</u>:   (Under de jure, common-law, Sovereign
                   National State Reservation of Rights)

STATE OF HAWAII   )
)   ss.

CITY AND COUNTY OF HONOLULU   )

On this _____19th_____ day of __January__ A. D. 2002, in the Year of Our Lord Jesus Christ, before me personally appeared _____Aran Alton: Ardaiz _(on Page Five)_____ to me known to be the Living Soul and person described herein and who executed the foregoing instrument and I further acknowledge that he did execute same of his own free will and deed.

My Commission Expires _____4/19/03_____.   (L. S.)

               Notary Public, _Bruce Ishibashi_
                      STATE OF HAWAII

6

EXHIBIT E

Treaties of the Hawaiian Kingdom with other nations

TREATIES OF THE HAWAIIAN NATION AT TIME OF OVERTHROW IN 1893

Other Nations with which the Hawaiian Kingdom (A Nation titled *"Ko Hawaii Pae Aina"* or in English, *"The Hawaiian Islands"*) possesses lawful International Treaties, follows:

1.   United States of America, December 23, 1826 *(Treaty)*
2.   Great Britain, November 13, 1836 *(Lord E. Russell's Treaty)*
3.   France, July 17, 1839 *(Captain La Place's Convention)*
4.   Great Britain, March 26, 1846 *(Treaty)*
5.   Denmark, October 19, 1846 *(Treaty)*
6.   Hamburg, January 8, 1848 *(Treaty)*
7.   United States of America, December 20, 1849 *(Treaty)* Hawaii signed in 1850.
8.   Sweden and Norway, July 1, 1852 *(Treaty)*
9.   Tahiti, November 24, 1853 (Agreement)
10. Bremen, March 27, 1854 *(Treaty)*
11. France, September 8, 1858 *(Treaty)*
12. Belgium, October 4, 1862 *(Treaty)*
13. Netherlands, October 16, 1862 *(Treaty)*
14. Italy, July 22, 1863 *(Treaty)*
15. Spain, October 9, 1863 *(Treaty)*
16. Swiss Confederation, July 20, 1864 *(Treaty)*
17. Russia, June 19, 1869 *(Treaty)*
18. Japan, August 17, 1871 *(Treaty)*
19. United States of America, January 30, 1875 *(Reciprocity Treaty)*
20. German Empire, 1879-80 *(Treaty)*
21. Samoa, March 20, 1887 *(Treaty)*

There are also many Conventions, Postal, monetary, trade, etc. made between the Hawaiian Kingdom Nation and other world governments, too numerous to list here.

Of note is the fact that Treaties are only made between nations. Therefore the Hawaiian Kingdom Nation by evidence of the Treaties shown above was and still is a nation among nations, occupied, yet presently functioning <u>under extreme duress</u> with oppression of its nationals by a Godless world power functioning without integrity.

EXHIBIT F

Newlands Resolution (1898)

THE

STATUTES AT LARGE

OF THE

UNITED STATES OF AMERICA,

FROM

MARCH, 1897, TO MARCH, 1899,

AND

RECENT TREATIES, CONVENTIONS, EXECUTIVE PROCLAMATIONS,

AND

THE CONCURRENT RESOLUTIONS OF THE TWO HOUSES OF CONGRESS.

EDITED, PRINTED, AND PUBLISHED BY AUTHORITY OF
CONGRESS, UNDER THE DIRECTION OF
THE SECRETARY OF STATE.

VOL. XXX.

WASHINGTON:
GOVERNMENT PRINTING OFFICE.
1899.

750 FIFTY-FIFTH CONGRESS. Sess. II. Res. 53–55. 1898.

newspapers for any Department shall not apply to the purchase of newspapers for military use by the military information division of the Adjutant-General's Office from the appropriations for the support of the Army for the fiscal years herein named.

Approved, June 29, 1898.

July 1, 1898.

[No. 54.] Joint Resolution For improvement of San Joaquin River and Stockton and Mormon channels, California.

Improvement of San Joaquin River and Stockton and Mormon channels, California.

Resolved by the Senate and House of Representatives of the United States of America in Congress assembled, That the Secretary of War be, and he is hereby, authorized to expend for improvements and surveys of the waterways hereinafter named and their tributaries any sums of money now to the credit of and heretofore appropriated for the improvement of the San Joaquin River and Stockton and Mormon channels, California, as and where, in his discretion, will best improve the commercial capacity of said waterways.

Approved, July 1, 1898.

July 7, 1898.

[No. 55.] Joint Resolution To provide for annexing the Hawaiian Islands to the United States.

Annexation of the Hawaiian Islands. Preamble.

Whereas the Government of the Republic of Hawaii having, in due form, signified its consent, in the manner provided by its constitution, to cede absolutely and without reserve to the United States of America all rights of sovereignty of whatsoever kind in and over the Hawaiian Islands and their dependencies, and also to cede and transfer to the United States the absolute fee and ownership of all public, Government, or Crown lands, public buildings or edifices, ports, harbors, military equipment, and all other public property of every kind and description belonging to the Government of the Hawaiian Islands, together with every right and appurtenance thereunto appertaining: Therefore,

Cession of Hawaiian sovereignty, etc., accepted.

Resolved by the Senate and House of Representatives of the United States of America in Congress assembled, That said cession is accepted, ratified, and confirmed, and that the said Hawaiian Islands and their dependencies be, and they are hereby, annexed as a part of the territory of the United States and are subject to the sovereign dominion thereof, and that all and singular the property and rights hereinbefore mentioned are vested in the United States of America.

Congress to enact special public-land laws.

Proviso.
—revenues for educational purposes, etc.

The existing laws of the United States relative to public lands shall not apply to such lands in the Hawaiian Islands; but the Congress of the United States shall enact special laws for their management and disposition: *Provided,* That all revenue from or proceeds of the same, except as regards such part thereof as may be used or occupied for the civil, military, or naval purposes of the United States, or may be assigned for the use of the local government, shall be used solely for the benefit of the inhabitants of the Hawaiian Islands for educational and other public purposes.

Existing powers of officers continued.

Removal of officers.

Until Congress shall provide for the government of such islands all the civil, judicial, and military powers exercised by the officers of the existing government in said islands shall be vested in such person or persons and shall be exercised in such manner as the President of the United States shall direct; and the President shall have power to remove said officers and fill the vacancies so occasioned.

Existing treaties replaced by United States treaties.

Municipal legislation continued.

The existing treaties of the Hawaiian Islands with foreign nations shall forthwith cease and determine, being replaced by such treaties as may exist, or as may be hereafter concluded, between the United States and such foreign nations. The municipal legislation of the Hawaiian Islands, not enacted for the fulfillment of the treaties so extinguished, and not inconsistent with this joint resolution nor contrary to the Constitution of the United States nor to any existing treaty of the United States, shall remain in force until the Congress of the United States shall otherwise determine.

Until legislation shall be enacted extending the United States customs laws and regulations to the Hawaiian Islands the existing customs relations of the Hawaiian Islands with the United States and other countries shall remain unchanged. *Existing customs laws continued.*

The public debt of the Republic of Hawaii, lawfully existing at the date of the passage of this joint resolution, including the amounts due to depositors in the Hawaiian Postal Savings Bank, is hereby assumed by the Government of the United States; but the liability of the United States in this regard shall in no case exceed four million dollars. So long, however, as the existing Government and the present commercial relations of the Hawaiian Islands are continued as hereinbefore provided said Government shall continue to pay the interest on said debt. *United States to assume the public debt of Hawaii. —limit. —interest.*

There shall be no further immigration of Chinese into the Hawaiian Islands, except upon such conditions as are now or may hereafter be allowed by the laws of the United States; and no Chinese, by reason of anything herein contained, shall be allowed to enter the United States from the Hawaiian Islands. *Chinese immigration prohibited.*

The President shall appoint five commissioners, at least two of whom shall be residents of the Hawaiian Islands, who shall, as soon as reasonably practicable, recommend to Congress such legislation concerning the Hawaiian Islands as they shall deem necessary or proper. *Commissioners to recommend legislation.*

SEC. 2. That the commissioners hereinbefore provided for shall be appointed by the President, by and with the advice and consent of the Senate. *—appointment of.*

SEC. 3. That the sum of one hundred thousand dollars, or so much thereof as may be necessary, is hereby appropriated, out of any money in the Treasury not otherwise appropriated, and to be immediately available, to be expended at the discretion of the President of the United States of America, for the purpose of carrying this joint resolution into effect. *Appropriation for enforcing resolution.*

Approved, July 7, 1898.

[No. 56.] Joint Resolution Authorizing the Librarian of Congress to accept the collection of engravings proposed to be donated to the Library of Congress by Mrs. Gertrude M. Hubbard. *July 7, 1898.*

Resolved by the Senate and House of Representatives of the United States of America in Congress assembled, That the Librarian of Congress is hereby empowered and directed to accept the offer of Mrs. Gertrude M. Hubbard, widow of the late Gardiner Greene Hubbard, communicated to him by the following letter, on the terms and conditions therein stated, except that instead of naming the gallery in the Library as therein proposed, the collection shall be known and styled as the Gardiner Greene Hubbard Collection, it not being, in the opinion of Congress, desirable to call parts of the public buildings after the names of individual citizens, and that the bust therein named be accepted and kept in a suitable place, to be designated by the Joint Committee on the Library; and to communicate to Mrs. Hubbard the grateful appreciation of Congress of the public spirit and munificence manifested by said gift: *Library of Congress. Acceptance of engravings, etc., from Mrs. Gertrude M. Hubbard.*

WASHINGTON, D. C., March 21, 1898.

MY DEAR SIR: I hereby offer to the Congressional Library, for the benefit of the people of the United States, the collection of engravings made by my husband, the late Gardiner Greene Hubbard, and, in addition thereto, the art books, to be treated as part of the collection.

This disposition of the collection, the gathering of which was to him the pleasure of many years chiefly devoted to the welfare of his fellow-

EXHIBIT G

State of Hawaii Voter Registration Form

AFFIDAVIT ON APPLICATION FOR VOTER REGISTRATION

STATE OF HAWAII

☐ County of Hawaii
☐ County of Kauai
☐ County of Maui
☐ City and County of Honolulu

} SS.

IMPORTANT: PRINT CLEARLY IN BLACK INK. FAILURE TO COMPLETE ALL ITEMS WILL PREVENT ACCEPTANCE OF THIS APPLICATION.

AFFIDAVIT NO.

(FOR OFFICE USE ONLY)

I HEREBY SWEAR (OR AFFIRM) THAT THE FOLLOWING INFORMATION IS TRUE AND CORRECT:

1 SOCIAL SECURITY NUMBER*
_ _ _ - _ _ - _ _ _ _

2 DATE OF BIRTH
_ _ / _ _ / _ _
Month Day Year

3 TELEPHONE
Home: Business:

4 LAST NAME   FIRST NAME   MIDDLE INITIAL(S)

5 RESIDENCE ADDRESS IN HAWAII (Must be completed. P.O. Box, R.R., S.R. are **not** acceptable)   CITY/TOWN   ZIP CODE

6 MAILING ADDRESS IN HAWAII (Street address or P.O. Box)   CITY/TOWN   ZIP CODE

7 If no street/residence address, describe location of residence (leave blank if box #5 is completed)   CITY/TOWN   ZIP CODE

8 GENDER
☐ Female
☐ Male

9 ARE YOU A REGISTERED VOTER IN ANOTHER STATE?
If "yes", please complete the following: I was last registered to vote at:
_____ in the county of _____
(Last Registered Address)   (County)   (State)   (Zip Code)
and hereby authorize cancellation of my previous voter registration.

10 READ CAREFULLY, MARK APPROPRIATE "YES" OR "NO" BOX, AND SIGN BELOW.

I hereby swear (or affirm) that:

FOR FEDERAL, STATE, and COUNTY ELECTIONS:

a. I am a citizen of the United States of America (Non-U.S. citizens including U.S. nationals <u>do not</u> qualify).   ☐ Yes ☐ No

b. I am at least 16 years of age. I understand that I must be 18 years old by election day to vote.   ☐ Yes ☐ No

c. I am a resident of the State of Hawaii.
The residence stated in this affidavit is not simply because of my presence in the State, but that the residence was acquired with the intent to make Hawaii my legal residence with all the accompanying obligations therein.........   ☐ Yes ☐ No

SIGNATURE >   DATE _____

11 WITNESS SIGNATURE (required only if applicant makes a mark)   DATE

ADDRESS OF WITNESS   PHONE NO. OF WITNESS

WARNING ANY PERSON WHO KNOWINGLY FURNISHES FALSE INFORMATION MAY BE GUILTY OF A CLASS C FELONY, PUNISHABLE BY UP TO 5 YEARS OF IMPRISONMENT AND/OR $10,000 FINE.

* **Notice:** Section 11-15 of the Hawaii Revised Statutes requires that a person registering to vote provide, under oath, his or her social security number, if any. An application lacking this information will, therefore, be denied. Pursuant to Section 7 of the Federal Privacy Act (P.L. 93-579), be advised that this information may be released to government agencies for government purposes.

For Office Use Only

12 I.D. No.
E 0 9 6

13 LOCATION CODE
_ _

14 REPRESENTATIVE DISTRICT/PRECINCT
_ _ _ _ _ _

The office at which a person registers to vote is confidential. A person's declination to register to vote is also confidential and is used for voter registration purposes only (National Voter Registration Act of 1993).

06/04

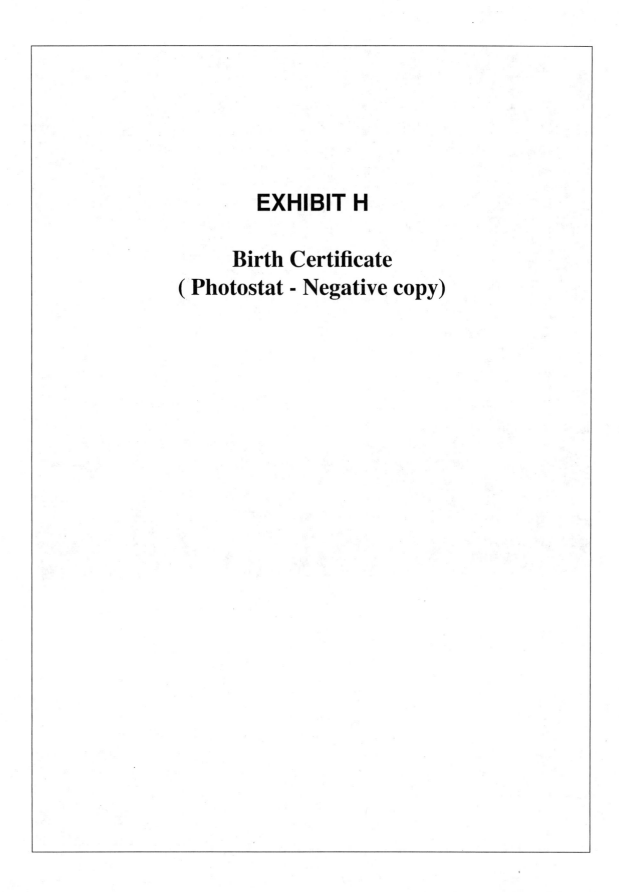

EXHIBIT H

Birth Certificate
(Photostat - Negative copy)

STATE OF CALIFORNIA
DEPARTMENT OF PUBLIC HEALTH
VITAL STATISTICS

197

STANDARD CERTIFICATE OF BIRTH

1. PLACE OF BIRTH. Dist. No. 2751

LOCAL REGISTERED No. 54

County of **Monterey**

City or
Rural Registration District **Monterey U.S.**

No. **Hamilton Ave** St. Ward
If birth occurred in a hospital or institution, give its NAME instead of street and number

2. FULL NAME OF CHILD **Aran Alton Ardaiz**

(If child is not yet named, make supplemental report as directed.)

3. Sex **Male** | If plural births | 4. Twin, triplet, or other 5. Number, in order of birth | 6. Premature Full term **X** | 7. Date of birth (month, day, year) **March 21st, 1939**

FATHER	MOTHER
8. Full name **Severino Ardaiz**	17. Full maiden name **Martha P.Cano**
9. Residence (usual place of abode; if nonresident, give place and State) **Monterey,Calif.**	18. Residence (usual place of abode; if nonresident, give place and State) **Monterey,Calif.**
10. Color or race **White** 11. Age at last birthday **49** years	19. Color or race **White** 20. Age at last birthday **39** years
12. Birthplace **California** State or country	21. Birthplace **California** State or country
13. Trade, profession, or particular kind of work done, as spinner, sawyer, bookkeeper, etc. **Millman**	22. Trade, profession, or particular kind of work done, as housekeeper, typist, nurse, clerk, etc. **Housekeeper**
14. Industry or business in which work was done, as silk mill, sawmill, bank, etc. **Millman**	23. Industry or business in which work was done, as own home, lawyer's office, silk mill, etc. **Home**
15. Date (month and year) last engaged in this work **March 21** 19 **39** 16. Total time (years) spent in this work **39**	24. Date (month and year) last engaged in this work **March 21** 19 **39** 25. Total time (years) spent in this work **19**

26. If stillborn, period of gestation { months or weeks | 27. Cause of stillbirth | Before labor ___ During labor ___

28. Was a prophylactic for Ophthalmia Neonatorum used? **Yes** If so, what? **Silver Nitrate** | 29. Specify congenital crippling deformities

30. Number of children of this mother (At time of this birth and including this child) **4** (a) Born alive and now living **4** (b) Born alive but now dead **0** (c) Stillborn **0**

31. CERTIFICATE OF ATTENDING PHYSICIAN OR MIDWIFE*

I hereby certify that I attended the birth of this child, who was **born alive** at **12:12 a** m.
on the date above stated. Born alive or stillborn

*When there was no attending physician or midwife, then the father, householder, etc., should make this return. A stillborn child is one that neither breathes nor shows other evidence of life after birth.

[SIGNED] **John H.Gratiot**

Physician
Physician, midwife, father, etc.

Given name added from a supplemental report ___ Date of ___

Address **Monterey, Calif.**

32. Filed **4/3/39**
Date

D.M.Bissell M.D.
Clyde A.Dorsey
Registrar

Registrar

EXHIBIT I

Birth Certificate
(certified copy)

CERTIFIED COPY OF BIRTH RECORD

	2751	54
STATE FILE NUMBER	LOCAL REGISTRATION DISTRICT AND CERTIFICATE NUMBER	

NAME OF CHILD—FIRST (GIVEN)	MIDDLE	LAST (FAMILY)
ARAN	ALTON	ARDAIZ

SEX	RACE	DATE OF BIRTH—MONTH, DAY, YEAR
Male	White	March 21, 1939

CITY OF BIRTH	COUNTY OF BIRTH
Monterey	Monterey

FULL NAME OF FATHER	DATE OF BIRTH—MONTH, DAY, YEAR
SEVERINO ARDAIZ	AGE 49

FULL MAIDEN NAME OF MOTHER	DATE OF BIRTH—MONTH, DAY, YEAR
MARTHA P CANO	AGE 39

DATE ACCEPTED FOR REGISTRATION	DATE(S) OF CORRECTION(S), IF ANY
April 3, 1939	--

This is to certify that the foregoing is a true and correct copy of statements appearing on the record of birth of the above named child, as registered in this office.

SIGNATURE OF CERTIFYING OFFICIAL	OFFICIAL TITLE
▶	Deputy Clerk

PLACE OF CERTIFICATION		DATE CERTIFIED
Monterey county Courthouse, Salinas, CA	93901	MAY 2 8 1998

STATE OF CALIFORNIA, DEPARTMENT OF HEALTH SERVICES, OFFICE OF STATE REGISTRAR   VS 61 (REV. 1/89)

EXHIBIT J

Bearer Bond Birth Certificate
(positive copy)

STATE OF CALIFORNIA
CERTIFICATION OF VITAL RECORD

COUNTY OF MONTEREY
SALINAS, CALIFORNIA

STATE OF CALIFORNIA
DEPARTMENT OF PUBLIC HEALTH
VITAL STATISTICS

197

STANDARD CERTIFICATE OF BIRTH

Local Registered No. 54

1. PLACE OF BIRTH. Dist. No. 2751

County of Monterey

City or Rural Registration District Monterey U.S.

No. Hamilton Ave St. Ward
If birth occurred in a hospital or institution, give its NAME instead of street and number
[If child is not yet named, make supplemental report as directed.]

2. FULL NAME OF CHILD Aran Alton Ardaiz

	FATHER		MOTHER
3. Sex Male	If plural births / 4. Twin, triplet, or other / 5. Number, in order of birth	6. Premature __ Full term X	7. Date of birth (month, day, year) March 21st, 1939
8. Full name Severino Ardaiz		17. Full maiden name Martha P. Cano	
9. Residence (usual place of abode) If nonresident, give place and State Monterey, Calif.		18. Residence (usual place of abode) If nonresident, give place and State Monterey, Calif.	
10. Color or race White 11. Age at last birthday 40 years		19. Color or race White 20. Age at last birthday 39 years	
12. Birthplace California State or country		21. Birthplace California State or country	
13. Trade, profession, or particular kind of work done, as spinner, lawyer, bookkeeper, etc. Millman		22. Trade, profession, or particular kind of work done, as housekeeper, typist, nurse, clerk, etc. Housekeeper	
14. Industry or business in which work was done, as silk mill, sawmill, bank, etc. Millman		23. Industry or business in which work was done, as own home, lawyer's office, silk mill, etc. Home	
15. Date (month and year) last engaged in this work March 21, 1939 16. Total time (years) spent in this work 39		24. Date (month and year) last engaged in this work March 21 1939 25. Total time (years) spent in this work 19	

Before labor
During labor

26. If stillborn, period of gestation { months or weeks 27. Cause of stillbirth

28. Was a prophylactic for Ophthalmia Neonatorum used? Yes If so, what? Silver Nitrate 29. Specify congenital crippling deformities

30. Number of children of this mother (At time of this birth and including this child) 4 (a) Born alive and now living 4 (b) Born alive but now dead 0 (c) Stillborn 0

31. CERTIFICATE OF ATTENDING PHYSICIAN OR MIDWIFE*

I hereby certify that I attended the birth of this child, who was born alive at 12:12 a m. on the date above stated. Born alive or stillborn

*When there was no attending physician or midwife, then the father, householder, etc., should make this return. A stillborn child is one that neither breathes nor shows other evidence of life after birth.

[SIGNED] John H. Gratiot

Physician
Physician, midwife, father, etc.

Given name added from a supplemental report _____ Date of _____

Address Monterey, Calif.
D. M. Bissell M.D.
32. Filed 4/5/39 Clyde A. Dorsey Registrar
Date

Registrar

128077

CERTIFIED COPY OF VITAL RECORDS

STATE OF CALIFORNIA } ss
COUNTY OF MONTEREY

This is a true and exact reproduction of the document officially registered and placed on file in the office of the Monterey County Clerk-Recorder.

Bruce A. Reeves

DATE ISSUED MAY 28 1998

BRUCE A. REEVES
County Clerk-Recorder

This copy not valid unless prepared on engraved border displaying seal and signature of County Clerk-Recorder.

ANY ALTERATION OR ERASURE VOIDS THIS CERTIFICATE

MIDWEST BANK NOTE COMPANY

EXHIBIT K

Liliuokalani letter 1897

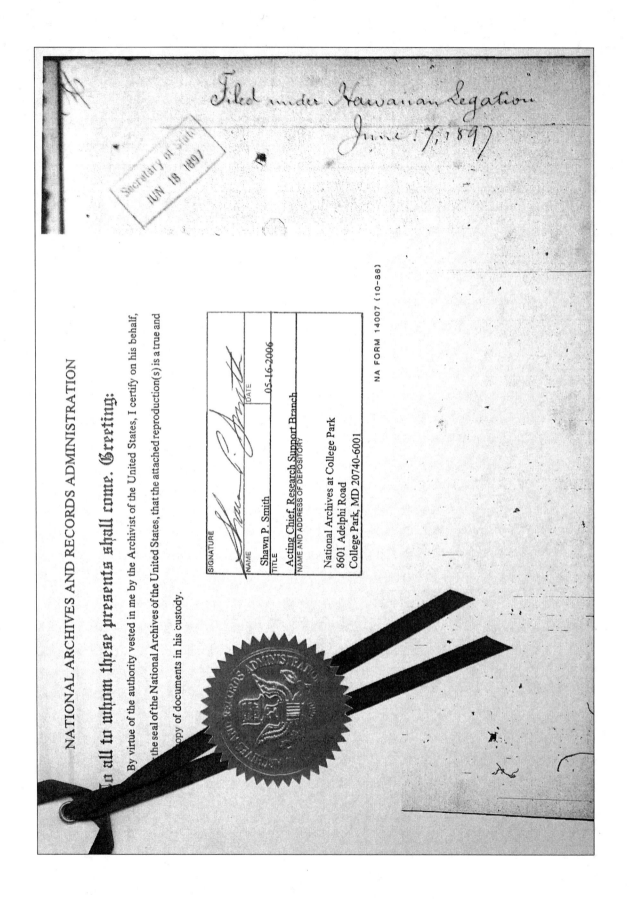

I, LILIUOKALANI of HAWAII , by the Will of God, named heir-apparent on
the tenth day of April A. D. 1877, and by the Will of God, Queen of the
Hawaiian Islands on the 17th. day of January, A. D. 1893, do hereby protest against the ratification of a certain treaty which so I am informed
has been signed at Washington by Messrs. Hatch, Thurston and Kinney, purporting to cede those Islands to the territory and dominion of the United
States . I declare such treaty to be an act of wrong towards the native
and part-native people of Hawaii , an invasion of the rights of the ruling
chiefs , in violation of international rights both towards my people and
towards friendly nations with whom they have made treaties , the perpetu-
ation of the fraud whereby the constitutional government was overthrown
and finally an act of gross injustice to me :-

BECAUSE,- The official protest made by me on the 17th day of January, 1893,
to the so-called Provisional Government was signed by me and received by
said government with the assurance that the case was referred to the United States for arbitration .

BECAUSE,- That protest and my communications to the United States government immediately thereafter expressly declares that I yielded my authority
to the forces of the United States , in order to avoid bloodshed , and because I recognized the futility of a conflict with so formidable a power.

BECAUSE,- The President of the United States , the Secretary of State, an
envoy commissioned by them reported in official documents that my government was unlawfully coerced by the forces, diplomatic and naval, of the U-
nited States , that I was at the date of their investigations the constitutional ruler of my people .

BECAUSE,- Such decision of the recognized magistrates of the United States
was officially communicated to me and to Sanford B. Dole , and said Dole's
resignation requested by Albert S. Willis , the recognized agent and minister of the government of the United States .

BECAUSE,- Neither the above-named commission nor the government which send
it has ever received any such authority from the registered voters of Hawaii but derives its assumed powers from the so-called Committee of Public
Safety organized on or about said 17th. day of January, 1893, said committee
being composed largely of persons claiming American citizenship, and not
one single Hawaiian was a member thereof or in any way participated in
the demonstration leading to its existence .

BECAUSE,- My people, about forty-thousand in number , have in no way been
consulted by those, three-thousand in number , who claim the right to de-

II.

stroy the independence of Hawaii My people constitute four-fifths of the legally qualified voters of Hawaii, and excluding those imported for the demands of labor, about the same proportion of the inhabitants.

BECAUSE,- Said treaty ignores not only the civic rights of my people, but further the hereditary property of their chiefs . Of the four million acres composing the territory said treaty offers to annex ,one million or 915 000 acres has in no way been heretofore recognized as other than the private property of the constitutional monarch ,subject to a control in no way differing from other items of a private estate.

BECAUSE.- It is proposed by said treaty to confiscate said property, technically called the Crown Lands ,those legally entitled thereto ,either now or in succession receiving no consideration whatever for estates their title to which has always been undisputed and which is legitimately in my name at this date.

BECAUSE,- Said treaty ignores not only all professions of perpetual amity and good faith made by the United States in former treaties with the sovereigns representing the Hawaiian people ,but all treaties made by those sovereigns with other and friendly powers ,and it is thereby in violation of international law .

BECAUSE ,- By treating with the parties claiming at this time the right to cede said territory of Hawaii ,the government of the United States receives such territory from the hands of those whom its own magistrates legally elected by the people of the United States and in office in 1893 pronounced fraudulently in power and unconstitutionally ruling Hawaii.

THEREFORE , I, LILIUOKALANI of HAWAII do hereby call upon the President of that nation to whom alone I yielded my property and my authority to withdraw said treaty (ceding said Islands) from further consideration .I ask the honorable Senate of the United States to decline to ratify said treaty and I implore the people of this great and good nation from whom my ancestors learned the Christian religion ,to sustain their representatives in such acts of justice and equity as may be in accord with the principles of their fathers ,and to the Almighty Ruler of the Universe ,to Him who judgeth righteously I commit my cause.

DONE at Washington, District of Columbia ,United States of America this Seventeenth Day of June in the year Eighteen Hundred and Ninety-seven.

Joseph Heleluhe

Liliuokalani

Wakeki Heleluhe

Julius A. Palmer

Witnesses to signature

To Hon John Sherman ,
        Secretary of State
           United States of America,

Dear Sir,

        On behalf of the Hawaiian Patriotic League , on behalf of the Hui Kalaiaina, organizations of the native and part native people of the Hawaiian Islands for the restoration of Constitutional Government , and the perpetuation of the Independence under their own rulers of the Islands , and by Commissions duly executed by such organizations conferring upon me authority , as well as in my own right as a representative of the people of Hawaii I herewith hand to you the duly executed protest of Her Majesty, Liliuokalani , by the grace of God , the reigning sovereign of those Islands on the seventeenth day of January, A. D. 1893 , at which date she yielded her property and authority as our Queen to the forces , diplomatic and naval of the Uited States of America.

        In the name of said associations of the people , and in the name of The majority of the voters registered at the date of such submission of our cause to the government of the United States , I do hereby support and confirm each and every representation of the said protest of our said Queen Liliuokalani , do add thereto the protest of the people I represent against the consideration , ratification or enforcement of a certain treaty as therein stated which purports to cede the territory of the Hawaiian Islands to the United States of America , and for the reasons stated to you in such protest made on our behalf by our aforesaid Queen Liliuokalani,

        Done at Washington , this 17th. day of June, 1897.

Joseph Heleluhe

EXHIBIT L

United States Code Title 4
Section 453, Federal Oath

Annotations:

Recall of appellate mandate directing action by federal agency. 44 ALR Fed 831.

Orders or penalties against state or its officials for failure to comply with regulations directing state to regulate pollution-creating activities of private parties, under § 113 of Clean Air Act (42 USCS § 1857c-8). 31 ALR Fed 79.

INTERPRETIVE NOTES AND DECISIONS

Under 28 USCS § 452, in spite of ending of term at which its mandate went down, it had power over such mandate not only to declare what it meant, but also to change it as situation demanded. National Comics Publications, Inc. v Fawcett Publications, Inc. (1952, CA2) 198 F2d 927, 94 USPQ 289.

Expiration of term does not deprive Court of Appeals of jurisdiction to make necessary correction of clerical error in opinion rendered in prior term. Kinnear-Weed Corp v Humble Oil & Refining Co. (1961, CA5 Tex) 296 F2d 215, 132 USPQ 305, cert den 368 US 890, 7 L Ed 2d 89, 82 S Ct 142, reh den 368 US 936, 7 L Ed 2d 198, 82 S Ct 359.

The fact that a request for recall of mandate is filed within the same term as the mandate, although of decisive significance under the common law "term" rule applied by the federal courts, has no significance since the enactment of this section in 1948; the continuance of the "term" is without importance and the 1963 amendment changing "term" to "session" wrought no substantive change; a court's decision whether to use the power to recall a mandate may be affected by the timeliness of the request, but a request may reflect untimeliness even though filed at the same term 11 months after judgment, and may reflect diligence even though filed at a different "term" if filed only two months after mandate. Greater Boston Television Corp. v FCC (1971) 149 App DC 322, 463 F2d 268, 31 ALR Fed 765, cert den 406 US 950, 32 L Ed 2d 338, 92 S Ct 2042.

Concept of "term" no longer retains much significance especially since enactment of 28 USCS § 452. American Iron & Steel Institute v Environmental Protection Agency (1977, CA3) 560 F2d 589, 7 ELR 20624, 44 ALR Fed 813, cert den 435 US 914, 55 L Ed 2d 505, 98 S Ct 1467.

§ 453. Oaths of justices and judges

Each justice or judge of the United States shall take the following oath or affirmation before performing the duties of his office: "I, _____, do solemnly swear (or affirm) that I will administer justice without respect to persons, and do equal right to the poor and to the rich, and that I will faithfully and impartially discharge and perform all the duties incumbent upon me as _____ according to the best of my abilities and understanding, agreeably to the Constitution and laws of the United States. So help me God."
(June 25, 1948, ch 646, § 1, 62 Stat. 907.)

HISTORY; ANCILLARY LAWS AND DIRECTIVES

Prior law and revision:
Based on title 28, U.S.C., 1940 ed., §§ 241, 372, and District of Columbia Code, 1940 ed., §§ 11-203, 11-303 (R.S.D.C., § 752, 18 Stat. pt. II, 90; Feb. 9, 1893, ch. 74, § 3, 27 Stat. 435; Mar. 3, 1901, ch. 854, § 223, 31 Stat. 1224; Mar. 3, 1911, ch. 231, §§ 136, 137, 257, 36 Stat. 1135, 1161; Feb. 25, 1919, ch. 29, § 4, 40 Stat. 1157).
This section consolidates sections 11-203 and 11-303 of District of Columbia Code, 1940 ed., and section 372 of title 28, U.S.C., 1940 ed.,

573

with that portion of section 241 of said title 28 providing that judges of the Court of Claims shall take an oath of office. The remainder of said section 241 comprises sections 171 and 173 of this title.

The phrase "justice or judge of the United States" was substituted for "justices of the Supreme Court, the circuit judges, and the district judges" appearing in said section 372, in order to extend the provisions of this section to judges of the Court of Claims, Customs Court, and Court of Customs and Patent Appeals and to all judges of any court which may be created by enactment of Congress. See definition in section 451 of this title.

The Attorney General has ruled that the expression "any judge of any court of the United States" applied to the Chief Justice and all judges of the Court of Claims. (21 Op. Atty. Gen. 449.)

CROSS REFERENCES

This section is referred to in 28 USCS §§ 460, 631.

RESEARCH GUIDE

Federal Procedure L Ed:

Courts and Judicial System, Fed Proc, L Ed §§ 20:24, 124, 174.

Am Jur:

32 Am Jur 2d, Federal Practice and Procedure §§ 26, 126, 200.
46 Am Jur 2d, Judges § 12.

Annotations:

Marital privilege under Rule 501 of Federal Rules of Evidence. 46 ALR Fed 735.

INTERPRETIVE NOTES AND DECISIONS

1. Generally
2. Ground for disqualification
3. Oath as basis of cause of action

1. Generally

No position can be more clear than that all federal judges are bound by solemn obligation of religion to regulate their decisions agreeably to Constitution of United States, and that it is standard of their determination in all cases that come before them. United States v Callender (1800, CC Va) F Cas No 14709.

Judge's duty to decide whatever cases come before him to best of his ability imposes obligation not to disqualify himself solely by reason of personal burdens related to task; duty is more compelling when single judge has acquired by experience familiarity with protracted complex case which could not easily be passed on to second judge. Bradley v School Board of Richmond (1971, ED Va) 324 F Supp 439.

2. Ground for disqualification

While every litigant in federal courts is entitled to have his case heard by judge mindful of oath required under 28 USCS § 453 to administer justice without respect to persons and to do equal right to poor and to rich, faithfully discharging all duties agreeably to Constitution and laws of United States, nevertheless neither oath, statute for disqualification of judges (28 USCS § 455), nor practice of Justices of the United States Supreme Court as to disqualification guarantee litigant that each judge will start off from dead center in his willingness or ability to reconcile opposing arguments of counsel with his understanding of Constitution and law; thus, it is not ground for disqualification that judge has prior to his nomination expressed his then understanding of meaning of some particular provision of Constitution. [Per Rehnquist, J., on motion to recuse.] Laird v Tatum (1972) 409 US 824, 34 L Ed 2d 50, 93 S Ct 7.

GENERAL PROVISIONS

3. Oath as basis of cause of action

28 USCS § 453, which sets forth oath of allegiance to Constitution taken by federal judges, does not create substantive cause of action against federal judges for violating oath by acting contrary to Constitution. Lewis v Green (1986, DC Dist Col) 629 F Supp 546.

§ 454. Practice of law by justices and judges

Any justice or judge appointed under the authority of the United States who engages in the practice of law is guilty of a high misdemeanor.
(June 25, 1948, ch 646, § 1, 62 Stat. 908.)

HISTORY; ANCILLARY LAWS AND DIRECTIVES

Prior law and revision:

Based on title 28, U.S.C., 1940 ed., § 373 (Mar. 3, 1911, ch. 231, § 258, 36 Stat. 1161).

Changes in phraseology were made.

CROSS REFERENCES

Clerks of justices not to practice, USCS Rules of the Supreme Court, Rule 7. This section is referred to in 28 USCS § 460.

RESEARCH GUIDE

Federal Procedure L Ed:

Bankruptcy, Fed Proc, L Ed §§ 9:27.

Courts and Judicial System, Fed Proc, L Ed § 20:25.

Am Jur:

9 Am Jur 2d, Bankruptcy § 133.

9A Am Jur 2d, Bankruptcy § 932.

32 Am Jur 2d, Federal Practice and Procedure § 27.

46 Am Jur 2d, Judges §§ 52, 54.

Law Review Articles:

Freedman, Removal and Discipline of Federal Judges. 31 Mercer L Rev 681, Spring, 1980.

INTERPRETIVE NOTES AND DECISIONS

Whenever Congress has intended to prohibit practice of law by officers of United States it has done so by specific enactment, whether such enactment relates to judges of court (28 USCS § 454), marshals (28 USCS § 556), or court clerks (28 USCS § 955). Audett v United States (1959, CA9 Idaho) 265 F2d 837, cert den 361 US 815, 4 L Ed 2d 62, 80 S Ct 54, reh den 361 US 926, 4 L Ed 2d 241, 80 S Ct 290.

Assumption by attorney of office of federal judge by operation of law effected termination of theretofore existing relation of attorney and client; but, where there was no substitution of any other attorney and notice of appeal was not served on any of the defendants, plaintiff's appeal would be dismissed. Endresse v Van Vleet (1946) 118 Mont 533, 169 P2d 719.

575

EXHIBIT M

Hawaii's Federal Judge's Oath

Form No. G-22
(Ed. 6-29-55)

OATH OF OFFICE FOR UNITED STATES JUDGES

(Title 28, Sec. 453 and Title 5, Sec. 16, United States Code)

I, _____ SAMUEL P. KING _____, do solemnly swear (or affirm) that I will administer justice without respect to persons, and do equal right to the poor and to the rich, and that I will faithfully and impartially discharge and perform all the duties incumbent upon me as _____ United States District Judge _____ according to the best of my abilities and understanding, agreeably to the Constitution and laws of the United States; and that I will support and defend the Constitution of the United States against all enemies, foreign and domestic; that I will bear true faith and allegiance to the same; that I take this obligation freely, without any mental reservation or purpose of evasion; and that I will well and faithfully discharge the duties of the office on which I am about to enter. SO HELP ME GOD.

(signature)

Subscribed and sworn to (or affirmed) before me this _____ 21st _____ day of _____ July _____, 19 72.

(signature)

Judge, 9th Circuit Court of Appeals

Actual abode _____ Chambers T _____

Official station _____ Honolulu, Hawaii _____

Date of birth _____ 4-13-16 _____

Date of entry on duty 7-21-72

NOTE.—The Act of May 1, 1876 (Title 48, sec. 1466, United States Code), provides that the oaths of Territorial Officers shall be administered in the Territory in which the office is held.

* Title 28, sec. 456 United States Code, as amended.

ATTEST: A True Copy

(signature)
WALTER A/Y.H. CHINN
Clerk, United States District
Court, District of Hawaii

EXHIBIT N

Court Docket Sheet

```
                                                     TERMED
                   U.S. District Court
     U.S. District Court for the District of Hawaii (Hawaii)

              CIVIL DOCKET FOR CASE #: 02-CV-198

Ebarez, et al v. Tamanaha, et al              Filed: 04/04/02
Assigned to: Judge Alan C. Kay
              Referred to: Mag Judge Leslie E Kobayashi
Demand: $0,000                        Nature of Suit: 870
Lead Docket: None                     Jurisdiction: US Defendant
Dkt# in other court: None

Cause: 26:7426 IRS: Wrongful Levy for Taxes


JOHN ALFRED EBAREZ,                John Alfred Ebarez
individually and jointly           [COR LD NTC] [PRO SE]
     plaintiff                     91-680 Kilipoe Street
                                   Ewa Beach, HI 96707
                                   689-7427


DARCY JEAN MAPUANA EBANEZ,         Darcy Jean Mapuana Ebanez
Individually and Jointly           [COR LD NTC] [PRO SE]
     plaintiff                     91-680 Kilipoe Street
                                   Ewa Beach, HI 96707
                                   689-7427



     v.



EMY TAMANAHA, A Private Party      David M. Lum
     defendant                     [COR LD NTC]
                                   Char Sakamoto Ishii & Lum
                                   841 Bishop St.
                                   850 Davies Pacific Center
                                   Honolulu, HI 96813
                                   522-5133

                                   Keith S. Agena
                                   [COR LD NTC]
                                   Char Sakamoto Ishii & Lum
                                   Davies Pacific Center
                                   Suite 850
                                   841 Bishop St.
                                   Honolulu, HI 96813
                                   522-5133


ALOHA AIRLINES, INCORPORATED       David M. Lum
     defendant                     (See above)
                                   [COR LD NTC]

Docket as of August 5, 2002 2:42 pm            Page 1
```

Proceedings include all events.   TERMED
1:02cv198 Ebarez, et al v. Tamanaha, et al

                                    Keith S. Agena
                                    (See above)
                                    [COR LD NTC]

SUSAN MEREDITH
     defendant

INTERNAL REVENUE SERVICE   Michael Chun
     defendant   [COR LD NTC]
                                    Office of the United States
                                    Attorney
                                    Prince Kuhio Federal Building
                                    300 Ala Moana Blvd Ste 6100
                                    Honolulu, HI 96850
                                    541-2850

                                    Charles M. Duffy
                                    [COR LD NTC]
                                    U.S. Department of Justice
                                    Ben Franklin Station
                                    P O Box 683
                                    Washington, DC 20044-0683
                                    202 307-6406

Proceedings include all events.   TERMED
1:02cv198 Ebarez, et al v. Tamanaha, et al

4/4/02   1   Conspiracy to extort in violation of law; threat and
                 intimidation under color of law; securing of compensation
                 for labor under false pretenses; failure to give lawful
                 notice prior to threat of levy; violation of national and
                 jurisdictional right of citizenship (byy)
                 [Entry date 04/05/02]

4/4/02   2   ORDER by Judge David A. Ezra rule 16 conference set for
                 9:00 7/1/02 before Mag Judge Leslie E. Kobayashi (byy)
                 [Entry date 04/05/02]

4/4/02   --   FILING FEE PAID in the amount of $ 150.00, receipt # 207940
                 (byy) [Entry date 04/05/02]

4/5/02   3   SUMMONS issued (byy)

4/10/02   4   REQUEST by plaintiffs for immediate permanent restraining
                 order and injunction against Aloha Airlines and the Internal
                 Revenue Service acting in open defiance of justice and this
                 court for proceeding with unlawful and fraudulent attachment
                 of compensation for labor after receipt of a lawful service
                 and summons - referred to Judge Alan C. Kay (byy)
                 [Entry date 04/11/02] [Edit date 04/17/02]

4/11/02   5   NOTICE of setting hearing on: Request for immediate
                 permanent restraining order and injunction against Aloha
                 Airlines and the Internal Revenue Service acting in open
                 defiance of justice and this court for proceeding with
                 unlasful and fraudulent attachment of compensation for
                 labor after receipt of a lawful service and summons [4-1]
                 set for hearing at 10:00 4/24/02 before Judge Alan Kay (cc:
                 John Alfred Ebanez and Darcy Jean Mapuana Ebanez; Michael
                 Chun, AUSA, David Lum) (byy) [Entry date 04/12/02]

4/15/02   6   NOTICE of setting hearing on Request for immediate
                 permanent restraining order and injunction against Aloha
                 Airlines and the Internal Revenue Service acting in open
                 defiance of justice and this court for proceeding with
                 unlasful and fraudulent attachment of compensation for
                 labor after receipt of a lawful service and summons [4-1]
                 set for 10:00 4/29/02 before Judge Alan C. Kay; NOTE: per
                 earlier conversation, the Court will expect defendants'
                 responses by Thursday, 4/8/02 (cc: John Alfred Ebanez and
                 Darcy Jean Mapuana Ebanez; Michael Chun, David Lum) (byy)
                 [Entry date 04/16/02]

4/17/02   7   NOTICE of setting hearing on: motion for immediate
                 permanent restraining order and injunction against Aloha
                 Airlines and the Internal Revenue Service acting in open
                 defiance of justice and this court for proceeding with
                 unlawful and fraudulent attachment of compensation for
                 labor after receipt of a lawful service and summons [4-1]
                 hrg set for 2:00 4/29/02 (cc: all parties and counsel) (byy)

Docket as of August 5, 2002 2:42 pm   Page 3

Proceedings include all events.   TERMED
1:02cv198 Ebarez, et al v. Tamanaha, et al

4/17/02   8   MEMORANDUM by defendant United States in opposition to
               motion for immediate permanent restraining order and
               injunction [4-1]; certificate of service (byy)
               [Entry date 04/18/02] [Edit date 04/26/02]

4/18/02   9   OBJECTIONS by defendants Emy Tamanaha and Aloha Airlines,
               Inco to complainants request for immediate permanent
               restraining order and injunction filed 4/10/02 [4-1];
               declaration of Emy Tamanaha; exhibits a-c; certificate of
               service (byy)

4/24/02   10   Second REQUEST by plaintiffs John Alfred Ebarez and Darcy
               Jean Mapuana Ebanez re motion for immediate permanent
               restraining order and injunction against Aloha Airlines and
               the Internal Revenue Service acting in open defiance of
               justice and this court for proceeding with unlawful and
               fraudulent attachment of compensation for labor after
               receipt of a lawful service and summons [4-1]; under FRCP
               Rule 65 (byy) [Entry date 04/25/02]

4/25/02   11   NOTICE OF MOTION and motion by defendant Emy Tamanaha, and
               Aloha Airlines, Inco to dismiss and for more definite
               statement pursuant to FRCP 9(b) and 12 (b)(6); memorandum
               of law; certificate of service - set for 10:30 6/17/02
               before Judge Alan C. Kay (byy) [Entry date 04/26/02]

4/26/02   12   RETURN OF SERVICE executed upon defendant Emy Tamanaha on
               4/5/02 of Finances department, 2828 Paa St., Hono, HI (byy)

4/26/02   13   RETURN OF SERVICE executed upon defendant Aloha Airlines,
               Inco on 4/5/02 thru Emy Tamanaha, Finance Dept (byy)

4/26/02   14   RETURN OF SERVICE executed upon defendant Susan Meredith on
               4/8/02 via certified mail, RRR 7002 0460 0001 4067 6962 (byy)

4/26/02   15   RETURN OF SERVICE executed upon defendant Internal Revenue
               Ser on 4/8/02 via certified mail, RRR 7002 0460 0001 4067
               6979 (byy)

4/26/02   16   DECLARATION of counsel by defendant re [1-1]; exhibits a
               and b; certificate of service (byy)

4/27/02   17   MOTION for termination by plaintiff of two requests for
               temporary restraining order and injunction against Aloha
               airlies and Internal Revenue Service, et al, for failure to
               affirm competent jurisdiction of the court [4-1], [10-1];
               certificate of service (byy) [Entry date 04/29/02]

Proceedings include all events.   TERMED
1:02cv198 Ebarez, et al v. Tamanaha, et al

4/29/02   18   EP :Request For Immediate Permanent Restraining Order And
                   Injunction Against Aloha Airlines And The Internal Revenue
                   Service Acting In Open Defiance Of Justice And This Court
                   For Proceeding With Unlawful And Fraudulent Attachment Of
                   Compensation For Labor After Receipt Of A Lawful Service:
                   Three calls made outside of Courtroom Aha Kaulike in the
                   names of John Alfred Ebanez and Darcy Jean Mapuana Ebanez
                   with no response. Arguments made. Since plaintiffs filed a
                   Motion For Termination, Court GRANTED the Motion for
                   Termination. Court to prepare Order - re [4-1], granting
                   motion to dismiss and for more definite statement pursuant
                   to FRCP 9(b) and 12(b)(6) [11-1] (Ct Rptr : Cynthia
                   Fazio) JUDGE Alan C. Kay (byy) [Entry date 04/30/02]

5/1/02   19   ORDER by Judge Alan C. Kay granting plaintiffs' motion for
                   termination of two requests for temporary restraining order
                   and injunction re [18-1] (cc: all counsel) (byy)

5/16/02   20   NOTICE OF MOTION and motion by defendant Internal Revenue
                   Ser to dismiss; memorandum in support of motion to
                   dismiss; certificate of service - set for 10:30 6/17/02
                   before Judge Alan C. Kay (eps) [Entry date 05/17/02]

5/30/02   21   NOTICE of default of respondents by plaintiff; Clerical
                   claim for damages by default under common-law and as
                   affirmed by FRCP 55(a); and lawful rejection of unlawful
                   responses by fraud on court and inability of judges to
                   affirm competency by written, lawful oaths of office;
                   affidavit and attachments (byy) [Entry date 05/31/02]

5/30/02   22   Entry of Default - automatic judgment (by plaintiffs) re:
                   [21-1] DENIED BY WALTER A.Y.H. CHINN, Clerk (byy)
                   [Entry date 05/31/02]

5/3/02   23   NOTICE of non-acceptance of service by the plaintiffs by
                   defendant Internal Revenue Ser; exhibit a; certificate of
                   service (byy) [Entry date 06/04/02]

5/10/02   24   NOTICE OF MOTION and motion by defendant Emy Tamanaha, and
                   Aloha Airlines, Inco to excuse them from provisions of
                   Fed,R.CIV.P 26(f) requiring a meeting of and report from
                   the parties; memorandum of law; declaration of counsel
                   certificate of service - non-hrg before Mag Judge Leslie E.
                   Kobayashi (byy)

5/13/02   25   DECLARATION of counsel regarding service upon defendants;
                   exhibits a-c; certificTE OF SERVICE - by defendants Emy
                   Tamanaha and Aloha Airlines, Inco (byy)
                   [Entry date 06/17/02]

Docket as of August 5, 2002 2:42 pm   Page 5

Proceedings include all events.   TERMED
1:02cv198 Ebarez, et al v. Tamanaha, et al

6/13/02   26   EO :Continued : [Rule 16 Scheduling Conference] from
                  07/01/2002 09:00:00 AM to 09/09/2002 09:00:00 AM, LEK.
                  Order to issue continuing date rule 16 conference set for
                  9:00 9/9/02 before Mag Judge Leslie E. Kobayashi (Ct Rptr
                  :) Mag Judge Leslie E. Kobayashi (byy)
                  [Entry date 06/17/02]

6/14/02   27   ORDER by Mag Judge Leslie E. Kobayashi granting defendants'
                  motion to excuse them from provisions of Fed,R.CIV.P 26(f)
                  requiring meeting of and report from the parties [24-1]
                  (cc: all counsel) (byy) [Entry date 06/17/02]

6/17/02   28   EP :1) Government's Motion to Dismiss and 2) Defendants Emy
                  Tamanaha and Aloha Airlines, Inc.'s Motion to Dismiss and
                  for More Definite Statement Pursuant to Federal Rules of
                  Civil Procedure 9 (b) and 12(b)(6) Three calls made outside
                  of Courtroom Aha Kaulike in the names of John Alfred
                  Ebanez and Darcy Jean Mapuana Ebanez with no response.
                  Arguments made. Government's Motion to Dismiss and
                  Defendant Emy Tamanaha and Aloha Airlines, Inc's Motion to
                  Dismiss and for More Definite Statement Pursuant to Federal
                  Rules of Civil Procedure 9 (b) and 12(b)(6) GRANTED.
                  Counsels to prepare Order. [20-1], [11-1] (Ct Rptr : Steve
                  Platt) JUDGE Judge Alan C. Kay (byy) [Entry date 06/18/02]

5/27/02   29   ORDER by Judge Alan C. Kay granting United States' motion
                  to dismiss [20-1]; certificate of service - on behalf of
                  USA - the plaintiffs have failed to state a claim against
                  the United States upon which relief can be granted (byy)
                  [Entry date 07/02/02]

5/27/02   30   ORDER by Judge Alan C. Kay granting defendants Emy
                  Tamanaha and Aloha Airlines, Inc.'s motion to dismiss and
                  for more definite statement pursuant to FRCP 9(b) and 12
                  (b)(6) [11-1] - on behalf of Emy Tamanaha and Aloha Airles,
                  Inc. (byy) [Entry date 07/02/02]

7/3/02   31   JUDGMENT in a civil case: that the Complaint is DISMISSED,
                  pursuant to "Order Granting United States' Motion to
                  Dismiss" and "Order Granting Defendants' Emy Tamanaha and
                  Aloha Airlines, Inc.'s Motion to Dismiss and For More
                  Definite Statement Pursuant to Federal Rules of Civil
                  Procedure 9 (b) and 12 (b) (6) Filed April 25, 2002", filed
                  on June 27, 2002 - by WALTER A.Y.H. CHINN, Clerk/Barbara
                  Yamada (cc: all counsel) (byy)

Docket as of August 5, 2002 2:42 pm   Page 6

EXHIBIT O

Entry of Automatic Default Judgment

John Alfred Ebanez and
Darcy Jean Mapuana Ebanez,
Individually and Jointly, as
Husband and Wife, In Propia Persona.
91-680 Kilipoe Street
Ewa Beach, Oahu, Hawaii Nei (96706)
(808) 689-7427
Complainants.

Emy Tamanaha, A Private Party, and,
ALOHA AIRLINES INCORPORATED,
A STATE OF HAWAII CORPORATION;
And,
Susan Meredith, A Private Party, and,
THE INTERNAL REVENUE SERVICE,
A UNITED STATES RELATED ENTITY,
Respondents.

IN THE UNITED STATES COURT

FOR THE HAWAII DISTRICT

John Alfred Ebanez and Darcy Jean Mapuana Ebanez, Individually and Jointly,) Complainants,) vs.) Emy Tamanaha, A Private Party, and,) ALOHA AIRLINES INCORPORATED;) AND, Susan Meredith, A Private Party, and,) THE INTERNAL REVENUE SERVICE, A) PRIVATE ENTITY,) Respondents.) _____)	**CIVIL CASE NO. CV 02 00198 ACK / LEK** **ENTRY OF DEFAULT – AUTOMATIC JUDGMENT** (FOR DAMAGES BY DEFAULT UNDER THE COMMON-LAW AND (FRCP 55 [b][1]) AGAINST Emy Tamanaha AND Susan Meredith, BOTH PRIVATE PARTIES: ALOHA AIRLINES, INC. AND INTERNAL REVENUE SERVICE A PRIVATE ENTITY, FOR EXTORTION AND FRAUD.) By Special Appearance, under the common-law. Federal Question under 28 USC § 1331/1332 Under Reservation of Rights / Jurisdiction

Justice, without the Grace of Almighty God, becomes a plague of corruption and death upon the innocent as well as those who execute justice by the abuse of the law.   (Unknown)

ENTRY OF DEFAULT – AUTOMATIC JUDGMENT

Now come John Ebanez and Darcy-Jean Ebanez, his wife, Plaintiffs, in Propia Persona, both individually and jointly under the common-law and stated reservation of rights in filing of this lawful **Entry of Default – Automatic Judgment** and clerical claim for damages under the common-law (and Federal Rules of Civil Procedure (FRCP) Rule 55 [a]), regarding **Complaint No. CV 02 00198 ACK / LEK** filed on April 4, 2002 against the named Respondents who failed to lawfully respond or defend.

"ENTRY OF NOTICE OF DEFAULT OF RESPONDENTS" was previously filed with this Court.

Complaint was for the unlawful assessment and fraudulent extortion of Complainant's compensation for labor owed by ALOHA AIRLINES, INC. and administered by Emy Tamanaha, a Private Party and Agent, and THE INTERNAL REVENUE SERVICE, A PRIVATE CORPORATION and Susan Meredith, a Private Party, (hereinafter, "Respondents"). **NOTICE:** There has been no lawful response in the lawful birth names to the lawful domicile of record of the real parties in interest nor has there been any lawful attempt to defend by Respondents since filing of the Complaint.

RESERVATION OF RIGHTS:

Judges and Clerks under Constitutional and Statutory Oaths of Office are bound to honor the American Constitution and must have full respect of the Superior law of all treaties made, specifically, the ratified, non-abrogated Treaty of 1850 between the Nations of America and Hawaii. Lawfully distinct Hawaiians under their own de jure birth names and birth law are "favored citizens" under "favored nation" status of said Treaty possessing the same rights as Americans born to that continent. Judges of this Court have ignored and abused that Treaty right while representing a foreign corporation on de jure Hawaiian Kingdom National soil.

1

Complainants have reserved their rights to be heard in a court of competent jurisdiction under the common-law in this matter of fraud, extortion and violation of International Law, before a Jury of Peers. That reservation of rights under the common-law of the Complaint has never been waived by the Complainants and is in lawful evidence on the ORDER SETTING RULE 16 SCHEDULING CONFERENCE STATEMENT, filed on April 4, 2002.

NOTICE TO CLERK OF NOTICE OF ENTRY OF DEFAULT:

This is a notice to the clerk of an *Entry of Default* by Complainants against the above and below captioned parties who have, *"...failed to plead or otherwise defend as provided by these rules and that fact is made to appear by affidavit or otherwise, the clerk shall enter his default."* Said right of default for damages is affirmed by the common law and previous filing under the Federal Rules of Civil Procedure (FRCP) Rule 55 (a). Default is for lawful lack of truthful and lawful response or substantiated response by Respondents to the Complaint filed on April 4, 2002, supra, as evidenced and documented in the *Notice of Default*, filed previously.

Under FRCP Rule 55 (a) ("affidavit") *"judgment by default"* is automatic as affirmed under FRCP Rule 55 (b)(1), is requiring of the clerk to enter *Default*, supra. This Default comes under the common-law and conditions set forth in Rule 55 (a) after previous filing of *Notice of Default*, and wherein Respondents *"...has failed to plead or otherwise defend..."* and, as affirmed by the wording, *"...or otherwise, the clerk shall enter his default."* (Underlined emphasis by Complainant).

ACTUAL NOTICE TO PARTIES IN DAFAULT:

Parties, acting without proving jurisdiction and participating in fraud, conspiracy, extortion and criminal misrepresentation in violation of law under "color of United States

Law", holding office under "color of Office" <u>do not possess lawful right, being in violation of law, to use the law to dismiss a lawful filing under the law</u>; i.e. specifically, the unlawful attempt to set aside this Default by use of Rule 55 (c); or Rule 54 (c) (NOTE: Rule 55 [c] and 54 [c] are not applicable, as this is an automatic default under Rule 55 [b][1] and therefore not a judgment under Rule 55 [b][2], "By the Court"); NOR DOES Rule 55 (e) apply for the very same reason, supra. Default is for fraud; conspiracy and extortion by the Respondents who are Private Parties, a Hawaiian Corporation and a United States Entity, all acting outside of law against Complainants.

<u>NOTICE TO THE CLERK: FEDERAL RULES OF CIVIL PROCEDURE (FRCP) RULE 55 (b)(1) – CLERK IS RESPONSIBLE FOR COMPUTING CLAIM</u>:

Notice to the clerk is hereby given that computation of claim is *"...for a sum certain"* and can be entered by the clerk against the parties in violation in this <u>automatic judgment by default</u>.

<u>DAMAGES OWED TO John Alfred Ebanez and Darcy Jean Mapuana Ebanez, Husband and Wife BY DEFAULT OF RESPONDENTS</u>:

Complainants, falsely and unlawfully damaged, possess Default for damages under right of law against the <u>non-responsive and defaulting Respondents</u> ALOHA AIRLINES, INC., A HAWAII STATE CORPORATION and Emy Tamanaha, a Private Party; and, THE INTERNAL REVENUE SERVICE, A PRIVATE ENTITU AND CORPORATION, and, Susan Meredith, a Private Party for conspiracy, fraud and extortion.

<u>DAMAGES OWED AND COMPUTABLE</u>:

Emy Tamanaha, a Private Party $500,000.00

ALOHA AIRLINES, INC.	$500,000.00
Susan Meredith, a Private Party	$500,000.00
THE INTERNAL REVENUE SERVICE, A	
PRIVATE ENTITY	$500,000.00

PUNITIVE DAMAGES (TREBLE):

Complainant waives punitive damages against the two Private Parties, Emy Tamanaha and Susan Meredith but not against the other two persons.

ALOHA AIRLINES, INC.	$1,500,000.00
THE INTERNAL REVENUE SERVICE,	
A PRIVATE ENTITY	$1,500,000.00.

The total amount of damages and punitive damages are as stated, and Complainants waive at this time all costs of legal fees incurred in their behalf.

DEMAND FOR IMMEDIATE LAWFUL ENTRY BY THE CLERK:

Clerk, under lawful obligation to honor the law and the Federal Rules of Civil Procedure is not under order of any judge of incompetent authority in this matter required by and before the Clerk of the Court. Demand is for the Clerk of the Court not to yield to unlawful intimidation, as the Oath of Office of the Clerk requires this "Entry of Default and Automatic Judgment" to be immediately filed.

DATED: May 10, 2002 in Ewa Beach, Oahu, Hawaii Nei.

_____
John Alfred: Ebanez, Husband and
Complainant as an Individual and Jointly,
in Propia Persona.

_____
Darcy-Jean Ebanez, Wife and Complainant
as and Individual and Jointly, in Propia
Persona.

IN THE UNITED STATES COURT

FOR THE DISTRICT OF HAWAII

John Alfred Ebanez and Darcy –Jean Ebanez, Complainants, vs. ALOHA AIRLINES, INC. AND, THE INTERNAL REVENUE SERVICE, Respondents.	)))))))))))))

Case No. CV 02 00198 ACK/LEK

CERTIFICATE OF SERVICE

CERTIFICATE OF LAWFUL SERVICE

      I HEREBY CERTIFY that a true and correct copy of the foregoing to which this Certificate of Service is attached, was duly served upon the following by hand delivery or by depositing said copies into the United States mail at Honolulu, Hawaii Nei, First Class postage prepaid and addressed as follows:

Emy Tamanaha, A Private Party
P. O. Box 30028
Honolulu, Hawaii 96820

Susan Meredith, A Private Party
P. O. Box 24017
Fresno, California 93779-4017

ALOHA AIRLINES INCORPORATED
A HAWAII CORPORATION
C/O: Emy Tamanaha, Director
    Accounting Department
P. O. Box 30028
Honolulu, Hawaii 96820

INTERNAL REVENUE SERVICE
A UNITED STATES RELATED
ENTITY (Fresno Office)
Susan Meredith, Operations Manager
P. O. Box 24017
Fresno, California 93779-4017

DATED: May 9, 2002 in Ewa Beach, Oahu, Hawaii Nei.

John Alfred: Ebanez Complainant In Propia Persona

EXHIBIT P

Docket Sheet, Johnson Case
#CV 98-00089 SPK

Proceedings include all events.   TERMED
1:98cv89   Johnson v. First Hawaiian Bank, et al

                                                          TERMED

                    U.S. District Court
    U.S. District Court for the District of Hawaii (Hawaii)

              CIVIL DOCKET FOR CASE #: 98-CV-89

Johnson v. First Hawaiian Bank, et al   Filed: 01/30/98
Assigned to: Judge Samuel P. King   Jury demand: Both
          Referred to: Mag Judge Francis I. Yamashita
Demand: $10,400,000   Nature of Suit: 890
Lead Docket: None   Jurisdiction: Federal Question
Dkt# in other court: None

Cause: 28:1331 Fed. Question

1/30/98 1   COMPLAINT in tort for bad faith, false pretense, frivolous
               claim pertaining to nonexistent loan contract, and
               collusion; violation of U.S. Constitutional rights of
               plaintiff; request for jury trial (wn)

1/30/98 2   ORDER by Judge Alan C. Kay rule 16 pretrial conference
               set for 8:30 5/4/98 before Mag Judge Francis I. Yamashita
               (wn)

3/9/98   3   First AMENDED COMPLAINT [1-1] in tort for bad faith, false
               pretense, frivolous claim, malice and racketeering by
               non-existant contract, collusion of parties, violation of
               U.S. constitutional rights of plaintff by plaintiff Jon
               Robert Johnson; pltf requests common-law jury trial of his
               peers; pltf requests use of everyday, common, English
               language - [terminating defendant Norman Doi, defendant
               Cedric Yamamoto; adding Norman Doi, Cedric Yamamoto, Norman
               Doi, Cedric Yamamoto, Watanabe, Ing & Kawa, William H.
               Galardy, Jonathan W.Y. Lai, Peter A. Horovitz, Eric
               Kashibawara, Hawaii, State of, T, Ben Cayetano, Kevin
               Chang, Kevin S.C. Chang] (mm) [Entry date 03/10/98]

3/9/98   4   SUMMONS (issued) (mm) [Entry date 03/10/98]

3/26/98 5   RETURN OF SERVICE executed upon defendant First Hawaiian
               Bank thru Norman Doi, agent on 3/11/98 (wn)
               [Entry date 03/27/98]

3/26/98 6   RETURN OF SERVICE executed upon defendant Norman Doi on
               3/11/98 (wn) [Entry date 03/27/98]

3/26/98 7   RETURN OF SERVICE unexecuted - attempted as to defendant
               Eric Kashibawara (refused) (wn) [Entry date 03/27/98]

3/26/98 8   RETURN OF SERVICE executed upon defendant Cedric Yamamoto
               on 3/11/98 (wn) [Entry date 03/27/98]

3/26/98 9   RETURN OF SERVICE executed upon defendant Cedric Yamamoto
               on 3/11/98 (wn) [Entry date 03/27/98]

Docket as of May 5, 1998 12:39 pm   Page 1

Proceedings include all events.   TERMED
1:98cv89   Johnson v. First Hawaiian Bank, et al

3/26/98 10   RETURN OF SERVICE executed upon defendant Kevin Chang thru
               Wilma Arakaki, clerk on 3/11/98 (wn) [Entry date 03/27/98]

3/26/98 11   RETURN OF SERVICE executed upon defendant Kevin S.C. Chang
               thru Wilma Arakaki, clerk on 3/11/98 (wn)
               [Entry date 03/27/98]

3/26/98 12   RETURN OF SERVICE executed upon defendant Peter A. Horovitz
               thru John A. Komeiji, atty on 3/11/98 (wn)
               [Entry date 03/27/98]

3/26/98 13   RETURN OF SERVICE executed upon defendant Watanabe, Ing &
               Kawa thru John T. Komeiji, atty on 3/11/98 (wn)
               [Entry date 03/27/98]

3/26/98 14   RETURN OF SERVICE executed upon defendant Jonathan W.Y. Lai
               on 3/11/98 (wn) [Entry date 03/27/98]

3/26/98 15   RETURN OF SERVICE unexecuted - attempted as to defendant
               Hawaii, State of, T; sent by US Mail (wn)
               [Entry date 03/27/98] [Edit date 03/27/98]

3/26/98 16   RETURN OF SERVICE unexecuted - attempted as to defendant
               William H. Galardy; sent by US Mail (wn)
               [Entry date 03/27/98]

3/26/98 17   CERTIFICATE of service; of first amended complaint and
               original complaint via US Mail on: Gov. Ben Cayetano, State
               of Hawaii, William H. Galardy, Eri Kashibawara; in person:
               State of Hawaii, Deloitte and Touche, Reinwald, O'Connor &
               Playdon (wn) [Entry date 03/27/98] [Edit date 03/27/98]

3/31/98 18   NOTICE OF MOTION and motion by defendant Hawaii, State of,
               T, defendant Ben Cayetano, defendant Kevin Chang, defendant
               Kevin S.C. Chang to dismiss first amended complaint or
               alternatively for summary judgment; memorandum in support
               of motion; certificate of service - set for 10:00 5/21/98
               before Judge Samuel P. King (mm) [Entry date 04/01/98]

3/31/98 19   NOTICE OF MOTION and motion by defendant First Hawaiian
               Bank, defendant Norman Doi, defendant Cedric Yamamoto,
               defendant Norman Doi, defendant Cedric Yamamoto, defendant
               Watanabe, Ing & Kawa, defendant William H. Galardy,
               defendant Jonathan W.Y. Lai, defendant Peter A. Horovitz,
               defendant Eric Kashibawara to dismiss first amended
               complaint; memorandum in support of motion; declaration of
               Patsy H. Kirio; exhibits "a"-"m"; certificate of service -
               set for 3:00 6/8/98 before Judge Samuel P. King (wn)
               [Entry date 04/02/98]

4/9/98   20   MOTION by plaintiff to strike motions to dismiss set for
               3:00 6/8/98 before Judge Samuel P. King (wn)
               [Entry date 04/10/98]

Docket as of May 5, 1998 12:39 pm   Page 2

Proceedings include all events.   TERMED
1:98cv89   Johnson v. First Hawaiian Bank, et al

4/9/98   21   NOTICE by plaintiff of hearing setting hearing on motion to
                strike motions to dismiss [20-1] 3:00 6/8/98 (wn)
                [Entry date 04/10/98]

4/9/98   22   MOTION by plaintiff to strike motions to dismiss set for
                3:00 6/8/98 before Judge Samuel P. King (wn)
                [Entry date 04/10/98]

4/9/98   23   MOTION by plaintiff to strike motions to dismiss set for
                3:00 6/8/98 before Judge Samuel P. King (wn)
                [Entry date 04/10/98]

4/9/98   24   MOTION by plaintiff to strike motions to dismiss set for
                3:00 6/8/98 before Judge Samuel P. King (wn)
                [Entry date 04/10/98]

4/9/98   25   MOTION by plaintiff to strike motions to dismiss set for
                3:00 6/8/98 before Judge Samuel P. King (wn)
                [Entry date 04/10/98]

4/9/98   26   MOTION by plaintiff to strike motions to dismiss set for
                3:00 6/8/98 before Judge Samuel P. King (wn)
                [Entry date 04/10/98]

4/9/98   27   MOTION by plaintiff to strike motions to dismiss set for
                3:00 6/8/98 before Judge Samuel P. King (wn)
                [Entry date 04/10/98]

4/9/98   28   (Proposed) REQUEST by plaintiff for entry of default and
                entry of default by clerk (against defendant Jonathan W.Y.
                Lai) (wn) [Entry date 04/10/98]

4/9/98   29   (Proposed) REQUEST by plaintiff for entry of default and
                entry of default by clerk (against defnedant Watanabe Ing &
                Kawashima) (wn) [Entry date 04/10/98]

4/9/98   30   (Proposed) REQUEST by plaintiff for entry of default and
                entry of default by clerk (against defendant Cedric
                Yamamoto) (wn) [Entry date 04/10/98]

4/9/98   31   (Proposed) REQUEST by plaintiff for entry of default and
                entry of default (against defendant First Hawaiian Bank,
                Norman Doi, agent and Cedric Yamamoto, agent) (wn)
                [Entry date 04/10/98]

4/9/98   32   (Proposed) REQUEST for entry of default and entry of
                default by clerk (against Peter A. Horovitz) (wn)
                [Entry date 04/10/98]

4/9/98   33   (Proposed) REQUEST by plaintiff for entry of default and
                entry of default by clerk (against Kevin S.C. Chang) (wn)
                [Entry date 04/10/98]

Docket as of May 5, 1998 12:39 pm   Page 3

Proceedings include all events.   TERMED
1:98cv89   Johnson v. First Hawaiian Bank, et al

4/9/98 34 (Proposed) REQUEST by plaintiff for entry of default and
            entry of default (against Norman Doi) (wn)
            [Entry date 04/10/98]

4/9/98 35 (Proposed) REQUEST by plaintiff for default judgment by
            clerk (against defendant Cedric Yamamoto) (wn)
            [Entry date 04/10/98]

4/9/98 36 (Proposed) DEFAULT JUDGMENT (against Cedric Yamamoto) (wn)
            [Entry date 04/10/98]

4/9/98 37 (Proposed) REQUEST by plaintiff for default judgment by
            clerk (against defendant First Hawaiian Bank) (wn)
            [Entry date 04/10/98]

4/9/98 38 (Proposed) DEFAULT JUDGMENT (against defendant First
            Hawaiian Bank) (wn) [Entry date 04/10/98]

4/9/98 39 (Proposed) REQUEST by plaintiff for default judgment by
            clerk (against Peter A. Horovitz) (wn) [Entry date 04/10/98]

4/9/98 40 (Proposed) DEFAULT JUDGMENT (against defendant Peter A.
            Horovitz) (wn) [Entry date 04/10/98]
            [Edit date 04/10/98]

4/9/98 41 (Proposed) REQUEST by plaintiff for default judgment
            (against defendant Watanabe Ing & Kawashima) (wn)
            [Entry date 04/10/98]

4/9/98 42 (Proposed) DEFAULT JUDGMENT (against defendant Watanabe
            Ing & Kawashima) (wn) [Entry date 04/10/98]

4/9/98 43 (Proposed) REQUEST by plaintiff for default judgment
            (against Jonathan W.Y. Lai) (wn) [Entry date 04/10/98]

4/9/98 44 (Proposed) DEFAULT JUDGMENT (against Jonathan W.Y. Lai) (wn)
            [Entry date 04/10/98]

4/9/98 45 (Proposed) REQUEST by plaintiff for default judgemnt
            (against defendant Kevin S.C. CHang) (wn)
            [Entry date 04/10/98]

4/9/98 46 (Proposed) DEFAULT JUDGMENT (against defendant Kevin S.C.
            Chang) (wn) [Entry date 04/10/98]

4/9/98 47 (Proposed) REQUEST by plaintiff for default judgment
            (against Norman Doi) (wn) [Entry date 04/10/98]

4/9/98 48 (Proposed) DEFAULT JUDGMENT (against Norman Doi) (wn)
            [Entry date 04/10/98]

4/9/98 49 ORDER by Judge Samuel P. King sua sponte dismissing
            complaint for failure to include statement of jurisdiction
            (cc: all counsel) (wn) [Entry date 04/13/98]

Docket as of May 5, 1998 12:39 pm   Page 4

Proceedings include all events.   TERMED
1:98cv89   Johnson v. First Hawaiian Bank, et al

4/13/98   50   JUDGMENT: by Walter A.Y.H. CHINN, Clerk/Warren N. Nakamura,
                Deputy Clerk - plaintiff's complaint is hereby dismissed
                without prejudice for failure to include a statement of
                jurisdiction; it is further ordered that plaintiff has 30
                days from the date he receives the 4/9/98 "order sua sponte
                dismissing complaint for failure to include statement of
                jurisdiction," to amend his complaint - terminating case
                (cc: Jon Robert Johnson, Patsy H. Kirio, Russell A. Suzuki)
                (wn)

4/13/98   51   MOTION by plaintiff Jon Robert Johnson to correct
                jurisdictional error by the clerk of court - referred to
                before Judge Samuel P. King (wn)

4/13/98   52   MOTION by plaintiff Jon Robert Johnson to correct
                malfeasance and egregious misconduct by Judge for fraud on
                court - referred to Judge Samuel P. King (wn)

4/13/98   52   MOTION by plaintiff Jon Robert Johnson to strike
                fraudulent "order sua sponte dismissing complaint for
                failure to include statement of jurisdiction" - referred
                to Judge Samuel P. King (wn)

4/13/98   52   MOTION by plaintiff Jon Robert Johnson to grant default
                judgments against defendants as filed - referred to Judge
                Samuel P. King (wn)

4/15/98   53   ORDER DENYING plaintiff's motion for reconsideration of
                order sua sponte dismissing complaint for failure to
                include statement of jurisdiction by Judge Samuel P. King
                [denying motion to correct jurisdictional error by the
                clerk of court [51-1], denying motion to correct
                malfeasance and egregious misconduct by Judge for fraud on
                court [52-1], denying motion to strike fraudulent "order
                sua sponte dismissing complaint for failure to include
                statement of jurisdiction" [52-1], denying motion to grant
                default judgments against defendants as filed [52-1]] (cc:
                all counsel) (wn)

4/20/98   54   MOTION by plaintiff Jon Robert Johnson to strike Judge
                King's ficticious order for reconsideration, a relabeling
                of plaintiff's motion to correct malfeasance and egregious
                misconduct by Judge for fraud on court; motion to strike
                fraudulent order sua sponte dismissing complaint for
                failure to include statement of juridiction; and motion to
                grant default judgment against defendants, as filed; second
                act of fraud on court - referred to Judge Samuel P. King (wn)
                [Entry date 04/21/98]

Docket as of May 5, 1998 12:39 pm   Page 5

1:98cv89   Johnson v. First Hawaiian Bank, et al

4/24/98 55   ORDER OF ASSIGNMENT of PETITION FOR RECUSAL by Judge Alan C.
                Kay - [court construes 4/20/98 petition as a petition to
                recuse Judge Samuel P. King; the motion to strike Judge
                King's ficticious order for reconsideration, a relabeling of
                plaintiff's motion to correct malfeasance and egregious
                misconduct by Judge for fraud on court; motion to strike
                fraudulent order sua sponte dismissing complaint for failure
                to include statement of juridiction; and motion to grant
                default judgment against defendants, as filed; second act of
                fraud on court [54-1] is REFERRED TO JUDGE MARTIN PENCE to
                decide] (cc: all counsel, Judge Pence) (wn)
                [Entry date 04/27/98] [Edit date 04/27/98]

4/27/98 56   MOTION by plaintiff Jon Robert Johnson to the judiciary of
                the Hawaii District Court to cease acts of collusion, fraud
                on court and corruption; fourth and fifth actions of fraud
                on court by the judiciary of the District Court for the
                Hawaii District - referred to Judge Samuel P. King (wn)
                [Edit date 04/27/98]

4/27/98 57   MOTION by plaintiff Jon Robert Johnson to strike Judge
                Kay's improper "order for assignment of petition for
                recusal;" third action of fraud on court by judiciary of
                the Hawaii District; exhibit "a" and "b" - referred to
                Judge Samuel P. King (wn)

4/27/98 58   SECOND MOTION by plaintiff Jon Robert Johnson to correct
                jurisdictional error by the Clerk of Court; declaration of
                Jon Robert Johnson, Aran Alton Ardaiz - referred to Judge
                Samuel P. King (wn) [Edit date 04/29/98]

4/29/98 59   ORDER denying plaintiff's motion for reconsideration by
                Judge Alan C. Kay [denying motion to strike Judge Kay's
                improper "order for assignment of petition for recusal;"
                third action of fraud on court by judiciary of Hawaii
                District [57-1]] (cc: all counsel) (seal)

4/30/98 60   ORDER of DENIAL of MOTION to RECUSE by Judge Martin Pence
                [denying motion to strike Judge King's ficticious order for
                reconsideration, a relabeling plaintiff's motion to correct
                malfeasance and egregious misconduct by Judge for fraud on
                court; motion to strike fraudulent order sua sponte
                dismissing complaint for to include statement of
                juridiction; and motion to grant default judgment against
                defendants, as filed; second act fraud on court [54-1]]
                (cc: all counsel) (wn)

5/4/98   61   Pltf's Second MOTION to the judiciary of the Hawaii
                District Court to cease acts of collusion fraud on court
                and corruption; motion to strike Judge Pence's "denial of
                motion to recuse"; sixth action on court by the judiciary
                of the Federal Court for the Hawaii District - referred to
                Judge Alan C. Kay (mm)

Docket as of May 5, 1998 12:39 pm   Page 6

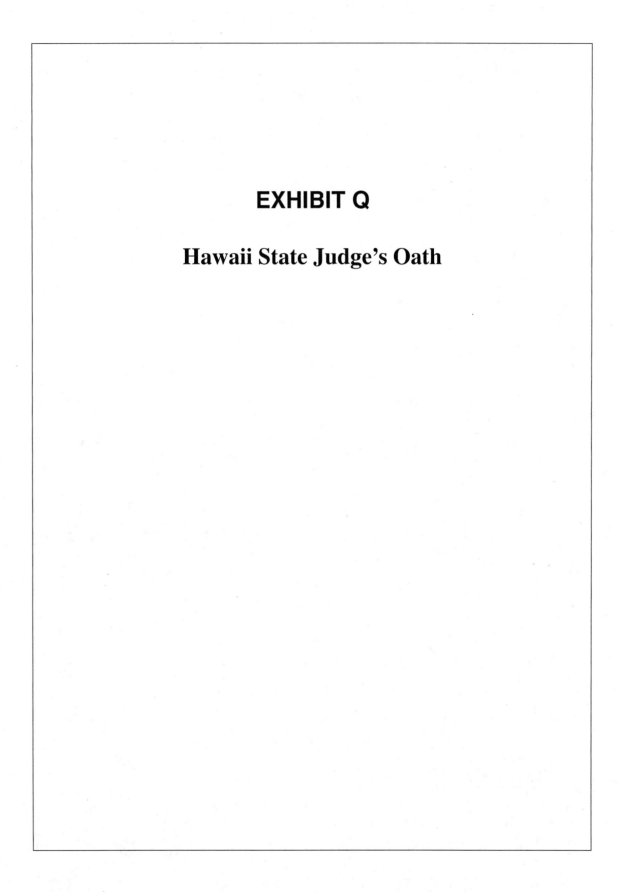

EXHIBIT Q

Hawaii State Judge's Oath

State of Hawaii
Oath of Office

State of Hawaii

City and County of Honolulu

⎫
⎬ ss.
⎭

I, _____ RONALD T. Y. MOON _____

do solemnly swear that I will support and defend the Constitution of the United States, and the Constitution of the State of Hawaii, and that I will faithfully discharge my duties as ____Chief Justice of the Supreme Court____ for the State of Hawaii to the best of my ability.

_____
RONALD T. Y. MOON

Subscribed and sworn to before me this

____31st____ day of ____March____

A. D. 19 93

_____
State of Hawaii
HERMAN LUM
Chief Justice
Supreme Court of Hawaii

SUPREME COURT
Seal
STATE OF HAWAII

State of Hawaii
Oath of Office

State of Hawaii

City and County of Honolulu } ss.

I, _____ KEVIN S. C. CHANG _____

do solemnly swear that I will support and defend the Constitution of the United States, and the Constitution of the State of Hawaii, and that I will faithfully discharge my duties as _____ Judge of the Circuit Court of the First Circuit _____ for the State of Hawaii to the best of my ability.

_____
KEVIN S. C. CHANG

Subscribed and sworn to before me this
_____ 30th _____ day of _____ April _____
A. D. 19 93

_____
State of Hawaii
RONALD T. Y. MOON
Chief Justice
Supreme Court

SUPREME COURT
Seal
STATE OF HAWAII

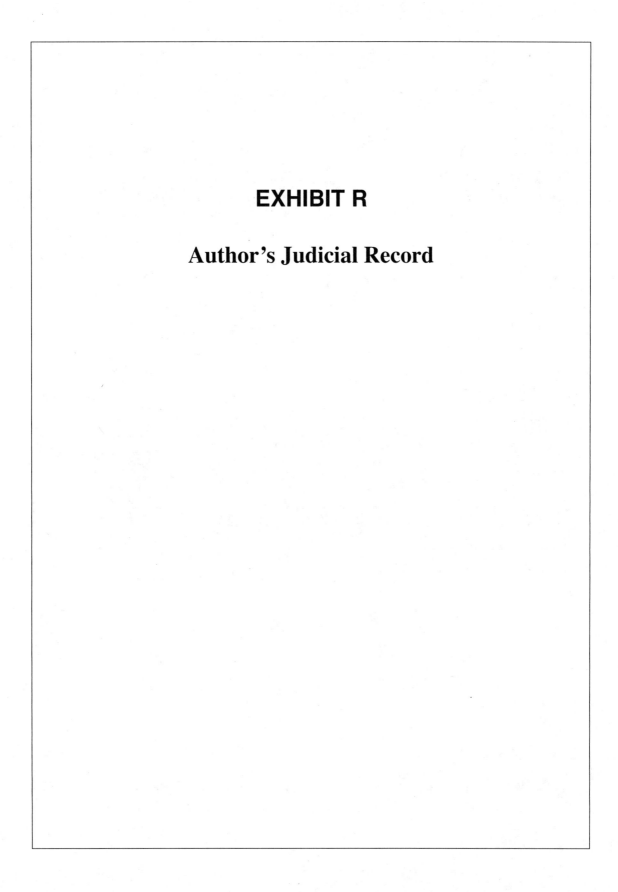

EXHIBIT R

Author's Judicial Record

Person/Case Type Search Results

▶ New Search

Phonetic Search: off **Person ID:** @432747

ID	Name/Corporation	Case	Party Type	Filing Date
@432747	Alton, Aran	000062658 State v. Aran Ardaiz	Defendant	17-FEB-2000
@432747	Alton, Aran	002169300 State v. Aran Ardaiz	Defendant	06-MAY-2002
@432747	Alton, Aran	002169301 State v. Aran Ardaiz	Defendant	06-MAY-2002
@432747	Alton, Aran	002169302 State v. Aran Ardaiz	Defendant	06-MAY-2002
@432747	Alton, Aran	002169304 State v. Aran Ardaiz	Defendant	06-MAY-2002
@432747	Alton, Aran	002169306 State v. Aran Ardaiz	Defendant	06-MAY-2002
@432747	Alton, Aran	097297760 State v. Aran Ardaiz	Defendant	01-AUG-1997
@432747	Alton, Aran	098373038 State v. Aran Ardaiz	Defendant	08-OCT-1998
@432747	Alton, Aran	4204579MO State v. Aran Ardaiz	Defendant	10-FEB-1997
@432747	Alton, Aran	4476119MO State v. Aran Ardaiz	Defendant	07-JUL-1997
@432747	Alton, Aran	4476118MO State v. Aran Ardaiz	Defendant	07-JUL-1997
@432747	Alton, Aran	4476117MO State v. Aran Ardaiz	Defendant	07-JUL-1997
@432747	Alton, Aran	4476116MO State v. Aran Ardaiz	Defendant	07-JUL-1997
@432747	Alton, Aran	4476115MO State v. Aran Ardaiz	Defendant	07-JUL-1997
@432747	Alton, Aran	4447912MO State v. Aran Ardaiz	Defendant	25-AUG-1997
@432747	Alton, Aran	4414915MO State v. Aran Ardaiz	Defendant	07-MAR-1997
@432747	Alton, Aran	4414914MO State v. Aran Ardaiz	Defendant	07-MAR-1997
@432747	Alton, Aran	4414913MO State v. Aran Ardaiz	Defendant	07-MAR-1997
@432747	Alton, Aran	4693643MO State v. Aran Ardaiz	Defendant	09-OCT-1998
@432747	Alton, Aran	4693642MO State v. Aran Ardaiz	Defendant	09-OCT-1998

Page: 1 **Records:** 1 - 20

Next->

| Search Home | Search Help |

https://jimspss1.courts.state.hi.us/court/ck_public_qry_cpty.cp_personcase_details_idx?backto=P&so... 11/10/2005

Hawaii – The Fake State

Person/Case Type Search Results

▶ New Search

Phonetic Search: off   **Person ID:** @432747

ID	Name/Corporation	Case	Party Type	Filing Date
@432747	Alton, Aran	4677714MO State v. Aran Ardaiz	Defendant	09-OCT-1998
@432747	Alton, Aran	4677713MO State v. Aran Ardaiz	Defendant	09-OCT-1998
@432747	Alton, Aran	4489498MO State v. Aran Ardaiz	Defendant	04-AUG-1997
@432747	Alton, Aran	4489497MO State v. Aran Ardaiz	Defendant	04-AUG-1997
@432747	Alton, Aran	4489496MO State v. Aran Ardaiz	Defendant	04-AUG-1997
@432747	Alton, Aran	4484004MO State v. Aran Ardaiz	Defendant	05-AUG-1997
@432747	Alton, Aran	4476120MO State v. Aran Ardaiz	Defendant	07-JUL-1997
@432747	Alton, Aran	5083038MO State v. Aran Ardaiz	Defendant	05-DEC-2001
@432747	Alton, Aran	5083037MO State v. Aran Ardaiz	Defendant	05-DEC-2001
@432747	Alton, Aran	5083036MO State v. Aran Ardaiz	Defendant	05-DEC-2001
@432747	Alton, Aran	5083035MO State v. Aran Ardaiz	Defendant	05-DEC-2001
@432747	Alton, Aran	5083034MO State v. Aran Ardaiz	Defendant	05-DEC-2001
@432747	Alton, Aran	4897962MO State v. Aran Ardaiz	Defendant	07-APR-2000
@432747	Alton, Aran	4897961MO State v. Aran Ardaiz	Defendant	07-APR-2000
@432747	Alton, Aran	4897371MO State v. Aran Ardaiz	Defendant	10-APR-2000
@432747	Alton, Aran	4897370MO State v. Aran Ardaiz	Defendant	10-APR-2000
@432747	Alton, Aran	4879497MO State v. Aran Ardaiz	Defendant	22-FEB-2000
@432747	Alton, Aran	4879496MO State v. Aran Ardaiz	Defendant	22-FEB-2000
@432747	Alton, Aran	4879495MO State v. Aran Ardaiz	Defendant	22-FEB-2000
@432747	Alton, Aran	4879494MO State v. Aran Ardaiz	Defendant	22-FEB-2000

Page: 2 Records: 21 - 40

<-Previous   Next->

Search Home   Search Help

https://jimspss1.courts.state.hi.us/court/ck_public_qry_cpty.cp_personcase_details_idx?backto=P&so... 11/10/2005

Person/Case Type Search Results

▶ New Search

Phonetic Search: off   Person ID: @432747

ID	Name/Corporation	Case		Party Type	Filing Date
@432747	Alton, Aran	4830772MO	*State v. Aran Ardaiz*	Defendant	20-DEC-1999
@432747	Alton, Aran	4830771MO	*State v. Aran Ardaiz*	Defendant	20-DEC-1999
@432747	Alton, Aran	4693644MO	*State v. Aran Ardaiz*	Defendant	09-OCT-1998
@432747	Alton, Aran	5528293MO	*State v. Aran Ardaiz*	Defendant	02-JUN-2003
@432747	Alton, Aran	5528292MO	*State v. Aran Ardaiz*	Defendant	02-JUN-2003
@432747	Alton, Aran	5528291MO	*State v. Aran Ardaiz*	Defendant	02-JUN-2003
@432747	Alton, Aran	5528290MO	*State v. Aran Ardaiz*	Defendant	02-JUN-2003
@432747	Alton, Aran	5528289MO	*State v. Aran Ardaiz*	Defendant	02-JUN-2003
@432747	Alton, Aran	5287685MO	*State v. Aran Ardaiz*	Defendant	06-DEC-2001
@432747	Alton, Aran	5287684MO	*State v. Aran Ardaiz*	Defendant	06-DEC-2001
@432747	Alton, Aran	5282616MO	*State v. Aran Ardaiz*	Defendant	26-NOV-2001
@432747	Alton, Aran	5282615MO	*State v. Aran Ardaiz*	Defendant	26-NOV-2001
@432747	Alton, Aran	5191640MO	*State v. Aran Ardaiz*	Defendant	15-AUG-2001
@432747	Alton, Aran	5191639MO	*State v. Aran Ardaiz*	Defendant	15-AUG-2001
@432747	Alton, Aran	5191638MO	*State v. Aran Ardaiz*	Defendant	15-AUG-2001
@432747	Alton, Aran	5133819MO	*State v. Aran Ardaiz*	Defendant	29-MAY-2001
@432747	Alton, Aran	5133818MO	*State v. Aran Ardaiz*	Defendant	29-MAY-2001
@432747	Alton, Aran	5133817MO	*State v. Aran Ardaiz*	Defendant	29-MAY-2001
@432747	Alton, Aran	5083039MO	*State v. Aran Ardaiz*	Defendant	05-DEC-2001
@432747	Alton, Aran	4204578MO	*State v. Aran Ardaiz*	Defendant	10-FEB-1997

Page: 3 Records: 41 - 60

<-Previous   Next->

Search
Home

Search
Help

https://jimspss1.courts.state.hi.us/court/ck_public_qry_cpty.cp_personcase_details_idx?backto=P&so...   11/10/2005

Person/Case Type Search Results

▶ New Search

Phonetic Search: off   **Person ID:** @432747

ID	Name/Corporation	Case	Party Type	Filing Date
@432747	Alton, Aran	098373037 *State v. Aran Ardaiz*	Defendant	08-OCT-1998
@432747	Alton, Aran	003210111 *State v. Aran Ardaiz*	Defendant	30-MAY-2003
@432747	Alton, Aran	002169305 *State v. Aran Ardaiz*	Defendant	06-MAY-2002
@432747	Alton, Aran	002169303 *State v. Aran Ardaiz*	Defendant	06-MAY-2002
@432747	Alton, Ardaiz	000062658 *State v. Aran Ardaiz*	Defendant	17-FEB-2000
@432747	Alton, Ardaiz	002169301 *State v. Aran Ardaiz*	Defendant	06-MAY-2002
@432747	Alton, Ardaiz	002169303 *State v. Aran Ardaiz*	Defendant	06-MAY-2002
@432747	Alton, Ardaiz	4447912MO *State v. Aran Ardaiz*	Defendant	25-AUG-1997
@432747	Alton, Ardaiz	4414915MO *State v. Aran Ardaiz*	Defendant	07-MAR-1997
@432747	Alton, Ardaiz	4414914MO *State v. Aran Ardaiz*	Defendant	07-MAR-1997
@432747	Alton, Ardaiz	4414913MO *State v. Aran Ardaiz*	Defendant	07-MAR-1997
@432747	Alton, Ardaiz	4204579MO *State v. Aran Ardaiz*	Defendant	10-FEB-1997
@432747	Alton, Ardaiz	4204578MO *State v. Aran Ardaiz*	Defendant	10-FEB-1997
@432747	Alton, Ardaiz	098373038 *State v. Aran Ardaiz*	Defendant	08-OCT-1998
@432747	Alton, Ardaiz	098373037 *State v. Aran Ardaiz*	Defendant	08-OCT-1998
@432747	Alton, Ardaiz	097297760 *State v. Aran Ardaiz*	Defendant	01-AUG-1997
@432747	Alton, Ardaiz	5083038MO *State v. Aran Ardaiz*	Defendant	05-DEC-2001
@432747	Alton, Ardaiz	5083037MO *State v. Aran Ardaiz*	Defendant	05-DEC-2001
@432747	Alton, Ardaiz	5083036MO *State v. Aran Ardaiz*	Defendant	05-DEC-2001
@432747	Alton, Ardaiz	5083035MO *State v. Aran Ardaiz*	Defendant	05-DEC-2001

Page: 4   Records: 61 - 80

<-Previous   Next->

Search Home   Search Help

https://jimspss1.courts.state.hi.us/court/ck_public_qry_cpty.cp_personcase_details_idx?backto=P&so... 11/10/2005

Hawaii – The Fake State

Person/Case Type Search Results

▶ New Search

Phonetic Search: off   **Person ID:** @432747

ID	Name/Corporation	Case	Party Type	Filing Date
@432747	Alton, Ardaiz	5083034MO State v. Aran Ardaiz	Defendant	05-DEC-2001
@432747	Alton, Ardaiz	4897962MO State v. Aran Ardaiz	Defendant	07-APR-2000
@432747	Alton, Ardaiz	4897961MO State v. Aran Ardaiz	Defendant	07-APR-2000
@432747	Alton, Ardaiz	4897371MO State v. Aran Ardaiz	Defendant	10-APR-2000
@432747	Alton, Ardaiz	4830772MO State v. Aran Ardaiz	Defendant	20-DEC-1999
@432747	Alton, Ardaiz	5528293MO State v. Aran Ardaiz	Defendant	02-JUN-2003
@432747	Alton, Ardaiz	5528292MO State v. Aran Ardaiz	Defendant	02-JUN-2003
@432747	Alton, Ardaiz	5528291MO State v. Aran Ardaiz	Defendant	02-JUN-2003
@432747	Alton, Ardaiz	5528290MO State v. Aran Ardaiz	Defendant	02-JUN-2003
@432747	Alton, Ardaiz	5528289MO State v. Aran Ardaiz	Defendant	02-JUN-2003
@432747	Alton, Ardaiz	5287685MO State v. Aran Ardaiz	Defendant	06-DEC-2001
@432747	Alton, Ardaiz	5287684MO State v. Aran Ardaiz	Defendant	06-DEC-2001
@432747	Alton, Ardaiz	5282616MO State v. Aran Ardaiz	Defendant	26-NOV-2001
@432747	Alton, Ardaiz	5282615MO State v. Aran Ardaiz	Defendant	26-NOV-2001
@432747	Alton, Ardaiz	5191640MO State v. Aran Ardaiz	Defendant	15-AUG-2001
@432747	Alton, Ardaiz	5191639MO State v. Aran Ardaiz	Defendant	15-AUG-2001
@432747	Alton, Ardaiz	5191638MO State v. Aran Ardaiz	Defendant	15-AUG-2001
@432747	Alton, Ardaiz	5133819MO State v. Aran Ardaiz	Defendant	29-MAY-2001
@432747	Alton, Ardaiz	5133818MO State v. Aran Ardaiz	Defendant	29-MAY-2001
@432747	Alton, Ardaiz	5133817MO State v. Aran Ardaiz	Defendant	29-MAY-2001

Page: 5   **Records:** 81 - 100

<-Previous   Next--

https://jimspss1.courts.state.hi.us/court/ck_public_qry_cpty.cp_personcase_details_idx?backto P&so... 11-10-2005

▶ New Search

Phonetic Search: off   **Person ID:** @432747

ID	Name/Corporation	Case	Party Type	Filing Date
@432747	Alton, Ardaiz	5083039MO State v. Aran Ardaiz	Defendant	05-DEC-2001
@432747	Alton, Ardaiz	4830771MO State v. Aran Ardaiz	Defendant	20-DEC-1999
@432747	Alton, Ardaiz	4693644MO State v. Aran Ardaiz	Defendant	09-OCT-1998
@432747	Alton, Ardaiz	4693643MO State v. Aran Ardaiz	Defendant	09-OCT-1998
@432747	Alton, Ardaiz	4693642MO State v. Aran Ardaiz	Defendant	09-OCT-1998
@432747	Alton, Ardaiz	4677714MO State v. Aran Ardaiz	Defendant	09-OCT-1998
@432747	Alton, Ardaiz	4677713MO State v. Aran Ardaiz	Defendant	09-OCT-1998
@432747	Alton, Ardaiz	4489498MO State v. Aran Ardaiz	Defendant	04-AUG-1997
@432747	Alton, Ardaiz	4489497MO State v. Aran Ardaiz	Defendant	04-AUG-1997
@432747	Alton, Ardaiz	4897370MO State v. Aran Ardaiz	Defendant	10-APR-2000
@432747	Alton, Ardaiz	4879497MO State v. Aran Ardaiz	Defendant	22-FEB-2000
@432747	Alton, Ardaiz	4879496MO State v. Aran Ardaiz	Defendant	22-FEB-2000
@432747	Alton, Ardaiz	4879495MO State v. Aran Ardaiz	Defendant	22-FEB-2000
@432747	Alton, Ardaiz	4879494MO State v. Aran Ardaiz	Defendant	22-FEB-2000
@432747	Alton, Ardaiz	4489496MO State v. Aran Ardaiz	Defendant	04-AUG-1997
@432747	Alton, Ardaiz	4484004MO State v. Aran Ardaiz	Defendant	05-AUG-1997
@432747	Alton, Ardaiz	4476120MO State v. Aran Ardaiz	Defendant	07-JUL-1997
@432747	Alton, Ardaiz	4476119MO State v. Aran Ardaiz	Defendant	07-JUL-1997
@432747	Alton, Ardaiz	4476118MO State v. Aran Ardaiz	Defendant	07-JUL-1997
@432747	Alton, Ardaiz	4476117MO State v. Aran Ardaiz	Defendant	07-JUL-1997

Page: 6   **Records:** 101 - 120

‹-Previous   Next-›

https://jimspss1.courts.state.hi.us/court/ck_public_qry_cpty.cp_personcase_srch_details?backto=P&s... 11/10/2005

▶ New Search

Phonetic Search: off   Person ID: @432747

ID	Name/Corporation	Case	Party Type	Filing Date
@432747	Alton, Ardaiz	4476116MO State v. Aran Ardaiz	Defendant	07-JUL-1997
@432747	Alton, Ardaiz	4476115MO State v. Aran Ardaiz	Defendant	07-JUL-1997
@432747	Alton, Ardaiz	003210111 State v. Aran Ardaiz	Defendant	30-MAY-2003
@432747	Alton, Ardaiz	002169306 State v. Aran Ardaiz	Defendant	06-MAY-2002
@432747	Alton, Ardaiz	002169305 State v. Aran Ardaiz	Defendant	06-MAY-2002
@432747	Alton, Ardaiz	002169304 State v. Aran Ardaiz	Defendant	06-MAY-2002
@432747	Alton, Ardaiz	002169302 State v. Aran Ardaiz	Defendant	06-MAY-2002
@432747	Alton, Ardaiz	002169300 State v. Aran Ardaiz	Defendant	06-MAY-2002
@432747	Ardaiz, Aran Alton	000062658 State v. Aran Ardaiz	Defendant	17-FEB-2000
@432747	Ardaiz, Aran Alton	003210111 State v. Aran Ardaiz	Defendant	30-MAY-2003
@432747	Ardaiz, Aran Alton	5528293MO State v. Aran Ardaiz	Defendant	02-JUN-2003
@432747	Ardaiz, Aran Alton	5528292MO State v. Aran Ardaiz	Defendant	02-JUN-2003
@432747	Ardaiz, Aran Alton	5528291MO State v. Aran Ardaiz	Defendant	02-JUN-2003
@432747	Ardaiz, Aran Alton	5528290MO State v. Aran Ardaiz	Defendant	02-JUN-2003
@432747	Ardaiz, Aran Alton	5528289MO State v. Aran Ardaiz	Defendant	02-JUN-2003
@432747	Ardaiz, Aran Alton	5287685MO State v. Aran Ardaiz	Defendant	06-DEC-2001
@432747	Ardaiz, Aran Alton	5287684MO State v. Aran Ardaiz	Defendant	06-DEC-2001
@432747	Ardaiz, Aran Alton	5282616MO State v. Aran Ardaiz	Defendant	26-NOV-2001
@432747	Ardaiz, Aran Alton	5083038MO State v. Aran Ardaiz	Defendant	05-DEC-2001
@432747	Ardaiz, Aran Alton	5083037MO State v. Aran Ardaiz	Defendant	05-DEC-2001

Page: 7   **Records:** 121 - 140

<-Previous   Next-

https://jimspss1.courts.state.hi.us/court/ck_public_qry_cpty.cp_personcase_srch_details?backto=P&s...   11 10 2005

Big

▶ New Search

Phonetic Search: off   Person ID: @432747

ID	Name/Corporation	Case	Party Type	Filing Date
@432747	Ardaiz, Aran Alton	5083036MO State v. Aran Ardaiz	Defendant	05-DEC-2001
@432747	Ardaiz, Aran Alton	5083035MO State v. Aran Ardaiz	Defendant	05-DEC-2001
@432747	Ardaiz, Aran Alton	5083034MO State v. Aran Ardaiz	Defendant	05-DEC-2001
@432747	Ardaiz, Aran Alton	4897962MO State v. Aran Ardaiz	Defendant	07-APR-2000
@432747	Ardaiz, Aran Alton	4897961MO State v. Aran Ardaiz	Defendant	07-APR-2000
@432747	Ardaiz, Aran Alton	4897371MO State v. Aran Ardaiz	Defendant	10-APR-2000
@432747	Ardaiz, Aran Alton	4830771MO State v. Aran Ardaiz	Defendant	20-DEC-1999
@432747	Ardaiz, Aran Alton	5282615MO State v. Aran Ardaiz	Defendant	26-NOV-2001
@432747	Ardaiz, Aran Alton	5191640MO State v. Aran Ardaiz	Defendant	15-AUG-2001
@432747	Ardaiz, Aran Alton	5191639MO State v. Aran Ardaiz	Defendant	15-AUG-2001
@432747	Ardaiz, Aran Alton	5191638MO State v. Aran Ardaiz	Defendant	15-AUG-2001
@432747	Ardaiz, Aran Alton	5133819MO State v. Aran Ardaiz	Defendant	29-MAY-2001
@432747	Ardaiz, Aran Alton	5133818MO State v. Aran Ardaiz	Defendant	29-MAY-2001
@432747	Ardaiz, Aran Alton	5133817MO State v. Aran Ardaiz	Defendant	29-MAY-2001
@432747	Ardaiz, Aran Alton	5083039MO State v. Aran Ardaiz	Defendant	05-DEC-2001
@432747	Ardaiz, Aran Alton	4693644MO State v. Aran Ardaiz	Defendant	09-OCT-1998
@432747	Ardaiz, Aran Alton	4693643MO State v. Aran Ardaiz	Defendant	09-OCT-1998
@432747	Ardaiz, Aran Alton	4693642MO State v. Aran Ardaiz	Defendant	09-OCT-1998
@432747	Ardaiz, Aran Alton	4677714MO State v. Aran Ardaiz	Defendant	09-OCT-1998
@432747	Ardaiz, Aran Alton	4677713MO State v. Aran Ardaiz	Defendant	09-OCT-1998

Page: 8 Records: 141 - 160

Previous   Next

https://jimspss1.courts.state.hi.us/court/ck_public_qry_cpty.cp_personcase_srch_details?backto=P&s... 11/10/2005

Big

▶ New Search

Phonetic Search: off   Person ID: @432747

ID	Name/Corporation	Case	Party Type	Filing Date
@432747	Ardaiz, Aran Alton	4489498MO *State v. Aran Ardaiz*	Defendant	04-AUG-1997
@432747	Ardaiz, Aran Alton	4489497MO *State v. Aran Ardaiz*	Defendant	04-AUG-1997
@432747	Ardaiz, Aran Alton	4447912MO *State v. Aran Ardaiz*	Defendant	25-AUG-1997
@432747	Ardaiz, Aran Alton	4897370MO *State v. Aran Ardaiz*	Defendant	10-APR-2000
@432747	Ardaiz, Aran Alton	4879497MO *State v. Aran Ardaiz*	Defendant	22-FEB-2000
@432747	Ardaiz, Aran Alton	4879496MO *State v. Aran Ardaiz*	Defendant	22-FEB-2000
@432747	Ardaiz, Aran Alton	4879495MO *State v. Aran Ardaiz*	Defendant	22-FEB-2000
@432747	Ardaiz, Aran Alton	4879494MO *State v. Aran Ardaiz*	Defendant	22-FEB-2000
@432747	Ardaiz, Aran Alton	4830772MO *State v. Aran Ardaiz*	Defendant	20-DEC-1999
@432747	Ardaiz, Aran Alton	4414915MO *State v. Aran Ardaiz*	Defendant	07-MAR-1997
@432747	Ardaiz, Aran Alton	4414914MO *State v. Aran Ardaiz*	Defendant	07-MAR-1997
@432747	Ardaiz, Aran Alton	4414913MO *State v. Aran Ardaiz*	Defendant	07-MAR-1997
@432747	Ardaiz, Aran Alton	4204579MO *State v. Aran Ardaiz*	Defendant	10-FEB-1997
@432747	Ardaiz, Aran Alton	4204578MO *State v. Aran Ardaiz*	Defendant	10-FEB-1997
@432747	Ardaiz, Aran Alton	098373038 *State v. Aran Ardaiz*	Defendant	08-OCT-1998
@432747	Ardaiz, Aran Alton	098373037 *State v. Aran Ardaiz*	Defendant	08-OCT-1998
@432747	Ardaiz, Aran Alton	097297760 *State v. Aran Ardaiz*	Defendant	01-AUG-1997
@432747	Ardaiz, Aran Alton	4489496MO *State v. Aran Ardaiz*	Defendant	04-AUG-1997
@432747	Ardaiz, Aran Alton	4484004MO *State v. Aran Ardaiz*	Defendant	05-AUG-1997
@432747	Ardaiz, Aran Alton	4476120MO *State v. Aran Ardaiz*	Defendant	07-JUL-1997

Page: 9   Records: 161 - 180

‹-Previous   Next-›

https://jimspss1.courts.state.hi.us/court/ck_public_qry_cpty.cp_personcase_srch_details?backto=P&s...   11/10/2005

Big

▶ New Search

Phonetic Search: off   Person ID: @432747

ID	Name/Corporation	Case		Party Type	Filing Date
@432747	Ardaiz, Aran Alton	4476119MO	State v. Aran Ardaiz	Defendant	07-JUL-1997
@432747	Ardaiz, Aran Alton	4476118MO	State v. Aran Ardaiz	Defendant	07-JUL-1997
@432747	Ardaiz, Aran Alton	4476117MO	State v. Aran Ardaiz	Defendant	07-JUL-1997
@432747	Ardaiz, Aran Alton	4476116MO	State v. Aran Ardaiz	Defendant	07-JUL-1997
@432747	Ardaiz, Aran Alton	4476115MO	State v. Aran Ardaiz	Defendant	07-JUL-1997
@432747	Ardaiz, Aran Alton	002169306	State v. Aran Ardaiz	Defendant	06-MAY-2002
@432747	Ardaiz, Aran Alton	002169305	State v. Aran Ardaiz	Defendant	06-MAY-2002
@432747	Ardaiz, Aran Alton	002169304	State v. Aran Ardaiz	Defendant	06-MAY-2002
@432747	Ardaiz, Aran Alton	002169302	State v. Aran Ardaiz	Defendant	06-MAY-2002
@432747	Ardaiz, Aran Alton	002169303	State v. Aran Ardaiz	Defendant	06-MAY-2002
@432747	Ardaiz, Aran Alton	002169301	State v. Aran Ardaiz	Defendant	06-MAY-2002
@432747	Ardaiz, Aran Alton	002169300	State v. Aran Ardaiz	Defendant	06-MAY-2002

Page: 10   Records: 181 - 192

◄ Previous

https://jimspss1.courts.state.hi.us/court/ck_public_qry_cpty.cp_personcase_srch_details?backto=P&s...   11/10/2005

- Not an Official Document

Report Selection Criteria

Case ID: 5528289MO
Docket Start Date:
Docket Ending Date:

Case Description

Case ID: 5528289MO - State v. Aran Ardaiz - -NON JURY-
Filing Date: Monday , June 02nd, 2003
Type: TC - Traffic Crime
Status: INACTIVE - Inactive Case

Violation

| | Violation | | | Disposition | | | Sentence | |
No.	Code	Description	Date	Code	Description	Date	Code	Description
1	HRS 286-102	NO MOTOR VEH DRIVER'S LICENSE	30-MAY-2003					

Related Cases

No related cases were found

Case Event Schedule

Event	Date/Time	Room	Location	Judge
Arraignment and Plea	15-JUL-2003 08:30 AM	HONOLULU DIVISION	Honolulu Courtroom 4B	*unassigned*

Case Parties

Seq #	Assoc	Expn Date	Type	ID	Name
1			Defendant	@432747	Ardaiz, Aran Alton
			Aliases:	Alton, Aran Alton, Ardaiz	
2			Law Enforcement Officer	101100344	Yi, Rick Sung Yong
			Aliases:	none	

https://jimspss1.courts.state.hi.us/court/ck_public_qry_doct.cp_dktrpt_docket_report?backto=P&case... 11 10 2005

326

Docket Entries

Filing Date	Description	Name	Monetary
15-JUL-2003 08:00 AM	Penal Summons Ordered		
Entry:	PSO 071503 KOYANAGI O11		
15-JUL-2003 08:30 AM	TRAVIS Minutes Code		
Entry:	AP: 07/15/03. DEFENDANT NOT PRESENT. PS ISSUED. JUDGE: KOYANAGI CASE NO: 4B0013A 4B0013A		
05-AUG-2003 08:00 AM	TRAVIS Generic Code		
Entry:	PST 080503 CERT MAIL CRT: 093003 O11		
19-AUG-2003 08:00 AM	TRAVIS Generic Code		
Entry:	COM 081903 RUS O11		
10-MAR-2004 08:00 AM	TRAVIS Generic Code		
Entry:	COM 031004 PS/RUS-SHERIFFS O11		

Report Selection Criteria

Case ID: 5528290MO
Docket Start Date:
Docket Ending Date:

Case Description

Case ID: 5528290MO - State v. Aran Ardaiz - -*NON JURY*-
Filing Date: Monday , June 02nd, 2003
Type: TI - Traffic Infraction
Status: INACTIVE - Inactive Case

Violation

No.	Violation			Disposition			Sentence	
	Code	Description	Date	Code	Description	Date	Code	Description
1	HRS 286-25	NO SAFETY CHECK	30-MAY-2003					

Related Cases

No related cases were found.

Case Event Schedule

Event	Date/Time	Room	Location	Judge
Hearing	15-JUL-2003 08:30 AM	HONOLULU DIVISION	Honolulu Courtroom 4B	*unassigned*

Case Parties

Seq #	Assoc	Expn Date	Type	ID	Name
1			Defendant	@432747	**Ardaiz, Aran Alton**
			Aliases:	Alton, Aran Alton, Ardaiz	
2			Law Enforcement Officer	101100344	**Yi, Rick Sung Yong**
			Aliases:	*none*	

https://jimspss1.courts.state.hi.us/court/ck_public_qry_doct.cp_dktrpt_docket_report?backto=P&case... 11/10/2005

Docket Entries

Filing Date	Description	Name	Monetary
15-JUL-2003 08:00 AM	Penal Summons Ordered		
Entry:	PSO 071503 KOYANAGI O11		
15-JUL-2003 08:30 AM	TRAVIS Minutes Code		
Entry:	AP: 07/15/03: DEFENDANT NOT PRESENT. PS ISSUED. JUDGE: KOYANAGI CASE NO: 4B0014A 4B0014A		
05-AUG-2003 08:00 AM	TRAVIS Generic Code		
Entry:	PST 080503 CERT MAIL CRT: 093003 O11		
19-AUG-2003 08:00 AM	TRAVIS Generic Code		
Entry:	COM 081903 RUS O11		
10-MAR-2004 08:00 AM	TRAVIS Generic Code		
Entry:	COM 031004 PS/RUS-SHERIFFS O11		

Report Selection Criteria

Case ID: 5528291MO
Docket Start Date:
Docket Ending Date:

Case Description

Case ID: 5528291MO - State v. Aran Ardaiz - -*NON JURY*-
Filing Date: Monday , June 02nd, 2003
Type: TI - Traffic Infraction
Status: INACTIVE - Inactive Case

Violation

No.	Code	Description	Date	Code	Description	Date	Code	Description
	Violation			**Disposition**			**Sentence**	
1	HRS 249-10	DELINQUENT MOTOR VEHICLE TAX	30-MAY-2003					

Related Cases

No related cases were found.

Case Event Schedule

Event	Date/Time	Room	Location	Judge
Hearing	15-JUL-2003 08:30 AM	HONOLULU DIVISION	Honolulu Courtroom 4B	*unassigned*

Case Parties

Seq #	Assoc	Expn Date	Type	ID	Name
1			Defendant	@432747	**Ardaiz, Aran Alton**
			Aliases:	Alton, Aran Alton, Ardaiz	
2			Law Enforcement Officer	101100344	**Yi, Rick Sung Yong**
			Aliases:	*none*	

https://jimspss1.courts.state.hi.us/court/ck_public_qry_doct.cp_dktrpt_docket_report?backto_P&case... 11 10 2005

Hawaii – The Fake State

Docket Entries

Filing Date	Description	Name	Monetary
15-JUL-2003 08:00 AM	Penal Summons Ordered		
Entry:	PSO 071503 KOYANAGI O11		
15-JUL-2003 08:30 AM	TRAVIS Minutes Code		
Entry:	AP: 07/15/03: DEFENDANT NOT PRESENT. PS ISSUED. JUDGE: KOYANAGI CASE NO: 4B0015A 4B0015A		
05-AUG-2003 08:00 AM	TRAVIS Generic Code		
Entry:	PST 080503 CERT MAIL CRT: 093003 O11		
19-AUG-2003 08:00 AM	TRAVIS Generic Code		
Entry:	COM 081903 RUS O11		
10-MAR-2004 08:00 AM	TRAVIS Generic Code		
Entry:	COM 031004 PS/RUS-SHERIFFS O11		

Report Selection Criteria

Case ID: 5528292MO
Docket Start Date:
Docket Ending Date:

Case Description

Case ID: 5528292MO - State v. Aran Ardaiz - -NON JURY-
Filing Date: Monday , June 02nd, 2003
Type: TC - Traffic Crime
Status: INACTIVE - Inactive Case

Violation

No.	Violation Code	Violation Description	Violation Date	Disposition Code	Disposition Description	Disposition Date	Sentence Code	Sentence Description
1	HRS 431:10C-104	NO MOTOR VEH INSURANCE	30-MAY-2003					

Related Cases

No related cases were found.

Case Event Schedule

Event	Date/Time	Room	Location	Judge
Arraignment and Plea	15-JUL-2003 08:30 AM	HONOLULU DIVISION	Honolulu Courtroom 4B	*unassigned*

Case Parties

Seq #	Assoc	Expn Date	Type	ID	Name
1			Defendant	@432747	**Ardaiz, Aran Alton**
			Aliases:	Alton, Aran Alton, Ardaiz	
2			Law Enforcement Officer	101100344	**Yi, Rick Sung Yong**
			Aliases:	*none*	

https://jimspssl.courts.state.hi.us/court/ck_public_qry_doct.cp_dktrpt_docket_report?backto_P&case   11-10-2005

Hawaii – The Fake State

Docket Entries

Filing Date	Description	Name	Monetary
15-JUL-2003 08:00 AM	Penal Summons Ordered		
Entry:	PSO 071503 KOYANAGI O11		
15-JUL-2003 08:30 AM	TRAVIS Minutes Code		
Entry:	AP: 07/15/03: DEFENDANT NOT PRESENT. PS ISSUED. JUDGE: KOYANAGI CASE NO: 4B0016A 4B0016A		
05-AUG-2003 08:00 AM	TRAVIS Generic Code		
Entry:	PST 080503 CERT MAIL CRT: 093003 O11		
19-AUG-2003 08:00 AM	TRAVIS Generic Code		
Entry:	COM 081903 RUS O11		
10-MAR-2004 08:00 AM	TRAVIS Generic Code		
Entry:	COM 031004 PS/RUS-SHERIFFS O11		

Report Selection Criteria

Case ID: 5528293MO
Docket Start Date:
Docket Ending Date:

Case Description

Case ID: 5528293MO - State v. Aran Ardaiz - -*NON JURY*-
Filing Date: Monday , June 02nd, 2003
Type: TI - Traffic Infraction
Status: INACTIVE - Inactive Case

Violation

No.	Code	Violation Description	Date	Disposition Code	Description	Date	Sentence Code	Description
1	*HRS 249-11	FRAUD USE VEH PLATES,EMBL,DECL	30-MAY-2003					

Related Cases

No related cases were found.

Case Event Schedule

Event	Date/Time	Room	Location	Judge
Hearing	15-JUL-2003 08:30 AM	HONOLULU DIVISION	Honolulu Courtroom 4B	*unassigned*

Case Parties

Seq #	Assoc	Expn Date	Type	ID	Name
1			Defendant	@432747	**Ardaiz, Aran Alton**
			Aliases:	Alton, Aran Alton, Ardaiz	
2			Law Enforcement Officer	101100344	**Yi, Rick Sung Yong**

https://jimspss1.courts.state.hi.us/court/ck_public_qry_doct.cp_dktrpt_docket_report?backto=P&case... 11/10/2005

Aliases: none

Docket Entries

Filing Date	Description	Name	Monetary
15-JUL-2003 08:00 AM	Penal Summons Ordered		
Entry:	PSO 071503 KOYANAGI O11		
15-JUL-2003 08:30 AM	TRAVIS Minutes Code		
Entry:	AP: 07/15/03: DEFENDANT NOT PRESENT. PS ISSUED. JUDGE: KOYANAGI CASE NO: 4B0017A 4B0017A		
05-AUG-2003 08:00 AM	TRAVIS Generic Code		
Entry:	PST 080503 CERT MAIL CRT: 093003 O11		
19-AUG-2003 08:00 AM	TRAVIS Generic Code		
Entry:	COM 081903 RUS O11		
10-MAR-2004 08:00 AM	TRAVIS Generic Code		
Entry:	COM 031004 PS/RUS-SHERIFFS O11		

EXHIBIT S

48 Star vs 50 Star E.O. and Fringe on the Flag

TITLE 4 — FLAG AND SEAL, SEAT OF GOVERNMENT, AND THE STATES

[This title was revised and enacted into positive law by Act July 30, 1947, ch 389, § 1, 61 Stat. 641.]

HISTORY; ANCILLARY LAWS AND DIRECTIVES

Amendments:

1951. Act Oct. 31, 1951, ch 655, § 11, 65 Stat. 713, amended the analysis of this title by adding Chapter 5.

Other provisions:

Positive law. Act July 30, 1947, ch 389, 61 Stat. 641, § 1, provided in part that: "title 4 of the United States Code, entitled 'Flag and seal, Seat of Government, and the States', is codified and enacted into positive law.".

Repeals. Section 2 of Act July 30, 1947, provided that the sections or parts thereof of the Statutes at Large or the Revised Statutes covering provisions codified in this Act are repealed insofar as such provisions appeared in former Title 4, and provided that any rights or liabilities now existing under such repealed sections or parts thereof shall not be affected by such repeal.

TABLE OF DISPOSITIONS

The following table shows where former sections of Title 4, and the laws from which such former sections were derived, have been incorporated in revised Title 4, as revised by Act July 30, 1947, ch 389, § 1:

Title 4 former sections	Revised Statutes Statutes at Large	Title 4 new sections
1	R.S. §§ 1791, 1792	1
2	R.S. § 1792	2
3	Feb. 8, 1917, ch 34, 39 Stat. 900	3
4	R.S. § 1793	41
5	R.S. §§ 203 (first clause), 1794	42
6	R.S. § 1795	71
7	R.S. § 1796	72
8	R.S. § 4798	73
9	R.S. § 1836	101
10	R.S. § 1837	102
11	R.S. § 1838	103
12	June 16, 1936, ch 582, § 10, 49 Stat. 1521	104
	Oct. 9, 1940, ch 787, § 7, 54 Stat. 1060.	

675

13	Oct. 9, 1940, ch 787, § 1, 54 Stat. 1059	105
14	Oct. 9, 1940, ch 787, § 2, 54 Stat. 1060	106
15	Oct. 9, 1940, ch 787, § 3, 54 Stat. 1060	107
16	Oct. 9, 1940, ch 787, § 4, 54 Stat. 1060	108
17	Oct. 9, 1940, ch 787, § 5, 54 Stat. 1060	109
18	Oct. 9, 1940, ch 787, § 6, 54 Stat. 1060	110

Auto-Cite®: Cases and annotations referred to herein can be further researched through the Auto-Cite® computer-assisted research service. Use Auto-Cite to check citations for form, parallel references, prior and later history, and annotation references.

CHAPTER 1.   THE FLAG

Section
1.   Flag; stripes and stars on.
2.   Same; additional stars.
3.   Use of flag for advertising purposes; mutilation of flag.

§ 1.   Flag; stripes and stars on

The flag of the United States shall be thirteen horizontal stripes, alternate red and white; and the union of the flag shall be forty-eight stars, white in a blue field.

(July 30, 1947, ch 389, 61 Stat. 642.)

HISTORY; ANCILLARY LAWS AND DIRECTIVES

Other provisions:

Proportions and sizes of flags until July 4, 1960. Ex. Or. No. 10798 of Jan. 3, 1959, 24 Fed. Reg. 79, which prescribed the proportion and sizes of flags until July 4, 1960, was revoked by § 33 of Ex. Or. No. 10834 of Aug. 21, 1959, 24 Fed. Reg. 6365, which appears as a note to this section.

Proportions and sizes of flags and positioning of stars after July 4, 1960. Ex. Or. No. 10834 of Aug. 21, 1959, 24 Fed. Reg. 6865 provided:

"PART I—DESIGN OF THE FLAG

"Section 1. The flag of the United States shall have thirteen horizontal stripes, alternate red and white, and a union consisting of white stars on a field of blue.

"Sec. 2. The positions of the stars in the union of the flag and in the union jack shall be as indicated on the attachment to this order, which is hereby made a part of this order.

"Sec. 3. The dimensions of the constituent parts of the flag shall conform to the proportions set forth in the attachment referred to in section 2 of this order.

"PART II—REGULATIONS GOVERNING EXECUTIVE AGENCIES

676

"Sec. 21. The following sizes of flags are authorized for executive agencies:

Size	Dimensions of flag	
	Hoist (width)	Fly (length)
	Feet	Feet
(1)	20.00	38.00
(2)	10.00	19.00
(3)	8.95	17.00
(4)	7.00	11.00
(5)	5.00	9.50
(6)	4.33	5.50
(7)	3.50	6.65
(8)	3.00	4.00
(9)	3.00	5.70
(10)	2.37	4.50
(11)	1.32	2.50

"Sec. 22. Flags manufactured or purchased for the use of executive agencies:

"(a) Shall conform to the provisions of Part I of this order, except as may be otherwise authorized pursuant to the provisions of section 24, or except as otherwise authorized by the provisions of section 21, of this order.

"(b) Shall conform to the provisions of section 21 of this order, except as may be otherwise authorized pursuant to the provisions of section 24 of this order.

"Sec. 23. The exterior dimensions of each union jack manufactured or purchased for executive agencies shall equal the respective exterior dimensions of the union of a flag of a size authorized by or pursuant to this order. The size of the union jack flown with the national flag shall be the same as the size of the union of that national flag.

"Sec. 24. (a) The Secretary of Defense in respect of procurement for the Department of Defense (including military colors) and the Administrator of General Services in respect of procurement for executive agencies other than the Department of Defense may, for cause which the Secretary or the Administrator, as the case may be, deems sufficient, make necessary minor adjustments in one or more of the dimensions or proportionate dimensions prescribed by this order, or authorize proportions or sizes other than those prescribed by section 3 or section 21 of this order.

"(b) So far as practicable, (1) the actions of the Secretary of Defense under the provisions of section 24(a) of this order, as they relate to the various organizational elements of the Department of Defense, shall be coordinated, and (2) the Secretary and the Administrator shall mutually coordinate their actions under that section.

"Sec. 25. Subject to such limited exceptions as the Secretary of Defense in respect of the Department of Defense, and the Administrator of General Services in respect of executive agencies other than the Department

677

of Defense, may approve, all national flags and union jacks now in the possession of executive agencies, or hereafter acquired by executive agencies under contracts awarded prior to the date of this order, including those so possessed or so acquired by the General Services Administration, for distribution to other agencies, shall be utilized until unserviceable.

"PART III—GENERAL PROVISIONS

"Sec. 31. The flag prescribed by Executive Order No. 10798 of January 3, 1959, shall be the official flag of the United States until July 4, 1960, and on that date the flag prescribed by Part I of this order shall become the official flag of the United States; but this section shall neither derogate from section 24 or section 25 of this order nor preclude the procurement, for executive agencies, of flags provided for by or pursuant to this order at any time after the date of this order.

"Sec. 32. As used in this order, the term "executive agencies" means the executive departments and independent establishments in the executive branch of the Government, including wholly-owned Government corporations.

"Sec. 33. Executive Order No. 10798 of January 3, 1959, is hereby revoked."

CROSS REFERENCES

Penalty for desecration of the flag, 18 USCS § 700.

Display and use of flag by civilians, 36 USCS § 174.

Manner of display of flag, 36 USCS § 175.

Respect for flag, 36 USCS § 176.

Police uniforms to display U.S. flag emblem or colors, 40 USCS § 210a.

This section is referred to in 36 USCS § 173.

RESEARCH GUIDE

Am Jur:

35 Am Jur 2d, Flag §§ 1, 7.

Annotations:

Supreme Court's views as to constitutionality of laws prohibiting, or of criminal convictions for, desecration, defiance, disrespect, or misuse of American flag. 105 L Ed 2d 809.

INTERPRETIVE NOTES AND DECISIONS

Placing of fringe on national flag, dimensions of flag, and arrangement of stars in union are matters of detail not controlled by statute, but are within discretion of President as Commander-In-Chief of Army and Navy. (1925) 34 Op Atty Gen 483.

§ 2. Same; additional stars

On the admission of a new State into the Union one star shall be added to the union of the flag; and such addition shall take effect on the fourth day of July then next succeeding such admission.

(July 30, 1947, ch 389, 61 Stat. 642.)

678

THE U.S. NATIONAL ARCHIVES & RECORDS ADMINISTRATION

www.archives.gov — Wednesday, February 20, 2008

Executive Order 10834--The flag of the United States

Source: The provisions of Executive Order 10834 of Aug. 21, 1959, appear at 24 FR 6865, 3 CFR, 1959-1963 Comp., p. 367, unless otherwise noted.

WHEREAS the State of Hawaii has this day been admitted into the Union; and

WHEREAS section 2 of title 4 of the United States Code provides as follows: "On the admission of a new State into the Union one star shall be added to the union of the flag; and such addition shall take effect on the fourth day of July then next succeeding such admission."; and

WHEREAS the Federal Property and Administrative Services Act of 1949 (63 Stat. 377), as amended, authorizes the President to prescribe policies and directives governing the procurement and utilization of property by executive agencies; and

WHEREAS the interests of the Government require that orderly and reasonable provision be made for various matters pertaining to the flag and that appropriate regulations governing the procurement and utilization of national flags and union jacks by executive agencies be prescribed:

NOW, THEREFORE, by virtue of the authority vested in me as President of the United States and as Commander in Chief of the armed forces of the United States, and the Federal Property and Administrative Services Act of 1949, as amended, it is hereby ordered as follows:

Part I--Design of the Flag

Section 1. The flag of the United States shall have thirteen horizontal stripes, alternate red and white, and a union consisting of white stars on a field of blue.

Sec. 2. The positions of the stars in the union of the flag and in the union jack shall be as indicated on the attachment to this order, which is hereby made a part of this order.

Sec. 3. The dimensions of the constituent parts of the flag shall conform to the proportions set forth in the attachment referred to in section 2 of this order.

Part II--Regulations Governing Executive Agencies

Sec. 21. The following sizes of flags are authorized for executive agencies:

Size	Dimensions of flag	
	Hoist (width) Feet	Fly (length) Feet
(1)	20.00	38.00
(2)	10.00	19.00
(3)	8.95	17.00
(4)	7.00	11.00
(5)	5.00	9.50
(6)	4.33	5.50

http://www.archives.gov/federal-register/codification/executive-order/10834.html?templat... 2/20/2008

(7)		3.50	6.65
(8)		3.00	4.00
(9)		3.00	5.70
(10)		2.37	4.50
(11)		1.32	2.50

Sec. 22. Flags manufactured or purchased for the use of executive agencies:
(a) Shall conform to the provisions of Part I of this order, except as may be otherwise authorized pursuant to the provisions of section 24, or except as otherwise authorized by the provisions of section 21, of this order.
(b) Shall conform to the provisions of section 21 of this order, except as may be otherwise authorized pursuant to the provisions of section 24 of this order.

Sec. 23. The exterior dimensions of each union jack manufactured or purchased for executive agencies shall equal the respective exterior dimensions of the union of a flag of a size authorized by or pursuant to this order. The size of the union jack flown with the national flag shall be the same as the size of the union of that national flag.

Sec. 24. (a) The Secretary of Defense in respect of procurement for the Department of Defense (including military colors) and the Administrator of General Services in respect of procurement for executive agencies other than the Department of Defense may, for cause which the Secretary or the Administrator, as the case may be, deems sufficient, make necessary minor adjustments in one or more of the dimensions or proportionate dimensions prescribed by this order, or authorize proportions or sizes other than those prescribed by section 3 or section 21 of this order.
(b) So far as practicable, (1) the actions of the Secretary of Defense under the provisions of section 24(a) of this order, as they relate to the various organizational elements of the Department of Defense, shall be coordinated, and (2) the Secretary and the Administrator shall mutually coordinate their actions under that section.

Sec. 25. Subject to such limited exceptions as the Secretary of Defense in respect of the Department of Defense, and the Administrator of General Services in respect of executive agencies other than the Department of Defense, may approve, all national flags and union jacks now in the possession of executive agencies, or hereafter acquired by executive agencies under contracts awarded prior to the date of this order, including those so possessed or so acquired by the General Services Administration for distribution to other agencies, shall be utilized until unserviceable.

Part III--General Provisions

Sec. 31. The flag prescribed by Executive Order No. 10798 of January 3, 1959, shall be the official flag of the United States until July 4, 1960, and on that date the flag prescribed by Part I of this order shall become the official flag of the United States; but this section shall neither derogate from section 24 or section 25 of this order nor preclude the procurement, for executive agencies, or flags provided for by or pursuant to this order at any time after the date of this order.

Sec. 32. As used in this order, the term "executive agencies" means the executive departments and independent establishments in the executive branch of the Government, including wholly-

http://www.archives.gov/federal-register/codification/executive-order/10834.html?templat... 2/20/2008 owned Government corporations.

Sec. 33. Executive Order No. 10798 of January 3, 1959, is hereby revoked.

Editorial note: The attachment detailing the proportions of the constituent parts of the flag, which was attached to and made a part of Executive Order 10834, is printed in 3 CFR, 1959-1963 Comp., p. 368.

Page URL: http://www.archives.gov/federal-register/codification/executive-order/10834.html

The U.S. National Archives and Records Administration
8601 Adelphi Road, College Park, MD 20740-6001 • Telephone: 1-86-NARA-NARA or 1-866-272-6272

EXHIBIT T

Bernice Pauahi Bishop Trust

Will of Bernice Pauahi Bishop

Know all Men by these Presents, That I, Bernice Pauahi Bishop, the wife of Charles R. Bishop, of Honolulu, Island of Oahu, Hawaiian Islands, being of sound mind and memory, but conscious of the uncertainty of life, do make, publish and declare this my last Will and Testament in manner following, hereby revoking all former wills by me made:

First. I give and bequeath unto my namesakes, E. Bernice Bishop Dunham, niece of my husband, now residing in San Joaquim County, California, Bernice Parke, daughter of W. C. Parke Esq., of Honolulu, Bernice Bishop Barnard, daughter of the late John E. Barnard Esq. of Honolulu, Bernice Bates, daughter of Mr. Dudley C. Bates, of San Francisco, California, Annie Pauahi Cleghorn of Honolulu, Lilah Bernice Wodehouse, daughter of Major J. H. Wodehouse, of Honolulu, and Pauahi Judd the daughter of Col. Charles H. Judd of Honolulu, the sum of Two hundred Dollars ($200.) each.

Second. I give and bequeath unto Mrs. William F. Allen, Mrs. Amoe Haalelea, Mrs. Antone Rosa, and Mrs. Nancy Ellis, the sum of Two Hundred Dollars ($200.) each.

Third. I give and bequeath unto Mrs. Caroline Bush, widow of A .W. Bush, Mrs. Sarah Parmenter, wife of Gilbert Parmenter Mrs. Keomailani Taylor, wife of Mr. Wray Taylor, to their sole and separate use free from the control of their husbands, and to Mrs. Emma Barnard, widow of the late John E .Barnard Esq. the sum of Five hundred dollars ($500.) each.

15

Fourth. I give, devise and bequeath unto H. R. H. Liliuokalani, the wife of Gov. John O. Dominis, all of those tracts of land known as the "Ahupuaa of Luumahai," situated on the Island of Kauai, and the "Ahupuaa of Kealia", situated in South Kona Island of Hawaii; to have and to hold for and during the term of her natural life; and after her decease to my trustees upon the trusts below expressed.

Fifth. I give and bequeath unto Kahakuakoi (w) and Keolohapauole, her husband, and to the survivor of them, the sum of Thirty Dollars ($30.) per month, (not $30. each) so long as either of them may live. And I also devise unto them and to their heirs of the body of either, the lot of land called "Mauna Kamala", situated at Kapalama Honolulu; upon default of issue the same to go to my trustees upon the trusts below expressed.

Sixth. I give and bequeath unto Mrs. Kapoli Kamakau, the sum of Forty Dollars ($40.) per month during her life; to my servant woman Kaia the sum of Thirty Dollars ($30.) per month during her life, and to Nakaahiki (w) the sum of Thirty Dollars ($30.) per month during her life.

Seventh. I give, devise and bequeath unto Kapaa (k) the house-lot he now occupies, situated between Merchant and Queen Streets in Honolulu, to have and to hold for and during the term of his natural life; upon his decease to my trustees upon the trusts below expressed.

Eighth. I give, devise and bequeath unto Auhea (w) the wife of Lokana (k) the house-lot situated on the corner of Richard and Queen Streets, now occupied by G. W. Macfarlane & Co; to have and to hold for and during the term of her natural life; upon her decease to my trustees upon the trusts below expressed.

Ninth. I give, devise and bequeath unto my husband, Charles R. Bishop, all of the various tracts and parcels of land situated upon the Island of Molokai, comprising the

16

"Molokai Ranch", and all of the live-stock and personal property thereon; being the same premises now under the care of R. W. Myer Esq.; and also all of the real property wherever situated, inherited by me from my parents, and also all of that devised to me by my aunt Akahi, except the two lands above devised to H. R. H. Liliuokalani for her life; and also all of my lands at Waikiki, Oahu, situated makai of the government main road leading to Kapiolani Park; to have and to hold together with all tenements, hereditaments, rights, privileges and appurtenances to the same appertaining, for and during the term of his natural life; and upon his decease to my trustees upon the trusts below expressed.

Tenth. I give, devise and bequeath unto Her Majesty Emma Kaleleonalani, Queen Dowager, as a token of my good will, all of the premises situated upon Emma Street in said Honolulu, known as "Kaakopua," lately the residence of my cousin Keelikolani; to have and to hold with the appurtenances for and during the term of her natural life; and upon her decease to my trustees upon the trusts below expressed.

Eleventh. I give and bequeath the sum of Five thousand Dollars ($5000.) to be expended by my executors in repairs upon Kawaiahao Church building in Honolulu, or in improvements upon the same.

Twelfth. I give and bequeath the sum of Five thousand Dollars ($5000.) to be expended by my executors for the benefit of the Kawaiahao Family School for Girls (now under charge of Miss Norton) to be expended for additions either to the grounds, buildings or both.

Thirteenth. I give, devise and bequeath all of the rest, residue and remainder of my estate real and personal, wherever situated unto the trustees below named, their heirs and assigns forever, to hold upon the following trusts, namely: to erect and maintain in the Hawaiian Islands two schools, each for boarding and day scholars, one for

17

347

boys and one for girls, to be known as, and called the Kamehameha Schools. I direct my trustees to expend such amount as they may deem best, not to exceed however one-half of the fund which may come into their hands, in the purchase of suitable premises, the erection of school buildings, and in furnishing the same with the necessary and appropriate fixtures furniture and apparatus. I direct my trustees to invest the remainder of my estate in such manner as they may think best, and to expend the annual income in the maintenance of said schools; meaning thereby the salaries of teachers, the repairing buildings and other incidental expenses; and to devote a portion of each years income to the support and education of orphans, and others in indigent circumstances, giving the preference to Hawaiians of pure or part aboriginal blood; the proportion in which said annual income is to be divided among the various objects above mentioned to be determined solely by my said trustees they to have full discretion. I desire my trustees to provide first and chiefly a good education in the common English branches, and also instruction in morals and in such useful knowledge as may tend to make good and industrious men and women; and I desire instruction in the higher branches to be subsidiary to the foregoing objects. For the purposes aforesaid I grant unto my said trustees full power to lease or sell any portion of my real estate, and to reinvest the proceeds and the balance of my estate in real estate, or in such other manner as to my said trustees may seem best. I also give unto my said trustees full power to make all such rules and regulations as they may deem necessary for the government of said schools and to regulate the admission of pupils, and the same to alter, amend and publish upon a vote of a majority of said trustees. I also direct that my said trustees shall annually make a full and complete report of all receipts and expenditures, and of the condition of said schools to the Chief Justice of the Supreme Court, or other highest judicial officer in this country; and shall also file before him annually an inventory of the property in their hands

18

and how invested, and to publish the same in some Newspaper published in said Honolulu; I also direct my said trustees to keep said school buildings insured in good Companies, and in case of loss to expend the amounts recovered in replacing or repairing said buildings. I also direct that the teachers of said schools shall forever be persons of the Protestant religion, but I do not intend that the choice should be restricted to persons of any particular sect of Protestants.

Fourteenth. I appoint my husband Charles R. Bishop, Samuel M. Damon, Charles M. Hyde, Charles M. Cooke, and William O. Smith, all of Honolulu, to be my trustees to carry into effect the trusts above specified. I direct that a majority of my said trustees may act in all cases and may convey real estate and perform all of the duties and powers hereby conferred; but three of them at least must join in all acts. I further direct that the number of my said trustees shall be kept at five; and that vacancies shall be filled by the choice of a majority of the Justices of the Supreme Court, the selection to be made from persons of the Protestant religion.

Fifteenth. In addition to the above devise to Queen Emma, I also give, devise and bequeath to her (said Emma Kaleleonalani Queen Dowager (sic) the Fish-pond in Kawaa, Honolulu near Oahu Prison, called "Kawa", for and during the term of her natural life; and after her decease to my trustees upon the trusts aforesaid.

Sixteenth. In addition to the above devise to my husband, I also give and bequeath to him, said Charles R. Bishop all of my personal property of every description, including cattle at Molokai; to have and to hold to him, his executors, administrators and assigns forever.

Seventeenth. I hereby nominate and appoint my husband Charles R. Bishop and Samuel M. Damon, executors of this my will.

19

In witness whereof I, said Bernice Pauahi Bishop, have hereunto set my hand and seal this thirty-first day of October A. D. Eighteen hundred and eighty-three.

BERNICE P. BISHOP (SEAL)

The foregoing instrument, written on eleven pages, was signed, sealed, published and declared by said Bernice Pauahi Bishop, as and for her last will and testament in our presence, who at her request, in her presence, and in the presence of each other, have hereunto set our names as witnesses thereto, this 31st day of October A. D. 1883.

F. W. MACFARLANE
FRANCIS M. HATCH

20

CODICIL NO. 1.

This is a Codicil to the last Will and Testament of me, Bernice P. Bishop, dated October thirty-first A. D. Eighteen hundred and eighty-three:

1st I give and bequeath unto Mrs William F. Allen the sum of One thousand Dollars ($1000.) in place of the amount given to her in my said will.

2nd I revoke the devise to Her Majesty Emma Kaleleonalani of the premises situated upon Emma Street in Honolulu, known as "Kaakopua", contained in the tenth article of my said will; and in place thereof I give, devise and bequeath unto her, said Emma Kaleleonalani, all of those parcels of land situated in Nuuanu Valley, Oahu, on both sides of the road, known as "Laimi"; to hold for and during the term of her natural life; and upon her decease to my trustees upon the trusts expressed in my said will. Said Emma to also have the fish pond known as "Kawa", as provided in the fifteenth article of my said will.

3rd In addition to the bequests to my husband named in my said will I also give, devise and bequeath unto my said husband, Charles R. Bishop, the land known as Waialae-nui, as well as Waialae-iki and also the land known as "Maunalua", Island of Oahu; and also all of the premises situated in said Honolulu, known as the Ili of "Kaakopua", extending from Emma to Fort Street and also all kuleanas in the same, and everything appurtenant to said premises; to hold for his life, remainder to my trustees.

4th I give, devise and bequeath unto Kuaiwa (k) and Kaakaole (w), old retainers of my parents, that piece of land now occupied by them, situated in upper Kapalama,

21

ORDER OF PROBATE OF WILL

SUPREME COURT OF THE HAWAIIAN ISLANDS.

In the Matter of the Estate
of
Bernice Pauahi Bishop, Deceased.
} In Probate. No. 2425.

The Petition of Charles R. Bishop and Samuel M. Damon praying for the admission to Probate of a document alleged to be the Last Will and Testament of said deceased and also two Codicils to the same and that Letters Testamentary thereon be granted to them coming on this day to be heard; due proof was made that notice had been given that said petition had been filed in this Court, and that a hearing of all concerned therein would be had in the Court-room of the Supreme Court, in the City of Honolulu, on the second day of December A. D. 1884, at ten o'clock in the forenoon, and that said notice has been published in the "Hawaiian Gazette" & "Kuokoa" Newspapers, for three consecutive weeks, the last publication being not less than seven days previous to the day therein appointed for said hearing.

And, it appearing by the testimony of F. W. Macfarlane, F. M. Hatch W. W. Hall, G. Trousseau & J. Brodie subscribing witnesses of said documents . . . . that said documents are the last Will and Testament and Codicils of the said deceased, executed in all particulars as required by law, and that the Testator was of sound mind at the time of its execution; that the said Bernice Pauahi Bishop died on or about the sixteenth day of October A. D. 1884, at Honolulu, Oahu being at the time of death a native born citizen of this Kingdom and a resident of said Honolulu, leaving real and personal estate in the Hawaiian Islands and no objections being made thereto, and said Charles R. Bishop & Samuel M. Damon appearing to be competent to perform this trust:

28

IT IS ORDERED: that the said documents be admitted to Probate as, and for the last Will and Testament and Codicils of said Bernice Pauahi Bishop deceased, and that Letters Testamentary be issued to the said Charles R. Bishop and Samuel M. Damon as Executors.

Dated at Honolulu, Island of Oahu, December 2d, A. D. 1884.

L. McCULLY

Justice of the Supreme Court.

29

EXHIBIT U

IRS Tax Audit Service

State of Delaware

SECRETARY OF STATE
DIVISION OF CORPORATIONS
P.O. BOX 898
DOVER, DELAWARE 19903

PAGE   1

960071123

9229727
ARAN A. ARDAIZ
P. O. BOX 62199
HONOLULU   HI   96839

03-14-96

DESCRIPTION	AMOUNT
INTERNAL REVENUE TAX AND AUDIT SERVICE, INC.	
0325720 4100 Plain Copy	
Plain Copy Fee	7.00
FILING TOTAL	7.00
TOTAL PAYMENTS	10.00
CHARGED TO ACCOUNT	3.00CR

The Corp Tr. Co
of Del. $20,000 = 200 shs $100 = 10

Certificate of Incorporation

Name

First.—The name of this Corporation shall be ....

.... INTERNAL REVENUE TAX AND AUDIT SERVICE, INC. ....

Registered Office.

Second.—Its principal office or place of business in the State of Delaware shall be located at 15-17 Dover Green in the City of Dover, County of Kent, and its resident agent shall be The Capital Trust Company of Delaware.

Objects and Powers.

Third.—The nature of the business and the objects and purposes proposed to be transacted, promoted and carried on, are to do any or all of the things herein set forth, as fully and to the same extent as natural persons might or could do, and in any part of the world, viz:

To own, hold, sell and dispose of the right to the use, and in the sale of a Copyright Book, printed therein, new and improved Forms, for use of business and professional men, and for the purpose of compiling accounting records and figures, and other purposes, from which INCOME TAX RETURNS of any manner, kind, class and description may be prepared in conformity with the Internal Revenue Laws of the United States, and in conformity with any and all Taxing Laws enacted by any of the States, Counties, Municipalities, Cities, Towns, or other taxing divisions or subdivisions. Generally to conduct an Income Tax Accounting and Auditing business, and to act as Income Tax Accountants and Auditors for persons, firms, corporations, syndicates and others, and to make charges for the sale of said Income Tax Accounting Book of Forms, and for such other services as may be rendered.

To examine, audit and certify to the correctness of Corporation reports, Corporation books and accounts of persons, firms, partnerships, associations, public, quasi-public and private Corporations including any State or Government, estates and public and private institutions of all kinds, to install and maintain systems of Corporations analysis, and for other purposes, and for the keeping of records and accounts of all kinds, and to install and operate cost systems, and to make investigations as to the business affairs and property of any of the foregoing, and to render reports in connection therewith, and to make Corporation analysis, appraisals and valuations of all kinds, and to maintain, prepare and certify to the correctness of reports, balance sheets and statements, including Tax Reports and Tax Returns, for any and all purposes, State, Government or otherwise.

To manufacture, purchase or acquire in any lawful manner and to hold, own, mortgage, pledge, sell, transfer, or in any manner dispose of, and to deal and trade in goods, wares, merchandise, and property of any and every class and description, and in any part of the world.

To acquire the good will, rights and property, and to undertake the whole or any part of the assets or liabilities of any person, firm, association or corporation; to pay for the same in cash, the stock of this company, bonds or otherwise; to hold or in any manner to dispose of the whole or any part of the property so purchased; to conduct in any lawful manner the whole or any part of any business so acquired, and to exercise all the powers necessary or convenient in and about the conduct and management of such business.

To apply for, purchase, or in any manner to acquire, and to hold, own, use and operate, and to sell or in any manner dispose of, and to grant license or other rights in respect of, and in any manner deal with, any and all rights, inventions, improvements and processes used in connection with or secured under letters patent or copyrights of the United States or other countries, or otherwise, and to work, operate or develop the same, and to carry on any business, manufacturing or otherwise, which may directly or indirectly effectuate these objects or any of them.

353

To guarantee, purchase, hold, sell, assign, transfer, mortgage, pledge, or otherwise dispose of the shares of the capital stock of, or any bonds, securities or evidences of indebtedness created by any other corporation or corporations of this State or any other State, country, nation or government, and while owner of said stock may exercise all the rights, powers and privileges of ownership, including the right to vote thereon, to the same extent as natural persons might or could do.

To enter into, make and perform contracts of every kind with any person, firm, association or corporation, municipality, body politic, country, territory, State, government or colony or dependency thereof, and without limit as to amount to draw, make, accept, endorse, discount, execute and issue promissory notes, drafts, bills of exchange, warrants, bonds, debentures, and other negotiable or transferable instruments and evidences of indebtedness whether secured by mortgage or otherwise, as well as to secure the same by mortgage or otherwise.

To conduct business in any of the States, territories, colonies or dependencies of the United States, in the District of Columbia, and in any and all foreign countries, to have one or more offices therein, and therein to hold, purchase, mortgage and convey real and personal property, without limit as to the amount.

To do any or all of the things herein set forth to the same extent as natural persons might or could do and in any part of the world, as principals, agents, contractors, trustees, or otherwise, and either alone or in company with others.

To purchase, hold and reissue any of the shares of its capital stock.

In General to carry on any other business in connection therewith, whether manufacturing or otherwise, not forbidden by the laws of the State of Delaware, and with all the powers conferred upon corporations by the laws of the State of Delaware.

Strike out 1, 2, 3 or 4 if not desired

Fourth.—The total authorized capital stock of this corporation consists of ....

.... shares of Common stock without nominal or par value AND

... Two Hundred (200) .... shares of Common stock with the par value

of. One Hundred ...... Dollars ($100.00) each AND ....

.... shares of Preferred stock with the par value of ....

Dollars ($ ....) each AND .... shares of Preferred

stock without nominal or par value.

If preferred stock is desired, fill in these blanks. If only common is wanted, leave blank.

The preferred stock may be issued as and when the Board of Directors shall determine, and shall entitle the holder thereof to receive out of the net earnings, and the Corporation shall be bound to pay .... dividends at the rate of .... per centum per annum, payable before any dividend shall be set apart or paid on the common stock, provided however, that when and as dividends their preferred stock the directors shall have power in their discretion to declare and pay a dividend for the period on the common stock.

The holders of preferred stock shall, in case of liquidation or dissolution of the Corporation before any amount shall be paid to the holders of the general or common stock, be entitled to be paid the amount paid up on their shares and the dividends accrued and unpaid thereon, but shall not participate in any surplus assets after paying off the whole of the paid up capital.

The preferred stock, at the discretion of the Company, shall be subject to redemption at .... on .... 19.... or any dividend day thereafter.

Strike out if not desired.

The sole voting power shall be vested in the holders of the common stock and the preferred stock shall have no voting power, nor shall the holders thereafter at any meeting of the stockholders, and the holders of the common stock shall have the exclusive right to vote for the election of directors and for all other purposes, and the preferred stock shall have no voting power nor right to participate in the management or control of the business.

Not less than $1000.

This corporation will commence business with a capital of at least. One .... Thousand Dollars.

Incorporators.

Fifth.—The names and places of residence of the incorporators are as follows:

Name	Residence
.... E. CLIFTON BARTON	.... NEW YORK, N.Y. ....
.... HELEN E'DELE BARTON	.... NEW YORK, N.Y. ....
.... LAWRENCE ECHEVARRIA	.... NEW YORK, N.Y. ....

Liability of Stockholders.

Seventh.—The private property of the stockholders shall not be subject to the payment of corporate debts to any extent whatever.

Powers of Directors.

Eighth.—The Directors shall have power to make and to alter or amend the By-laws; to fix the amount to be reserved as working capital, and to authorize and cause to be executed, mortgages and liens without limit as to amount, upon the property and franchises of this Corporation.

Inspection of Corporate Books.

The By-laws shall determine whether and to what extent the accounts and books of this corporation, or any of them, shall be open to the inspection of the stockholders; and no stockholder shall have any right of inspecting any account, or book, or document of this Corporation, except as conferred by law or the By-laws, or by resolution of the stockholders or directors.

Meetings.

The stockholders and directors shall have power to hold their meetings and keep the books, documents and papers of the corporation outside of the State of Delaware, at such places as may be from time to time designated by the By-laws or by resolution of the stockholders or directors.

Executive Committee.

The directors shall have power by a resolution passed by a majority vote of the whole Board, under suitable provision of the By-laws, to designate two or more of their number to constitute an Executive Committee, which Committee shall for the time being, as provided in said resolution or in the By-laws, have and exercise any or all the powers of the Board of Directors which may be lawfully delegated in the management of the business and affairs of the Company, and shall have power to authorize the seal of the said Company to be affixed to all papers which may require it.

There shall be no preemptive right in the stockholders of subscribing to any additional issues of any class of stock of this corporation now or hereafter authorized unless hereafter conferred by resolution of the directors.

Amendments.

This Corporation reserves the right to amend, alter, change or repeal any provision contained in this Certificate of Incorporation, in the manner now or hereafter prescribed by the statutes of the State of Delaware, and all rights conferred on officers, directors and stockholders herein are granted subject to this reservation.

It is the intention that each of the objects, purposes and powers specified in all the paragraphs of the Third Section hereof shall be regarded as independent objects, purposes and powers.

We, the Undersigned, for the purpose of forming a Corporation under the laws of the State of Delaware, do make, file and record this Certificate, and do certify that the facts herein stated are true; and we have accordingly hereunto set our respective hands and seals.

Dated at ....NEW YORK CITY, N.Y.....

July 11th 19 33

In presence of ....

State of .....New York.....

County of .....New York..... } ss:

Be It Remembered, That on this................11....th.. day of ....July..... A. D. 1933....personally appeared before me, the subscriber, a Notary Public for the State of ....parties to the foregoing Certificate of Incorporation, known to me personally to be such, and severally acknowledged the said Certificate of Incorporation to be their act and deed, and that the facts therein stated are truly set forth.

Given Under my hand and seal of office the day and year aforesaid.

.... Notary Public.

Must be acknowledged before a Notary Public with seal.

Seventh.—The private property of the stockholders shall not be subject to the payment of corporate debts to any extent whatever.

Eighth.—The Directors shall have power to make and to alter or amend the By-laws; to fix the amount to be reserved as working capital, and to authorize and cause to be executed, mortgages and liens without limit as to amount, upon the property and franchises of this Corporation.

The By-laws shall determine whether and to what extent the accounts and books of this corporation, or any of them, shall be open to the inspection of the stockholders; and no stockholder shall have any right of inspecting any account, or book, or document of this Corporation, except as conferred by law or the By-laws, or by resolution of the stockholders or directors.

The stockholders and directors shall have power to hold their meetings and keep the books, documents and papers of the corporation outside of the State of Delaware, at such places as may be from time to time designated by the By-laws or by resolution of the stockholders or directors.

The directors shall have power by a resolution passed by a majority vote of the whole Board, under suitable provision of the By-laws, to designate two or more of their number to constitute an Executive Committee, which Committee shall for the time being, as provided in said resolution or in the By-laws, have and exercise any or all the powers of the Board of Directors which may be lawfully delegated in the management of the business and affairs of the Company, and shall have power to authorize the seal of the said Company to be affixed to all papers which may require it.

There shall be no preemptive right in the stockholders of subscribing to any additional issues of any class of stock of this corporation now or hereafter authorized unless hereafter conferred by resolution of the directors.

This Corporation reserves the right to amend, alter, change or repeal any provision contained in this Certificate of Incorporation, in the manner now or hereafter prescribed by the statutes of the State of Delaware, and all rights conferred on officers, directors and stockholders herein are granted subject to this reservation.

It is the intention that each of the objects, purposes and powers specified in all the paragraphs of the Third Section hereof shall be regarded as independent objects, purposes and powers.

We, the Undersigned, for the purpose of forming a Corporation under the laws of the State of Delaware, do make, file and record this Certificate, and do certify that the facts herein stated are true; and we have accordingly hereunto set our respective hands and seals.

Dated at ... NEW YORK CITY, N.Y. ...

July 11th 1933

In presence of ...

State of New York
County of New York } ss:

Be It Remembered, That on this 11th day of July A.D. 1933 personally appeared before me, the subscriber, a Notary Public for the State of New York, ... E. Clifton Barton Helen E'dele Barton and Laurence Echevarria parties to the foregoing Certificate of Incorporation, known to me personally to be such, and severally acknowledged the said Certificate of Incorporation to be their act and deed, and that the facts therein stated are truly set forth.

Given Under my hand and seal of office the day and year aforesaid.

Notary Public.

356

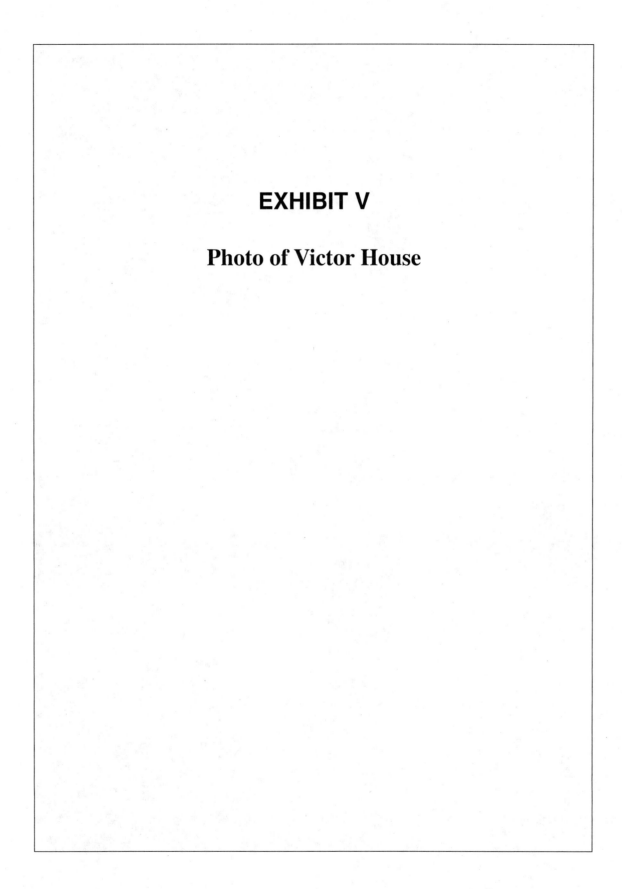

EXHIBIT V

Photo of Victor House

EXHIBIT W

Pua Victor's Certified Mail Letters

Lily Liliaokekomahana Victor
Hawaiian National Citizen
General Delivery: Box 994
Kaneohe, Oahu, Hawaii Nei
(U. S. P. Z. Exempt)

August 28, 2007

via U. S. Postal Service Certified Mail
7003 1680 0002 5391 0999

Bank of Hawaii
Legal and Custody Department
130 Merchant Street, 16th Floor
Honolulu, Hawaii 96813

Attention: Legal Department

Regarding: **ACTUAL NOTICE OF: LAWFULLY <u>UNSUPPORTED</u> "NOTICE OF LEVY" FOR $11,138.51 FROM THE INTERNAL REVENUE SERVICE DATED 08-08-2007 BY Gwen Kai, IRS Agent.**

NOTICE OF UNLAWFUL CONFISCATION OF MY SAVINGS IN COLLUSION WITH THE INTERNAL REVENUE SERVICE.

DEMAND FOR IMMEDIATE RELEASE OF MONEY UNLAWFULLY SEIZED BY BANK OF HAWAII

To Whom It May Concern:

Aloha. Please be informed that the above "Notice of Levy" provided you (supra) by the IRS is not lawfully supported by a "Perfected Lien" requiring a signature by a judge of the court. Secondly, I am not a **"person"** subject to lien as affirmed by Title 26 Section 6331, (a) of the IRS Code, quoted below. <u>Deliberately missing</u> in the documentation provided you by the IRS is subparagraph (a) of United States Code, Title 26 Section 6331 *(Levy and distraint.)* which states:

(a) Authority of Secretary.
If any person liable to pay any tax neglects or refused to pay the same within 10 days after notice and demand, it shall be lawful for the Secretary to collect such tax (and such further sum as shall be sufficient to cover the expenses of the levy) by levy upon all property and rights to property (Except such property as is exempt under section 6334) belonging to such person or on which there is a lien provided in this chapter for the payment of such tax. **Levy may be made upon the accrued salary or wages of any officer, employee, or elected official, of the United States, the District of Columbia, or any agency or instrumentality of the United States or the District of Columbia, by serving a notice of levy on the employer (as defined in section 3401 (d) of such officer, employee, or elected official.** *If the secretary makes a finding that the collection of such tax is in jeopardy, notice and demand for immediate payment of such tax may be made by the Secretary and upon failure or refusal to pay such tax, collection thereof by levy shall be lawful without regard to the 10-day prior provided in this section.* **(Bold emphasis by me)**

<u>**NOTICE OF VIOLATION OF LAW BY BANK OF HAWAII:**</u> **Please be noticed** that <u>Section (b) cannot be applicable</u> being it applies to and references Section (a) which

1

defines those who are liable under Title 26 Section 6331. This deception by the IRS in regard to who is liable for taxes and your permitting the IRS to use Bank of Hawaii as the seizure and conversion agent to perpetuate a fraud and unlawful conversion of assets is a criminal act by Bank of Hawaii in violation of United States Criminal Law.

Please be noticed that I, Pua Victor, age 78, am not an "...officer, employee, or elected official of the United States or the District of Columbia..." as stated in the Section 6331(a) for which a perfected lien does not exist and for which this unsupported "Notice of Levy" would be applicable *(i.e. officer of a corporation, employee or elected official of the U. S. or Washington D. C.)*

Please be further noticed that the IRS through Bank of Hawaii has made a false claim for payment for "income" *(under Subsection (a) above)* never received by me or my deceased husband *(during our time of retirement on fixed income),* and are doing so under threat, extortion and *"libel"* claim. The IRS has consistently refused to provide answers to questions of law regarding their basis of claim on these supposed taxes.

ACTUAL NOTICE: You and Bank of Hawaii in conjunction with the Hawaii USA Federal Credit Union have unlawfully seized money in excess of the falsified IRS claim of supposed taxes owed, a criminal act. Both you and Bank of Hawaii have violated the law by participation with the IRS in a fraudulent claim by the IRS for taxes on retirement income never received by either myself or my deceased husband George Victor.

NOTICE TO RELEASE AND RETURN FUNDS UNLAWFULLY SEIZED: This is demand for immediate release by Bank of Hawaii of my unlawfully seized and retained money secured under false and fraudulent pretense by the IRS. Please immediately contact me by telephone notifying me of the availability of my money.

I am enclosing two letters to the IRS regarding this false claim for your records and to substantiate my position. The letters are dated June 18, 2007 and August 27, 2007, both of which may help you in becoming aware of the fraud being perpetuated on Bank of Hawaii, myself and my late husband, George Victor.

Mahalo for your assistance in this matter.

Respectfully,

Pua Liliaokekomahana Victor, a Widow
HA 098 139 888; Lawfully Documented
Hawaiian National Citizen

Enclosure: Copies of U. S. Certified mailings of June 18, 2007 (U. S. Certified Mail No. 7003 3110 0000 7308 4559 and August 27, 2007 (U. S. Certified Mail No. 7003 3110 000 7308 4597)

Lily Liliaokekomahana Victor
Hawaiian National Citizen
General Delivery: Box 994
Kaneohe, Oahu, Hawaii Nei
(U. S. P. Z. Exempt)

August 27, 2007

via U. S. Postal Service Certified Mail
7003 3110 0000 7308 4597

Internal Revenue Service
300 Ala Moana Boulevard
RO GROUP 35, M/S H212
Honolulu, Hawaii 96850-4994

Attention: G. Kai, I. D. No. 99-20022; Phone Number: (808) 539-2094

Regarding: **OFFER TO PAY IN FULL**

                SECOND REQUEST FOR IRS RESPONSE TO LETTER OF 07-19-007 (Attached)

                ACTUAL NOTICE OF FRAUDULENT CLAIM AND REGARDING PROPER BIRTH NAME

Aloha Ms. Kai:

I wish to settle this IRS claim with a payment in full and will make the payment in full on the following condition being met: (1) that you and your agency provide me a Certified Copy of the *"Verified Charging Document"* as required by law, affirming the amount owed to your agency. (2) upon receipt, I may provide you full payment immediately.

This is also to inform you that I, Pua Victor, age 78, am again in receipt of another unsubstantiated billing from your office after my formal U. S. Certified Mail to you was received by your agency office on June 19th, 2007, and obviously ignored. A copy of that certified letter sent you, your office and your agency is attached.

Please know that I do not have difficulty with paying any debt that is verifiable and justly owed. Whereas you are demanding payment for an unsubstantiated claim, based upon income never affirmed, **I reserve all of my rights.**

I find the following to be fact:

1.   That the IRS, you and your superiors are making false claim for payment of "income" never received by me or my deceased husband, and are doing so under threat, extortion and *"libel"* claim.

1

2.   That you and your agency have lawful obligation to respond to the U. S. Certified Mailing received by Adam Quinn of your office in your behalf on June 19th, 2007 (attached), prior to any further actions by your agency. <u>That request for information has been ignored to date.</u>

ACTUAL NOTICE: <u>Regarding my desire to pay your claim in full</u>. If you cannot affirm the supposed IRS debt you claim as owed, by providing a <u>Certified Copy</u> of the *"Verified Charging Document,"* **as required by law,** it shall be assumed that you personally and your agency have no claim and that you will henceforth not contact me any more by mail or telephone, as doing so will be considered harassment and an attempt to libel and extort under false pretenses by you individually, your superiors and the agency you represent.

I will look forward to your immediate <u>written response</u> enclosing the Certified Copy of the *"Verified Charging Document"*. Thank you.

My proper birth name is, *"Pua Liliaokekomahana Victor"*, not "LILY VICTOR" as falsely claimed and addressed in your correspondence. Please correct all your future correspondence with respect for me and my proper birth name. Thank you.

Respectfully,

Pua Liliaokekomahana Victor, a Widow
HA 098 139 888; Lawfully Documented
Hawaiian National Citizen

Enclosure: Copy of U. S. Certified mailing of June 18, 2007 (U. S. Certified Mail No. 7003 3110 0000 7308 4559.

Lily Liliaokekomahana Victor
Hawaiian National Citizen
General Delivery: Box 994
Kaneohe, Oahu, Hawaii Nei
(U. S. P. Z. Exempt)

June 18, 2007
via U. S. Postal Service Certified Mail
7003 3110 0000 7308 4559

Internal Revenue Service
300 Ala Moana Boulevard
RO GROUP 35, M/S H212
Honolulu, Hawaii 96850-4994

Attention: G. Kai, I. D. No. 99-20022; Phone Number: (808) 539-2094

Regarding: CLAIM BY IRS BASED UPON FRAUD, DECEPTION AND A
FALSIFIED "INCOME" NEVER RECEIVED BY SUPPOSED
"TAXPAYER"

FORMAL REQUEST FOR AFFIRMATION AND CERTIFIED
COPIES OF THE FOLLOWING FORMS: "CONTROL NUMBER-
ED DOCUMENT 1545-1654" USED IN THIS ACTION AGAINST ME,
AND "ASSESSMENT CERTIFICATES No. 23C," SIGNED BY IRS
ASSESSMENT OFFICERS FOR EACH YEAR OF ATTACHMENTS

Aloha Ms. Kai:

This is to inform you that I, Pua Victor, age 78, *(after considering your telephone call demand for my presence at your office on June 20, 2007 @ 9:30 AM)*, do not feel it appropriate regarding your falsified claim and illegal created lien against my deceased husband George Victor, and myself.

An unlawful and falsified claim of supposed income was claimed by the Internal Revenue Service (IRS) in 2001 and the basis of your claim was never confirmed, i. e. that my husband and I had ever received additional income, as falsely claimed. Your IRS claim was without foundation and that fact was established by failure of the IRS to provide my deceased husband and me with any substantiated source or basis of your falsified IRS claim, yet, you continued to attach our retirement checks causing us painful financial damage, extreme emotional stress and hurt. My deceased husband was greatly torn and extremely stressed by the actions of your agency which contributed to his passing.

1

A *"Notice of Federal Tax Lien" (Form 668 YC)* was filed by a J. Pruett and John Ta *(Sp?)* against my late husband and me on April 4, 2002 without a lawful basis of claim. We had no obligation and no affidavit of claim had ever been provided us.

Under United States Law, specifically, the **Code of Federal Regulations**, the IRS is required to comply with **"26CFR602.101"** and **"26 CFR601.104."** I also have never been made aware that there was ever a **"Document Control Number"** *(upper right hand corner)* on any forms submitted to me or my late husband, at any time in the past.

At this time <u>I am making a formal request</u> for a signed and dated *"Assessment Certificate Form No. 23C,"* <u>signed under penalty of perjury by an IRS Assessment Officer previous to 2002</u> *(date of claimed lien)* and for each year thereafter that the IRS has been collecting *(by attachment)*, verifying that the collection process being utilized against me is true and correct according to law, as required by **26CFR602.101** and **26CFR601.104**.

I believe thirty (30) days from receipt of this *U. S. Postal Service "Certified Mail"* letter is adequate time for response. If there is no response affirming compliance to the law received by me by that time, then <u>please be noticed</u> that I intend to seek a civil actions against yourself, the parties mentioned herein, and the Internal Revenue Service on the basis of fraud, false statements, false claims, misrepresentation of facts, emotional stress, hurt, injury and criminal (felonious) actions exercised outside of law. If you feel that my rights have in fact been violated, you may voluntarily lift the false lien; return the monies unlawfully taken from my late husband and me with interest at 10% per annum; clear my record with your agency and my late husband's and my good name with all parties involved of any wrongdoing and provide me with a written letter of apology. If that is done, I would then be willing to cease any actions against you, your agency, and others.

I will look forward to your immediate <u>written response</u>. Thank you.

Respectfully,

Pua Liliaokekomahana Victor, a Widow
HA 098 139 888; Lawfully Documented
Hawaiian National Citizen

EXHIBIT X

Citizen Application Form

(Do not write above this line, for Official filing purposes only, Under Protest)

Government Document:

Notice:
You must file
two (2) sets.
One Original
will be
returned.

After recordation return by mail ___ or pick-up ___

DO NOT MARK IN THIS SPACE

"And you shall love the Lord your God with all your heart, and with all your soul, and with all your might." (Deut. 6:5) "There is no fear in love but perfect love casts out fear, because fear has punishment. He that fears is not made perfect in love." (1 John 4:18)

AFFIDAVIT AND DECLARATION:

I, _____, **Affiant**,

born on the date of A. D. _____, in _____,

_____, am presently domiciled at the following address:

_____.

To the best of my awareness and knowledge, I have <u>never knowingly</u> made any foreign allegiance nor commitment severing my birthright Citizenship rights to the de jure "common-law" of **Ko Hawaii Pae Aina**. Although I may have been a resident in foreign lands and resided under foreign governments other than my own, <u>I have never knowingly forfeited nor abandoned my birthrights or my rights as a Hawaiian National, Citizen / Subject</u>. Although I may have honored foreign laws, statutes and ordinances on my own birth soil, <u>those actions are void ab initio</u>. I was never properly informed that such actions were contrary to my birthrights, birth name and Hawaiian National rights.

I was never informed that my <u>birthrights under Almighty God</u> were still in existence within the de jure National Jurisdiction of the Hawaiian Kingdom, under its "common-law," wherein now I reserve my rights. I claim my primary Hawaiian National Citizenship, allegiance and obligation to the Nation and laws of Ke Aupuni O Hawaii Nei o *Ko Hawaii Pae Aina*, and its "common-law," as defined in the *Sessions Laws of 1892, Chapter LVII, Section 5*, **and the lawful Constitution** thereof.

OPTIONAL: (IF FILING WITHIN THE DEFACTO STATE OF HAWAII)

_____

Signature: Affiant/Declarant for STATE OF HAWAII filing.

_____

(Typewrite your name on this line <u>before</u> notarizing)

NOTARIZATION: **FOR DE FACTO PUBLIC FILING (IF REQUIRED)**

JURAT

STATE OF HAWAII   )
)   ss:
CITY AND COUNTY OF _____)

Subscribed and sworn to before me on this _____ day of _____ in the

year _____ .

_____

My Commission Expires: _____ . (Signature)_____

Notary Public, _____ (Print Name)
                          STATE OF HAWAII

Copyright 2002/ Rev. 06 - _Ke Aupuni O Hawaii Nei_ (Form C-77) Government Document - **Do not duplicate.**

4

ISBN 142517524-4

AFFIRMATION: This Affidavit and Declaration, made by the Affiant/Declarant herein, a Hawaiian Kingdom Citizen/Subject is lawfully affirmed by Almighty God and documented and recorded within this dejure Government, *Ke Aupuni O Hawaii Nei o Ko Hawaii Pae Aina.* Affiant/Declarant declares to be a God-fearing Citizen/Subject of this jurisdiction of law.

Affirmation of Type of Hawaiian Kingdom Citizenship:

The following are the types of Citizenship that exist under Hawaiian Kingdom Law. There are five (5) distinct types of citizenship that apply to Hawaiians. **"Hawaiian" is a nationality, not just a bloodline of the aboriginal Hawaiian People. Circle the one that Applies:**

1. The first and primary type of citizenship is that of the natural born **"Hawaiian" of aboriginal Hawaiian ancestry**. These Hawaiians have the greatest interest being stewards of the aina under Almighty God. These Hawaiians have a vested interest in the aina, as affirmed by the Great Mahele.

2. The second type of **"Hawaiian,"** is one who does not have aboriginal Hawaiian blood, but is born in the Hawaiian Islands.

3. The third type of citizenship is that of one **"born abroad"** to parents of Hawaiian Nationals. This individual has the choice of dual citizenship. At the age of consent, this foreign born has choice of citizenship of the nation of birth or that of their Hawaiian parents.

4. The fourth type of citizenship is that of a **"naturalized"** citizen, who has taken an oath to become a Hawaiian National after first renouncing his or her country of birth citizenship. This is accomplished in a Circuit Court of the Hawaiian Kingdom.

5. The fifth type is a "Denizen" or dual citizenship. A **"denizen"** is a Hawaiian National who retains his foreign citizenship but is under lawful oath of allegiance to the Hawaiian Kingdom Constitution and Hawaiian Kingdom laws.

After circling and initialing the citizenship type that is applicable to you, sign below: If you are a denizen or to be naturalized, you must take an oath of citizenship before any further processing can be done. The official providing you this form can administer your denizen oath. The Naturalization oath must be administered by a Circuit or Supreme Court Judge.

Date: _____   Name: _____
                     (Typewrite name above this line before notarizing)

Official administering denizen oath: _____ Position: _____

Department: _____ (Signature) _____

2

Naturalization Affirmation:

Name: _____
(Typewrite your birth name above this line <u>before</u> notarizing)

_____   _____
Printed Name of Judge   Signature: Affiant/Declarant

Circuit Court of the ____ Circuit

Judge: _____
       Signature of Judge

Ke Aupuni O Hawaii Nei
Ko Hawaii Pae Aina
General Delivery (Box 62107)
Manoa, Oahu, Hawaii Nei
(U. S. P. Z. Exempt)

Court Seal

NOTARIZATION: FOR LAWFUL PUBLIC FILING (IF REQUESTED)

Ko Hawaii Pae Aina, de jure)
)   Scilicet:
Island of Oahu, Hawaii Nei   )

On this _____ day of _____, in the Year of Our Lord Jesus the Christ, A. D. 20____, the above natural person, a Living Soul, personally appeared before me and executed the foregoing instrument. Said Affiant is known to me as:

_____.

I do further acknowledge that Affiant executed same of his or her own free will, act and deed.

My Commission Expires: _____. (L. S.) _____

    Notary Public, _____
       Ko Hawaii Pae Aina, dejure

Seal

Copyright 2002/ Rev 06 - *Ke Aupuni O Hawaii Nei* (Form C-77) Government Document - **Do not duplicate.**

3